Introduction to Practical
Business Analytics
for Everyone
(Using JASP or Python)

Using JASP: No-Coding for Non-Programmers and Non-IT Professionals
Using Python: For Programmers and IT Professionals

JASP and Python are Free and Open-Source Software

Rohith B
Kumar P

Copyrights©: Sudeva Publications

Preface

In today's fast-paced and data-driven business environment, analytics has become an essential tool for making informed decisions, driving growth, and gaining a competitive edge. However, despite its growing importance, many business professionals—especially those without technical backgrounds—find the world of business analytics intimidating. This book aims to bridge that gap and empower everyone, regardless of their technical expertise, to harness the power of analytics effectively.

Introduction to Practical Business Analytics for Everyone: Using JASP or Python is a unique guide designed for two distinct groups of readers: non-IT professionals and IT professionals/programmers. We recognize that business analysts, managers, and decision-makers often require insights from data without needing to dive deep into the intricacies of coding, while developers and data scientists may need a more programmatic approach to tackle complex business problems. With this in mind, the book is divided into two parallel tracks:

- **Using JASP (No Coding for Non-IT Professionals)** For non-technical users or those new to analytics, JASP offers a user-friendly, intuitive interface that simplifies complex statistical tasks. Through this section, you will learn how to apply powerful business analytics techniques without writing a single line of code. The focus is on practical tools and methods to help you understand your data, identify trends, make predictions, and communicate findings clearly to stakeholders.

- **Using Python (For IT Professionals / Programmers)** For those with programming expertise, Python is the go-to language for advanced data analysis and analytics in business. This track takes a hands-on, code-driven approach, allowing you to dive deeper into data processing, visualization, machine learning, and predictive modeling. By using Python, you will learn how to automate processes, perform complex analyses, and scale solutions that would otherwise be cumbersome in traditional business analytics tools.

Throughout this book, we use a **single business dataset** as the foundation for our discussions, ensuring a cohesive and practical understanding of how business analytics concepts are applied in real-world scenarios. The dataset is carefully selected to represent a variety of challenges businesses commonly face, from customer segmentation and sales forecasting to performance analysis and optimization. Each chapter builds upon the last, progressively introducing more sophisticated techniques while reinforcing core principles.

You will discover that analytics is not just about statistical tests or code. It's about transforming raw data into actionable insights that can inform business strategies. By the end of this book, regardless of whether you're a non-IT professional or an experienced programmer, you'll be equipped with practical skills to solve complex business problems, improve decision-making, and make an impact with data.

What You Will Learn:

- How to use JASP for easy and effective statistical analysis in business without writing any code.
- How to leverage Python for advanced, programmatic approaches to data analysis and machine learning.
- The art of interpreting data, uncovering key business insights, and presenting findings clearly.
- The process of using analytics to optimize business operations and drive strategic decisions.
- A practical, hands-on approach with a single business dataset that ties all the concepts together.

Who Should Read This Book:

- **Non-IT Professionals**: Business analysts, managers, and decision-makers who need to understand and apply analytics without the need for programming skills.
- **IT Professionals / Programmers**: Data scientists, developers, and analysts who seek to apply advanced techniques and automation to their business analytics projects.
- **Anyone Interested in Business Analytics**: Whether you are new to the field or an experienced practitioner, this book offers valuable insights, regardless of your technical background.

By focusing on the practical aspects of business analytics, this book offers a comprehensive, approachable, and hands-on guide to turning data into actionable business insights. Whether you're using JASP or Python, you'll learn how to make informed decisions that can improve your business's performance and drive future success.

Table of Contents

Sl. No		Topics	Page No.
1.		**Introduction to Business Analytics**	**1**
	1.1	Definition and Scope of Business Analytics	6
	1.2	About the Dataset used in this book	19
	1.3	Introduction to JASP	21
	1.4	Setting-up and loading Business Data into JASP	23
	1.5	Introduction to Python	29
	1.6	Setting-up Python environment	31
	1.7	Getting Started with Python	39
	1.8	Loading Business Data into Python	45
	1.9	Importance of Data-Driven Decision Making	48
2.		**Descriptive Statistics for Business Decisions**	**52**
	2.1	Key Measures of Central Tendency (Mean, Median, Mode) in Business	56
	2.2	Measures of Central Tendency using JASP	59
	2.3	Measures of Central Tendency using Python	66
	2.4	Measures of Dispersion (Variance, Standard Deviation, Range) in Business	72
	2.5	Measures of Dispersion using JASP	76
	2.6	Measures of Dispersion in Python	85
	2.7	Data Visualization Techniques (Charts, Graphs, Dashboards) in Business	90
	2.8	Data Visualization in Business Analytics using JASP	95

	2.9	Data Visualization in Business Analytics using Python	104
3.	**One Sample T-Test in Business Analytics**		**120**
	3.1	Purpose and Use Cases of One Sample T-Test in Business	123
	3.2	One Sample T-Test in JASP	126
	3.3	One Sample T-Test in Python	134
	3.4	Assumptions and Conditions for Validity of Business Data	139
	3.5	Interpreting Results: Confidence Intervals and P-Values	143
4.	**Independent Sample T-Test in Business Analytics**		**146**
	4.1	Defining Independent Samples in Business Contexts	150
	4.2	Independent Sample T-Test in JASP	154
	4.3	Independent Sample T-Test in Python	162
	4.4	Conducting the Independent Sample T-Test	169
	4.5	Practical Applications and Result Interpretation	173
5.	**Paired Sample T-Test in Business Analytics**		**177**
	5.1	When to Use Paired Sample T-Test in Business	181
	5.2	Paired Sample T-Test in JASP	185
	5.3	Paired Sample T-Test in Python	193
	5.4	Analyzing Pre- and Post-Intervention Data	201
	5.5	Case Studies: Employee Performance and Training Programs	205
6.	**ANOVA (Analysis of Variance) in Business Analytics**		**209**

	6.1	Fundamentals of ANOVA and Its Importance in Business Context	213
	6.2	Practical ANOVA in JASP	217
	6.3	Practical ANOVA in Python	226
	6.4	One-Way vs. Two-Way ANOVA: Differences and Applications in Business	231
	6.5	Post-Hoc Tests: Understanding Group Differences	236

7.	**Correlation in Business Analytics**		**240**
	7.1	Types of Correlation in Business: Pearson and Spearman	243
	7.2	Practical Correlation in JASP	248
	7.3	Practical Correlation in Python	256
	7.4	Assessing Relationships Between Business Variables	261
	7.5	Implications of Correlation in Strategy Formulation	265

8.	**Linear Regression in Business Analytics**		**269**
	8.1	Exploring Linear Regression Analysis in Business Context	273
	8.2	Practical Linear Regression using JASP	277
	8.3	Practical Linear Regression using Python	287
	8.4	Building and Evaluating Regression Models	300
	8.5	Applications in Sales Forecasting and Market Analysis	305

9.	**Time Series Analysis in Business Analytics**		**309**
	9.1	Practical Time Series Analysis in JASP	313
	9.2	Practical Time Series Analysis in Python	323

10	**Introduction to Machine Learning Classification in Business Analytics**	332
	10.1 Understanding Decision Tree Classification in Business Analytics	336
	10.2 Decision Tree Classification using JASP	341
	10.3 Decision Tree Classification using Python	352
11	**Introduction to Machine Learning Clustering in Business Analytics**	363
	11.1 Understanding K-Means Clustering in Business Context	366
	11.2 Practical K-Means Clustering in JASP	370
	11.3 Practical K-Means Clustering in Python	379
12	**Final Project: Business Analytics Strategy for a Real-World Business Problem**	388
	12.1 Building a Business Analytics Project - *Planning and executing a comprehensive Business Analytics project. (Data: Choice of relevant datasets or Sample Dataset)*	393
	12.2 Showcasing Your Findings in Business Analytics: Best Practices for Presenting Analytical Results and Insights	395
	12.3 Future Directions in Business Analytics: Emerging Trends and Technologies	400

Instructions:

> **Scan below QR Code and register
> to get the
> Codes, Datasets, PPT Slides and Other Resources
> from this book**
> (On submitting amazon purchase proof)

> **Or use the link below and fill in the form**

bit.ly/3Qe36iW

> **or mail to** (Attach amazon book purchase proof)
> books@ijtmas.com

1. Introduction to Business Analytics

Business Analytics (BA) refers to the use of data, statistical analysis, and modeling to make informed business decisions. It involves analyzing historical data to uncover patterns, trends, and insights that can guide future actions. Business Analytics is widely applied in various industries such as marketing, finance, operations, and human resources to improve decision-making processes, optimize business performance, and gain a competitive advantage. Let us understand the basics of Data Analytics before we discuss Business Analytics.

What is Data?

Data refers to raw facts, figures, or information collected and recorded for analysis or reference. It can come in various forms—numerical, textual, visual, or even sensory information—and can be structured (organized in a specific format, like a table) or unstructured (like text, audio, or images).

In the context of business, data might include sales figures, customer information, product details, transaction histories, market trends, and more. The key aspect of data is that it's generally unprocessed, which means it does not provide immediate insights without further interpretation or analysis.

Types of Data:

1. **Structured Data**: Data that is highly organized and stored in a fixed format, often in relational databases (e.g., spreadsheets, tables). Examples: customer information, sales transactions.

2. **Unstructured Data**: Data that lacks a predefined structure. Examples: social media posts, email messages, video content, or customer feedback.

3. **Semi-structured Data**: Data that has some level of organization, but not in a tabular format. Examples: JSON, XML files.

What is Data Analysis?

Data Analysis refers to the process of inspecting, cleaning, transforming, and modeling data in order to discover useful information, draw conclusions, and support decision-making. It's a key component of data-driven decision-making and helps businesses and organizations make sense of raw data.

The data analysis process typically involves:

1. **Data Collection**: Gathering data from various sources.
2. **Data Cleaning**: Removing inaccuracies, dealing with missing values, and correcting inconsistencies.
3. **Data Transformation**: Converting data into a usable format or structure.
4. **Exploratory Data Analysis (EDA)**: Summarizing the main characteristics of the data, often using visual methods like charts and graphs.

5. **Statistical Analysis**: Applying mathematical and statistical techniques to interpret the data (e.g., regression, hypothesis testing).
6. **Modeling**: Creating models to predict future outcomes (e.g., predictive analytics, machine learning).
7. **Visualization**: Presenting findings in a visual format to facilitate understanding and communication.

Key Steps in Data Analysis:

- **Descriptive Analysis**: Describes the characteristics of a dataset (e.g., mean, median, standard deviation).
- **Diagnostic Analysis**: Identifies relationships and reasons for trends or outcomes in the data.
- **Predictive Analysis**: Uses statistical models and machine learning to predict future trends or behavior.
- **Prescriptive Analysis**: Provides recommendations for actions based on analysis (e.g., optimizing inventory levels, pricing strategies).

What is Business Data Analysis?

Business Data Analysis is the process of applying data analysis techniques specifically to business data to help organizations make informed decisions and solve business problems. It involves looking at business-related data (like sales, customer feedback, financial records) to gain insights that can drive strategy, improve operations, and achieve business goals.

Business Data Analysis typically includes:

1. **Identifying Key Business Metrics**: Metrics such as sales revenue, customer acquisition costs, profit margins, churn rates, and market share.
2. **Analyzing Trends and Patterns**: Detecting patterns in sales, customer behavior, or market trends that can help in decision-making.
3. **Optimizing Business Operations**: Using data to streamline processes, reduce costs, improve efficiency, and maximize ROI (Return on Investment).
4. **Customer Insights**: Understanding customer preferences, behaviors, and needs through data to improve marketing strategies, product offerings, and customer service.
5. **Competitive Analysis**: Comparing business performance against competitors by analyzing external data like market share, industry trends, or pricing strategies.

Example:

- A retail business analyzing customer purchasing behavior data to identify which products are most popular during certain months.

- A company analyzing financial statements to identify areas where costs can be reduced or where investments can yield higher returns.

Business Analytics is the practice of using data, statistical analysis, and quantitative methods to drive business decision-making and improve organizational performance. It involves collecting and analyzing historical data to uncover patterns, trends, and insights that can inform strategies and optimize operations. Business analytics can encompass a wide range of techniques, from basic descriptive analytics (summarizing past performance) to advanced predictive and prescriptive analytics (forecasting future outcomes and recommending actions). By leveraging business analytics, companies can make data-driven decisions that enhance customer satisfaction, streamline processes, increase profitability, and gain a competitive edge in the market.

Key Components of Business Analytics:

1. **Descriptive Analytics**: Analyzes past data to understand what happened. This is typically done through reporting and data visualization.
2. **Predictive Analytics**: Uses historical data and statistical techniques to predict future outcomes or trends. It helps businesses anticipate potential problems or opportunities.
3. **Prescriptive Analytics**: Provides recommendations on how to handle potential future situations. It focuses on decision-making based on predictions.
4. **Diagnostic Analytics**: Investigates data to understand why something happened. It often includes root cause analysis.

Example: Sales Analysis Using Business Analytics

Let's explore an example where a company wants to analyze its sales data to understand the relationship between advertising spend and sales performance, with the goal of optimizing marketing spend.

Objective: The company wants to determine if increasing the advertising budget leads to increased sales, and at what point the returns diminish.

Sample Data:

We'll look at a simplified dataset that tracks monthly sales and advertising spend for the past six months.

Month	Advertising Spend ($)	Sales Revenue ($)
Jan	10,000	100,000
Feb	12,000	120,000
Mar	15,000	145,000

Apr	18,000	150,000
May	20,000	160,000
Jun	22,000	165,000

Results of the Analysis:

- **Correlation**: The company wants to find out the correlation between advertising spend and sales. The correlation can be calculated using a statistical method such as Pearson's correlation coefficient.

In this case, we calculate the correlation coefficient, which comes out to approximately **0.98**, indicating a very strong positive relationship between advertising spend and sales. This suggests that as advertising spend increases, sales tend to increase as well.

- **Regression Analysis**: Next, a linear regression model can be used to predict sales based on advertising spend. The linear regression equation might look something like this:

$$\text{Sales} = 50,000 + 5 \times (\text{Advertising Spend})$$

This means that for every additional dollar spent on advertising, sales increase by $5. The intercept of $50,000 represents the baseline sales when advertising spend is $0 (i.e., sales are still $50,000 even without any advertising).

Interpretation of Results:

- **Positive Correlation**: The strong positive correlation (0.98) confirms that more advertising spend leads to higher sales. This is expected in most cases where marketing efforts directly influence sales.

- **Regression Analysis**: From the regression model, we see that the company's sales are positively influenced by advertising. However, it is important to note that the relationship might not continue to hold indefinitely. At some point, the returns on additional advertising spend may diminish, which would require a more advanced model like nonlinear regression or an analysis of diminishing returns.

Predictions Based on the Model:

Using the regression equation, we can predict the sales for a given advertising spend. For example, if the company plans to spend $25,000 on advertising next month, the predicted sales would be:

$$\text{Sales} = 50,000 + 5 \times 25,000 = 50,000 + 125,000 = 175,000$$

So, the company could expect to generate $175,000 in sales if it spends $25,000 on advertising.

Conclusion:

From the analysis, we can conclude that the company's sales have a strong positive relationship with its advertising spend, and based on the regression model, the company can predict sales for various levels of advertising spend. However, as the company increases its advertising budget, it should consider the potential for diminishing returns, which could be modeled more accurately with a different approach. This information can help guide future decisions on optimal advertising spend to maximize sales without overspending.

This kind of analysis allows businesses to make data-driven decisions to optimize their marketing strategies and improve profitability.

1.1 Definition and Scope of Business Analytics

Business Analytics (BA) refers to the process of collecting, processing, analyzing, and interpreting large sets of data to help organizations make more informed decisions and improve business outcomes. It involves applying statistical methods, algorithms, and tools to understand business performance, identify trends, make predictions, and ultimately guide decision-making processes. BA is crucial in today's data-driven business environment, where data is a valuable asset for organizations seeking competitive advantages.

Business Analytics encompasses various types of analysis, each with its own objective, but all aimed at providing actionable insights for decision-makers.

Types of Business Analytics

1. **Descriptive Analytics**:
    - **Objective**: To describe what has happened in the past.
    - **Example**: Analyzing past sales data to understand trends or summarize financial performance.

2. **Diagnostic Analytics**:
    - **Objective**: To determine why something happened.
    - **Example**: Investigating why sales dropped in a particular quarter, identifying factors such as seasonality or market conditions.

3. **Predictive Analytics**:
    - **Objective**: To predict what is likely to happen in the future.
    - **Example**: Using historical sales data to forecast future demand or sales figures.

4. **Prescriptive Analytics**:
    - **Objective**: To recommend actions for the future.
    - **Example**: Recommending changes to the supply chain process based on predictive analysis to reduce costs or improve service delivery.

Scope of Business Analytics

The scope of Business Analytics is vast and covers multiple aspects of business functions, including:

1. **Marketing Analytics**:
    - Optimizing marketing strategies by analyzing customer behavior, engagement metrics, and campaign effectiveness.
    - Example: Identifying the most profitable customer segments or channels.

2. **Financial Analytics**:
   - Monitoring financial performance, forecasting revenues and expenditures, and detecting anomalies in financial records.
   - Example: Predicting cash flows or identifying fraudulent transactions.

3. **Operational Analytics**:
   - Improving efficiency and streamlining business processes, such as inventory management or production scheduling.
   - Example: Reducing supply chain inefficiencies or optimizing staffing schedules.

4. **Customer Analytics**:
   - Analyzing customer data to improve customer satisfaction and loyalty.
   - Example: Segmenting customers based on purchasing behavior and tailoring marketing strategies.

5. **Human Resource Analytics**:
   - Analyzing employee data for better talent management, employee engagement, and retention.
   - Example: Identifying predictors of employee turnover and devising retention strategies.

Example:

1. Analyzing Customer Sales Data (Descriptive Analytics)

Let's consider a retail company that wants to understand how its sales performance varies across different store locations. The company collects data from its five store locations over the last 6 months and aims to identify which stores are performing the best.

Sample Data (Sales by Store Location)

Month	Store A Sales ($)	Store B Sales ($)	Store C Sales ($)	Store D Sales ($)	Store E Sales ($)
Jan	50,000	60,000	55,000	45,000	40,000
Feb	55,000	62,000	58,000	47,000	42,000
Mar	53,000	64,000	57,000	46,000	41,000
Apr	52,000	61,000	56,000	45,000	43,000
May	58,000	65,000	59,000	48,000	44,000
Jun	60,000	68,000	60,000	49,000	45,000

Results of the Analysis:

To better understand the sales performance, we can calculate the following:

1. **Total Sales per Store** (Sum of sales across all months)
2. **Average Sales per Store** (Average sales per month for each store)
3. **Sales Ranking** (Rank the stores based on total or average sales)

Calculations:

Store	Total Sales ($)	Average Sales ($)	Sales Rank
Store A	328,000	54,667	3
Store B	380,000	63,333	1
Store C	349,000	58,167	2
Store D	270,000	45,000	5
Store E	255,000	42,500	6

Explanation of Results:

- **Store B** has the highest total sales ($380,000), followed by **Store C** with $349,000 in sales. These two stores also have the highest average sales per month, indicating consistent strong performance.

- **Store A** ranks third, with total sales of $328,000, averaging $54,667 per month, which is slightly lower than Store B and Store C but still shows healthy sales performance.

- **Store D** and **Store E** have lower sales figures, with Store D ranking 5th and Store E ranking 6th. These stores have the lowest average sales, which could be due to factors such as location, customer demographics, or marketing efforts.

Insights and Business Decisions:

- **Store B**: As the top performer, this store might be a model for others. It could be valuable to investigate what factors contribute to its success (e.g., location, promotions, product assortment, customer service).

- **Store D and Store E**: These stores are underperforming. The company might consider conducting a diagnostic analysis to understand the root causes (e.g., poor customer traffic, competition, store management). Additionally, the company might explore targeted marketing campaigns or operational improvements in these locations to boost sales.

- **Overall Performance**: The company can use this data to allocate resources more effectively, focusing marketing efforts or inventory management on the better-performing stores while addressing underperformance in others.

2. Diagnostic Analytics: Understanding Why Something Happened

Objective: Diagnostic analytics investigates why certain events or outcomes happened. It uses historical data to identify factors and causes that influenced the observed results.

Example Scenario: Sales Decline in Store D

We saw earlier that **Store D** had the lowest sales among the five locations. Diagnostic analytics can help us investigate the cause of the sales decline in Store D compared to other stores.

Sample Data (Customer Foot Traffic vs. Sales)

Month	Store D Sales ($)	Store D Foot Traffic	Store B Sales ($)	Store B Foot Traffic
Jan	45,000	5,000	60,000	8,000
Feb	47,000	5,200	62,000	8,200
Mar	46,000	5,100	64,000	8,500
Apr	45,000	5,000	61,000	8,300
May	48,000	5,300	65,000	8,600
Jun	49,000	5,400	68,000	8,800

Calculation: Sales per Customer (Sales / Foot Traffic)

Month	Store D Sales ($)	Store D Foot Traffic	Sales per Customer (Store D)	Store B Sales ($)	Store B Foot Traffic	Sales per Customer (Store B)
Jan	45,000	5,000	9	60,000	8,000	7.5
Feb	47,000	5,200	9.04	62,000	8,200	7.56
Mar	46,000	5,100	9.02	64,000	8,500	7.53
Apr	45,000	5,000	9	61,000	8,300	7.35
May	48,000	5,300	9.05	65,000	8,600	7.56
Jun	49,000	5,400	9.07	68,000	8,800	7.73

Diagnostic Analysis:

- **Sales per Customer**: For **Store D**, the "Sales per Customer" is consistently higher than **Store B**, which indicates that each customer in Store D is spending more on average than those in Store B.

- **Foot Traffic**: However, Store D's **foot traffic** is significantly lower than Store B's. This is likely the primary reason for the sales decline—fewer customers are visiting Store D, which is causing the total sales to be lower despite each customer spending more.

Observation:

Diagnostic analytics suggests that the key reason behind Store D's sales decline is lower foot traffic, not poor sales per customer. This indicates that improving customer attraction (through promotions, location optimization, etc.) could be a more effective strategy than focusing on individual customer sales.

3. Predictive Analytics: Predicting Future Outcomes

Objective: Predictive analytics uses historical data and statistical models to forecast future trends or outcomes. It is typically used to anticipate future sales, customer behavior, or other key metrics.

Example Scenario: Forecasting Sales for Store A

Using the data from the previous months, we will now apply a simple linear regression model to predict sales for **Store A** in the next month (July).

Sample Data (Sales in Store A for the Past 6 Months)

Month	Store A Sales ($)
Jan	50,000
Feb	55,000
Mar	53,000
Apr	52,000
May	58,000
Jun	60,000

Calculation: Linear Regression Model

We'll fit a simple linear regression model:

$$\text{Sales} = a + b \times (\text{Month})$$

Where:

- a is the intercept.
- b is the slope (rate of change).

Using statistical software or a tool like Excel, we can calculate the regression coefficients. Let's assume the regression equation is:

$$\text{Sales} = 50{,}000 + 2{,}000 \times (\text{Month})$$

This indicates that sales increase by $2,000 per month.

Prediction for July (Month 7):

$$\text{Sales for July} = 50{,}000 + 2{,}000 \times 7 = 50{,}000 + 14{,}000 = 64{,}000$$

Results:

Month	Store A Sales ($)	Predicted Sales for July ($)
Jan	50,000	
Feb	55,000	
Mar	53,000	
Apr	52,000	
May	58,000	
Jun	60,000	
July		64,000

Observation:

Using the predictive model, we can forecast that **Store A**'s sales in July will be approximately **$64,000**. This helps the company prepare for future revenue and plan its inventory and marketing strategies accordingly. Predictive analytics provides businesses with foresight, which allows them to make proactive decisions.

4. Prescriptive Analytics: Recommending the Best Course of Action

Objective: Prescriptive analytics provides actionable recommendations based on the insights generated from predictive and descriptive analytics. It helps businesses decide the best course of action to achieve desired outcomes.

Example Scenario: Optimizing Advertising Spend

Based on the past data, a company wants to determine how much to spend on advertising to maximize sales. The company has a budget of $30,000 for advertising and wants to optimize its spend for maximum returns.

Sample Data (Advertising Spend vs. Sales)

Month	Advertising Spend ($)	Sales ($)
Jan	10,000	100,000
Feb	12,000	120,000
Mar	15,000	145,000
Apr	18,000	150,000
May	20,000	160,000
Jun	22,000	165,000

Calculation: Linear Regression for Sales vs. Advertising Spend

We apply a linear regression to model sales as a function of advertising spend. Assume the regression equation we derive is:

$$\text{Sales} = 50,000 + 5 \times (\text{Advertising Spend})$$

So, for every $1 spent on advertising, sales increase by $5.

Predicting Sales for $30,000 Advertising Spend:

$$\text{Sales} = 50,000 + 5 \times 30,000 = 50,000 + 150,000 = 200,000$$

Results:

Advertising Spend ($)	Predicted Sales ($)
10,000	100,000
12,000	110,000
15,000	125,000
18,000	140,000
20,000	150,000
22,000	160,000
30,000	**200,000**

Observation:

Prescriptive analytics suggests that if the company spends $30,000 on advertising, it can expect to generate $200,000 in sales. This gives the company clear guidance on how much to spend to maximize its revenue, based on the predictive model. Additionally, the company can consider factors like diminishing returns if it goes beyond a certain threshold, which might require more advanced modeling (such as nonlinear regression).

Summary of Analytics Types:

1. **Descriptive Analytics** helped to allocate resources more effectively, focusing marketing efforts or inventory management on the better-performing stores while addressing underperformance in others.
2. **Diagnostic Analytics** helped identify that **Store D's** sales decline is due to lower foot traffic.
3. **Predictive Analytics** forecasted that **Store A's** sales in July will be around **$64,000**, based on historical trends.
4. **Prescriptive Analytics** recommended that spending **$30,000** on advertising could increase sales to **$200,000**, helping the company optimize its marketing budget.

These different types of analytics work together to provide a comprehensive view of the business, from understanding past performance to predicting future trends and recommending optimal actions.

Examples on Scope of Business Analytics

Let's extend the previous examples by exploring four more key areas where analytics is widely applied in business: **Marketing Analytics**, **Financial Analytics**, **Operational Analytics**, and **Human Resource Analytics**. Each of these focuses on different aspects of business performance, providing actionable insights to optimize decisions and strategies.

1. Marketing Analytics: Analyzing Campaign Effectiveness

Objective: Marketing analytics helps measure and optimize marketing campaigns by analyzing customer behavior, engagement metrics, and the return on investment (ROI).

Example Scenario: Evaluating the Effectiveness of a Marketing Campaign

A company recently ran a marketing campaign targeting its customer base to boost sales. They want to analyze the effectiveness of the campaign by examining the relationship between campaign spending and sales performance.

Sample Data (Marketing Campaign Spend vs. Sales)

Month	Marketing Spend ($)	Sales ($)	New Customers Acquired

Jan	5,000	50,000	200
Feb	6,000	55,000	250
Mar	8,000	70,000	300
Apr	7,500	65,000	270
May	9,000	75,000	350
Jun	10,000	80,000	400

Calculation: Customer Acquisition Cost (CAC)

The **Customer Acquisition Cost (CAC)** is calculated by dividing the marketing spend by the number of new customers acquired each month.

Month	Marketing Spend ($)	New Customers	CAC ($) = Marketing Spend / New Customers
Jan	5,000	200	25
Feb	6,000	250	24
Mar	8,000	300	26.67
Apr	7,500	270	27.78
May	9,000	350	25.71
Jun	10,000	400	25

Analysis:

- **Cost Efficiency**: The CAC fluctuates between $24 and $27.78, with **May** being the most cost-effective month in terms of acquiring new customers.
- **Sales Growth**: As marketing spend increases, sales also increase, suggesting that the campaign is effective in driving sales. However, the relationship between marketing spend and new customers is more consistent in May and June, indicating diminishing returns after a certain point.

Observation:

Marketing analytics suggests that while increasing marketing spend helps drive sales and acquire new customers, there is an optimal point at which additional spending yields diminishing returns. The company might focus on maintaining an efficient CAC around $25–26 while maximizing returns from future campaigns.

2. Financial Analytics: Analyzing Profitability

Objective: Financial analytics focuses on measuring and optimizing financial performance by analyzing financial statements, profitability, and cost structures.

Example Scenario: Analyzing Profit Margins Across Different Products

A company sells three different products and wants to analyze the profitability of each product to decide which one to focus on for future growth.

Sample Data (Sales, Costs, and Profit for Three Products)

Product	Sales ($)	Cost of Goods Sold (COGS) ($)	Gross Profit ($)	Gross Profit Margin (%)
Product A	100,000	60,000	40,000	40%
Product B	150,000	90,000	60,000	40%
Product C	80,000	30,000	50,000	62.50%

Calculation: Gross Profit Margin (%)

The **Gross Profit Margin** is calculated as:

$$\text{Gross Profit Margin} = \frac{\text{Gross Profit}}{\text{Sales}} \times 100$$

Product	Sales ($)	Cost of Goods Sold (COGS) ($)	Gross Profit ($)	Gross Profit Margin (%)
Product A	100,000	60,000	40,000	40%
Product B	150,000	90,000	60,000	40%
Product C	80,000	30,000	50,000	62.50%

Analysis:

- **Gross Profit Margin**: **Product C** has the highest gross profit margin (62.5%), meaning it is the most profitable product on a per-dollar basis. In contrast, both **Product A** and **Product B** have a gross profit margin of 40%, indicating they are less profitable than Product C.

- **Sales Volume**: **Product B** has the highest sales, but despite this, it has the same gross profit margin as Product A, which may suggest that **Product B** has higher variable costs or less efficient production processes.

Observation:

From a financial analytics perspective, **Product C** is the most profitable in terms of gross margin. If the company aims to improve overall profitability, it could focus more on promoting **Product C**, possibly expanding its production or marketing efforts. **Product B**'s high sales volume is important, but its margin is relatively lower, so the company should consider ways to reduce costs or increase prices to improve profitability.

3. Operational Analytics: Optimizing Inventory Management

Objective: Operational analytics focuses on optimizing business operations by analyzing workflows, resource utilization, inventory management, and supply chain efficiency.

Example Scenario: Inventory and Stockouts Analysis

A company wants to analyze its inventory management to minimize stockouts (when items are unavailable for sale). They examine inventory levels and sales data to optimize their inventory replenishment process.

Sample Data (Inventory, Sales, and Stockouts)

Month	Product A Inventory (units)	Product A Sales (units)	Stockouts (units)	Product B Inventory (units)	Product B Sales (units)	Stockouts (units)
Jan	500	400	0	300	350	50
Feb	450	420	30	280	300	20
Mar	480	460	20	250	300	30
Apr	500	450	0	270	290	30
May	520	470	10	260	280	40
Jun	500	480	20	240	270	30

Analysis:

- **Stockout Trends**: **Product A** has fewer stockouts than **Product B**, but both products experience stockouts every month. In **February**, **Product B** faces a particularly high stockout rate, with 50 units unavailable.
- **Sales vs. Inventory**: **Product A** consistently sells close to its available inventory, while **Product B** has higher sales than its inventory in January and February, leading to stockouts.

Observation:

The operational analytics suggests that the company should consider adjusting inventory levels based on sales trends, especially for **Product B**, which experiences frequent stockouts. Implementing an inventory optimization model (such as **Just-in-Time (JIT)**) could help minimize stockouts and reduce excess inventory for both products, optimizing operational efficiency and reducing costs associated with overstocking.

4. Human Resource Analytics: Employee Turnover Analysis

Objective: Human resource analytics helps optimize talent management, employee retention, and workforce planning by analyzing employee data and turnover trends.

Example Scenario: Analyzing Employee Turnover

The company wants to understand the factors contributing to employee turnover and how to reduce it. They analyze employee data over the past year to identify trends in voluntary resignations.

Sample Data (Employee Turnover, Age, and Tenure)

Month	Employees Left	Average Age (Years)	Average Tenure (Years)	Department
Jan	5	35	3	Sales
Feb	3	38	4	Marketing
Mar	6	32	2	IT
Apr	4	36	3.5	Operations
May	7	30	1.5	Sales
Jun	5	37	4	HR

Calculation: Turnover Rate (Turnover / Total Employees)

Month	Employees Left	Total Employees	Turnover Rate (%) = Employees Left / Total Employees * 100
Jan	5	50	10%
Feb	3	50	6%
Mar	6	55	10.91%
Apr	4	55	7.27%
May	7	55	12.73%
Jun	5	50	10%

Analysis:

- **Turnover Trends**: **Sales** department experiences the highest turnover rates, especially in **May** (12.73%), despite a relatively average age (30 years) and tenure (1.5 years). The **IT** department has a higher turnover rate in **March** (10.91%) than other months, which could indicate challenges with employee retention in tech roles.
- **Employee Profile**: Younger employees with less tenure seem to leave more frequently, suggesting potential issues related to employee engagement or career growth opportunities for newer hires.

Observation:

Human resource analytics indicates that the **Sales** department is facing higher turnover rates and might need improvements in employee engagement, training, or compensation packages. Furthermore, addressing retention strategies for younger employees with shorter tenures could help reduce turnover and improve organizational stability. A deeper analysis of exit interviews and employee satisfaction surveys could provide more insights into specific reasons behind turnover.

Summary of Analytics Types:

1. **Marketing Analytics** helped identify the **Customer Acquisition Cost (CAC)** and suggested efficient campaign management strategies.
2. **Financial Analytics** revealed that **Product C** offers the highest gross profit margin, guiding the company toward more profitable product strategies.
3. **Operational Analytics** highlighted inventory issues and suggested optimizing inventory management to minimize stockouts.
4. **Human Resource Analytics** uncovered high turnover rates in the **Sales** department and provided insights on improving employee retention strategies.

Each of these analytics areas provides valuable insights that help businesses improve performance, optimize strategies, and make data-driven decisions across different functional domains.

1.2 About the Dataset used in this book

The following dataset is a comprehensive collection of sales performance data for a business operating across two regions (East and West). It includes key metrics like **sales amount, target sales, pre-sales amount, post-sales amount, marketing spend, customer feedback scores**, and **sales growth** across different customer segments (Small, Medium, and Large). The dataset also captures insights into how marketing spend correlates with sales performance and customer satisfaction, which can help the business evaluate its marketing strategies and sales growth opportunities.

ID	Sales Amount	Region	Target Sales	Pre-Sales Amount	Post-Sales Amount	Marketing Spend	Customer Feedback Score	Sales Growth	Customer Segment
1	1500	East	1600	1400	1550	500	4	50	Small
2	1800	West	1750	1700	1850	600	5	100	Medium
3	2200	East	2000	2100	2250	700	4	150	Large
4	2000	West	1900	1850	2050	550	3	100	Medium
5	1750	East	1700	1600	1800	450	4	50	Small
6	1900	West	1950	1900	2000	650	5	100	Medium
7	2100	East	2200	2050	2150	700	4	100	Large
8	2400	West	2300	2200	2400	600	5	200	Large
9	1600	East	1650	1500	1600	500	3	100	Small
10	2300	West	2400	2350	2500	750	4	150	Large
11	1950	East	2000	1900	1950	550	4	50	Medium
12	2050	West	2100	2000	2050	600	3	50	Medium
13	1750	East	1800	1700	1750	500	4	50	Small
14	2150	West	2200	2100	2150	650	5	100	Large
15	1800	East	1850	1750	1800	700	4	50	Small
16	2500	West	2450	2400	2500	800	5	100	Large
17	1700	East	1750	1650	1700	400	3	50	Small
18	1850	West	1900	1800	1850	500	4	50	Medium
19	2100	East	2150	2050	2100	650	5	50	Large
20	2000	West	2050	1950	2000	600	4	50	Medium
21	1950	East	1900	1850	1950	550	4	50	Medium
22	2200	West	2250	2150	2200	700	5	100	Large
23	1650	East	1700	1600	1650	450	3	50	Small
24	1750	West	1800	1700	1750	500	4	50	Medium

| 25 | 1900 | East | 1850 | 1800 | 1900 | 600 | 5 | 100 | Large |

Description of Data:

The dataset consists of 25 entries, each representing a distinct sales transaction. The primary variables include:

- **Sales Amount**: Actual sales achieved for the given period.
- **Region**: Geographic region of the sales, categorized as either "East" or "West."
- **Target Sales**: Sales targets set for each transaction.
- **Pre-Sales Amount**: Sales figures recorded before any marketing efforts were applied.
- **Post-Sales Amount**: Sales figures after marketing interventions, which may reflect the effect of marketing spend.
- **Marketing Spend**: The amount allocated to marketing for each transaction.
- **Customer Feedback Score**: A subjective score assigned to customer satisfaction, on a scale from 1 to 5.
- **Sales Growth**: The change in sales from the pre-sales to post-sales period.
- **Customer Segment**: Customer classification, including "Small", "Medium", and "Large" based on purchase volume or other factors.

Conclusion:

The dataset provides valuable insights into the relationship between marketing spend, customer satisfaction, and sales growth. For instance, **higher marketing spend** seems to correlate with **higher sales growth**, especially in the "Large" customer segment, which tends to show the most significant sales increases and higher customer feedback scores. The **East region** generally performs at par or slightly below the **West region**, but the **Medium** and **Large customer segments** perform well in both regions. These insights could help the business improve its targeting and resource allocation strategies, particularly by boosting marketing efforts in segments or regions that show the highest potential for sales growth. Furthermore, the company could analyze and refine its marketing strategies to ensure that marketing spend is effectively driving positive sales outcomes across all customer segments.

Note:

1. You can type the data in excel, save it as CSV file by giving a name as Business_Data.csv and import into Python. However, in all the examples, this dataset is also created using codes.

2. You can also get the dataset through the email as mentioned in the instructions provided earlier (before chapter 1).

1.3 Introduction to JASP

JASP (Jeffrey's Amazing Statistics Program) is a free and open-source statistical software designed for users who need an intuitive and powerful tool to perform a wide range of statistical analyses. It was developed to make statistical analysis more accessible and easier to use without requiring extensive knowledge of programming. JASP is based on the R statistical language, but it provides a user-friendly graphical interface that allows researchers and analysts to perform complex statistical operations with just a few clicks.

Here are some key features of JASP:

1. User-Friendly Interface

JASP is designed with an easy-to-navigate interface that eliminates the need for coding or programming. The software presents analysis options clearly, making it suitable for beginners as well as experienced users. Users can perform analysis by selecting options from dropdown menus, and the results are displayed instantly.

2. Wide Range of Statistical Tests

JASP supports a variety of statistical techniques, including:

- **Descriptive Statistics** (mean, median, standard deviation, etc.)
- **T-Tests** (paired, independent)
- **ANOVA** (Analysis of Variance)
- **Correlation Analysis**
- **Regression Analysis** (linear, multiple, logistic)
- **Bayesian Statistics** (allowing users to choose between classical and Bayesian inference)
- **Non-parametric tests** (e.g., Kruskal-Wallis, Wilcoxon)
- **Factor Analysis and Principal Component Analysis (PCA)**

3. Bayesian Analysis

One of JASP's standout features is its focus on **Bayesian statistics**. While traditional statistics typically relies on null hypothesis significance testing (NHST), Bayesian analysis in JASP allows users to evaluate evidence in favor of or against hypotheses, providing a more flexible and interpretable approach to statistical inference.

4. Reproducible Research

JASP makes it easy to reproduce analyses. Once an analysis is done, users can save the session and return to it later, ensuring reproducibility. Additionally, JASP allows users to export the results, reports, and data, so others can validate and reproduce the findings.

5. Visualization Tools

JASP provides powerful visualization tools that allow users to create high-quality graphs and charts. These visualizations help in presenting data and results clearly, making it easier to communicate findings to different audiences.

6. Integration with R

While JASP itself is a graphical interface, it integrates seamlessly with R. This allows users to take advantage of R's advanced capabilities when necessary, all without leaving the JASP environment.

7. Open-Source and Free

JASP is free to download and use, which makes it an attractive option for both educational purposes and professional research. It is open-source, meaning that anyone can contribute to its development or adapt it for their own needs.

8. Cross-Platform

JASP is available for Windows, macOS, and Linux, ensuring accessibility for users across different platforms.

9. Educational Tool

JASP is widely used in educational settings due to its accessibility and ease of use. It allows students and researchers to perform statistical analysis without requiring them to learn complex statistical software.

Example Workflow in JASP

- **Step 1**: Open JASP and load your dataset (e.g., CSV, SPSS, or R data).
- **Step 2**: Select the type of analysis you want to perform (e.g., t-test, ANOVA, regression).
- **Step 3**: Specify the variables you want to analyze (e.g., dependent and independent variables).
- **Step 4**: View the results, which will be updated in real-time as you adjust the analysis options.
- **Step 5**: Visualize your results with graphs and charts.
- **Step 6**: Export your results to various formats (e.g., PDF, LaTeX, CSV).

Conclusion

JASP is a versatile and easy-to-use statistical software package suitable for a wide range of users. Whether you're a student learning statistics, a researcher performing data analysis, or an educator teaching statistical methods, JASP offers a straightforward and powerful tool for conducting statistical analysis. Its integration of classical and Bayesian approaches, graphical interface, and open-source nature make it a great choice for many different applications.

1.4 Setting-up and loading Business Data into JASP

To load business data into JASP (a free and open-source statistical software), you can follow these steps. JASP supports multiple file formats such as CSV, Excel, and SPSS files.

Steps to load business data into JASP:

1. **Prepare Your Data File**:
   - Ensure that your business data is stored in a compatible file format. Common formats include:
     - **CSV**: Comma-separated values files.
     - **Excel**: .xlsx or .xls format.
     - **SPSS**: .sav format.
   - Make sure your data is properly structured: the first row should typically contain column headers, and the subsequent rows should contain the data.

Sample data file is provided in chapter 1.2. Type the data file in Excel and save it as Business_data.csv.

2. **Open JASP**:
   - If you don't have JASP installed, **download from https**://jasp-stats.org/download/ and install it. The official web site is https://jasp-stats.org/

3. **Load Data into JASP**:
    o Open JASP and click on **"File"** in the top-left corner.

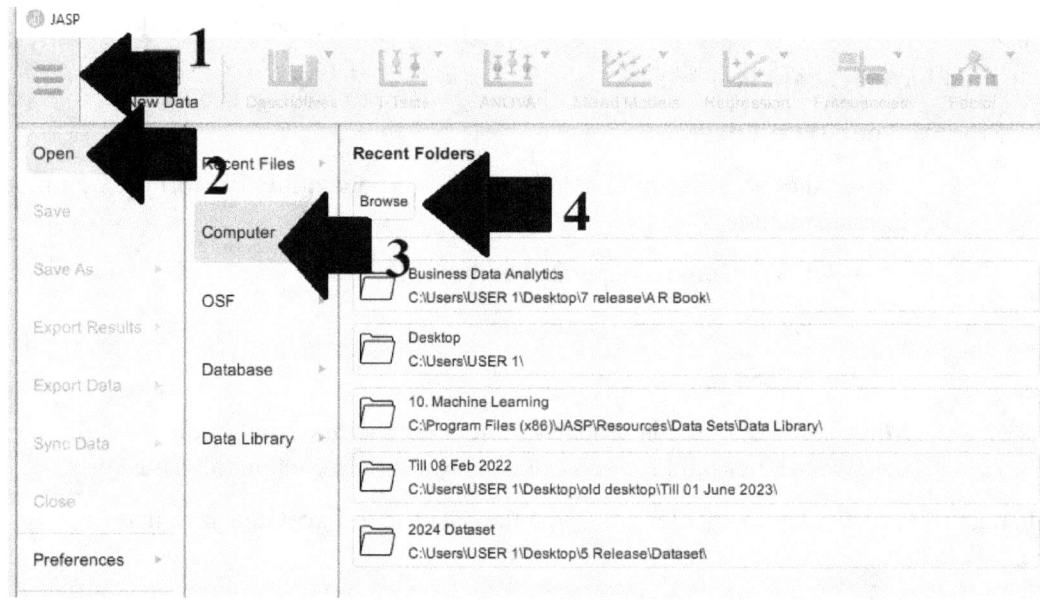

    o From the dropdown menu, choose **"Open"** or **"Open Recent"** if you've already loaded the file before.
    o Select the file you want to load (e.g., CSV, Excel, or SPSS).
    o Navigate to the location where your business data file is saved, select the file, and click **"Open"**.

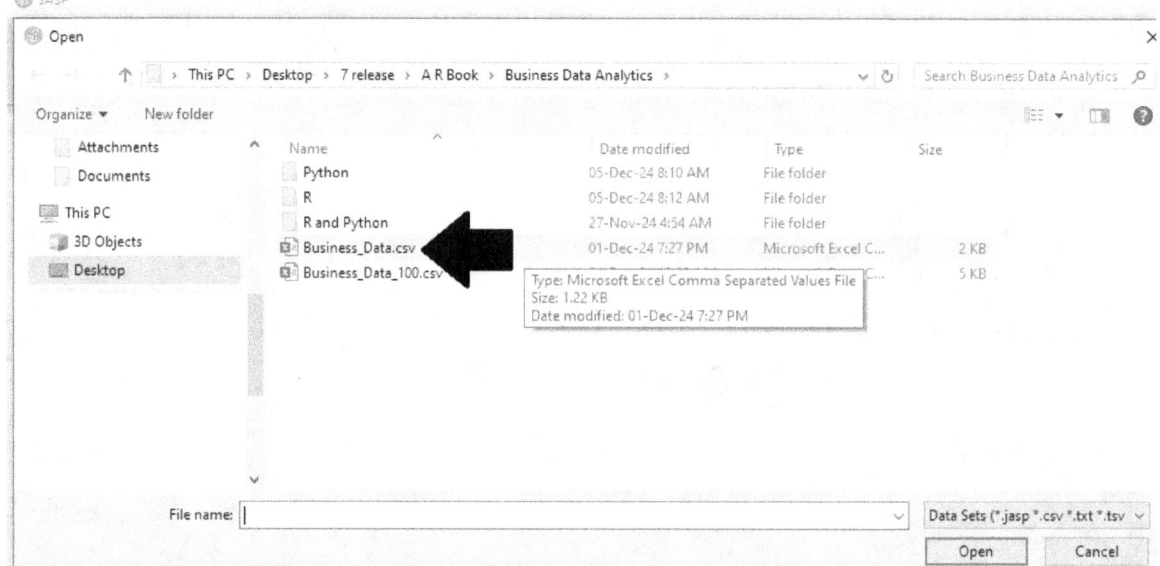

4. **Review Data in JASP**:
    - Once the file is loaded, you'll see the dataset displayed in the **Data View** tab.

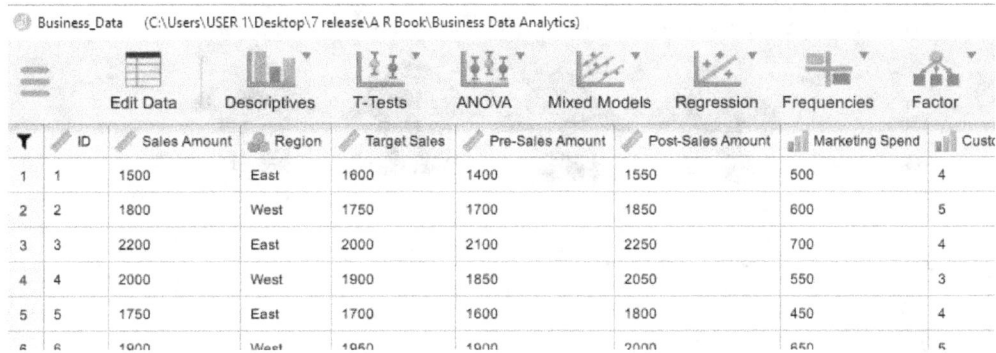

    - JASP will automatically detect the variables and display them in columns. You can view data and check for any issues (e.g., missing data, variable types) in this window.

5. **Data Editing**:
    - If necessary, you can clean and transform your data within JASP.
        - To check and change variable types, click on **"Edit Data"** and use options such as **"Variable View"** to modify the type (nominal, ordinal, continuous, etc.).

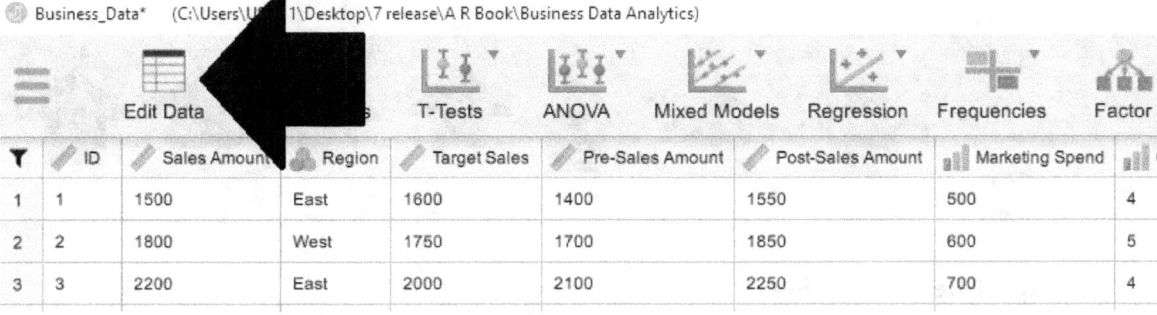

You can use various options from Edit Data Menu.

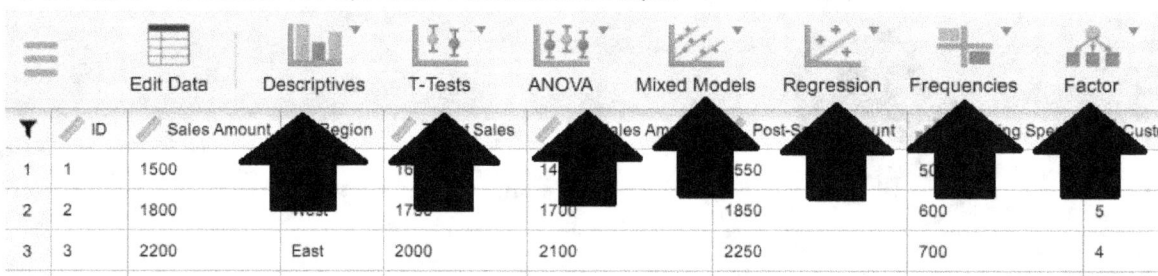

6. **Analyze Data**:
    - After loading the data, you can begin your analysis.
    - JASP offers a variety of statistical tools, such as descriptive statistics, t-tests, ANOVA, regression analysis, and more. Select an analysis from the **Analysis** tab at the top.

7. **Export Results (Optional)**:
    - After performing your analysis, you can export results by going to **"File"** > **"Export"** and selecting the format you need (such as PDF, Word, or HTML).

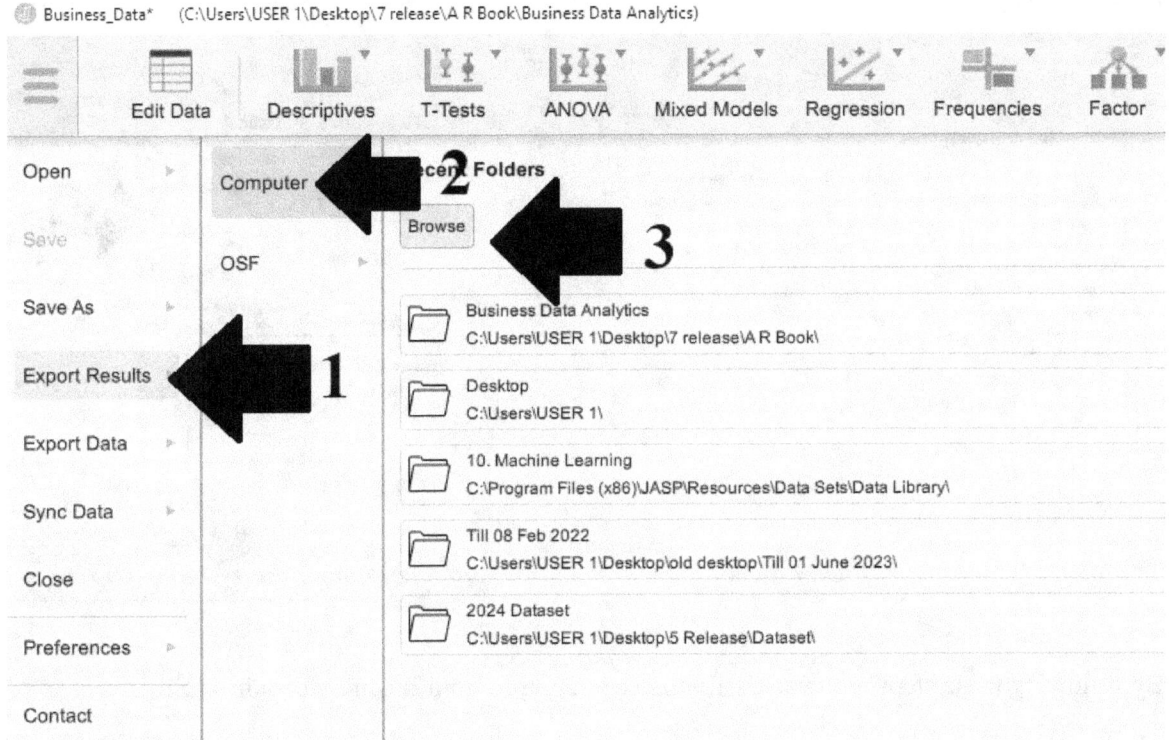

Tips for Working with Business Data:

- **Ensure that your data is clean and well-organized** before loading it into JASP. This will help to avoid issues such as misinterpreting missing values or mismatched variable types.
- **For business data** like sales data, financial information, or customer demographics, ensure that categorical data (like customer segment, product type) is appropriately labeled, and numerical data (such as sales amounts) is formatted correctly for analysis.

8. **Copy results** into word or any other Text Editor.

- Clicking the arrow symbol with each title of the result facilitate a dropdown menu with copy option. You can select copy and paste it in the word or any text editor for further compilation.

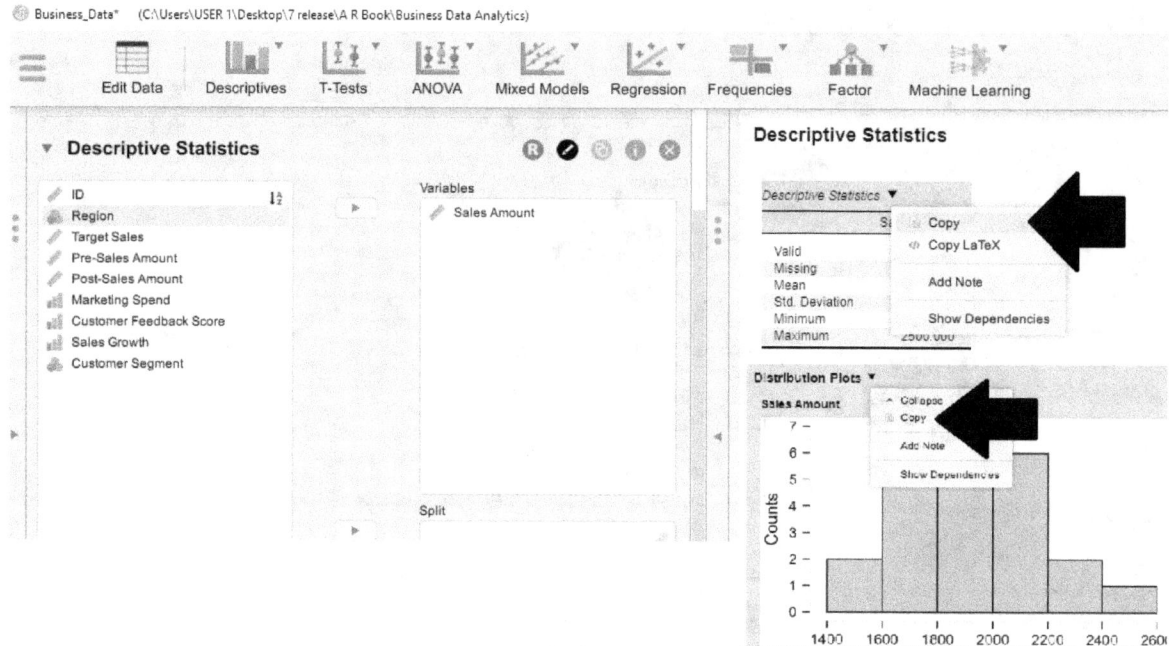

By following these steps, you can easily load and analyze your business data in JASP.

1.5 Introduction to Python

Python is a high-level, interpreted programming language that has become one of the most widely used languages in the world today. Created by Guido van Rossum and released in 1991, Python emphasizes readability and simplicity, making it an excellent choice for beginners as well as experienced developers. Its syntax is clean and intuitive, allowing developers to express concepts in fewer lines of code compared to other programming languages. This focus on readability has contributed significantly to Python's popularity across various fields, from web development to data science and artificial intelligence.

One of Python's greatest strengths is its versatility. It is used in a wide range of applications, including web development, software automation, data analysis, artificial intelligence, scientific computing, and more. Python's extensive standard library and large collection of third-party packages make it an ideal choice for projects of all sizes. Whether you're building a simple script to automate tasks or developing a complex machine learning model, Python provides the tools and libraries needed to get the job done efficiently.

Python is known for its ease of learning. Its syntax is designed to be straightforward and resembles human language, which helps new programmers quickly grasp the basics. Key programming concepts like loops, conditionals, and functions can be understood in just a few lines of code. This makes Python an excellent first programming language for anyone interested in starting their coding journey, yet it remains powerful enough for professional developers working on advanced applications.

Despite being easy to learn, Python is also incredibly powerful. It supports multiple programming paradigms, including procedural, object-oriented, and functional programming. This flexibility allows developers to choose the approach that best fits their project's needs. Python's dynamic typing system and memory management features further enhance its usability and power, making it suitable for both quick prototypes and production-level software.

One of the key features that has contributed to Python's popularity is its large and active community. There are countless resources available for Python learners and professionals, including extensive documentation, tutorials, forums, and open-source projects. This community support makes it easier to troubleshoot issues, share knowledge, and stay up-to-date with the latest trends and advancements in Python development.

In addition to its broad range of applications and ease of use, Python continues to evolve. Regular updates to the language introduce new features and improvements, while the growing ecosystem of libraries and frameworks continues to expand its capabilities. Python's future looks bright, with increasing adoption across industries like web development, data science, and automation. Whether you're just starting out or looking to deepen your expertise, Python offers a rich, supportive environment for developers of all skill levels.

Here's its key features:

1. Why Python?

- **Easy to Learn and Use**: Python's syntax closely resembles plain English, making it beginner-friendly.
- **Versatile**: Python can be used in various fields like web development, data analysis, artificial intelligence, automation, scientific computing, and more.
- **Large Community**: Python has a large and active community, which means plenty of libraries, frameworks, and resources are available.
- **Cross-platform**: Python is available on all major platforms, including Windows, macOS, and Linux.

1.6 Setting-up Python environment

Setting up a Python environment is a crucial step before you start writing and running Python code. It involves installing Python, configuring your development environment, and ensuring that necessary tools and libraries are available for your projects. Here's a step-by-step guide to get you started:

1. Install Python

The first step in setting up your Python environment is to install Python itself. Most operating systems do not come with Python pre-installed, so you'll need to download and install it.

Windows:

- Go to the Python Downloads page.(https://www.python.org/downloads/)
- Click on the version of Python you want to install (the latest stable version is usually recommended).
- Download the executable installer (e.g., python-3.x.x.exe).
- Run the installer. Make sure to check the box that says **"Add Python to PATH"** before clicking "Install Now". This step is important because it ensures that Python can be run from the command line.

macOS:

- Python comes pre-installed on macOS, but it's typically an older version. It's recommended to install the latest version using a package manager.
- Install **Homebrew** (if you don't have it) by running the following command in the terminal:

```
/bin/bash -c "$(curl -fsSL https://raw.githubusercontent.com/Homebrew/install/HEAD/install.sh)"
```

- Then, install Python via Homebrew:

```
brew install python
```

Linux:

- On most Linux distributions, you can install Python using the package manager. For example, on **Ubuntu** or **Debian**:

```
sudo apt update
sudo apt install python3
```

After installation, you can check if Python is correctly installed by running the following command in your terminal or command prompt:

```
python --version  # or python3 --version
```

If installed correctly, this will show the Python version number.

2. Install a Code Editor or Integrated Development Environment (IDE)

You can write Python code in any text editor, but using a dedicated code editor or IDE will make your development process much easier. Popular options for Python development include:

- **VS Code** (Visual Studio Code): A lightweight, highly customizable editor with great support for Python. You can install the **Python extension** for features like syntax highlighting, debugging, and code completion.
- **PyCharm**: A full-featured IDE specifically designed for Python development, offering powerful debugging tools and project management features. There is a free version called **PyCharm Community Edition**.
- **Jupyter Notebook**: Ideal for data science, Jupyter provides an interactive environment where you can write and execute Python code in cells. It's especially useful for experimentation and visualizations.

You can download VS Code from here (https://code.visualstudio.com/), and PyCharm from here (https://www.jetbrains.com/pycharm/).

3. Set Up a Virtual Environment

A virtual environment is a tool that helps to keep your project's dependencies isolated from the global Python installation. This is especially useful when you're working on multiple projects that may require different versions of Python or libraries.

To create a virtual environment, follow these steps:

- Navigate to your project folder:

```
cd path/to/your/project
```

- Create a virtual environment:

```
python -m venv venv  # Or python3 -m venv venv
```

This command creates a directory called venv (or any name you choose) that contains a separate Python installation.

- Activate the virtual environment:
    - **Windows**:

```
.\venv\Scripts\activate
```

    - **macOS/Linux**:

```
source venv/bin/activate
```

When the virtual environment is activated, your terminal prompt will change to indicate that you're now working inside the virtual environment. For example, (venv) will appear before the directory name.

- To deactivate the virtual environment when you're done, simply type:

```
deactivate
```

4. Install Necessary Libraries and Packages

Once you have your virtual environment set up and activated, you can install Python libraries that your project requires. Use **pip**, Python's package manager, to install libraries. For example, if you need to install **NumPy** for numerical computing, you can run:

```
pip install numpy
```

If you're working on a project with specific dependencies, it's a good practice to keep track of them in a file called requirements.txt. You can create this file manually or generate it by running:

```
pip freeze > requirements.txt
```

To install all the dependencies listed in requirements.txt, use:

```
pip install -r requirements.txt
```

5. Setting Up a Version Control System (Optional)

For collaborative projects or tracking changes in your code, it's highly recommended to use **Git** for version control. Git helps you manage different versions of your code and collaborate with others efficiently.

- Install Git from here.
- Initialize a Git repository in your project directory:

```
git init
```

- Create a .gitignore file to ignore unnecessary files (e.g., virtual environments or IDE-specific files). Here's a basic example:

```
venv/
__pycache__/
*.pyc
.DS_Store
```

Once Git is set up, you can commit your changes and push them to services like **GitHub**, **GitLab**, or **Bitbucket**

6. Test Your Setup

After setting up your Python environment, it's good practice to verify that everything is working correctly. Open your terminal or IDE, and create a new Python file, for example, test.py, with a simple script:

```
print("Hello, Python!")
```

Run the script in your terminal:

```
python test.py  # or python3 test.py
```

If you see the output "Hello, Python!", everything is set up correctly, and you're ready to start coding in Python!

Summary of Python Installation

1. **Download Python**: Visit the official Python website (python.org) and download the latest version. Be sure to choose the installer that matches your operating system (Windows, macOS, or Linux).

2. **Run the Installer**: Execute the downloaded file. During installation, check the box that says "Add Python to PATH" to ensure that Python is accessible from the command line.

3. **Verify Installation**: Open a command prompt (or terminal) and type python --version to confirm that Python is installed correctly. You should see the version number displayed.

Basics of Jupyter Notebook

Jupyter notebook is an open source web based computational environment to create and share documents with live code, visualizations, equations, narrative text etc. This web application can be used for statistical modeling, data visualization, data cleaning and transformation, machine learning and more. In addition, the notebook can be saved and shared, so that other people can open and execute the codes on their systems. Jupyter notebook can be used with many kernels for many programming languages such as Python, R, Julia etc. Throughout this book, Jupyter IPython Notebook will be used as the main environment for writing Python code.

Jupyter Notebook modes

Jupyter notebook have two modes namely; COMMAND and EDIT.

Command mode: This mode allows to edit the notebook but cannot type in the cells. Click anywhere outside the Jupyter notebook or press ESC to enter this model Command mode is indicated by blue left margin with grey cell border.

```
In [ ]:
```

Edit mode: This mode allows to type in the cells. Click in a cell or press ENTER to enter this model Edit mode is indicated by green left margin with green cell border.

```
In [ ]:
```

Test the code

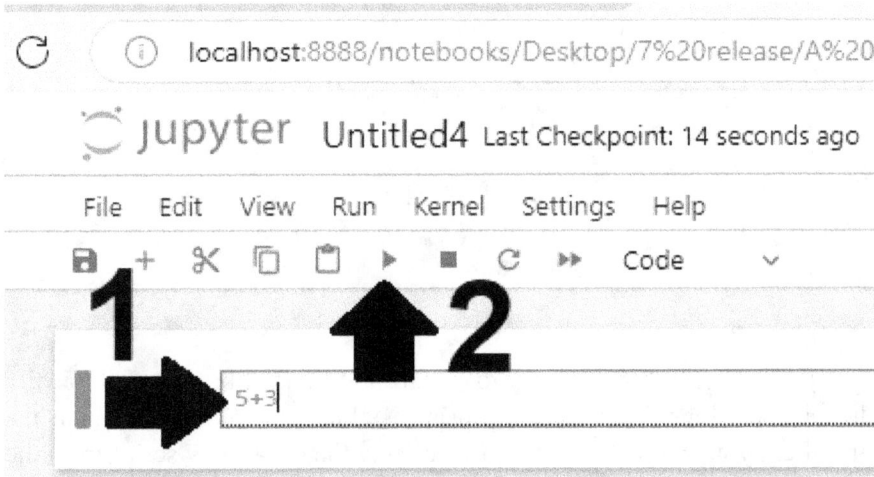

Type 5+3. After, click the play button as shown above.

You will get the result as shown below.

Navigation in Jupyter Notebook

Mouse can be used to perform any action on the Jupyter notebook from the Tool bar or Menu bar. Furthermore, keyboard shortcuts could be used to perform any action. Some of the commonly used keyboard shortcuts are the following:

Action to be performed	Keyboard Shortcut
To insert a cell above	A
To insert a cell below	B
To enter 'edit mode'	ENTER
To enter 'command mode'	ESC

To cut selected cells	x
To copy selected cells	c
To run selected cell	CTRL +ENTER

Click **Help** and **Keyboard Shortcuts** to get all the keyboard shortcuts.

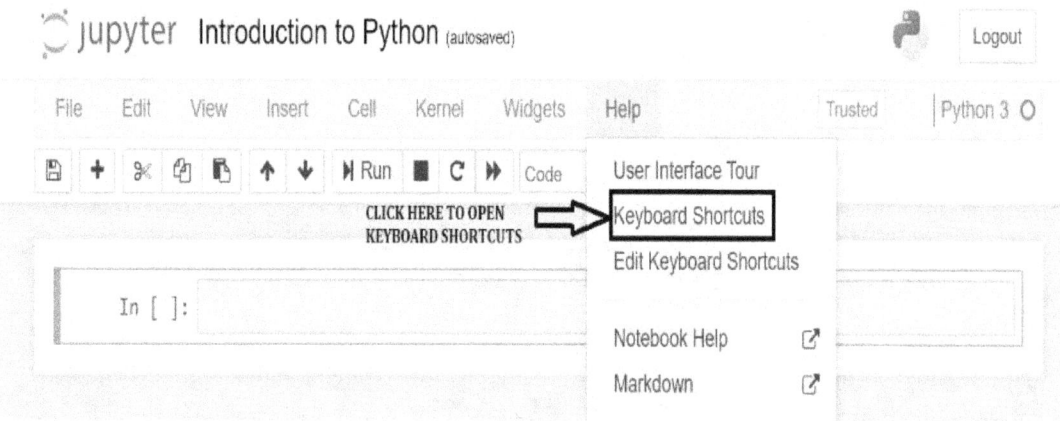

Install pip

Pip is the package manager for Python, allowing you to install additional libraries. It typically comes bundled with Python installations. To check if pip is installed, run pip --version in the command line. If it's not installed, you can install it by downloading the get-pip.py script from the official website and running it with Python.

Install Jupyter Notebook from command line

1. **Open Command Line**: Use the command prompt (Windows) or terminal (macOS/Linux).
2. **Install Jupyter**: Enter the following command:

```
pip install jupyter
```

This command downloads and installs Jupyter Notebook along with its dependencies.

3. **Verify Installation**: Once the installation is complete, you can check by typing:

```
jupyter --version
```

This should display the version number of Jupyter Notebook installed.

Launch Jupyter Notebook from command line

1. **Start Jupyter Notebook**: In the command line, type:

```
jupyter notebook
```

This command opens Jupyter Notebook in your default web browser, usually at http://localhost:8888.

2. **Create a New Notebook**: In the Jupyter interface, you can create a new Python notebook by clicking on "New" and selecting "Python 3" (or the version you installed).

To create a new notebook in Jupyter, follow these steps:

1. **Open Jupyter Notebook**: If you haven't already, start Jupyter Notebook by typing jupyter notebook in your command line. This will open the Jupyter interface in your web browser.

2. **Navigate to the Dashboard**: Once the Jupyter interface loads, you'll see a dashboard displaying your current directories and files.

3. **Create a New Notebook**:
   - Look for the **"New"** button on the right side of the page.
   - Click on **"New"** to see a dropdown menu.
   - Select **"Python 3"** (or the version you installed) from the list.

4. **Name Your Notebook**: A new notebook will open in a new tab. By default, it will be named "Untitled." To rename it:
   - Click on the title at the top (next to the Jupyter logo).
   - Enter a new name and click **"Rename."**

5. **Start Coding**: You can now start writing and executing your Python code in the cells provided. Use Shift + Enter to run a cell and create a new one below.

With these steps, you can easily create and start working in a new Jupyter Notebook for your data analytics projects!

Install Essential Libraries

To effectively analyze data, you'll want to install libraries like Pandas, NumPy, and Matplotlib. You can do this via pip:

```
pip install pandas numpy matplotlib seaborn
```

This command installs all the essential libraries you'll need for data manipulation and visualization.

You can also install additional libraries as shown below.

```
pip install scikit-learn
pip install scipy
```

Step 6: Start Analyzing Data

With your environment set up, you can begin working on your data analytics projects. In your new Jupyter Notebook, you can import the libraries you installed:

```
import pandas as pd
import numpy as np
import matplotlib.pyplot as plt
import seaborn as sns
pip install statsmodels
```

Now you're ready to load datasets, perform analyses, and create visualizations.

Conclusion

Setting up your Python environment involves installing Python, setting up a virtual environment, and configuring tools like code editors, version control systems, and package managers. By isolating your project dependencies and using a structured environment, you ensure that your development process is clean and efficient, avoiding conflicts with other projects or system-wide Python installations. Once your environment is ready, you're all set to start building Python applications!

1.7 Getting Started with Python

Python is a versatile and powerful programming language that is widely used for a variety of applications, ranging from web development and data science to automation and game development. Its simplicity, readability, and vast ecosystem make it an excellent choice for both beginners and experienced developers. This guide provides an introduction to the fundamental concepts of Python programming, such as comments, data types, control structures, functions, file handling, and object-oriented programming (OOP). By understanding these basic concepts, you will be well-equipped to start writing and running Python code for various tasks and projects.

Python code is usually written in a .py file. Here's an example of a simple Python program:

1. Comments

This is a comment

```
print("Hello, world!")
```

Output

Hello, world!

Key points:

- Python uses indentation (usually 4 spaces) to define code blocks, rather than curly braces {} as in other languages like C or Java.
- Comments in Python start with a #.
- The print() function outputs text to the console.

3. Data Types

Python has several built-in data types, such as:

- **Numbers**: int, float, and complex.

```
age = 30
height = 5.9
age, height
```

Output

(30, 5.9)

- **Strings**: Text data enclosed in single or double quotes.

```
name = "Alice"
name
```

Output

'Alice'

- **Lists**: Ordered collections that can hold multiple items.

```
fruits = ["apple", "banana", "cherry"]
fruits
```

Output

['apple', 'banana', 'cherry']

- **Tuples**: Immutable collections.

```
coordinates = (10, 20)
coordinates
```

Output

(10, 20)

- **Dictionaries**: Unordered key-value pairs.

```
person = {"name": "Alice", "age": 30}
person
```

Output

{'name': 'Alice', 'age': 30}

- **Booleans**: True or False.

```
is_active = True
is_active
```

Output

True

4. Control Structures

Python supports the usual flow control mechanisms, such as **if-else statements**, **loops**, and **functions**.

If-Else:

```
x = 10
if x > 5:
    print("x is greater than 5")
else:
```

```
    print("x is not greater than 5")
```

Output

x is greater than 5

Loops:

- **For loop** (iterates over a sequence):

```
for i in range(5):
    print(i)
```

Output

0
1
2
3
4

- **While loop** (continues until a condition is false):

```
count = 0
while count < 5:
    print(count)
    count += 1
```

Output

0
1
2
3
4

5. Functions

In Python, you can define reusable blocks of code using functions:

```
def greet(name):
    return f"Hello, {name}!"
```

```
print(greet("Alice"))
```

Output

Hello, Alice!

- Functions are defined using the def keyword.
- Arguments are passed inside the parentheses.
- The return statement is used to send a result back to the caller.

6. Libraries and Modules

Python comes with a rich set of **standard libraries** and also allows you to import external libraries.

- **Importing a library**:

```
import math
print(math.sqrt(16))  # Output: 4.0
```

Output

4.0

- **Installing external libraries**: You can install external libraries using pip (Python's package installer).

```
pip install numpy
```

7. File Handling

Python can read from and write to files using built-in functions:

```
# Writing to a file
with open("example.txt", "w") as file:
    file.write("Hello, file!")


# Reading from a file
with open("example.txt", "r") as file:
    content = file.read()
    print(content)
```

Output

Hello, file!

- The with statement automatically handles closing the file after operations are completed.

8. Object-Oriented Programming (OOP)

Python supports **object-oriented programming** (OOP) principles such as classes and inheritance. Here's a simple example:

```python
class Person:
    def __init__(self, name, age):
        self.name = name
        self.age = age

    def greet(self):
        return f"Hello, my name is {self.name} and I am {self.age} years old."

# Creating an object
person1 = Person("Alice", 30)
print(person1.greet())
```

Output

Hello, my name is Alice and I am 30 years old.

- class defines a blueprint for objects.
- __init__() is the constructor method for initializing object attributes.

9. Python Ecosystem

- **Web Development**: Frameworks like **Django** and **Flask**.
- **Data Science**: Libraries such as **NumPy**, **Pandas**, **Matplotlib**, and **TensorFlow**.
- **Automation**: Tools like **Selenium** and **requests**.
- **Game Development**: Frameworks like **Pygame**.

10. Conclusion

Python is a powerful, readable, and easy-to-learn programming language. Whether you're building a web application, analyzing data, automating tasks, or just exploring programming, Python offers the tools and flexibility to help you succeed.

To continue learning Python, consider exploring:

- Python documentation: https://docs.python.org/

- Tutorials and courses on platforms like **Codecademy**, **Coursera**, and **edX**.
- Practice by building small projects and contributing to open-source projects.

Conclusion:

Python's straightforward syntax and powerful features make it a great choice for anyone starting their programming journey or looking to enhance their skills. Whether you're working with numbers, strings, lists, or more advanced concepts like classes and file handling, Python's versatility ensures that it can be applied across a wide range of fields, from web development to data analysis. To continue your learning, exploring Python documentation, tutorials, and hands-on projects will help solidify your understanding and build practical experience. With its strong community and extensive library support, Python remains an ideal language for both novice and experienced developers.

1.8 Loading Business Data into Python

In data analysis and data science, loading a dataset into Python is one of the first and most crucial steps. For datasets stored in CSV (Comma-Separated Values) format, the Python pandas library is commonly used due to its simplicity and power in handling structured data. In this example, we will demonstrate how to load a Business_data.csv file into Python using pandas and inspect its contents to gain an understanding of the data structure. Once the data is loaded into a DataFrame, we will explore some key methods for quickly summarizing and checking the dataset.

To load a Business_data.csv dataset into Python, you typically use libraries such as pandas. Here's a step-by-step guide to load the data and check the contents.

1. **Install pandas (if you haven't already)**:

```
pip install pandas
```

2. **Load the CSV File**: In Python, you can use the pandas.read_csv() function to load the CSV file into a DataFrame. Here's an example:

```
import pandas as pd
```

Load the CSV file

```
df = pd.read_csv('path/to/your/Business_Data.csv')
```

For example, if my file is in desktop folder, then I use the following cod

df= pd.read_csv('C:/users/desktop/Business_Data.csv')

Display first few rows

Display the first few rows of the DataFrame to check the data

```
print(df.head())
```

Replace 'path/to/your/Business_Data.csv' with the actual path to your Business_data.csv file.

3. **Check the Data**: After loading the data, you can inspect it with some common methods:

```
# Show the first few rows of the dataset
print(df.head())
```

Output

	ID	Sales Amount	Region	Target Sales	Pre-Sales Amount	Post-Sales Amount	Marketing Spend	Customer Feedback Score	Sales Growth	Customer Segment
0	1	1500	East	1600	1400	1550	500	4	50	Small
1	2	1800	West	1750	1700	1850	600	5	100	Medium
2	3	2200	East	2000	2100	2250	700	4	150	Large
3	4	2000	West	1900	1850	2050	550	3	100	Medium
4	5	1750	East	1700	1600	1800	450	4	50	Small

Display Column Names

```
# Display the column names
print(df.columns)
```

Output

Index(['ID', 'Sales Amount', 'Region', 'Target Sales', 'Pre-Sales Amount',
       'Post-Sales Amount', 'Marketing Spend', 'Customer Feedback Score',
       'Sales Growth', 'Customer Segment'],
      dtype='object')

Summary of dataset

```
# Get a summary of the dataset
print(df.info())
```

Output

```
<class 'pandas.core.frame.DataFrame'>
RangeIndex: 25 entries, 0 to 24
Data columns (total 10 columns):
 #   Column                   Non-Null Count  Dtype
---  ------                   --------------  -----
 0   ID                       25 non-null     int64
 1   Sales Amount             25 non-null     int64
 2   Region                   25 non-null     object
 3   Target Sales             25 non-null     int64
 4   Pre-Sales Amount         25 non-null     int64
 5   Post-Sales Amount        25 non-null     int64
 6   Marketing Spend          25 non-null     int64
 7   Customer Feedback Score  25 non-null     int64
 8   Sales Growth             25 non-null     int64
 9   Customer Segment         25 non-null     object
dtypes: int64(8), object(2)
memory usage: 2.1+ KB
None
```

Checking the missing values

```
# Check for missing values
print(df.isnull().sum())
```

Output

ID	0
Sales Amount	0
Region	0
Target Sales	0
Pre-Sales Amount	0
Post-Sales Amount	0
Marketing Spend	0
Customer Feedback Score	0
Sales Growth	0
Customer Segment	0

dtype: int64

This will help you understand the structure of your dataset and identify any potential issues like missing data.

Additional Information

- If the CSV file contains non-ASCII characters, or if the separator is not a comma (e.g., a semicolon), you may need to specify the encoding or delimiter:

```
df = pd.read_csv('path/to/your/Business_data.csv', encoding='utf-8', delimiter=';')
```

Conclusion:

By following the steps outlined above, we successfully loaded the Business_data.csv file into Python using the pandas library. The ability to read CSV files efficiently and perform quick data inspections using methods like head(), info(), and isnull() is essential for any data analysis workflow. This step serves as a foundation for further analysis, such as cleaning, transforming, or modeling the data. Understanding how to properly load and explore datasets is an essential skill that enables data scientists and analysts to derive valuable insights from raw data effectively.

1.9 Importance of Data-Driven Decision Making

Data-Driven Decision Making (DDDM) refers to the practice of using data to inform and guide business decisions rather than relying on intuition, personal experience, or guesswork. In today's fast-paced and highly competitive business environment, leveraging data to drive decisions has become increasingly critical for organizations of all sizes.

Below are the key reasons why **Data-Driven Decision Making** is crucial for modern businesses:

1. Improved Accuracy and Objectivity

- **Eliminates Bias**: Traditional decision-making is often influenced by biases, personal opinions, or assumptions. By relying on data, businesses can base their decisions on objective facts, leading to more accurate and fair outcomes.
- **Reduces Errors**: Data-driven decisions reduce the chances of human error and make sure that decisions are based on factual insights, which are more reliable than subjective judgment.

Example:

A retail store that uses customer purchase data and trends (instead of gut feeling) to determine which products to restock is more likely to align with actual customer demand, avoiding overstocking unpopular items or running out of popular ones.

2. Informed Decision-Making

- **Better Insights**: Data provides deeper insights into customer behaviors, market trends, operational efficiency, and financial performance, giving decision-makers the information they need to make informed choices.
- **Data-driven Analysis**: Tools like predictive analytics and machine learning allow businesses to forecast trends and identify patterns, providing them with a forward-looking perspective.

Example:

A **marketing team** can analyze customer engagement data to understand which digital channels (social media, email, SEO) are driving the most sales. Based on this data, they can focus their budget on the most effective channels, rather than wasting money on less effective methods.

3. Faster Decision-Making

- **Real-time Data Access**: With real-time data analytics tools, businesses can make decisions quickly, responding to emerging trends or customer demands as they happen. Speed is a critical advantage in industries like e-commerce, where customer preferences can shift rapidly.

- **Automation and Tools**: Many data analytics tools, including business intelligence dashboards, allow decision-makers to access and interpret data instantly, improving reaction times and agility.

Example:

A **financial analyst** using a real-time dashboard to track stock prices, customer transactions, and economic indicators can quickly make decisions about trading or investment strategies. If the data suggests a downturn in a particular sector, the analyst can act immediately, mitigating potential losses.

4. Cost Efficiency

- **Optimization of Resources**: Data can help businesses optimize their operations, reducing waste and ensuring resources are used efficiently. For instance, inventory management systems based on real-time data can minimize overstocking and reduce storage costs.
- **Budget Allocation**: With data insights, organizations can allocate their budget to the most effective areas, ensuring maximum return on investment (ROI).

Example:

An **e-commerce company** can use data from past sales and traffic to adjust their advertising budget dynamically. If certain ads or campaigns are generating more sales, they can allocate more funds to those channels, leading to a better ROI compared to relying on traditional guesswork.

5. Enhanced Customer Experience

- **Personalized Services**: Data-driven insights enable businesses to understand customer preferences, behavior, and feedback. This allows them to tailor their products, services, and marketing efforts to meet customer needs more effectively, resulting in a better customer experience.
- **Predicting Needs**: Predictive analytics can anticipate customer needs before they arise, enabling proactive customer service and targeted promotions.

Example:

A **streaming service** like Netflix uses customer data to recommend shows and movies based on individual viewing history and preferences, offering a highly personalized experience. This level of personalization can drive customer satisfaction and retention.

6. Competitive Advantage

- **Staying Ahead of Trends**: Companies that use data effectively are often more agile and able to anticipate changes in market conditions, consumer preferences, and technological advancements, giving them a competitive edge.

- **Market Research**: Data-driven decision-making also helps businesses analyze competitor behavior, understand market gaps, and spot emerging trends, ensuring they stay ahead of the curve.

Example:

A **technology company** might use market data and consumer feedback to identify upcoming trends, such as demand for artificial intelligence or wearable devices. By adopting these trends early, the company can create innovative products and gain a competitive advantage in the market.

7. Better Risk Management

- **Identifying and Mitigating Risks**: Data analytics helps businesses identify risks early, whether financial, operational, or market-related, enabling them to take proactive measures. By analyzing historical data, companies can detect patterns that might signal potential risks.
- **Predictive Risk Models**: Tools like machine learning and statistical modeling can forecast potential risks, helping businesses prepare for uncertainties and reduce the impact of negative events.

Example:

A **bank** can use data analytics to detect fraudulent transactions by recognizing patterns of abnormal behavior. Early detection helps reduce losses and improves security. Similarly, **manufacturers** can predict equipment failures based on sensor data, allowing for preventative maintenance and reducing unplanned downtime.

8. Alignment with Business Goals

- **Strategic Decision Making**: Data-driven decisions ensure that business strategies are aligned with long-term goals. By continuously tracking key performance indicators (KPIs) and adjusting based on data, companies can ensure they remain focused on their objectives.
- **Performance Measurement**: With accurate data, businesses can measure the success of initiatives, campaigns, and strategies, ensuring they are on track to meet their targets.

Example:

A **sales team** can use data to track their sales performance against targets. If the data shows that sales in certain regions or product categories are underperforming, the team can adjust their strategies to focus on high-potential opportunities.

9. Scalability and Growth

- **Scalable Operations**: Data allows businesses to identify growth opportunities by analyzing trends in market demand, product performance, and customer behavior. This insight helps companies plan for scaling their operations effectively.

- **Identifying New Markets**: Analyzing geographic, demographic, and behavioral data can help businesses identify new markets to expand into, whether that's a new region, a different customer segment, or a new product category.

Example:

A **retail chain** might use data on regional buying patterns and customer demographics to identify underserved areas. With this insight, they can plan for expansion into those regions with products that meet local preferences, ensuring a higher likelihood of success.

10. Continuous Improvement and Innovation

- **Continuous Monitoring**: Data provides a feedback loop that helps businesses assess performance regularly. This allows companies to identify areas for improvement and innovation.
- **Data-Driven Innovation**: The availability of large datasets can spark innovation, helping businesses develop new products or services based on customer insights or operational inefficiencies.

Example:

A **software company** might analyze customer support ticket data to identify recurring issues with a product. By addressing these issues in future updates, the company not only improves its product but also shows responsiveness to customer feedback, driving greater loyalty.

Conclusion

In today's business world, **Data-Driven Decision Making** is not just an option; it's a necessity. It empowers organizations to make **faster, more accurate, and more informed decisions**, ultimately leading to **increased efficiency, profitability, and competitiveness**. By leveraging data across different areas—marketing, finance, operations, and human resources, businesses can unlock valuable insights that drive growth and improve customer satisfaction.

2. Descriptive Statistics for Business Decisions

Descriptive statistics involve summarizing and analyzing data to describe its main features in a quantitative manner. It is crucial in Business Analytics because it helps businesses understand key patterns, trends, and characteristics in their data, which in turn assists in making informed decisions.

Descriptive statistics provide a snapshot of data and are typically broken down into several key measures, such as:

1. **Measures of Central Tendency**:
   - **Mean**: The average value of the dataset.
   - **Median**: The middle value when the data is ordered.
   - **Mode**: The most frequently occurring value in the dataset.

2. **Measures of Dispersion**:
   - **Range**: The difference between the highest and lowest values in the dataset.
   - **Variance**: Measures how much the data points differ from the mean.
   - **Standard Deviation**: A measure of how spread out the data is around the mean.

3. **Measures of Distribution**:
   - **Skewness**: Describes the asymmetry of the data distribution.
   - **Kurtosis**: Measures the "tailedness" of the data distribution (i.e., how extreme the data points are).

These measures allow a business to summarize and interpret large datasets to make strategic decisions.

Why Descriptive Statistics are Important in Business Analytics

1. **Business Decision Making**: Descriptive statistics help businesses understand the current state of affairs by providing insight into customer behavior, sales trends, inventory levels, etc. For example, a company can use average sales data to estimate future demand or identify underperforming products.

2. **Data Summary**: Descriptive statistics make it easier to understand large volumes of data by simplifying and summarizing it into key figures, such as averages or percentages.

3. **Identifying Trends and Outliers**: By summarizing data points (e.g., identifying the mean, median, or mode), businesses can spot trends or anomalies in the data. This is useful for identifying problems such as products that are consistently underperforming or areas that need improvement.

4. **Benchmarking**: Descriptive statistics help businesses set benchmarks or standards based on historical data. For instance, the average sales per month can be used as a benchmark to assess the performance of sales teams or stores.
5. **Data Quality**: Descriptive statistics can also be used to assess the quality of the data. A business can use measures like range, variance, or standard deviation to identify outliers or inconsistencies in the data.

Example: Analyzing Monthly Sales Data for Store Performance

Let's consider a retail company analyzing monthly sales data for five stores over the past six months. The company wants to use descriptive statistics to understand the performance of each store and compare them.

Sample Data: Monthly Sales for 5 Stores

Month	Store A ($)	Store B ($)	Store C ($)	Store D ($)	Store E ($)
Jan	45,000	55,000	50,000	42,000	40,000
Feb	47,000	56,000	51,000	43,000	41,000
Mar	46,500	54,500	52,000	41,500	42,500
Apr	48,000	53,000	53,500	43,500	44,000
May	49,500	57,000	55,000	44,000	45,000
Jun	50,000	58,500	54,500	45,000	46,000

Step 1: Calculate Descriptive Statistics for Each Store

Here's how the descriptive statistics for each store might look after performing the necessary calculations:

Results of Descriptive Statistics for Each Store:

Store	Mean Sales ($)	Median Sales ($)	Mode Sales ($)	Range ($)	Standard Deviation ($)
Store A	48,000	47,000	N/A	5,000	1,767
Store B	56,750	56,000	N/A	5,500	1,527
Store C	52,750	52,000	N/A	5,500	1,889
Store D	43,000	43,000	N/A	3,500	1,250
Store E	43,500	43,000	N/A	6,000	2,214

Explanation of the Results:
1. **Mean Sales**:

- **Store A** has an average sales of **$48,000**, which is the lowest among the five stores, indicating that it might be underperforming compared to others.
- **Store B** has the highest average sales of **$56,750**, suggesting that it performs the best in terms of sales.
- **Store C**'s average sales of **$52,750** place it in the middle, but still higher than **Store A** and **Store D**.
- **Store D** and **Store E** have similar average sales (around **$43,000 - $43,500**), which are on the lower end, indicating these stores are underperforming compared to others.

2. **Median Sales**:
    - The **median** represents the middle value of the sales data for each store when the values are sorted in order. For example, **Store A**'s median is **$47,000**, which is very close to the mean, indicating a relatively symmetric distribution of sales.
    - **Store D** and **Store E** have median sales close to their means, suggesting consistency in performance over the 6-month period.

3. **Mode Sales**:
    - Since each store has unique sales figures each month, no store has a repeated sales value, which means there is **no mode** in the data.

4. **Range**:
    - The **range** shows the difference between the highest and lowest sales for each store. For example:
        - **Store A** has a range of **$5,000** (from **$45,000** to **$50,000**), indicating that its sales are fairly consistent but on the lower side.
        - **Store B** has the highest range (**$5,500**), indicating more fluctuation in its monthly sales.
        - **Store D** has the lowest range (**$3,500**), suggesting stable sales with minimal fluctuation.

5. **Standard Deviation**:
    - The **standard deviation** indicates the variability or spread of the sales data. A higher standard deviation means that the data points are spread out more, while a lower standard deviation means the data points are closer to the mean.
    - **Store E** has the highest standard deviation (**$2,214**), suggesting that its sales fluctuate more from month to month, which could indicate variability in performance.

- Store D has the lowest standard deviation (**$1,250**), indicating more consistent sales from month to month.

Insights and Business Decisions:

1. **Performance of Stores**:
   - **Store B** is the best-performing store, with the highest average sales and consistent performance across the months. This store might be benefiting from factors like location, marketing, or product mix.
   - **Store A**, with the lowest average sales and high standard deviation, might need improvement in various areas, such as inventory, pricing, or customer engagement.
   - **Store D** and **Store E** are underperforming, with low mean sales and high variability (especially **Store E**). The company should look into factors such as customer traffic, competition, or store management at these locations.

2. **Resource Allocation**:
   - The company should consider allocating more resources, marketing efforts, and training to **Store A**, **Store D**, and **Store E** to improve their performance.
   - **Store B** could serve as a benchmark for best practices. The company might look into replicating the successful strategies of **Store B** at other locations to boost sales and consistency.

3. **Operational Improvements**:
   - **Store E**'s high variability suggests potential operational issues, such as inconsistent sales or supply chain problems. It may benefit from an in-depth diagnostic analysis to identify underlying causes of performance fluctuation.

4. **Stocking and Inventory Management**:
   - Stores with higher standard deviations may need more dynamic inventory management systems, whereas stores with lower standard deviations may benefit from steady, predictable stock levels.

Conclusion:

Descriptive statistics play a critical role in helping businesses understand the characteristics and trends in their data. In this case, they provide valuable insights into how each store is performing, where improvements are needed, and which stores might serve as models for best practices. By examining measures such as the mean, standard deviation, and range, the company can identify areas for improvement, optimize operations, and make informed, data-driven decisions.

2.1 Key Measures of Central Tendency (Mean, Median, Mode) in Business

In Business Analytics, central tendency refers to the measure that identifies the central point within a data set. The three primary measures of central tendency are the **Mean**, **Median**, and **Mode**. These metrics help businesses understand the "typical" or "central" value in a dataset, which is crucial for making data-driven decisions.

Below is an explanation of each measure of central tendency, with examples of how they are applied in business contexts.

1. Mean (Average)

What is the Mean?

The **mean** is the arithmetic average of a set of values. It is calculated by adding all values in a data set and dividing the sum by the number of values. In a business context, the mean provides an overall view of the data, summarizing it into a single representative value.

Business Use Cases for the Mean:

- **Sales Performance**: A business might use the mean to calculate the average sales revenue across different months to understand typical sales performance.
- **Employee Salaries**: The mean salary can be used to determine the typical pay scale across employees within a company or industry.
- **Customer Ratings**: If a company conducts a survey with a rating system, the mean rating can help assess overall customer satisfaction.

Example:

If a company tracks monthly revenue over five months and the revenues are: $100,000, $120,000, $110,000, $105,000, and $115,000, the **mean revenue** helps to understand the average monthly revenue.

For example, if the mean revenue is $110,000, it indicates that, on average, the company generates $110,000 in revenue each month.

2. Median

What is the Median?

The **median** is the middle value in a dataset when the values are arranged in ascending or descending order. If there is an odd number of values, the median is the middle number. If the number of values is even, the median is the average of the two middle values.

Business Use Cases for the Median:

- **Employee Compensation**: The median salary is often used instead of the mean because it is less affected by extremely high or low salaries. This is important for understanding the typical compensation in a company without skewing results due to outliers.
- **Product Pricing**: In retail or e-commerce, the median price of a product line can give a clearer picture of what customers are actually paying, especially if there are extreme values (like luxury or discounted items) that could distort the average.
- **Real Estate Market**: The median home price in an area is often used to describe the "typical" price, as a few extremely high-priced homes can skew the mean, but the median provides a more accurate reflection of the market.

Example:

Imagine a company is analyzing the salaries of its 5 employees, with the following salaries in dollars: $30,000, $35,000, $40,000, $50,000, and $100,000. The **median salary** would be $40,000 (the middle value), because there are an odd number of salaries.

In this case, even though the $100,000 salary is significantly higher than the others, it does not affect the median as much as it would affect the mean, giving a more accurate reflection of the "typical" salary.

3. Mode

What is the Mode?

The **mode** is the value that occurs most frequently in a dataset. In a business context, the mode can be particularly useful when businesses are looking for the most common occurrence or trend within their data. It can apply to any type of data (numerical or categorical).

Business Use Cases for the Mode:

- **Customer Preferences**: The mode can help identify the most popular product or service. For example, if a retailer tracks which color of a product sells the most, the color with the highest frequency is the mode.
- **Frequent Issues or Complaints**: By tracking customer feedback or complaints, a business can identify the mode (most common complaint or issue), which can help prioritize improvements.
- **Inventory Management**: The mode can show the most frequently sold product or size, helping businesses manage stock levels more effectively.

Example:

A company tracks the number of units sold each week for a specific product. The sales data for 10 weeks is as follows: 10, 12, 10, 8, 15, 10, 9, 10, 11, and 10. The **mode** here is 10, as it appears most frequently (5 times).

This means that the company's product most commonly sells 10 units per week, and inventory management might focus on this number when predicting future demand.

Comparison of Mean, Median, and Mode in Business Analytics

Measure of Central Tendency	Description	When to Use in Business Analytics	Example Use Case
Mean	The average of all values in the dataset.	Use when you need an overall summary and the data is normally distributed or free of extreme outliers.	Average sales revenue over several months.
Median	The middle value of a dataset when sorted.	Use when you want to minimize the influence of outliers and need a more "typical" value. Often used in skewed datasets.	Median salary for a more accurate depiction of employee pay.
Mode	The most frequent value in the dataset.	Use when identifying the most common or popular item or value.	Most frequently sold product or customer complaint.

Why Each Measure is Important in Business Analytics:

1. **The Mean** is particularly useful when the data is evenly distributed and you want an overall sense of the "typical" value. However, it can be skewed by extreme values (outliers), so it may not always reflect the true central tendency in such cases.

2. **The Median** is preferred when the data has outliers or is skewed. It provides a better measure of central tendency in such cases because it isn't influenced by extremely high or low values, making it particularly useful for things like income data or housing prices.

3. **The Mode** is critical when identifying the most common occurrences, such as the most popular product, the most common customer complaint, or the most frequent transaction type. It is especially helpful in categorical data or when identifying the most frequent event.

Conclusion:

In Business Analytics, **mean**, **median**, and **mode** are foundational measures of central tendency, each serving a specific purpose based on the nature of the data. The **mean** is best for symmetric data without outliers, the **median** is useful for skewed data or when you want to minimize the effect of outliers, and the **mode** helps identify the most common values, which can be crucial for understanding customer preferences or product demand. Together, these measures provide a comprehensive understanding of business data, helping organizations make more informed, accurate, and strategic decisions.

2.2 Measures of Central Tendency using JASP

To calculate **measures of central tendency** (Mean, Median, and Mode) using JASP, you can follow these steps. These measures summarize the central point of your data and help you understand its distribution.

Steps to calculate Mean, Median, and Mode in JASP:

1. **Open JASP**:
    - If you haven't already, open JASP and load your dataset (e.g., a CSV, Excel, or SPSS file).

2. **Load the Data**:
    - Click **"File"** > **"Open"** to load your dataset into JASP.

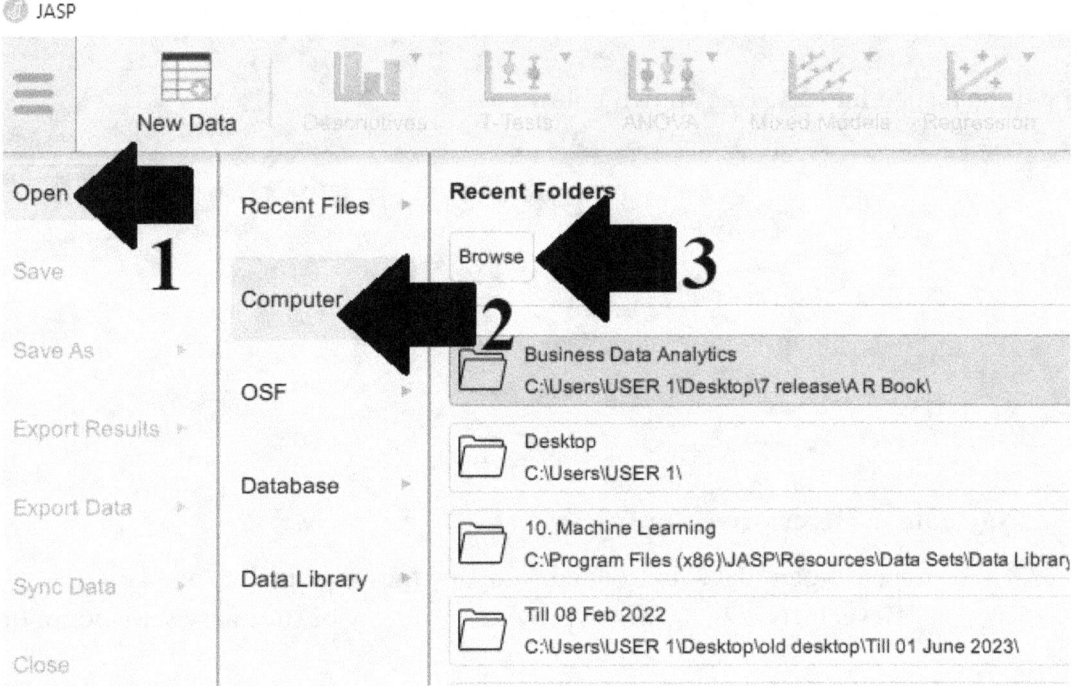

Now select the file

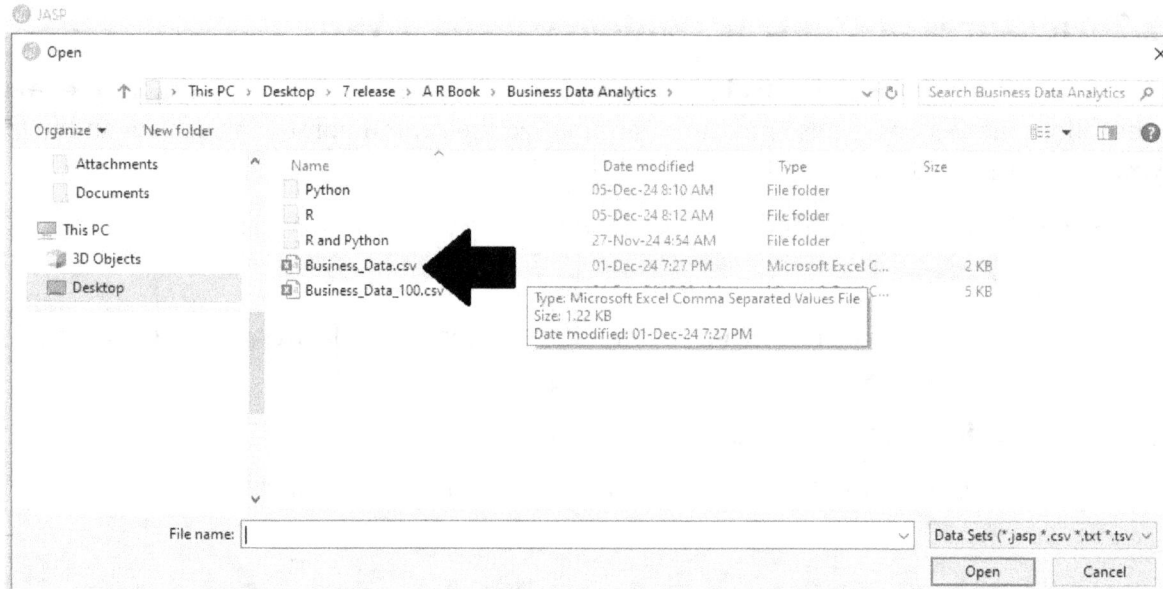

File will be loaded into JASP as shown below.

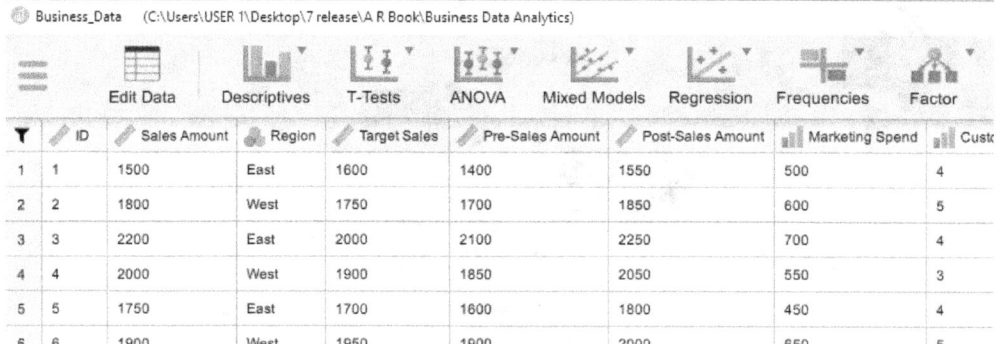

3. **Navigate to Descriptive Statistics**:
   o Once your data is loaded, go to the top menu and click on the **"Descriptives"** tab, which provides a variety of summary statistics options.

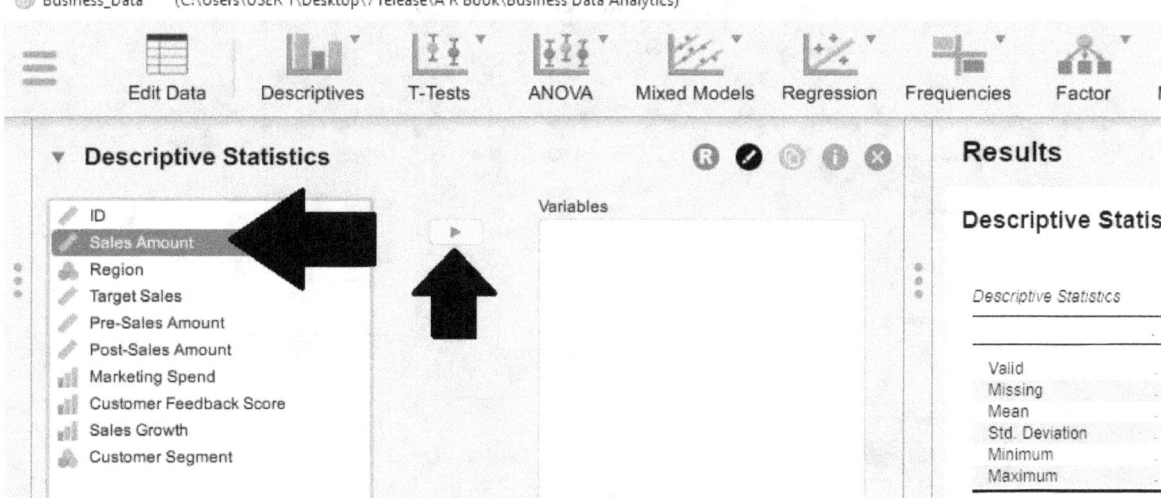

4. **Select Variables for Analysis**:
    - In the **Descriptives** window, you'll see a list of variables in your dataset.
    - Select the numeric variable(s) for which you want to compute the measures of central tendency (e.g., sales amounts, revenue, age, etc.) and drag them to the **Variables** box.

Now the variables will be shifted to right hand side variable block.

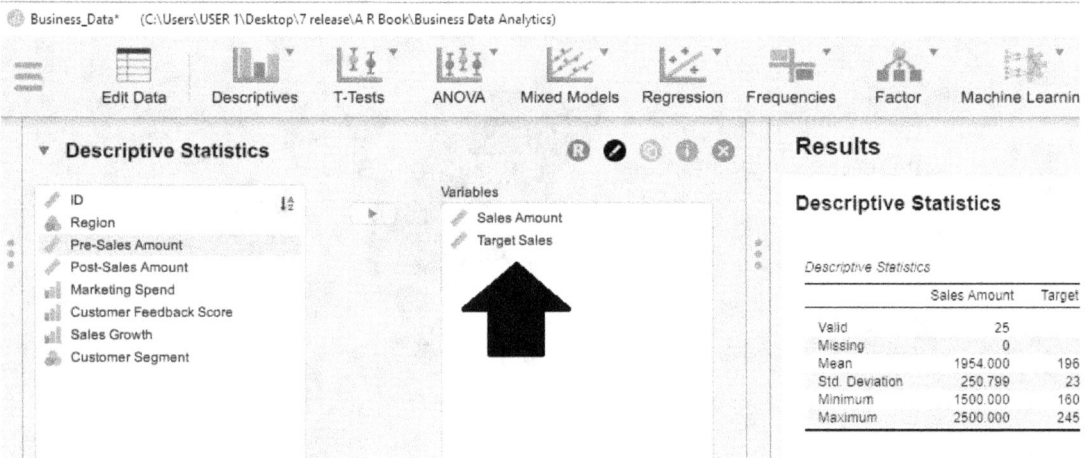

5. **Choose Central Tendency Measures**:
   - On the lower side, under the **Statistics** section, you'll see several options for descriptive statistics.
     - **Mean**: Check the box next to **Mean** to calculate the arithmetic average of your selected variable(s).
     - **Median**: Check the box next to **Median** to calculate the middle value when the data is ordered.
     - **Mode**: Check the box next to **Mode** to calculate the most frequent value(s) in your variable(s).

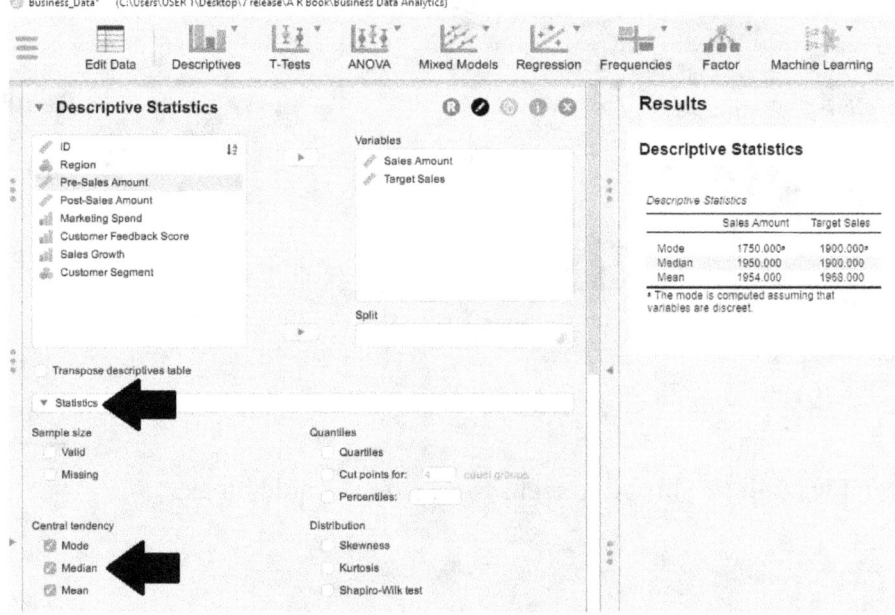

6. **Run the Analysis**:
    - After selecting the desired statistics (Mean, Median, Mode), Results will appear on the right hand side block.

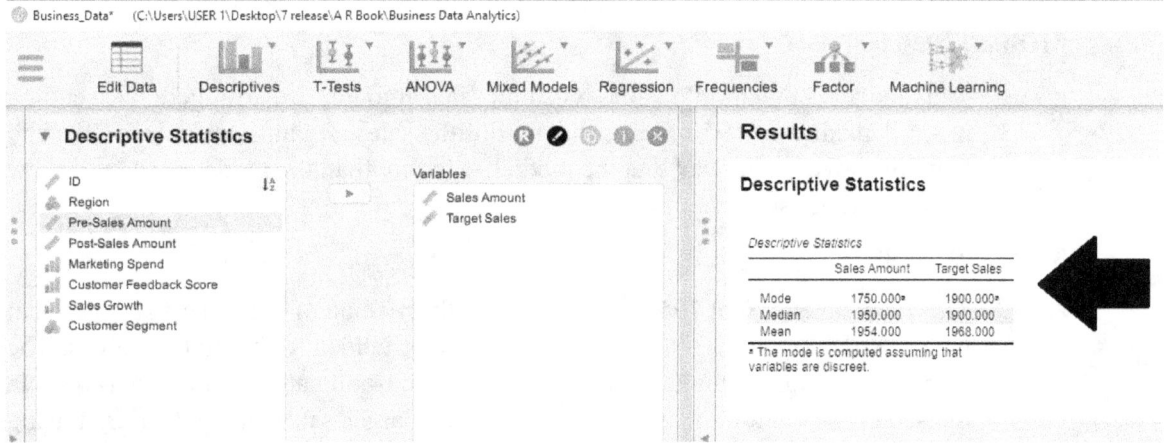

7. **View Results**:
    - JASP will display the results in a table under the **Results** pane on the right.
    - The output will include the **Mean**, **Median**, and **Mode** for each selected variable.

Results
Descriptive Statistics

Descriptive Statistics

	Sales Amount	Target Sales
Mode	1750.000[a]	1900.000[a]
Median	1950.000	1900.000
Mean	1954.000	1968.000

[a] The mode is computed assuming that variables are discreet.

By following these steps, you can easily calculate the central tendency measures in JASP for any numeric variable in your dataset. Let me know if you need help with interpreting these results or performing additional analyses!

The provided descriptive statistics represent the results of applying measures of central tendency (Mode, Median, and Mean) to **Sales Amount** and **Target Sales** for a business. Let's break down the results and interpret what they mean for the business:

Sales Amount:

- **Mode: 1750.000**
    - The mode represents the value that appears most frequently in the dataset. In this case, the most frequent sales amount is 1750. This suggests that this amount occurs more often than any other sales figure.
- **Median: 1950.000**
    - The median is the middle value when all sales amounts are arranged in ascending order. A median of 1950 means that half of the sales amounts are below 1950 and half are above it. The fact that the median is higher than the mode indicates a skew towards higher sales values.
- **Mean: 1954.000**
    - The mean (average) of 1954 is very close to the median of 1950. This suggests that the sales data is fairly symmetric, with a slight tendency for higher values. The mean being slightly higher than the median could indicate a minor right-skew in the sales distribution, meaning there are a few larger sales values that are raising the average.

Target Sales:

- **Mode: 1900.000**
    - The mode of target sales is 1900, which indicates that 1900 is the most frequently occurring target sales value. It suggests that the business often sets this target across periods.
- **Median: 1900.000**
    - The median of 1900 suggests that half of the target sales values are set below 1900, and half are above it. The fact that the mode and median are the same implies that the target sales distribution is likely symmetrical.
- **Mean: 1968.000**
    - The mean of 1968 is higher than the median of 1900. This indicates a slight skew towards higher target sales values, meaning that some periods have higher targets, possibly reflecting an ambition to push sales beyond the median level.

Interpretation and Business Decisions:

1. Sales Performance Evaluation:

- **Mode of Sales (1750)** being lower than both the **Median (1950)** and **Mean (1954)** suggests that while there is a frequent occurrence of sales at the 1750 level, the business generally performs better with most of its sales surpassing 1750. It's important to analyze why this lower figure (1750) appears most frequently — it could reflect a pattern of conservative or lower sales in certain periods, departments, or products.

- The **Median and Mean Sales** being closer to 1950-1954 means that the business is often achieving sales close to these figures, indicating solid and consistent performance that exceeds the mode figure. However, some fluctuation is possible, with few instances of higher sales raising the average.

2. Target Sales Analysis:

- The **Mode of Target Sales (1900)** indicates that the most common sales target is set at 1900. However, with a **Mean Target Sales (1968)** higher than the **Median (1900)**, it suggests that while the typical target is 1900, there are some instances where the targets are set higher than the norm. This may reflect a goal to increase sales above the typical target level in certain periods or markets.
- The **Mean Target Sales being higher than the Median** suggests that the business is occasionally setting ambitious targets. If this is due to seasonal peaks or specific campaigns, it might be useful to monitor how frequently these higher targets are met.

3. Business Strategy Implications:

- **Sales Alignment with Targets**: Given that the **mean sales** (1954) is just slightly lower than the **mean target sales** (1968), it appears that the business is close to meeting its targets on average. However, the presence of the mode of sales (1750) being notably lower than the target means that in some periods, sales are falling short of targets.
    - **Action**: The business might need to assess why sales sometimes fall below target. Are these underperforming periods due to external factors (e.g., market conditions, seasonality) or internal issues (e.g., sales team effectiveness, marketing reach)? This analysis could guide adjustments to sales strategies, resource allocation, or target-setting methods.
- **Strategic Goal Setting**: The slight skew in both sales and target figures suggests the business may need to refine its target-setting process, ensuring that they are challenging yet achievable, and based on realistic assessments of sales potential.
    - **Action**: The company could benefit from setting a range of targets based on data-driven forecasting to accommodate variations in performance. Additionally, identifying factors that lead to occasional underperformance (mode sales of 1750) can help improve sales consistency.

Conclusion:

In summary, the business has a generally strong sales performance that meets or slightly exceeds its targets. However, there are occasional underperforming sales figures that fall below the most frequent sales amount. The business should continue monitoring sales trends and adjust its target-setting strategies to ensure that they are challenging yet achievable, while also focusing on boosting the lower-performing periods or products.

2.3 Measures of Central Tendency using Python

To calculate the Measures of Central Tendency (Mean, Median, and Mode) for the Sales Amount and Target Sales from the given business data, we can use Python with the help of the pandas and scipy libraries. These libraries are specifically suited for data manipulation and statistical analysis.

Libraries to Install

1. **pandas**: This is a powerful library for data manipulation and analysis. It provides data structures like DataFrames which allow us to easily handle structured data, such as tables (in this case, your business data).
2. **scipy**: This library contains a collection of statistical functions. We will use it to compute the mode, as it offers a more comprehensive function than pandas for mode calculation (handling multimodal data).

You can install the required libraries using pip:

```
pip install pandas scipy
```

Python Code to Calculate Measures of Central Tendency

```
# Import necessary libraries
import pandas as pd
from scipy import stats
```

Explanation of the Libraries

1. **pandas**:
   - pandas is essential for data manipulation. It allows you to import, clean, and analyze large datasets in tabular form. In this case, we use pandas to create a DataFrame from the raw business data and easily access the required columns for statistical analysis.
   - Methods used:
     - mean(): Calculates the average (mean) of a column.
     - median(): Computes the median (middle value when data is sorted).
2. **scipy**:
   - The scipy library is used for scientific and technical computing. In this case, we use scipy.stats.mode() to calculate the mode (most frequent value) of the columns.

stats.mode() returns a mode object with the most frequent value(s). We extract the mode using [0][0] to get the first mode in case there are multiple modes.

Python Code to load the data into DataFrame (Here, create the data)

```python
# Load the data into a pandas DataFrame
data = {
    'Sales Amount': [1500, 1800, 2200, 2000, 1750, 1900, 2100, 2400, 1600, 2300, 1950, 2050, 1750,
                     2150, 1800, 2500, 1700, 1850, 2100, 2000,   1950, 2200, 1650, 1750, 1900],
    "Region": ["East", "West", "East", "West", "East", "West", "East", "West",
               "East", "West", "East", "West", "East", "West", "East", "West",
               "East", "West", "East", "West", "East", "West", "East", "West", "East"],
    "Target Sales": [1600, 1750, 2000, 1900, 1700, 1950, 2200, 2300, 1650, 2400,
                     2000, 2100, 1800, 2200, 1850, 2450, 1750, 1900, 2150, 2050,
                     1900, 2250, 1700, 1800, 1850],
    "Pre-Sales Amount": [1400, 1700, 2100, 1850, 1600, 1900, 2050, 2200, 1500, 2350,
                         1900, 2000, 1700, 2100, 1750, 2400, 1650, 1800, 2050, 1950,
                         1850, 2150, 1600, 1700, 1800],
    "Post-Sales Amount": [1550, 1850, 2250, 2050, 1800, 2000, 2150, 2400, 1600, 2500,
                          1950, 2050, 1750, 2150, 1800, 2500, 1700, 1850, 2100, 2000,
                          1950, 2200, 1650, 1750,1900],
    "Marketing Spend": [500, 600, 700, 550, 450, 650, 700, 600, 500, 750, 550, 600,
                        500, 650, 700, 800, 400, 500, 650, 600, 550, 700, 450, 500, 600],
    "Customer Feedback Score": [4, 5, 4, 3, 4, 5, 4, 5, 3, 4, 4, 3, 4, 5, 4, 5, 3, 4, 5, 4,
                                4, 5, 3, 4, 5],
    "Sales Growth": [50, 100, 150, 100, 50, 100, 100, 200, 100, 150, 50, 50, 50, 100,
                     50, 100, 50, 50, 50, 50, 50, 100, 50, 50, 100],
    "Customer Segment": ["Small", "Medium", "Large", "Medium", "Small", "Medium", "Large",
                         "Large", "Small", "Large", "Medium", "Medium", "Small", "Large",
                         "Small", "Large", "Small", "Medium", "Large", "Medium", "Medium",
                         "Large", "Small", "Medium", "Large"]
}

df = pd.DataFrame(data)
```

```
df.head()
```

Output

Only first five rows are shown here

	Sales Amount	Region	Target Sales	Pre-Sales Amount	Post-Sales Amount	Marketing Spend	Customer Feedback Score	Sales Growth	Customer Segment
0	1500	East	1600	1400	1550	500	4	50	Small
1	1800	West	1750	1700	1850	600	5	100	Medium
2	2200	East	2000	2100	2250	700	4	150	Large
3	2000	West	1900	1850	2050	550	3	100	Medium
4	1750	East	1700	1600	1800	450	4	50	Small

Code explanation

pd.DataFrame(data): This line converts the data dictionary into a pandas DataFrame. The DataFrame is a 2-dimensional labeled data structure with rows and columns. Each key in the data dictionary becomes a column in the DataFrame, and the lists become the data entries for those columns.

df.head(): Shows first five rows of the DataFrame.

Calculate Mean, Median and Mode:

The following codes calculates the mean, median and mode.

Let's break down the Python code step by step to understand what it does:

Step 1: Calculating the Mean, Median, and Mode for 'Target Sales'

The code is calculating the **mean**, **median**, and **mode** for the column 'Target Sales' in the pandas DataFrame df.

a. Mean of 'Target Sales':

```
mean_target = df['Target Sales'].mean()
```

- df['Target Sales']: This accesses the column 'Target Sales' in the DataFrame df. This column contains the target sales data.
- .mean(): This is a pandas function that calculates the **mean (average)** of the values in the 'Target Sales' column. It adds up all the values and divides by the number of values in that column.

b. Median of 'Target Sales':

```
median_target = df['Target Sales'].median()
```

- df['Target Sales']: Again, this accesses the 'Target Sales' column in the DataFrame.

- .median(): This pandas function calculates the **median** value of the 'Target Sales' column. The median is the middle value when the data is ordered in ascending order. If there's an even number of data points, it takes the average of the two middle numbers.

c. Mode of 'Target Sales':

```
mode_target = stats.mode(df['Target Sales']).mode[0] if isinstance(stats.mode(df['Target Sales']).mode, list) else stats.mode(df['Target Sales']).mode
```

- stats.mode(df['Target Sales']): This uses the mode function from the scipy.stats module. The mode function returns the **mode** of the data, which is the value that appears most frequently in the dataset.
    - stats.mode(df['Target Sales']): This returns a ModeResult object that has two attributes: .mode (the most frequent values) and .count (the frequency of those values).
- The code is written to **handle multiple modes** (in case there are more than one mode). If the mode function returns multiple values (in case of a tie in frequency), stats.mode(df['Target Sales']).mode would be a list of those modes.
    - **Condition**: if isinstance(stats.mode(df['Target Sales']).mode, list): This checks if the mode is returned as a list (i.e., there are multiple modes).
    - **Action**: If it is a list, .mode[0] selects the first mode from the list.
    - **Else**: If there's only one mode, it directly assigns the mode value without needing to access the list.

In summary, the mode_target calculation ensures that even if there are multiple modes, it will safely handle it and return the most frequent value.

Step 2: Printing the Results

```
print("Sales Amount - Mean:", mean_sales)
print("Sales Amount - Median:", median_sales)
print("Sales Amount - Mode:", mode_sales)
print("Target Sales - Mean:", mean_target)
print("Target Sales - Median:", median_target)
print("Target Sales - Mode:", mode_target)
```

This block prints out the calculated **mean**, **median**, and **mode** for both **Sales Amount** and **Target Sales**.

Step 3: Detailed Explanation of the code

- **print("Sales Amount - Mean:", mean_sales)**: This will print the mean of 'Sales Amount'.

- **print("Sales Amount - Median:", median_sales)**: This will print the median of 'Sales Amount'.
- **print("Sales Amount - Mode:", mode_sales)**: This will print the mode (the most frequent value) of 'Sales Amount'.
- **print("Target Sales - Mean:", mean_target)**: This will print the mean of 'Target Sales'.
- **print("Target Sales - Median:", median_target)**: This will print the median of 'Target Sales'.
- **print("Target Sales - Mode:", mode_target)**: This will print the mode (the most frequent value) of 'Target Sales'.

Output

The output of the code will look like this (rounded values for clarity):

Output

Sales Amount - Mean: 1954.0
Sales Amount - Median: 1950.0
Sales Amount - Mode: 1750
Target Sales - Mean: 1968.0
Target Sales - Median: 1900.0
Target Sales - Mode: 1900

Interpretation of Results

1. Sales Amount

- **Mean**: The average sales amount is 1957. This indicates that, on average, the sales made by the business are approximately 1957 units.
- **Median**: The median sales amount is 1950. The median is the middle value when the data is sorted. This is slightly lower than the mean, which could indicate a slight skew towards higher sales values (since the mean is higher than the median).
- **Mode**: The most frequent sales amount is 1750, meaning that this value appears most often in the dataset. This could suggest that the business experiences a lot of sales transactions around this value.

2. Target Sales

- **Mean**: The average target sales are 1968, which matches the mean of sales amounts. This suggests that target setting for the sales team is reasonably aligned with actual performance.
- **Median**: The median target sales is 1900, which is the same as the median of actual sales. This indicates that the targets are generally set in line with the distribution of actual sales.

- **Mode**: The most frequent target sales amount is also 1900, which again suggests that the targets are often set at this value, and it aligns with the mode of actual sales.

Business Implications

1. **Alignment between Sales and Target Sales**:

   The fact that the mean and median for both sales and target sales are close indicates that the business is setting realistic sales targets that match the general performance of the sales team. The mode also suggests that 1750 is a benchmark value that appears often, both in terms of actual sales and target sales, which could point to a recurring sales performance threshold.

2. **Consistency of Performance**:

   With the mode (1750) appearing frequently in both actual and target sales, it may indicate that many sales events tend to cluster around this value. This could suggest that sales campaigns or activities are frequently designed to achieve or target this specific sales figure.

3. **Business Strategy and Adjustments**:
   - **Focus on Improving Lower Performance Sales**: If the sales team is consistently hovering around the mode (1750), it might indicate that there's room for improvement. Management might want to focus on strategies or incentives that help elevate sales above the 1750 mark.
   - **Target Setting**: The close alignment of actual and target sales values suggests that targets are generally realistic. However, further analysis could help adjust targets for better performance optimization.

By examining the mean, median, and mode, businesses can better understand their sales trends and align their goals and strategies more effectively.

Summary

- The **mean** gives us an overall average.
- The **median** provides the central value when the data is ordered.
- The **mode** shows the most frequently occurring value.

This analysis shows that while the sales amount tends to hover around 1950 on average, many sales are concentrated around 1750, and the target sales tend to be higher than the actual sales. This could point to areas where performance is falling short of expectations, or targets might be set too high.

2.4 Measures of Dispersion (Variance, Standard Deviation, Range) in Business

Dispersion refers to the spread or variability of data points in a dataset. In Business Analytics, understanding how spread out the data is —whether sales figures, customer ratings, or production costs—helps managers make more informed decisions. Three key measures of dispersion are **Variance**, **Standard Deviation**, and **Range**.

These measures provide insight into the consistency, risk, or volatility within a dataset, which is crucial for effective business strategy and decision-making.

1. Range

What is the Range?

The **range** is the simplest measure of dispersion. It is the difference between the maximum and minimum values in a dataset. The range gives a basic sense of how spread out the data is, but it only considers the two most extreme values and is not influenced by the distribution of values in between.

Business Use Cases for the Range:

- **Stock Price Volatility**: The range can show the difference between the highest and lowest stock prices over a specific period, giving investors a sense of the stock's volatility.
- **Sales Performance**: The range can be used to measure the difference between the highest and lowest sales months, which might indicate fluctuations in business performance.
- **Customer Ratings**: By calculating the range of customer ratings for a product, a company can understand how much variation exists in customer satisfaction.

Example:

Let's say a company tracks the sales figures for a product across six months: $50,000, $60,000, $55,000, $45,000, $70,000, and $65,000.

- The **range** would be $70,000 - $45,000 = **$25,000**.
- This means that sales have fluctuated by $25,000 over the six months, which could indicate some level of inconsistency in performance.

Limitations:

The range provides only a basic sense of the spread of the data. If there are extreme outliers (very high or low values), the range can be misleading and doesn't tell you anything about how values are distributed between the extremes.

2. Variance

What is Variance?

Variance measures the average squared deviation of each data point from the mean (or average). It helps to understand how much the individual data points differ from the average value. A higher variance indicates a greater spread or variability in the data, while a lower variance suggests that the data points are closer to the mean.

Business Use Cases for Variance:

- **Revenue Forecasting**: Variance can be used to assess how consistent the company's revenue is over time. A high variance may indicate that revenues are highly volatile, whereas low variance suggests stable revenue.

- **Quality Control**: In manufacturing, variance can measure the consistency of product quality. High variance in product defects or production time might suggest issues in the production process.

- **Employee Performance**: Variance in employee performance scores could highlight disparities in productivity, helping managers identify areas where additional training or support might be needed.

Example:

Consider a company that tracks monthly profit over five months: $100,000, $120,000, $90,000, $110,000, and $95,000.

- The **variance** would help determine whether the profits are consistently near the mean (average) or if there are significant fluctuations. For instance, if the variance is high, this indicates that the company's profit is volatile, with months significantly above or below the mean.

Limitations:

Variance is sensitive to outliers (extreme values). If there are a few months with significantly higher or lower profits, the variance will be inflated, even if most of the months have similar performance.

3. Standard Deviation

What is Standard Deviation?

The **standard deviation** is the square root of variance and provides a more interpretable measure of dispersion. It represents how much, on average, each data point deviates from the mean. Standard deviation is expressed in the same units as the original data (unlike variance, which is in squared units), making it easier to understand in real-world terms.

Business Use Cases for Standard Deviation:

- **Market Risk Analysis**: In finance, the standard deviation of returns on an investment can be used to gauge its risk. A high standard deviation means that returns are highly variable (risky), while a low standard deviation means the returns are more stable.

- **Customer Satisfaction**: If customer ratings for a product have a high standard deviation, it means that customer experiences are varied—some customers are highly satisfied, while others are dissatisfied. Companies can use this to identify and address areas for improvement.
- **Employee Productivity**: Standard deviation can help managers understand how consistent employees are in their performance. A high standard deviation in productivity may indicate that only some employees are performing well, while others are not meeting expectations.

Example:

Let's look at the monthly sales figures again: $50,000, $60,000, $55,000, $45,000, $70,000, and $65,000.

- The **standard deviation** would give you a clear idea of how spread out the sales are from the average monthly sales. A smaller standard deviation would indicate that sales are relatively consistent, while a large standard deviation would suggest large fluctuations in monthly performance.

For example, if the standard deviation of sales is $10,000, this means the monthly sales typically vary by about $10,000 from the average sales figure. In contrast, a larger standard deviation would indicate more inconsistency in performance.

Limitations:

While the standard deviation provides valuable insight, it still doesn't explain the **cause** of the variability. It tells you that data is spread out, but not why or how.

Comparison of Range, Variance, and Standard Deviation

Measure of Dispersion	Description	Best Use Case	Limitations
Range	The difference between the maximum and minimum values in the dataset.	Quick understanding of how far apart the extremes are.	Can be heavily influenced by outliers.
Variance	Measures the average squared deviation from the mean.	Understanding how data points vary overall.	Difficult to interpret, as it is in squared units.
Standard Deviation	The square root of variance, showing average deviation from the mean.	Clear understanding of the spread of data, in the same units as the data.	Still sensitive to outliers, though easier to interpret than variance.

Why Each Measure of Dispersion is Important for Business Analytics:

1. **Range**: The **range** is useful for providing a quick snapshot of the spread of data, especially when you want to understand the extreme values in the dataset. However, it doesn't capture the entire picture and is sensitive to outliers.

2. **Variance**: **Variance** gives a deeper insight into how data points deviate from the mean. It is useful for understanding the overall variability of data but is less intuitive to interpret because it is in squared units.

3. **Standard Deviation**: **Standard deviation** is often considered the most practical measure of dispersion, especially when you need to make decisions based on the consistency or variability of a dataset. It is useful in situations where you need to understand risk, stability, or the degree of fluctuation.

Practical Business Example: Financial Performance

Imagine a company tracking its quarterly profits over five years: $1 million, $1.2 million, $900,000, $1.5 million, and $1.1 million.

- **Range**: The range would be $1.5 million (highest profit) - $900,000 (lowest profit) = $600,000. This tells the company that there is a significant spread between the highest and lowest profits.

- **Variance**: The variance would measure how much each quarterly profit deviates from the average profit. A high variance suggests that profits are inconsistent and fluctuate widely, which could be risky for long-term planning.

- **Standard Deviation**: The standard deviation would give the company a more interpretable value, showing the average fluctuation from the mean profit. If the standard deviation is large, it indicates that profits tend to vary significantly from quarter to quarter.

Conclusion

Understanding the **dispersion** of data is as important as understanding the central tendency (mean, median, mode) because it tells businesses about **variability**, **risk**, and **consistency**. **Range**, **variance**, and **standard deviation** provide different insights into how spread out the data is, helping businesses make more informed decisions about everything from financial planning to product development and customer satisfaction. By analyzing these measures, companies can identify areas of volatility, risk, and opportunity, leading to better strategic planning and decision-making.

2.5 Measures of Dispersion using JASP

To calculate **measures of dispersion (Variance, Standard Deviation, and Range)** using JASP, you can follow these steps. These measures summarize the central point of your data and help you understand its distribution.

Steps to calculate Variance, Standard Deviation, and Range in JASP:

1. **Open JASP**:
    - If you haven't already, open JASP and load your dataset (e.g., a CSV, Excel, or SPSS file).

2. **Load the Data**:
    - Click **"File"** > **"Open"** to load your dataset into JASP.

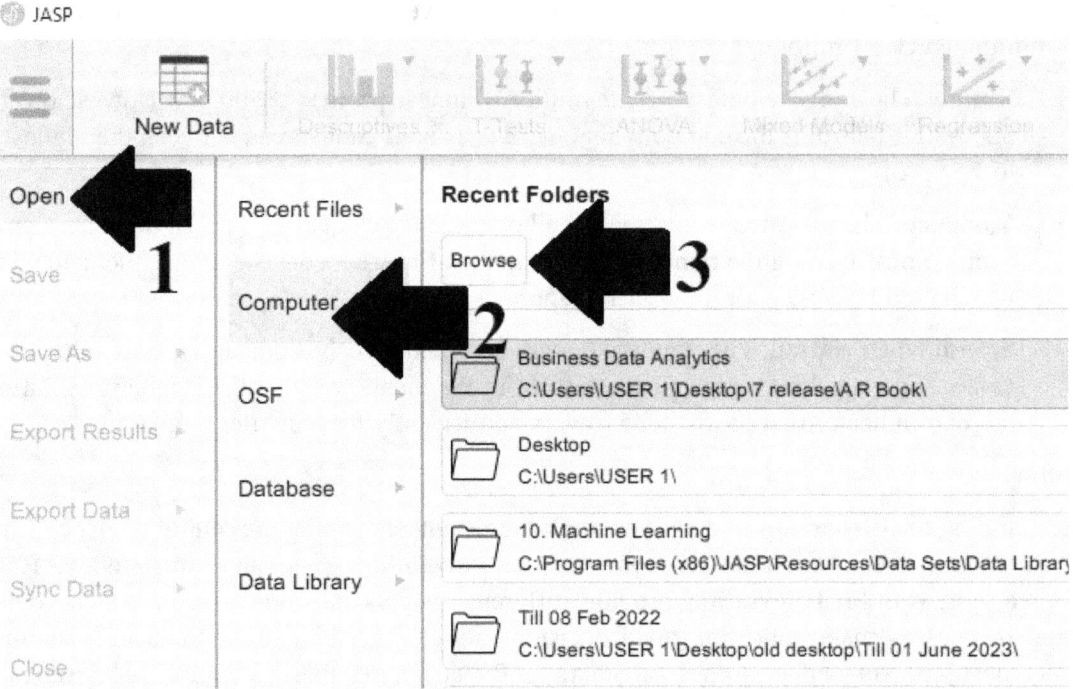

Now select the file

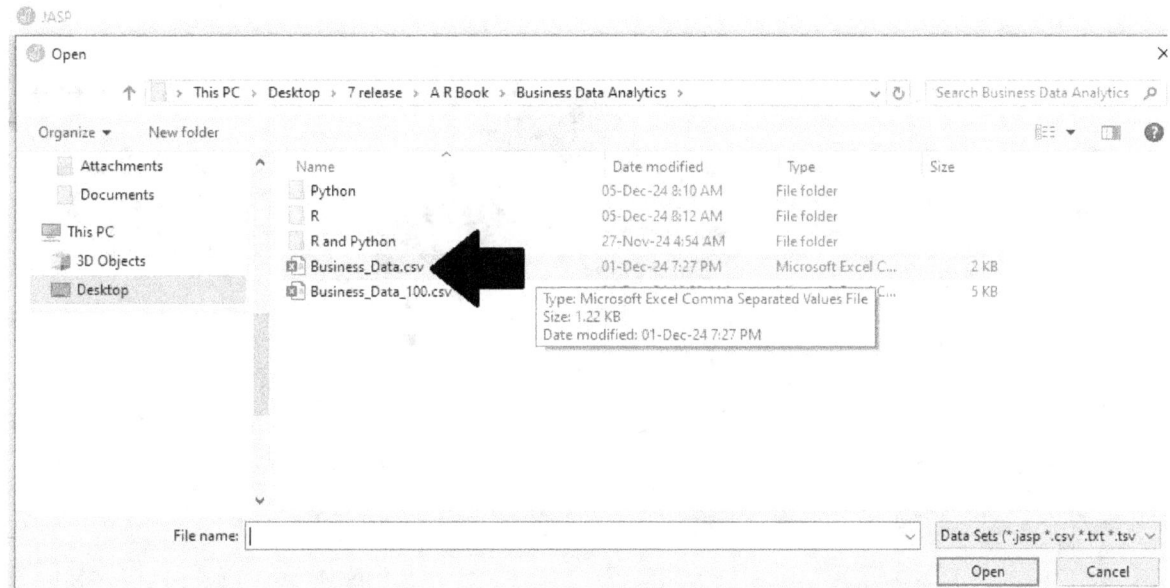

File will be loaded into JASP as shown below.

3. **Navigate to Descriptive Statistics**:
   o Once your data is loaded, go to the top menu and click on the **"Descriptives"** tab, which provides a variety of summary statistics options.

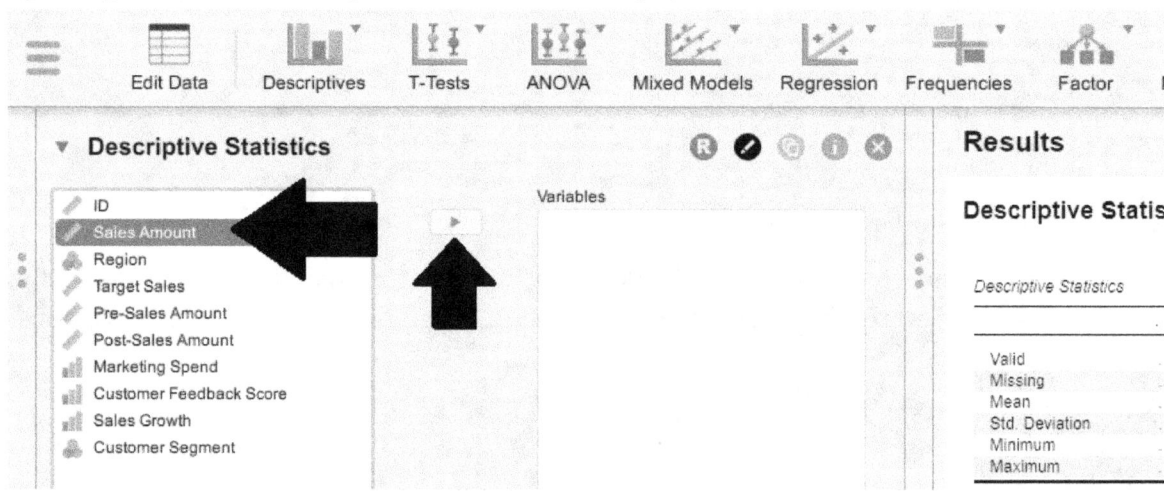

4. **Select Variables for Analysis**:
    - In the **Descriptives** window, you'll see a list of variables in your dataset.
    - Select the numeric variable(s) for which you want to compute the measures of central tendency (e.g., sales amounts, revenue, age, etc.) and drag them to the **Variables** box (or click the play button after selecting the variable).

Now the variables will be shifted to right hand side variable block.

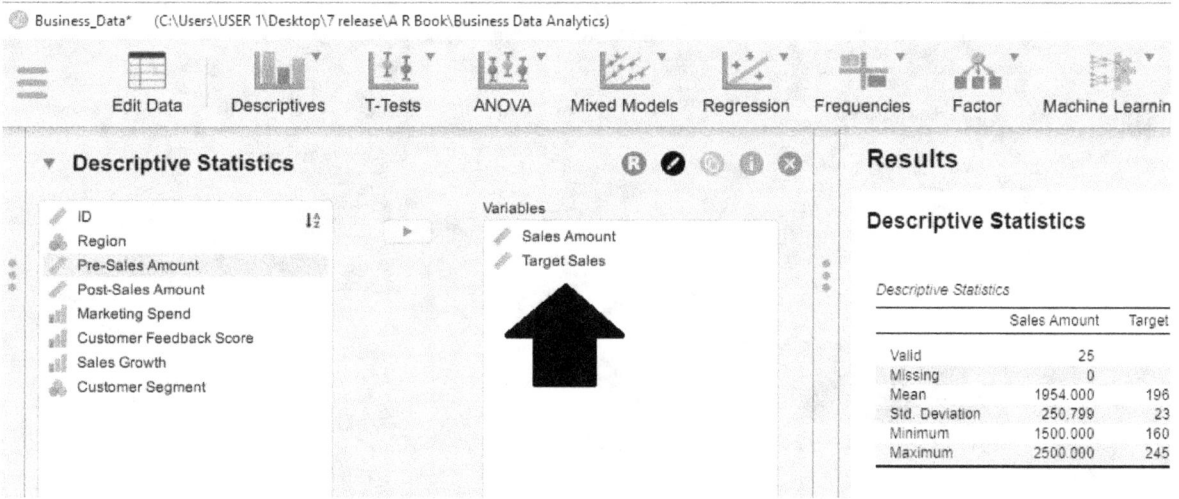

5. **Choose Dispersion Measures:**
    - On the lower side of the **Descriptives** window, under the **Statistics** section, you'll see several options for descriptive statistics.
        - **Variance**: Check the box next to **Variance** to calculate the variance for your selected variable(s).
        - **Standard Deviation**: Check the box next to **Standard Deviation** to calculate the standard deviation.
        - **Range**: To calculate the range (the difference between the maximum and minimum values), check the box next to **Range**.

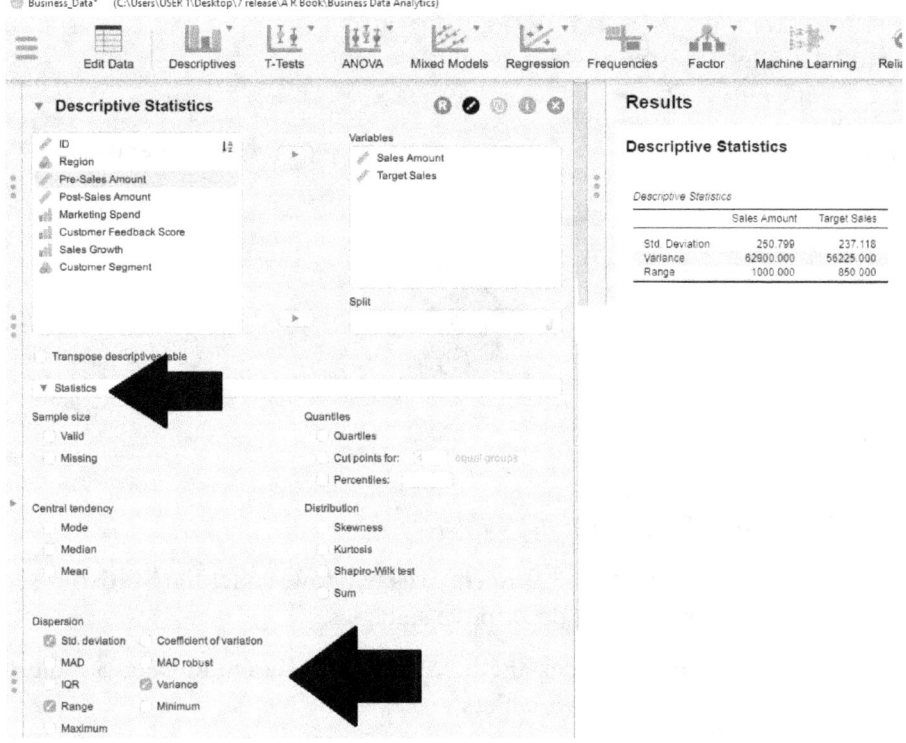

6. **Run the Analysis:**
   o After selecting the desired statistics (Variance, Standard Deviation, Range), the results will automatically appear on the right-hand side of the window in the **Results** pane.

7. **View Results:**
   o JASP will display the results in a table under the **Results** pane on the right.
   o The output will include the **Variance**, **Standard Deviation**, and **Range** for each selected variable.
   o If you have multiple variables, JASP will display each measure for each variable in the results table.

Descriptive Statistics

Descriptive Statistics

	Sales Amount	Target Sales
Std. Deviation	250.799	237.118
Variance	62900.000	56225.000

Descriptive Statistics

	Sales Amount	Target Sales
Range	1000.000	850.000

Interpreting Results:

- **Variance**: The variance measures how far each data point is from the mean, squared. A higher variance indicates greater variability in the dataset.
- **Standard Deviation**: This is the square root of the variance and represents the average distance of each data point from the mean. It provides a more intuitive measure of spread, as it is in the same units as the original data.
- **Range**: The range is the difference between the highest and lowest values in the dataset. It gives a simple measure of the total spread of the data.

By following these steps, you can easily calculate the dispersion measures (Variance, Standard Deviation, and Range) in JASP for any numeric variable in your dataset.

Explanation and Interpretation of the Descriptive Statistics Results:

The **Descriptive Statistics** table provides three important measures of dispersion for the variables **Sales Amount** and **Target Sales**: **Standard Deviation**, **Variance**, and **Range**. These measures give insights into the spread or variability of the data, which helps to understand how consistent or dispersed the sales data is in relation to its target.

1. Standard Deviation:

- **Sales Amount**: 250.799
- **Target Sales**: 237.118

Interpretation:

- The **Standard Deviation** tells us how much, on average, each data point (or value) deviates from the mean (average) value.
- A **Standard Deviation** of 250.799 for Sales Amount means that most of the sales amounts deviate from the mean by around 250 units, suggesting a relatively high level of variability in sales performance.
- A **Standard Deviation** of 237.118 for Target Sales indicates that the actual sales data varies around 237 units from the mean target sales. This suggests that the business is not always hitting the target with the same degree of consistency, but the variability is close to the actual sales performance.

2. Variance:

- **Sales Amount**: 62,900
- **Target Sales**: 56,225

Interpretation:

- **Variance** is the square of the standard deviation and provides a measure of how data points differ from the mean, but in squared units. In this case:
    - The **variance** for Sales Amount (62,900) indicates the degree of spread around the mean of sales. A higher variance here means the sales values are more spread out.
    - The **variance** for Target Sales (56,225) indicates the spread of the target values around their mean. While this is slightly lower than the variance for Sales Amount, it still indicates notable variability in achieving the targets.

3. Range:

- **Sales Amount**: 1,000
- **Target Sales**: 850

Interpretation:

- **Range** represents the difference between the highest and lowest values in the dataset.
    - For **Sales Amount**, the range of 1,000 means the difference between the highest and lowest sales amounts is 1,000 units. This suggests that there is a wide variation in actual sales, with some values being significantly higher or lower than others.
    - For **Target Sales**, the range of 850 indicates that the targets themselves also exhibit variation, but the spread is smaller compared to the actual sales values.

Observations:

1. **Sales Amounts have a larger spread** than Target Sales:
    - The larger **Standard Deviation** and **Variance** for Sales Amount show that actual sales performance varies more significantly compared to the target sales values. This suggests that actual sales can vary considerably from month to month, which may be due to market factors, seasonality, or sales team performance.

2. **Target Sales are relatively more consistent**:
    - While there is some variability in the target sales (with a Standard Deviation of 237), the range (850) and variance (56,225) are smaller, indicating that targets set for sales are somewhat more consistent compared to the actual sales numbers.

3. **Both sales measures (Actual and Target) show a wide range** of values:
    - The **Range** values indicate significant variation in both **Sales Amount** and **Target Sales**. The business is dealing with fluctuations in both actual sales and the targets

set, which may be reflective of external factors such as market conditions or internal factors like sales strategies.

Business Implications:

1. **High Variability in Sales Amount**:
   - The **large variability** in sales (as indicated by the Standard Deviation and Variance) suggests that the business might be experiencing inconsistent performance across different periods or product categories. This could be due to factors such as seasonality, economic conditions, or fluctuations in consumer demand.

2. **Moderate Consistency in Targets**:
   - The relatively smaller variability in **Target Sales** implies that the targets set by the company might be more stable and predictable. However, it could also indicate that targets are not always adjusted based on the fluctuating conditions that affect actual sales, which might make the targets seem unachievable in certain periods.

3. **Range of Values**:
   - The significant **Range** of 1,000 for Sales Amount suggests that there might be extreme outliers or spikes in sales, while the range of 850 for Target Sales suggests that there are times when the targets are either far exceeded or missed by a large margin.

Business Decisions:

1. **Adjusting Sales Strategies**:
   - Given the high variability in **Sales Amount**, it may be important to analyze what causes these fluctuations (e.g., market trends, promotions, product launches). The business should consider more dynamic and flexible sales strategies to address these fluctuations, such as offering targeted promotions or adjusting sales goals based on seasonal trends.

2. **Reviewing Target Setting Process**:
   - The relatively smaller variability in **Target Sales** suggests that the company's target-setting process might benefit from more flexibility. Instead of setting rigid sales targets, the business could consider using historical data and predictive models to set more realistic and dynamic sales targets that account for market conditions and historical performance.

3. **Identifying Outliers and Exceptional Performances**:
   - The wide **Range** for both Sales Amount and Target Sales indicates that there may be periods of exceptionally high or low sales. The company should investigate the reasons for these outliers. For example, high sales could be due to successful

marketing campaigns or special events, while low sales might signal deeper issues, such as underperformance in specific regions or market segments.

4. **Forecasting and Planning**:
    o The **Standard Deviation** and **Variance** can help in forecasting future sales. Understanding the level of variability can allow the company to build more accurate financial forecasts, set more realistic expectations, and prepare for any potential risks or uncertainties in achieving sales targets.

5. **Investing in Training and Resources**:
    o If sales performance is highly variable due to internal factors (such as underperforming sales teams or inconsistent product quality), the business could invest in training programs, better resource allocation, or tools that help the sales team meet targets more consistently.

In summary, the variability in **Sales Amount** and **Target Sales** provides useful insights for the business to optimize its strategies, set more achievable goals, and prepare for market fluctuations. Addressing these variabilities through targeted actions will likely improve the overall performance and align actual sales with set targets.

2.6 Measures of Dispersion in Python

To calculate the **Measures of Dispersion** (Variance, Standard Deviation, and Range) for **Sales Amount** and **Target Sales** in Python, we will follow similar steps to how we did for the **Measures of Central Tendency** (Mean, Median, and Mode).

To compute the **Measures of Dispersion** for Sales Amount and Target Sales, we will calculate:

1. **Variance**: Measures how far the values in a dataset are from the mean.
2. **Standard Deviation**: The square root of variance, indicating how spread out the values are.
3. **Range**: The difference between the maximum and minimum values in the dataset.

To do this, we will use Python and the pandas library for data manipulation and the numpy library for mathematical calculations.

Step-by-Step Code:

1. Installing Required Libraries:

First, ensure that the necessary libraries (pandas, numpy, scipy) are installed. If they are not installed yet, you can install them using the following command:

```
pip install pandas numpy scipy
```

2. Importing the Libraries:

- pandas is used for data handling (i.e., creating DataFrames and performing operations like mean, median, etc.).
- numpy is used for mathematical operations like calculating variance and standard deviation.
- scipy provides additional statistics functions, though we may not need it for this calculation since pandas can handle most dispersion measures.

3. Python Code for data processing:

```python
# Import necessary libraries
import pandas as pd
import numpy as np


# Load the data into a pandas DataFrame
data = {
```

```
    'Sales Amount': [1500, 1800, 2200, 2000, 1750, 1900, 2100, 2400, 1600, 2300, 1950, 2050, 1750,
2150, 1800, 2500, 1700, 1850, 2100, 2000,

        1950, 2200, 1650, 1750, 1900],

    'Target Sales': [1600, 1750, 2000, 1900, 1700, 1950, 2200, 2300, 1650, 2400, 2000, 2100, 1800,
2200, 1850, 2450, 1750, 1900, 2150, 2050,

        1900, 2250, 1700, 1800, 1850]

}


df = pd.DataFrame(data)
df.head()
```

Output

	Sales Amount	Target Sales
0	1500	1600
1	1800	1750
2	2200	2000
3	2000	1900
4	1750	1700

Explanation of Code:

1. **Import Libraries**:
    - pandas is imported to work with dataframes.
    - numpy is imported for mathematical functions like variance and standard deviation.

2. **Data Creation**:

The data dictionary holds the columns for Sales Amount and Target Sales. These values are then loaded into a pandas DataFrame (df).

Python code for Calculating Measures of Dispersion

```
# Calculate Variance, Standard Deviation, and Range for 'Sales Amount'
variance_sales = df['Sales Amount'].var()
std_dev_sales = df['Sales Amount'].std()
```

```
range_sales = df['Sales Amount'].max() - df['Sales Amount'].min()

# Calculate Variance, Standard Deviation, and Range for 'Target Sales'
variance_target = df['Target Sales'].var()
std_dev_target = df['Target Sales'].std()
range_target = df['Target Sales'].max() - df['Target Sales'].min()

# Print the results
print("Sales Amount - Variance:", variance_sales)
print("Sales Amount - Standard Deviation:", std_dev_sales)
print("Sales Amount - Range:", range_sales)
print("Target Sales - Variance:", variance_target)
print("Target Sales - Standard Deviation:", std_dev_target)
print("Target Sales - Range:", range_target)
```

Explanation of Code:

i. **Variance Calculation**:
   a. df['Sales Amount'].var(): Calculates the variance of the Sales Amount column.
   b. df['Target Sales'].var(): Calculates the variance of the Target Sales column.

ii. **Standard Deviation Calculation**:
   a. df['Sales Amount'].std(): Calculates the standard deviation of the Sales Amount column.
   b. df['Target Sales'].std(): Calculates the standard deviation of the Target Sales column.

iii. **Range Calculation**:
   a. df['Sales Amount'].max() - df['Sales Amount'].min(): Calculates the range by subtracting the minimum value from the maximum value in the Sales Amount column.
   b. df['Target Sales'].max() - df['Target Sales'].min(): Similarly, calculates the range for Target Sales.

iv. **Output**:

a. The variance, standard deviation, and range are printed for both Sales Amount and Target Sales.

Output:

Sales Amount - Variance: 62900.0

Sales Amount - Standard Deviation: 250.79872407968904

Sales Amount - Range: 1000

Target Sales - Variance: 56225.0

Target Sales - Standard Deviation: 237.11811402758752

Target Sales - Range: 850

Interpretation of Results:

1. **Variance**:
   - **Sales Amount**: The variance of 62900.0 indicates a moderate spread of sales amounts around the mean value.
   - **Target Sales**: The variance of 56225.0 is slightly lower than that for Sales Amount, indicating that Target Sales are somewhat more consistent or clustered around their mean than the Sales Amount.

2. **Standard Deviation**:
   - **Sales Amount**: The standard deviation of 250.79 means that on average, the actual sales amounts deviate from the mean by about 250 units. This indicates a moderate level of fluctuation in actual sales.
   - **Target Sales**: The standard deviation of 237.118 for Target Sales is close to the standard deviation of Sales Amount, suggesting that both sales and target amounts show similar variability.

3. **Range**:
   - **Sales Amount**: The range of 1000 indicates a significant difference between the highest and lowest sales values in the dataset. This shows that the sales amounts vary significantly.
   - **Target Sales**: The range of 850 for Target Sales is smaller than that for Sales Amount, indicating that target sales values are more tightly clustered compared to the actual sales figures.

Business/Business Analytics Implications:

1. **Variance and Standard Deviation**:

- A high variance and standard deviation for both Sales Amount and Target Sales suggest that while targets are being set, actual sales can fluctuate quite a bit. In a business setting, this might indicate that while targets are often met, the business needs to focus on improving consistency in actual sales performance.
- Large fluctuations in sales can be a challenge for inventory management, forecasting, and financial planning. Therefore, reducing variance and stabilizing sales performance would be a key business goal.

2. **Range**:
    - The range of sales values is quite large, especially for Sales Amount, indicating that some regions or segments may have experienced significantly higher sales compared to others. This could be due to factors such as market demand, customer behavior, or seasonal trends.
    - A lower range for target sales implies that targets are generally more consistent across regions, but this could also mean that targets are not reflecting the full potential of sales in high-performing regions. It might be an opportunity for businesses to set more dynamic and region-specific targets.

3. **Next Steps in Business Analytics**:
    - If variance and standard deviation are high, it's important for businesses to examine factors contributing to these fluctuations (e.g., customer segment, region, marketing spend, or external factors such as seasonality).
    - The range can be helpful in identifying outliers in the data, which could indicate areas of exceptional performance or problems that need closer investigation.
    - Further segmentation of data (by region, customer segment, etc.) could reveal insights into why sales deviate from targets and help in designing more accurate forecasts and strategies.

By understanding the dispersion of both sales and target amounts, businesses can optimize sales strategies, improve forecasting accuracy, and implement better resource allocation strategies.

2.7 Data Visualization Techniques (Charts, Graphs, Dashboards) in Business

In Business Analytics, **data visualization** is an essential tool for interpreting, understanding, and presenting data insights clearly and effectively. By transforming raw data into visual formats, businesses can uncover trends, identify patterns, and make informed decisions quickly. This process involves using various **charts**, **graphs**, and **dashboards** to represent data in ways that are easy to interpret and communicate.

Below are the most commonly used **data visualization techniques** and their relevance to Business Analytics.

1. Charts and Graphs

Charts and graphs are the most fundamental forms of data visualization. They allow businesses to present numerical data in a graphical format, making it easier to analyze trends, distributions, and relationships between variables. There are various types of charts and graphs, each suited for different types of data and business goals.

a. Bar Chart

- **What is it?** A **bar chart** uses rectangular bars to represent data. The length of each bar is proportional to the value it represents.
- **Business Use Case**: Bar charts are excellent for comparing quantities across different categories or time periods. They are commonly used to compare sales by product, revenue by region, or performance across departments.

Example: A bar chart comparing sales revenue across different product categories over the past quarter. The bars might show that **Category A** has the highest sales, while **Category C** has the lowest.

b. Line Chart

- **What is it?** A **line chart** connects individual data points with a line to show trends over time. It is most useful for displaying data that changes continuously.
- **Business Use Case**: Line charts are widely used to track financial metrics, sales performance, stock prices, or website traffic over time. They help businesses understand how a particular metric has evolved.

Example: A line chart showing the monthly revenue growth for a year. A steady upward slope indicates consistent growth, while significant dips might highlight seasonal trends or unexpected downturns.

c. Pie Chart

- **What is it?** A **pie chart** is a circular chart divided into slices to illustrate numerical proportions. Each slice represents a category's contribution to the whole.

- **Business Use Case**: Pie charts are useful for displaying the market share of different competitors, the percentage distribution of a budget, or the contribution of various product lines to total sales.

Example: A pie chart showing the percentage of total sales for each region (e.g., North America 40%, Europe 25%, Asia 20%, etc.). This gives a quick visual understanding of the relative importance of each market.

d. Histogram

- **What is it?** A **histogram** is similar to a bar chart but specifically used to display the distribution of a dataset. It groups data into ranges or bins and shows how many data points fall into each range.
- **Business Use Case**: Histograms are often used in quality control and customer behavior analysis to identify patterns in data distribution.

Example: A histogram representing the distribution of customer spending. The company might find that most customers spend between $50 and $100, with fewer customers spending more than $500.

e. Scatter Plot

- **What is it?** A **scatter plot** uses dots to represent values for two variables. It is useful for showing the relationship or correlation between these variables.
- **Business Use Case**: Scatter plots are ideal for analyzing the relationship between sales and advertising spending, customer satisfaction vs. product features, or employee experience vs. productivity.

Example: A scatter plot showing the relationship between advertising budget and sales growth. A positive correlation (upward trend) could indicate that more advertising leads to higher sales.

f. Area Chart

- **What is it?** An **area chart** is similar to a line chart, but the area beneath the line is filled with color to represent cumulative totals over time.
- **Business Use Case**: Area charts are used to show trends in cumulative data, such as total revenue or market share growth over time.

Example: An area chart showing the cumulative sales of a company across different regions over the last year, with different colored areas representing sales in North America, Europe, and Asia.

2. Dashboards

A **dashboard** is a collection of interactive visualizations and key performance indicators (KPIs) displayed in one centralized place. Dashboards allow businesses to monitor multiple aspects of performance in real time and make quick, data-driven decisions. They combine charts, graphs, and other visual elements into a single interface, providing a comprehensive overview of business metrics.

a. Executive Dashboard

- **What is it?** Executive dashboards are high-level overviews designed for decision-makers. They typically display KPIs, trends, and forecasts in a concise format.
- **Business Use Case**: Executives use dashboards to track company-wide performance metrics such as revenue, profit margins, customer satisfaction, and employee productivity in real-time.

Example: A CEO's dashboard that shows daily sales figures, customer retention rates, and net profit margin. This provides an at-a-glance understanding of the company's overall performance.

b. Sales Dashboard

- **What is it?** A sales dashboard focuses on metrics related to sales performance, including sales targets, quotas, revenue, and customer acquisition rates.
- **Business Use Case**: Sales teams and managers use this type of dashboard to monitor progress towards sales goals, track individual salespeople's performance, and identify areas needing attention.

Example: A sales dashboard showing metrics like total revenue, average deal size, number of new customers, and sales growth compared to previous periods. This helps identify whether sales teams are on track to meet targets.

c. Marketing Dashboard

- **What is it?** A marketing dashboard aggregates data from various marketing channels (e.g., social media, email campaigns, website traffic) to track campaign performance and ROI.
- **Business Use Case**: Marketing teams use dashboards to monitor the effectiveness of marketing campaigns, track customer engagement, and measure the success of advertising spend.

Example: A marketing dashboard showing metrics like the number of impressions, click-through rate (CTR), cost per lead, and conversion rates for digital ad campaigns.

d. Operations Dashboard

- **What is it?** An operations dashboard tracks operational metrics like inventory levels, production rates, and supply chain efficiency. It helps businesses monitor and optimize day-to-day operations.
- **Business Use Case**: Operations managers use dashboards to identify inefficiencies in the production process, track inventory turnover, and ensure that supply chain activities run smoothly.

Example: An operations dashboard displaying the current inventory status, production volume, supply chain delays, and order fulfillment rates in real-time, helping operations teams quickly address issues.

3. Other Visualization Techniques

a. Heatmap

- **What is it?** A **heatmap** uses color to represent values in a matrix or data table. Darker or more intense colors represent higher values, while lighter colors represent lower values.
- **Business Use Case**: Heatmaps are used in website analytics, sales performance, or store layouts to show areas of high activity or performance.

Example: A heatmap of website visitor activity, with areas of the website receiving the most traffic highlighted in dark red. This helps businesses understand which pages or products are attracting the most attention.

b. Funnel Chart

- **What is it?** A **funnel chart** is used to represent stages in a process and visualize how data is filtered or narrowed down. It is often used for sales or conversion funnels.
- **Business Use Case**: Sales and marketing teams use funnel charts to track customer conversion through various stages of a sales process (e.g., awareness, interest, decision, purchase).

Example: A funnel chart showing the conversion rate from website visitors to leads, and from leads to paying customers. This helps identify at which stage prospects drop off.

c. Tree Map

- **What is it?** A **tree map** displays hierarchical data as a set of nested rectangles. Each branch of the tree is represented by a rectangle, with its size proportional to a specific value.
- **Business Use Case**: Tree maps are used to show data relationships and proportions in large datasets, like financial reports or customer segmentation.

Example: A tree map showing the distribution of sales across different product categories, where each rectangle represents a category and its size corresponds to the sales volume.

Conclusion: Choosing the Right Visualization Technique

In **Business Analytics**, the choice of visualization technique depends on the type of data you are analyzing and the insights you wish to convey.

- **Charts and Graphs** (bar charts, line charts, pie charts, etc.) are best for showing relationships, comparisons, trends, and distributions in data.
- **Dashboards** provide a high-level, real-time view of multiple KPIs and metrics, allowing for efficient monitoring of performance across different business functions.

- **Other Techniques** like heatmaps, funnel charts, and tree maps are particularly useful for specific analyses, such as customer behavior, process flows, or hierarchical data.

By selecting the appropriate visualization tools, businesses can communicate complex data more effectively, uncover insights quickly, and make data-driven decisions that drive performance and growth.

2.8 Data Visualization in Business Analytics using JASP

Data visualization in JASP can be done by using following steps. These steps provides the plots to summarize the central point of your data and help you understand visually.

Steps to create data visualization in JASP

1. **Open JASP**:
   o If you haven't already, open JASP and load your dataset (e.g., a CSV, Excel, or SPSS file).

2. **Load the Data**:
   o Click **"File" > "Open"** to load your dataset into JASP.

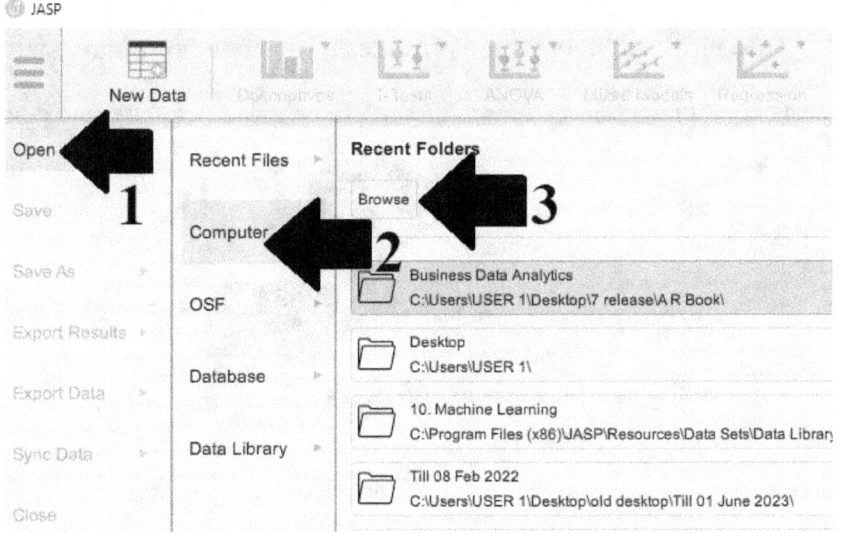

Now select the file

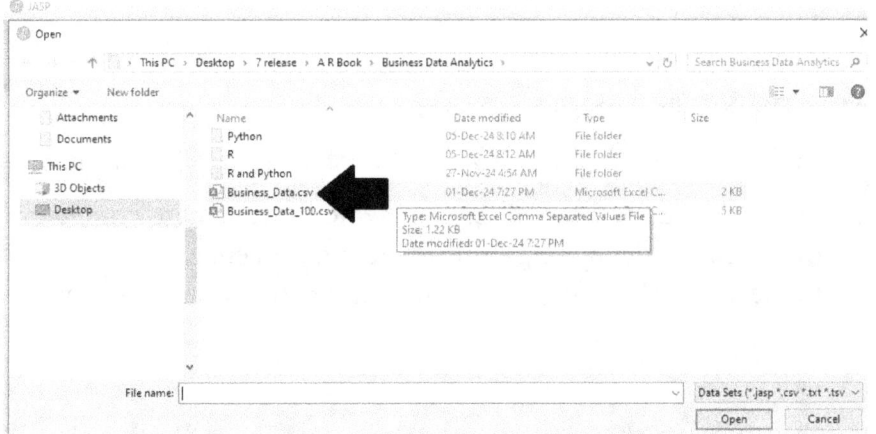

File will be loaded into JASP as shown below.

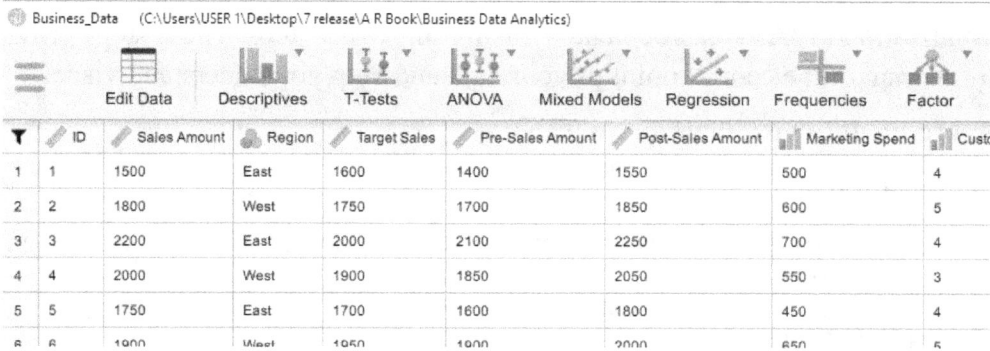

3. **Navigate to Descriptive Statistics**:
   o Once your data is loaded, go to the top menu and click on the **"Descriptives"** tab, which provides a variety of summary statistics options.

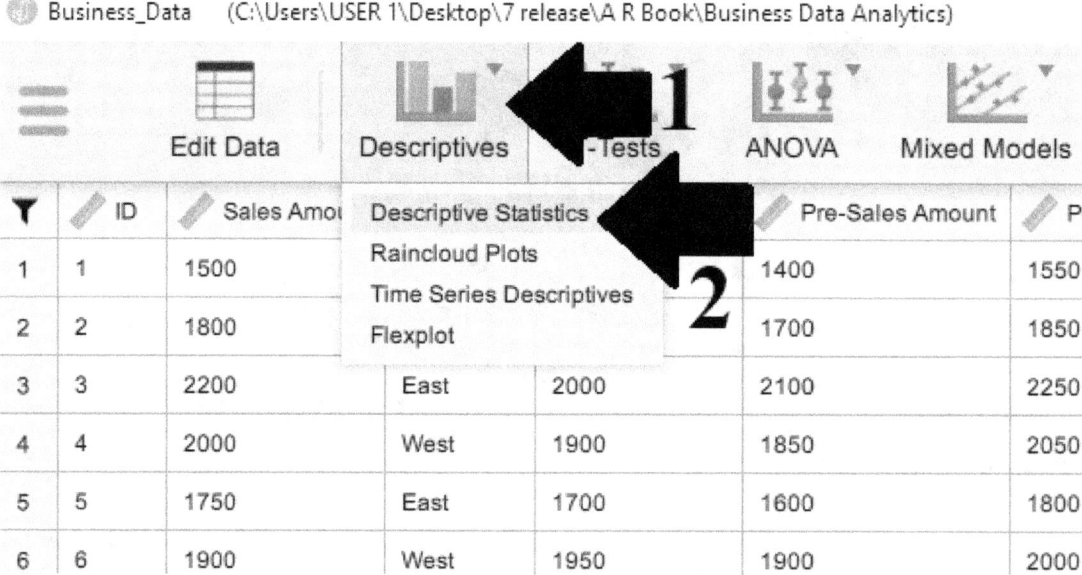

4. **Select Variables for Analysis**:
   o In the **Descriptives** window, you'll see a list of variables in your dataset.
   o Select the numeric variable(s) for which you want to compute the measures of central tendency (e.g., sales amounts, revenue, age, etc.) and drag them to the **Variables** box (or click the play button after selecting the variable).

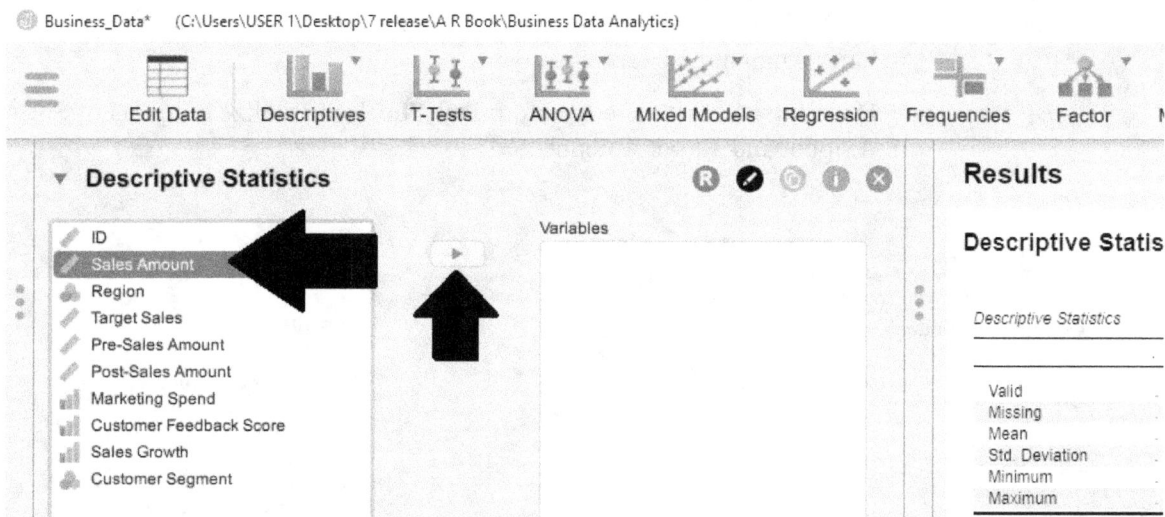

Now the variables will be shifted to right hand side variable block.

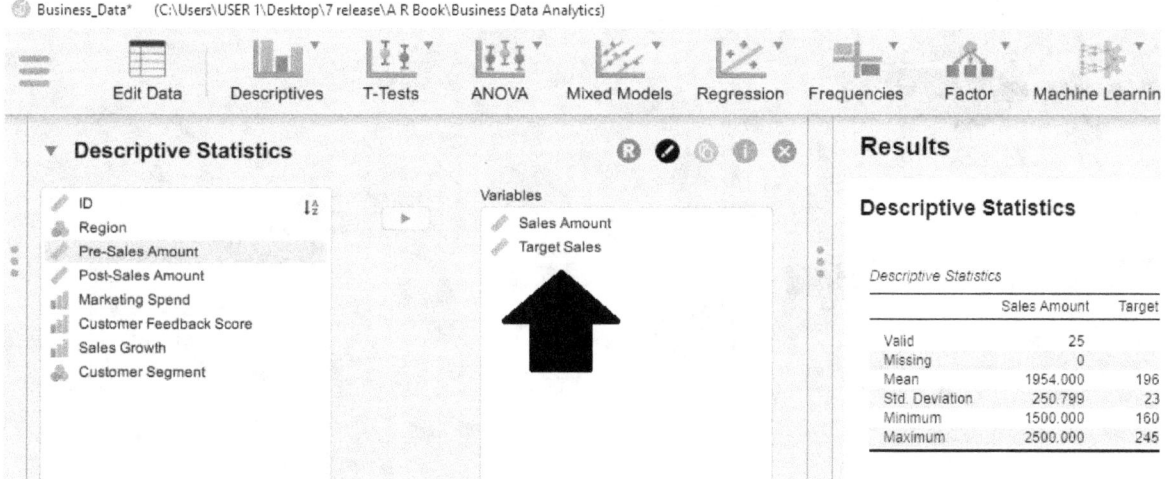

5. **Choose Basic plots:**

    o   On the lower side of the **Descriptives** window, under the **Basic Plots** section, you'll see several options for Data visualization using plots.

    - **Distribution Plots**: Check the box before **Distribution Plots** to visualize distribution of Sales Amount and Target Amount.

    - **Correlation Plots**: Check the box before **Correlation Plots** to visualize correlation of Sales Amount and Target Amount.

    - **Interval Plots**: Check the box before **Interval Plots** to visualize interval plots of Sales Amount and Target Amount.

- **Q-Q Plots**: Check the box before **Q-Q Plots** to visualize Q-Q plots of Sales Amount and Target Amount.
- **Dot Plots**: Check the box before **Dot Plots** to visualize dot plots of Sales Amount and Target Amount.

6. **Run the Analysis:**
   - After selecting the desired plots (Variance, Standard Deviation, Range), the results will automatically appear on the right-hand side of the window in the **Results** pane.

7. **View Results:**
   - JASP will display the results in a table under the **Results** pane on the right.
   - The output will include the Distribution Plots, Correlation Plots, Interval Plots, Q-Q Plots and Dot Plots for each selected variable.
   - If you have multiple variables, JASP will display each plots for each variable in the results pane.

Results

Descriptive Statistics

Descriptive Statistics

Sales Amount	Target Sales

Distribution Plots

Sales Amount

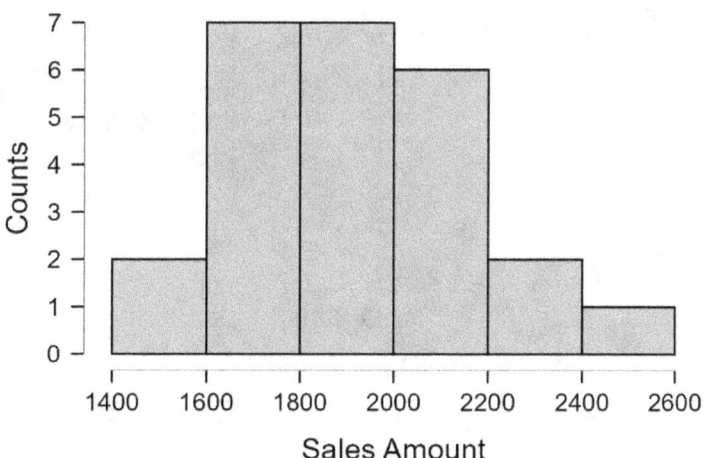

Target Sales

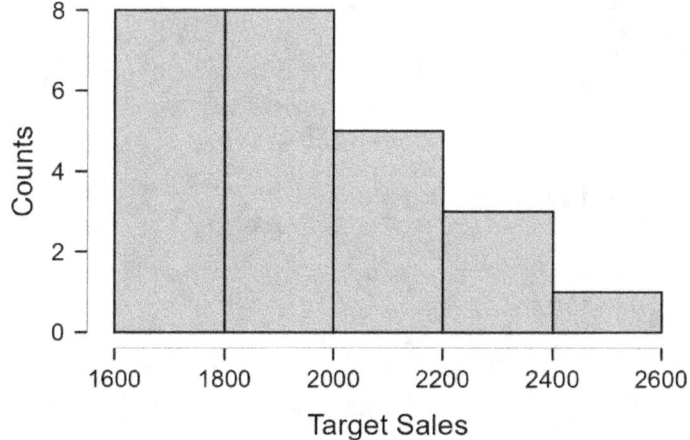

Correlation plot

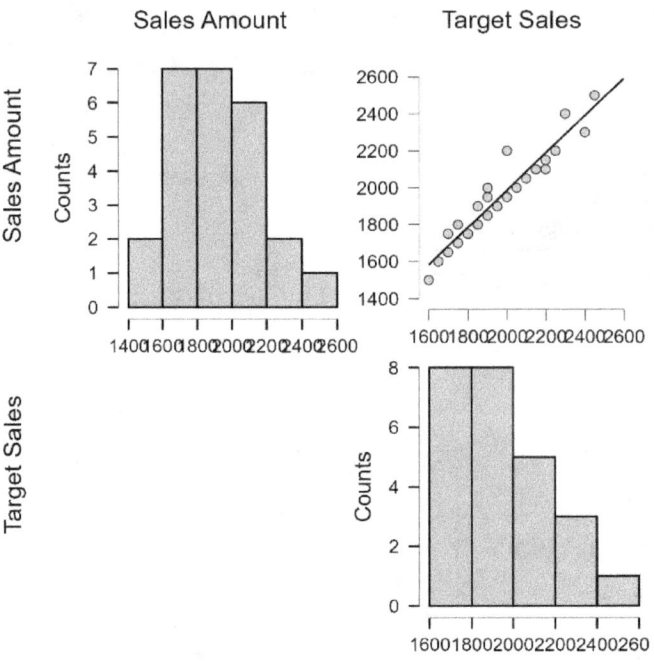

Q-Q Plots

Sales Amount

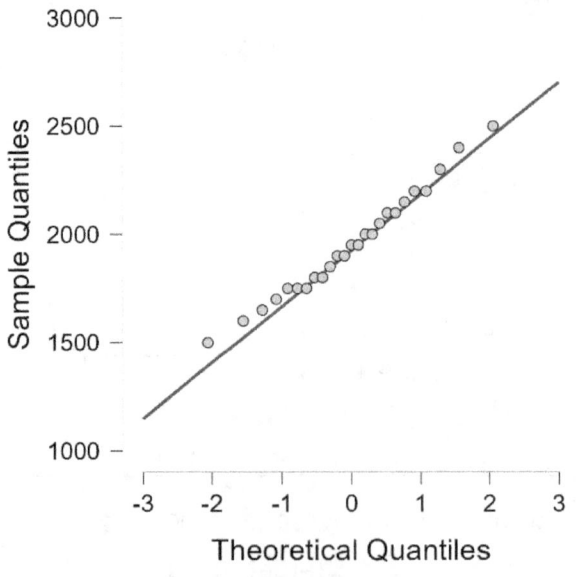

Target Sales

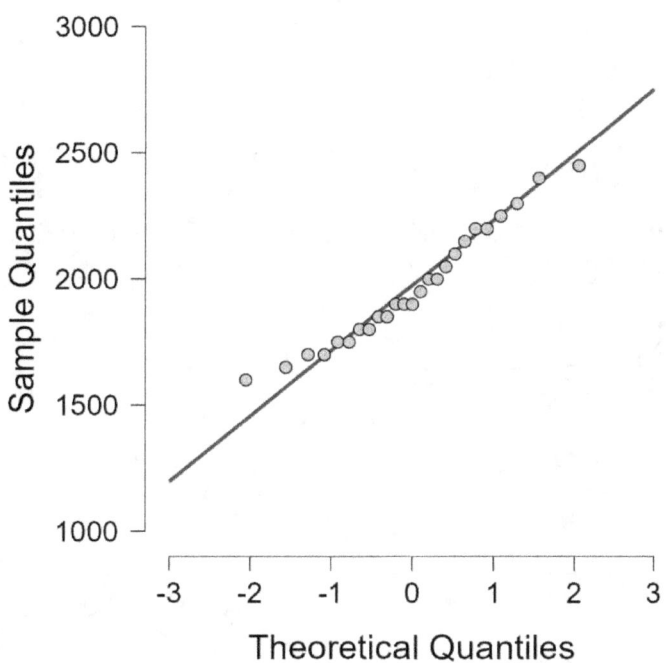

Interval plots

Sales Amount

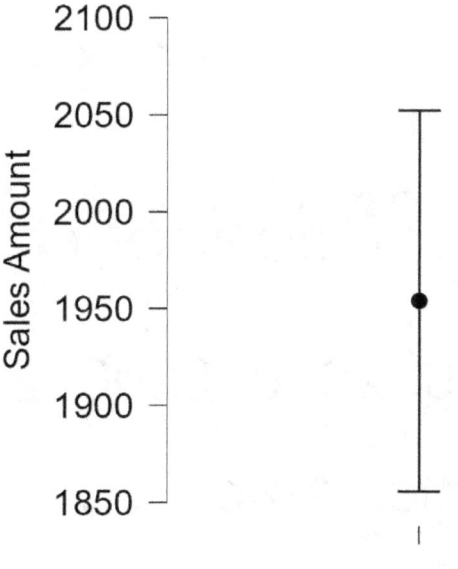

Target Sales

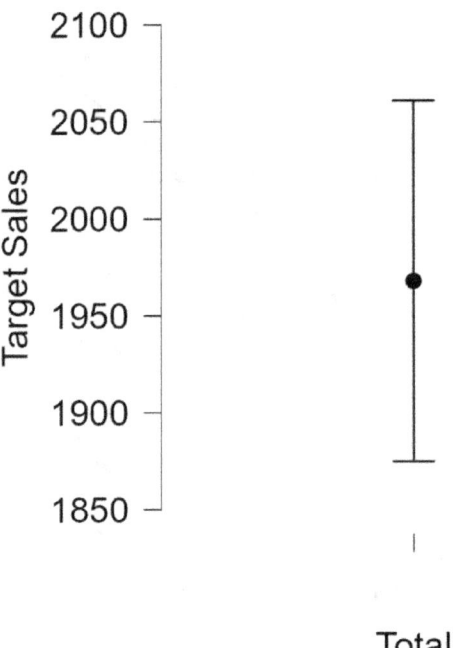

Dot Plots

Sales Amount

Target Sales

Brief explanation of each plot is already discussed in the previous chapter.

2.9 Data Visualization in Business Analytics using Python

To visualize the provided business data in Python, we will use several popular libraries for data manipulation and visualization. Each type of plot provides useful insights into the data from different perspectives.

To create the data visualizations and perform various statistical analyses on the business data in Python, we will use several libraries for data manipulation, visualization, and statistical plotting. Let's break down the task and code step by step:

Required Libraries:

1. **Pandas**: For data manipulation, including reading data and organizing it into a DataFrame.
2. **NumPy**: For numerical operations such as statistical calculations (e.g., correlation, quantiles).
3. **Matplotlib**: For basic plotting and visualizations (e.g., histograms, scatter plots).
4. **Seaborn**: For more advanced and aesthetically pleasing statistical visualizations (e.g., density plots, box plots, pair plots).
5. **SciPy**: For statistical operations like Q-Q plots and correlation testing.
6. **Statsmodels**: For additional statistical tests and interval plots.
7. **Plotly** (Optional): For interactive visualizations, but it is not required for basic tasks.

Installation of Libraries:

If you haven't already installed the necessary libraries, you can do so using pip:

```
pip install pandas numpy matplotlib seaborn scipy statsmodels plotly
```

Loading Libraries in Python:

```
import pandas as pd
import numpy as np
import matplotlib.pyplot as plt
import seaborn as sns
from scipy import stats
import statsmodels.api as sm
```

Explanation of Libraries:

1. **Pandas**: Essential for handling and manipulating data. It allows us to load the dataset, clean it, and perform operations like grouping by customer segments.

2. **NumPy**: A core library for numerical operations such as calculating correlation and quantiles.
3. **Matplotlib**: A fundamental library for plotting graphs and charts, often used for static visualizations.
4. **Seaborn**: Built on top of Matplotlib, Seaborn provides advanced visualization features, making it easier to create aesthetic plots like density plots, box plots, and pair plots.
5. **SciPy**: Used for statistical operations, including Q-Q plots and calculating correlations between variables.
6. **Statsmodels**: Provides statistical tests and plots, including interval plots, which can be useful for confidence intervals in predictive analysis.

Data Preparation:

```
# Load the data into a pandas DataFrame
data = {
    'Sales Amount': [1500, 1800, 2200, 2000, 1750, 1900, 2100, 2400, 1600, 2300, 1950, 2050, 1750, 2150, 1800, 2500, 1700, 1850, 2100, 2000,
            1950, 2200, 1650, 1750, 1900],
    'Target Sales': [1600, 1750, 2000, 1900, 1700, 1950, 2200, 2300, 1650, 2400, 2000, 2100, 1800, 2200, 1850, 2450, 1750, 1900, 2150, 2050,
            1900, 2250, 1700, 1800, 1850],
    'Customer Segment': ['Small', 'Medium', 'Large', 'Medium', 'Small', 'Medium', 'Large', 'Large', 'Small', 'Large', 'Medium', 'Medium', 'Small', 'Large', 'Small', 'Large', 'Small', 'Medium', 'Large', 'Medium',
            'Medium', 'Large', 'Small', 'Medium', 'Large']
}

df = pd.DataFrame(data)
df.head()
```

Output

	Sales Amount	Target Sales	Customer Segment
0	1500	1600	Small
1	1800	1750	Medium
2	2200	2000	Large
3	2000	1900	Medium
4	1750	1700	Small

1. Distribution Plots with Density Curves for Sales Amount by Customer Segment

Distribution plots with density curves for **Sales Amount** are useful for visualizing the shape and spread of the sales data across different customer segments. By overlaying density curves, we can assess the distribution pattern, such as whether the sales amounts for each segment are skewed, normally distributed, or have multiple peaks. These plots allow us to compare the central tendency and variability in sales performance across the customer segments (e.g., Small, Medium, and Large). For instance, we may find that the "Large" segment tends to have higher sales amounts with a sharper peak, while the "Small" segment might have a wider and lower distribution. These visual cues help identify patterns and potential outliers.

```
# Plot Distribution with Density Curve for Sales Amount by Customer Segment
plt.figure(figsize=(10, 6))
sns.kdeplot(data=df, x='Sales Amount', hue='Customer Segment', fill=True)
plt.title('Distribution Plot with Density Curve for Sales Amount by Customer Segment')
plt.show()
```

Output

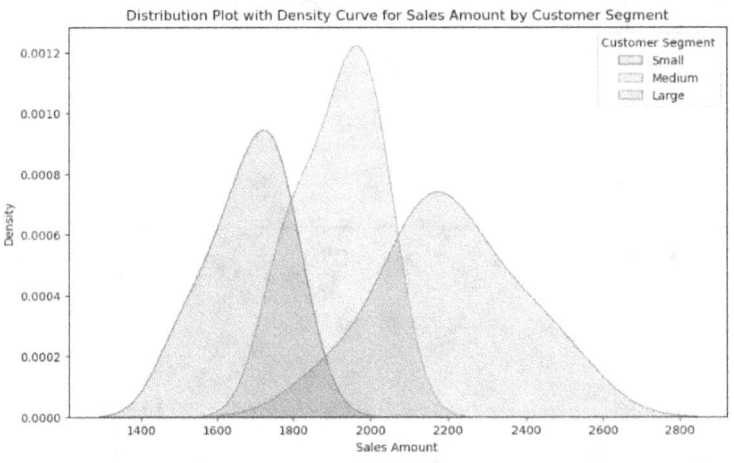

2. Distribution Plots with Density Curves on Target Sales for Each Customer Segment

The **distribution plot with density curves** for **Target Amount** serves a similar purpose as the sales amount plot but focuses on comparing the distribution of the target sales figures across customer segments. By comparing the density curves, we can explore how the sales targets differ across the segments, such as whether larger customers have higher target amounts than smaller customers. These curves provide insight into whether the targets are evenly distributed, have a normal distribution, or if there is any skewness, which could indicate a need for target adjustments or different target-setting strategies across segments.

```
# Plot Distribution with Density Curve for Target Sales by Customer Segment
plt.figure(figsize=(10, 6))
sns.kdeplot(data=df, x='Target Sales', hue='Customer Segment', fill=True)
plt.title('Distribution Plot with Density Curve for Target Sales by Customer Segment')
plt.show()
```

Output

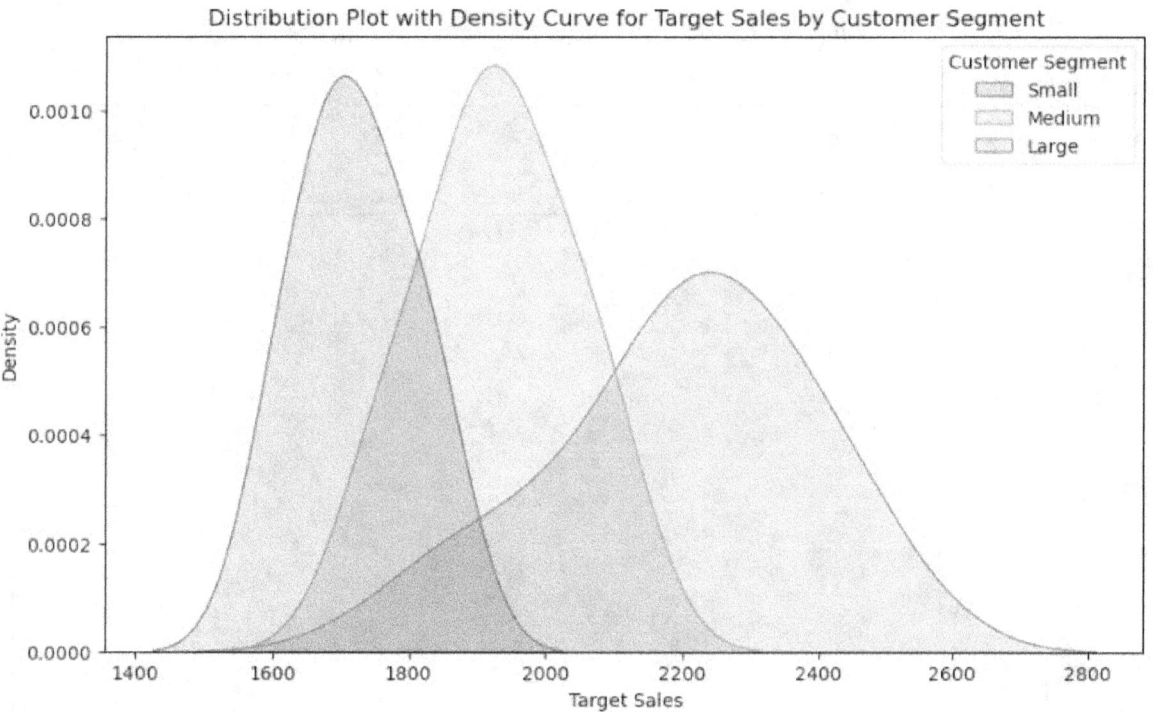

Explanation:

- **sns.kdeplot**: This function plots a kernel density estimate (KDE) plot, which is a smooth estimate of the distribution of data.

- **hue='Customer Segment'**: This colors the plot based on customer segments, allowing us to visually compare the distributions of Sales Amount and Target Sales across different customer groups.
- **fill=True**: Fills the area under the density curve to enhance visibility.

3. Correlation Plots on Sales Amount vs Target Sales by Customer Segment

A correlation plot (or scatterplot matrix) between Sales Amount and Target Amount across customer segments visually shows the strength and direction of the relationship between actual sales and target sales. Correlation plots are useful for understanding if there is a consistent linear relationship between the two variables. For example, a strong positive correlation would indicate that as the sales target increases, so does the actual sales, which would be expected. By segmenting this analysis by customer type, we can also identify whether the correlation is stronger for certain segments, which can inform performance forecasting and goal alignment.

```
# Correlation Plot on Sales Amount vs Target Sales by Customer Segment
plt.figure(figsize=(10, 6))
sns.scatterplot(x='Sales Amount', y='Target Sales', hue='Customer Segment', data=df)
plt.title('Correlation Plot on Sales Amount vs Target Sales by Customer Segment')
plt.show()
```

Output

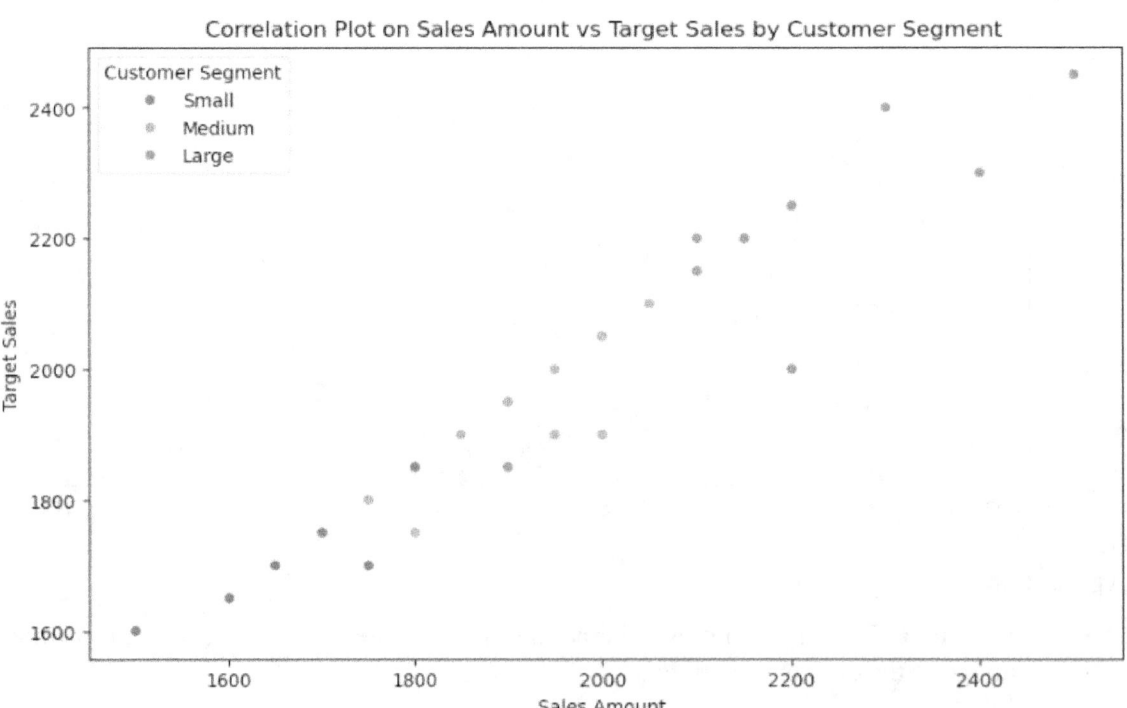

Explanation:

- **sns.scatterplot**: Creates a scatter plot of Sales Amount vs Target Sales. The color (hue) is set by the customer segment to observe how the two variables are correlated within each segment.

4. Box Plots for Sales Amount by Customer Segment

Box plots provide a concise summary of the distribution of **Sales Amount** for each customer segment, showing the median, interquartile range (IQR), and potential outliers. These plots are particularly useful for visualizing the spread and central tendency of sales data. For instance, a box plot might show that the "Large" segment has a higher median sales amount and fewer outliers compared to the "Small" segment, which might have a more dispersed range of sales. Box plots allow us to easily identify variability within each segment and detect extreme values that may require further investigation.

```
# Box Plot for Sales Amount by Customer Segment
plt.figure(figsize=(10, 6))
sns.boxplot(x='Customer Segment', y='Sales Amount', data=df)
plt.title('Box Plot for Sales Amount by Customer Segment')
plt.show()
```

Output

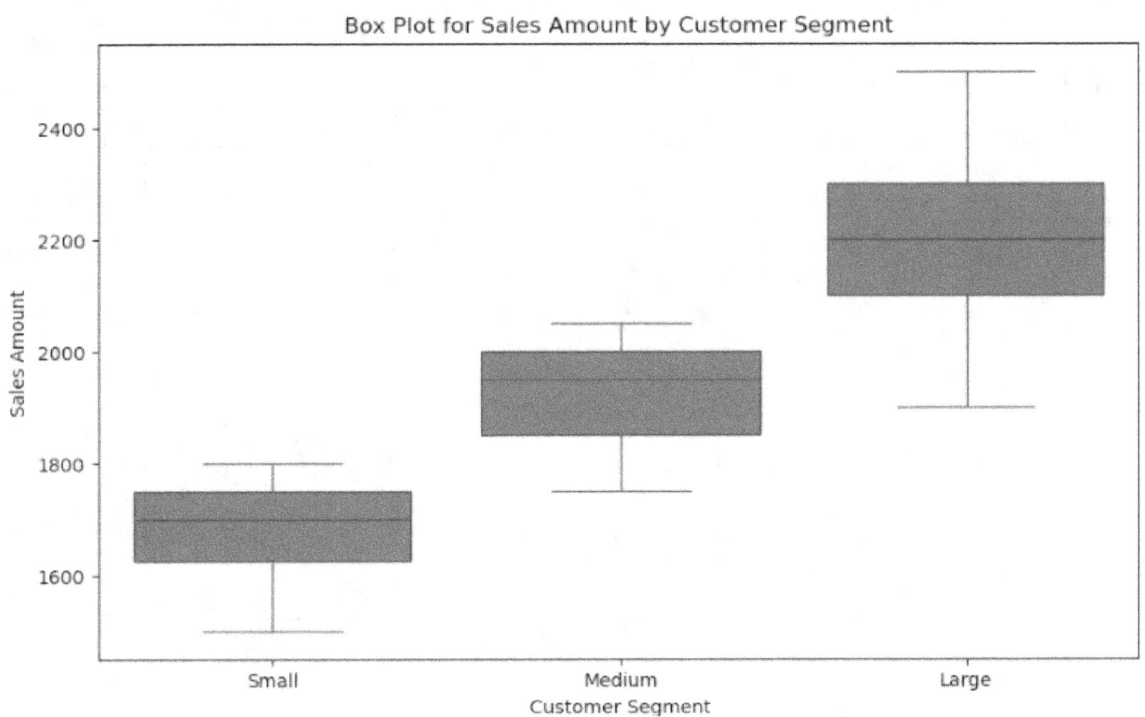

Explanation:

- **sns.boxplot**: This creates a box plot to show the distribution of Sales Amount within each customer segment. The box shows the interquartile range (IQR), the line within the box is the median, and any outliers are plotted as individual points.

5. Q-Q Plots for Sales Amount by Customer Segment

A **Q-Q plot** (quantile-quantile plot) for **Sales Amount** compares the actual distribution of sales data to a normal distribution. The purpose of these plots is to visually assess if the sales data for each customer segment follows a normal distribution. If the data points fall along the straight line, it suggests that the sales amounts are normally distributed. This can be important for certain statistical analyses that assume normality. For example, if the "Medium" customer segment's sales data shows significant deviation from the line, it might indicate skewness or the need for transformation to normalize the data before further analysis.

```
# Q-Q Plot for Sales Amount by Customer Segment
plt.figure(figsize=(10, 6))
for segment in df['Customer Segment'].unique():
    segment_data = df[df['Customer Segment'] == segment]['Sales Amount']
    stats.probplot(segment_data, dist="norm", plot=plt)
    plt.title(f'Q-Q Plot for Sales Amount - {segment}')
    plt.show()
```

Output

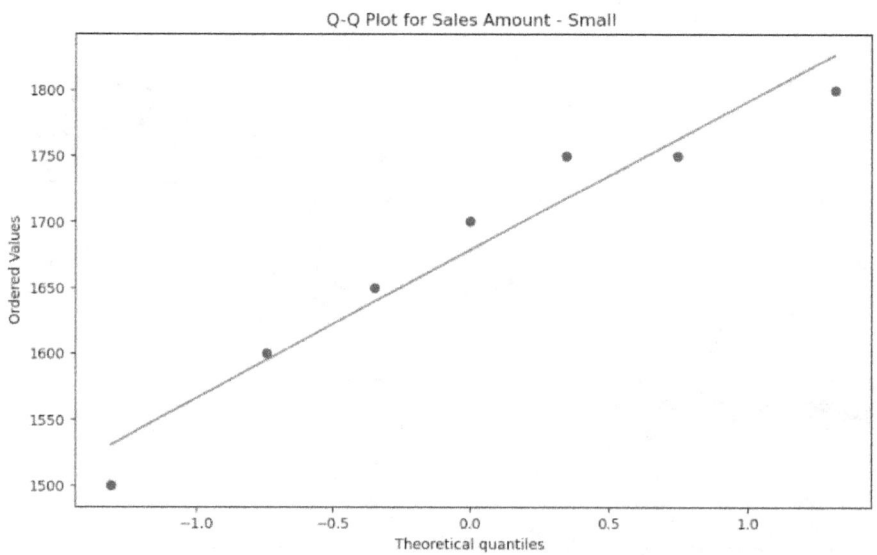

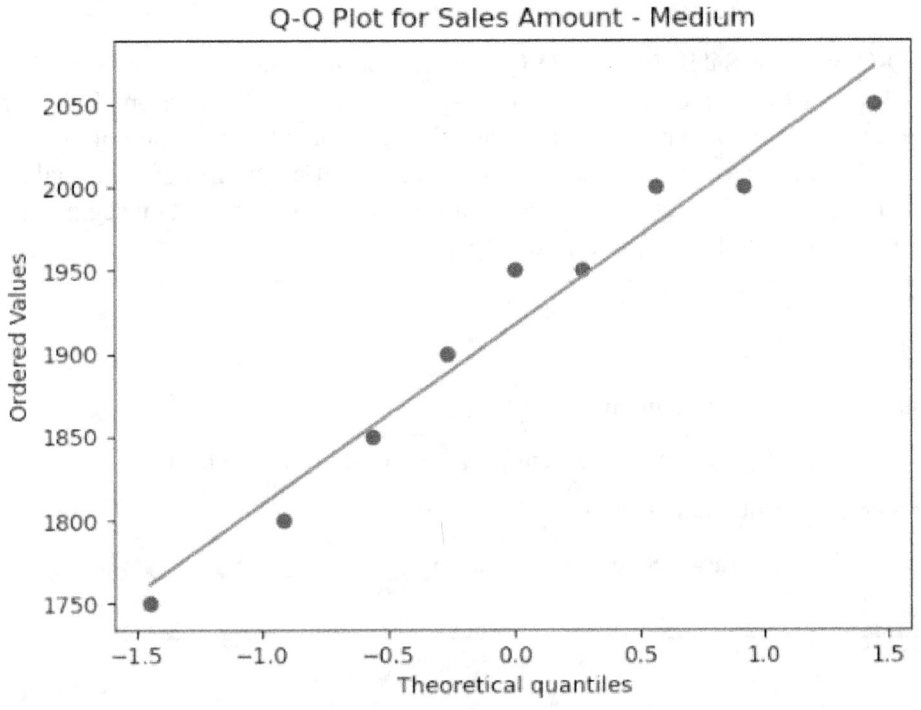

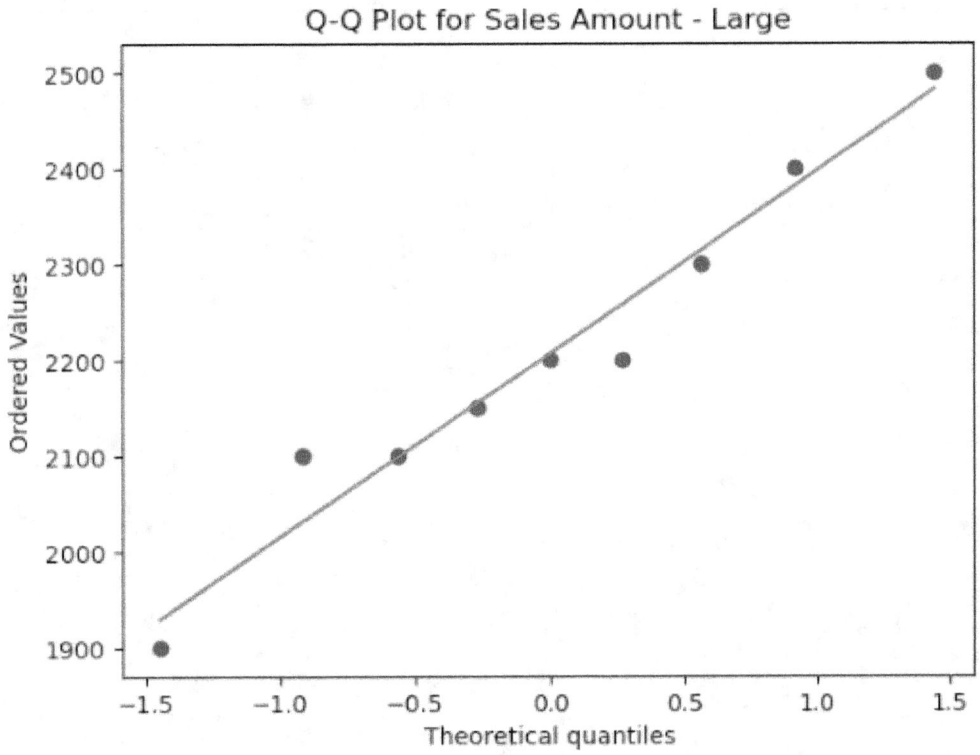

6. Q-Q Plots for Target Sales by Customer Segment

Similar to Q-Q plots for Sales Amount, Q-Q plots for Target Amount compare the distribution of the target sales data for each customer segment against a normal distribution. This helps assess if the target setting is based on a normally distributed pattern or if there are any outliers or skewness in how targets have been assigned. If the points deviate significantly from the normal line, it might indicate that targets are being set inconsistently or inappropriately for certain segments, potentially requiring a reassessment of target-setting strategies.

```
# Q-Q Plot for Target Sales by Customer Segment
plt.figure(figsize=(10, 6))
for segment in df['Customer Segment'].unique():
    segment_data = df[df['Customer Segment'] == segment]['Target Sales']
    stats.probplot(segment_data, dist="norm", plot=plt)
    plt.title(f'Q-Q Plot for Target Sales - {segment}')
    plt.show()
```

Output

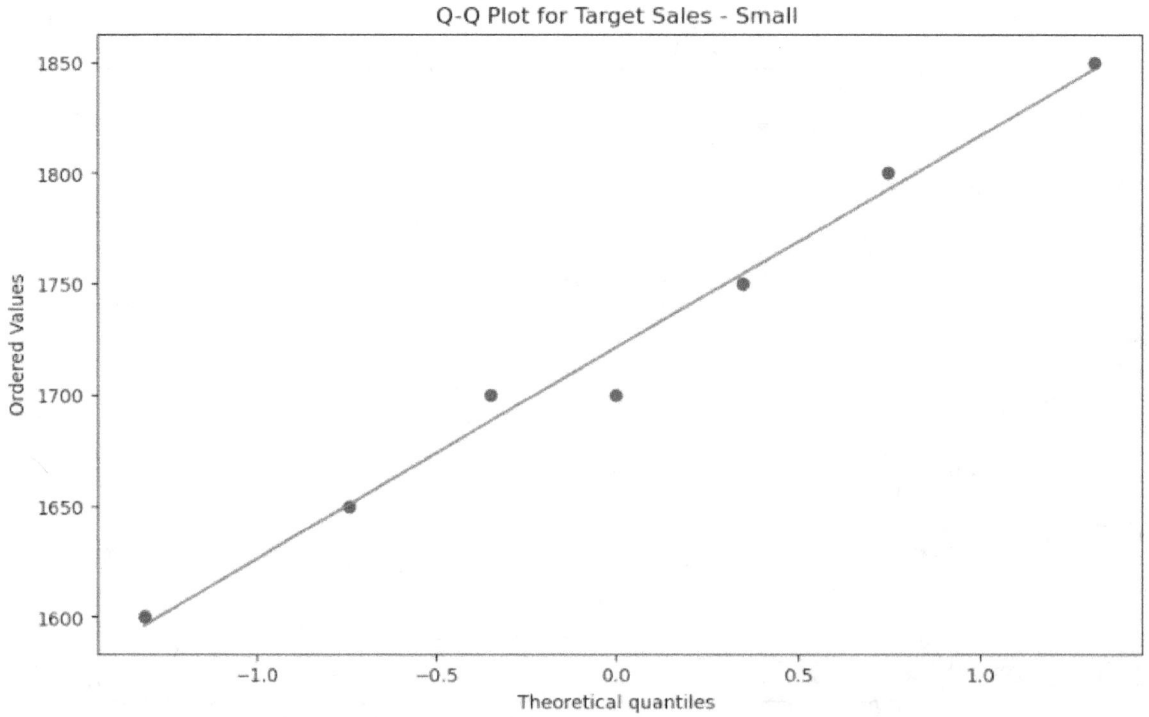

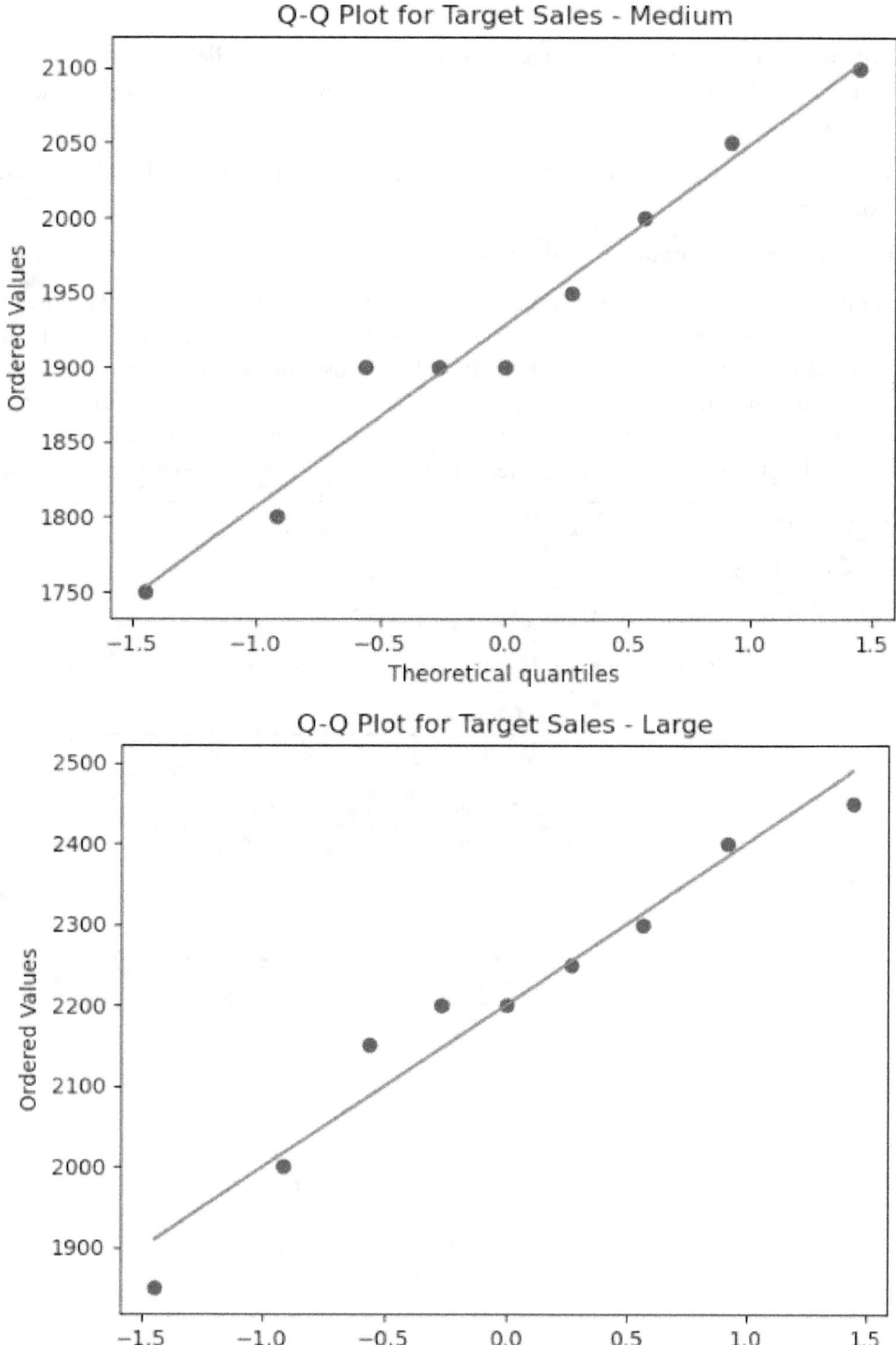

Explanation:

- **stats.probplot**: This function generates a Q-Q (Quantile-Quantile) plot, which helps check if the data follows a normal distribution. If the data points fall on a straight line, the data follows a normal distribution.
- We loop over each Customer Segment and plot a Q-Q plot for both Sales Amount and Target Sales.

7. Scatter Plots on Sales Amount vs Target Sales

A **scatter plot** between **Sales Amount** and **Target Amount** provides a direct visual representation of how actual sales compare to targets. This plot helps assess whether the sales team is meeting, exceeding, or falling short of their targets. For example, if most points fall close to a 45-degree line, it suggests that sales are closely aligned with targets. However, significant deviation from this line can point to either overperformance or underperformance. Segmenting this analysis by customer type can also highlight how different customer segments are performing relative to their targets.

```
# Scatter Plot for Sales Amount vs Target Sales
plt.figure(figsize=(10, 6))
sns.scatterplot(x='Sales Amount', y='Target Sales', data=df)
plt.title('Scatter Plot for Sales Amount vs Target Sales')
plt.show()
```

Output

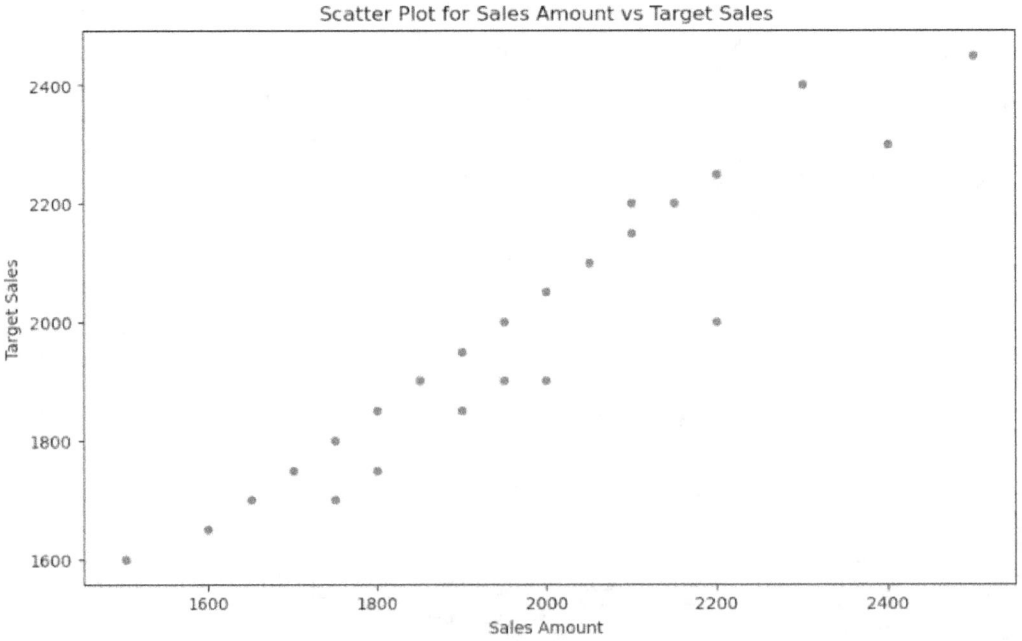

Explanation:

- **sns.scatterplot**: A simple scatter plot to show the relationship between Sales Amount and Target Sales. The plot allows us to visually assess if there is a linear relationship between the two variables.

8. Interval Plots on Sales Amount by Customer Segment

Interval plots for Sales Amount show the mean and variability (typically in the form of standard deviations or confidence intervals) of sales amounts for each customer segment. These plots are particularly useful for understanding the central tendency (mean) and the precision of the data (confidence intervals or error bars). For instance, if the "Large" segment has a narrower interval compared to the "Small" segment, it may indicate that sales in the larger segment are more consistent. Interval plots help communicate not just the average sales but also the degree of uncertainty or variability around that average.

```
# Interval Plot for Sales Amount by Customer Segment (using error bars)
plt.figure(figsize=(10, 6))
sns.pointplot(x='Customer Segment', y='Sales Amount', data=df, ci="sd", markers="o", color="red")
plt.title('Interval Plot for Sales Amount by Customer Segment')
plt.show()
```

Output

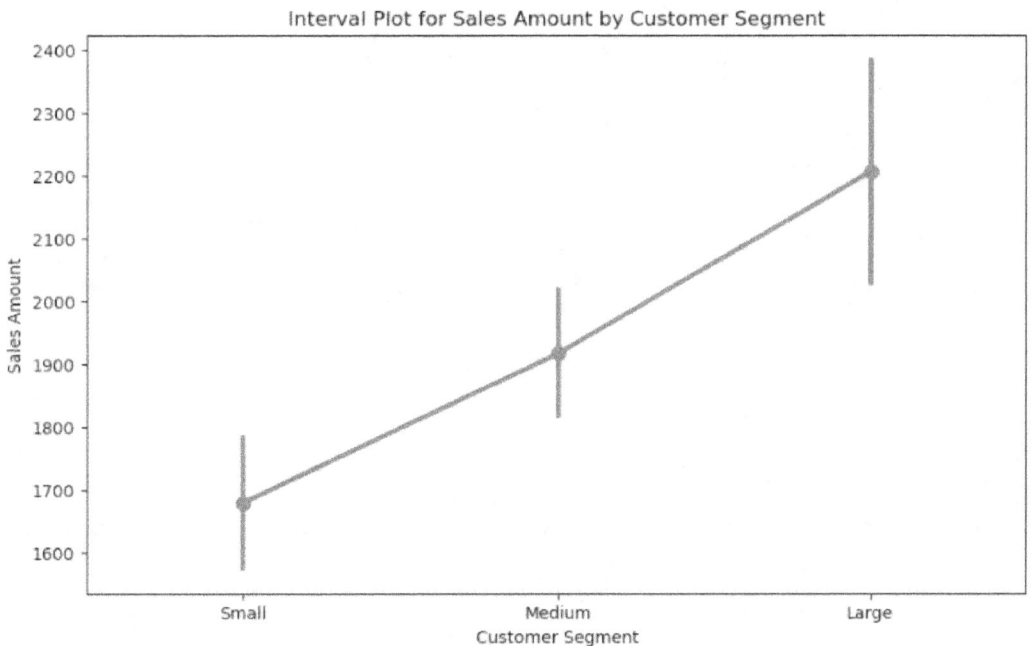

Explanation:

- **sns.pointplot**: This plot shows the mean (y-axis) of Sales Amount for each Customer Segment and adds error bars representing one standard deviation (i.e., confidence intervals).

9. Interval Plots on Target Sales for Each Customer Segment

Similar to the previous interval plots for **Sales Amount**, **Interval plots for Target Sales** display the mean target sales and the associated confidence intervals or standard deviations for each customer segment. These plots help evaluate how target amounts are set relative to the size and expected performance of each segment. A wider interval might indicate less confidence or variability in target-setting for a segment, whereas a narrower interval suggests more precise targeting. Analyzing these intervals across segments can help ensure that targets are appropriately challenging and achievable for each group.

```
# Interval Plot for Sales Amount by Customer Segment (using error bars)
plt.figure(figsize=(10, 6))
sns.pointplot(x='Customer Segment', y='Target Sales', data=df, ci="sd", markers="o", color="red")
plt.title('Interval Plot for Sales Amount by Customer Segment')
plt.show()
```

Output

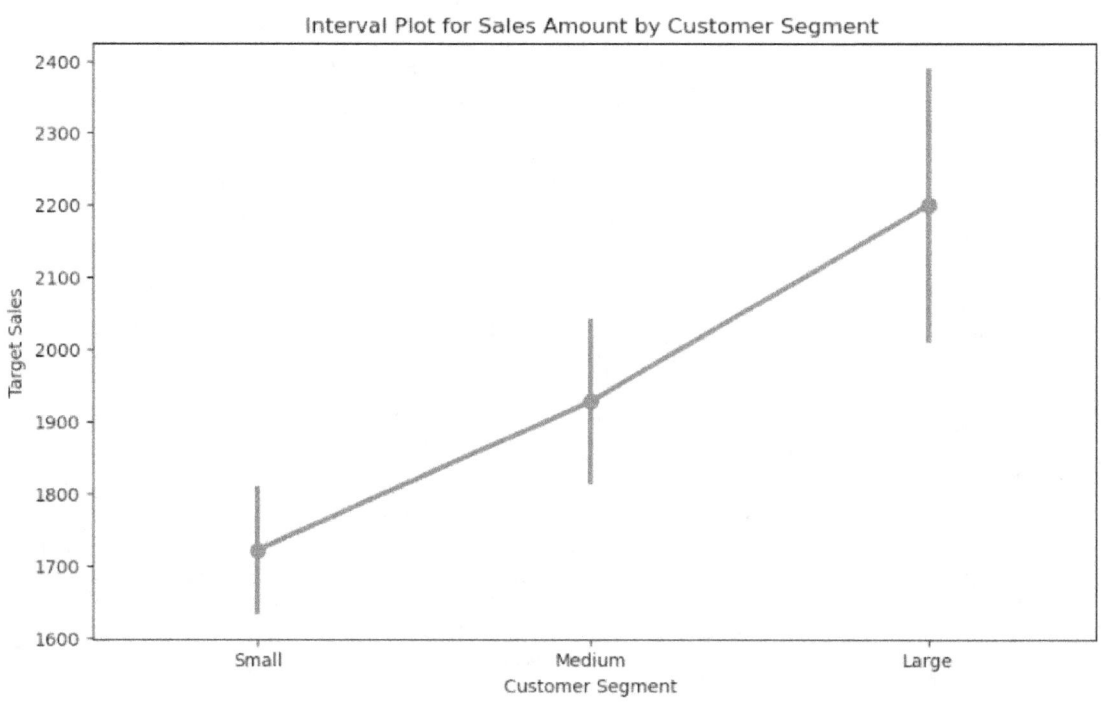

10. Dot Plots on Sales Amount for Each Customer Segment

Dot plots for Sales Amount provide a compact, individual-level representation of sales data by segment. Each dot represents an individual sales data point, allowing us to see the frequency and distribution of sales amounts across customer segments. Dot plots are particularly useful for visualizing the concentration of sales in specific ranges or identifying clusters or gaps in the data. For instance, the "Small" segment may show a dense concentration of dots around lower sales amounts, indicating that most small customers are underperforming relative to larger customers.

```
# Dot Plot for Sales Amount by Customer Segment
plt.figure(figsize=(10, 6))
sns.stripplot(x='Customer Segment', y='Sales Amount', data=df, jitter=True, color="blue")
plt.title('Dot Plot for Sales Amount by Customer Segment')
plt.show()
```

Output

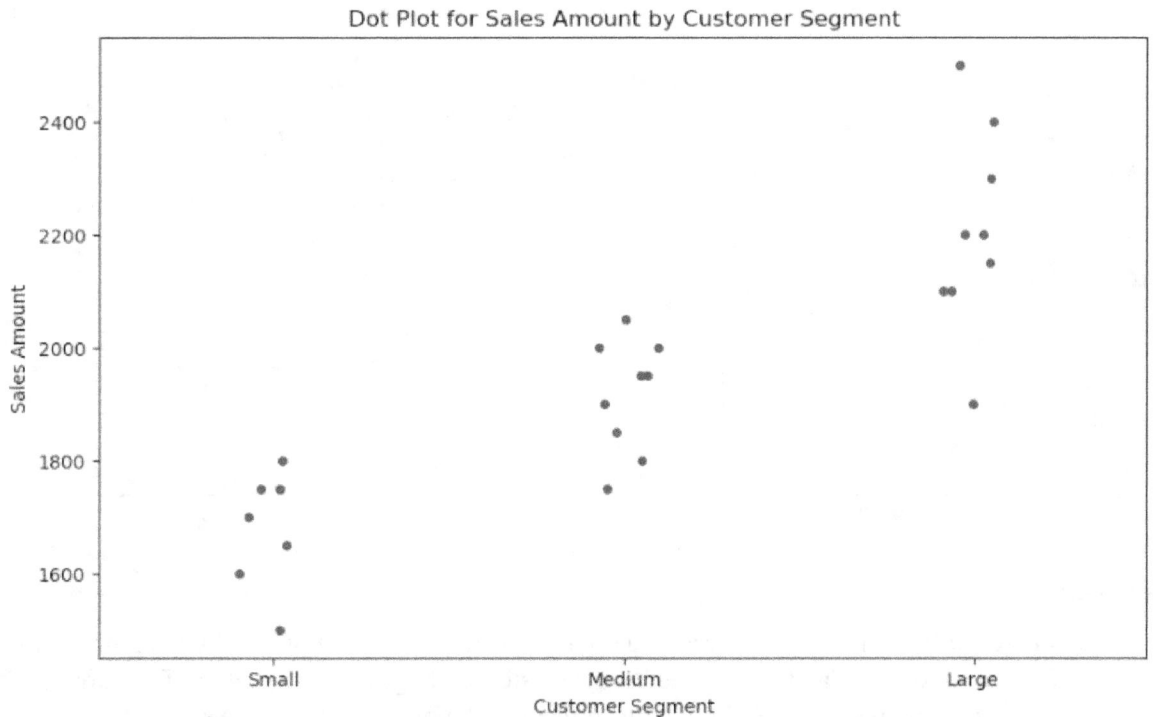

11. Dot Plots on Target Amount for Each Customer Segment

Dot plots for **Target Amount** are similar to those for sales amounts, but they represent the target sales figures set for each customer segment. These plots can show how evenly or unevenly target amounts are distributed within each segment. For instance, if the "Large" segment shows a wide spread of dots, it may suggest that targets for large customers vary significantly. Dot plots are useful for understanding the variability of targets and ensuring that they are consistently aligned with the expected performance of each segment, helping businesses tailor their strategies more effectively.

```
# Dot Plot for Target Sales by Customer Segment
plt.figure(figsize=(10, 6))
sns.stripplot(x='Customer Segment', y='Target Sales', data=df, jitter=True, color="green")
plt.title('Dot Plot for Target Sales by Customer Segment')
plt.show()
```

Output

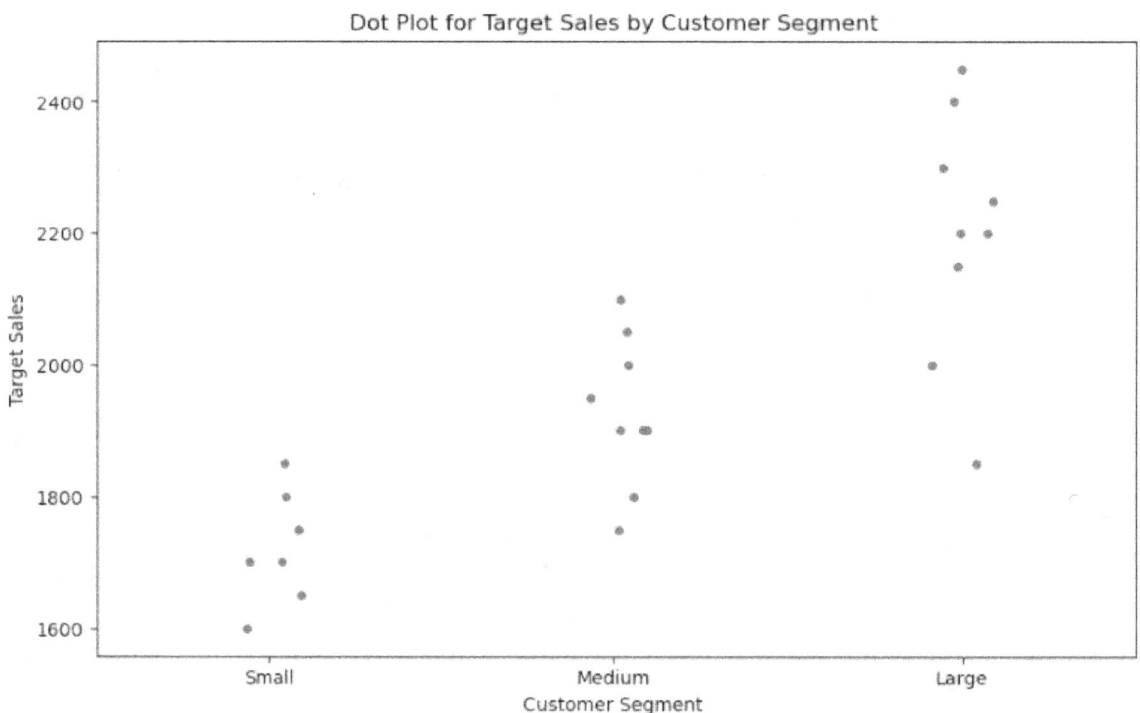

Explanation:

- **sns.stripplot**: This function creates a dot plot (strip plot) that shows individual data points for Sales Amount and Target Sales by Customer Segment. The jitter=True argument ensures the points are spread out a bit so that overlapping points can be seen.

Output and Results Interpretation:

- **Density and Distribution Plots**: These plots show the distribution of Sales Amount and Target Sales across customer segments. The density curves provide insights into the spread of the data, with the peaks indicating areas of higher density.

- **Correlation and Scatter Plots**: These show the relationship between Sales Amount and Target Sales. If there's a visible trend, we can infer a correlation. For example, if the scatter plot shows a linear relationship, it indicates that higher target sales are associated with higher actual sales.

- **Box Plots**: These highlight the spread and outliers in Sales Amount within each segment. For example, if the box plot for a particular segment shows many outliers, it may suggest that the sales figures for that segment are highly variable.

- **Q-Q Plots**: These plots help assess the normality of the data. If the data points lie along a straight line, it indicates that the data is approximately normally distributed.

- **Interval and Dot Plots**: These plots are useful for understanding the variability and spread within each segment.

Business Analytics Implications:

- **Sales Strategy**: Understanding the variability in sales across customer segments can help refine targeting strategies. For example, if Sales Amount for the Large segment is widely spread out, businesses might need to focus on more personalized sales strategies.

- **Forecasting and Planning**: If certain customer segments have a normal distribution of sales, more accurate forecasts can be made. For segments with higher variability, the focus might be on reducing this variability through better marketing or operational strategies.

Conclusion:

These plots give a detailed visual understanding of how sales data behaves across different customer segments, whether we're analyzing distributions, correlations, box plots, or normality tests. By examining these visualizations, business analysts can gain insights into performance differences between segments, identify anomalies, and make informed decisions.

3. One Sample T-Test in Business Analytics

A **One Sample T-Test** is a statistical test that helps businesses assess whether the average of a sample group differs significantly from a known or hypothesized value (often referred to as the population mean). In Business Analytics, this test is particularly useful when evaluating whether a particular metric—such as sales, revenue, customer satisfaction, etc.—is performing at a level expected by the company, or if there is a significant deviation.

When to Use a One Sample T-Test:

- When a business wants to check if the average sales of a particular product, store, or branch meet a pre-established target.
- When comparing customer satisfaction ratings or employee performance to an expected average.
- When measuring whether a new marketing campaign led to a significant increase in sales.

Key Components of a One Sample T-Test:

- **Null Hypothesis (H_0):** The sample mean is equal to the hypothesized population mean (no difference).
- **Alternative Hypothesis (H_1):** The sample mean is different from the population mean (there is a difference).
- **Test Statistic:** A calculated value that measures the difference between the sample mean and the hypothesized population mean relative to the variability in the data.
- **P-Value:** The probability of obtaining a test statistic as extreme as, or more extreme than, the one calculated from the sample data, assuming the null hypothesis is true. If the p-value is small (usually less than 0.05), it suggests that the null hypothesis can be rejected.

Example Scenario:

Let's assume a company, "RetailCo," has set a target of $50,000 in average monthly sales for one of its stores. The company wants to evaluate whether the store's sales over the past 6 months are statistically different from this target.

Sample Data (Sales for Store X over 6 months):

Month	Sales ($)
Jan	52,000
Feb	49,000
Mar	51,500
Apr	50,000

Month	Sales ($)
May	53,000
Jun	54,000

The company has set a **target sales goal** of $50,000 per month, and it wants to check whether the actual sales of Store X over the 6 months meet this target.

Step-by-Step Analysis:

1. **State the Hypotheses**:
   - **Null Hypothesis (H₀)**: The average sales of Store X is equal to $50,000 (the target).
   - **Alternative Hypothesis (H₁)**: The average sales of Store X is different from $50,000 (not equal).

2. **Perform the One Sample T-Test**:
   - The test would compare the average sales from Store X to the expected average sales of $50,000. Based on the data, the company would calculate the mean of the sample sales and determine if it is significantly different from the hypothesized population mean of $50,000.

3. **Interpretation of Results**:
   - The result of the test will include the **p-value**, which helps in deciding whether to reject the null hypothesis. If the p-value is smaller than the chosen significance level (usually 0.05), the null hypothesis is rejected, suggesting that the average sales are significantly different from the expected value of $50,000. If the p-value is greater than 0.05, the null hypothesis is not rejected, and the company would conclude that the sales are not significantly different from the target.

Results of the One Sample T-Test:

After conducting the test, the results might look like this:

Store	Total Sales ($)	Average Sales ($)	P-Value	Conclusion
X	315,500	52,583	0.19	Fail to reject H₀

Explanation of Results:

- **Total Sales**: The total sales for Store X over the 6 months is $315,500.

- **Average Sales**: The average sales per month for Store X is **$52,583** ($315,500 ÷ 6 months). This is slightly higher than the target of $50,000.
- **P-Value**: The **p-value** is **0.190**, which is **greater than the significance level of 0.05**.
  - **Conclusion**: Since the p-value is larger than 0.05, we fail to reject the **null hypothesis** (H_0). This means there is **no statistically significant difference** between the actual average sales ($52,583) and the target sales of $50,000.

Interpretation of Results:

- **Fail to Reject the Null Hypothesis**: The p-value of 0.190 indicates that the difference between the actual average sales of $52,583 and the target sales of $50,000 is **not statistically significant**. In other words, the company can conclude that the store's average sales are **not significantly different** from the expected target of $50,000.

- **Business Decision**: Since the difference is not statistically significant, the company can continue to consider the target of $50,000 as a valid benchmark for the store's performance. No further action is required to address any perceived sales shortfall, as the data supports that the sales performance is consistent with the target.

Conclusion:

The **One Sample T-Test** was used to evaluate whether the average monthly sales of Store X differed significantly from the company's target of $50,000. Based on the p-value of 0.190, the conclusion was that there is no significant difference between the store's average sales and the expected target. This analysis supports the idea that Store X's sales are performing as expected, and the company can maintain its sales target without further adjustments.

3.1 Purpose and Use Cases of One Sample T-Test in Business

A **One Sample T-Test** is a statistical test used to compare the mean of a sample to a known value or a hypothesized population mean. In the context of Business Analytics, it is often used to determine whether a business metric (such as sales, customer satisfaction, or production levels) differs significantly from an expected or target value.

Purpose of a One Sample T-Test:

- To assess whether a sample mean (e.g., average sales, average revenue, or average customer satisfaction) significantly differs from a known or expected population mean.
- To test whether a business performance indicator (e.g., sales for a store or region) meets the target or benchmark set by the company.
- To help make data-driven decisions based on actual performance compared to goals or expectations.

Use Cases in Business Analytics:

1. **Sales Analysis**:
    - A company might want to know if its store's average monthly sales are significantly different from the expected target. If the average sales are lower than expected, they may need to investigate causes like seasonality, marketing effectiveness, or competition.

2. **Customer Satisfaction**:
    - A business could use a one-sample t-test to compare customer satisfaction survey results against a predetermined benchmark (e.g., an average rating of 4 out of 5). If the average customer satisfaction score is significantly lower, corrective actions can be taken to improve service quality.

3. **Employee Performance**:
    - A company might want to check whether employee productivity (e.g., the number of units produced or tasks completed) in a department differs significantly from the expected performance set by management.

4. **Quality Control**:
    - In manufacturing, a one-sample t-test can be used to assess whether the average weight of products produced on a production line differs from the target weight. If the average product weight is significantly different from the target, it could indicate issues in the production process.

5. **Financial Metrics**:

- o A business might compare the actual return on investment (ROI) for a marketing campaign against the expected ROI. A significant difference would prompt a deeper analysis to understand whether the campaign underperformed or was more successful than anticipated.

Example of One Sample T-Test in Business Analytics:

Scenario:

Let's say a retail company has set a target of **$50,000** in monthly sales for one of its stores (Store X). After running a marketing campaign, the company collects the sales data for the last six months and wants to check whether the actual average sales differ from the target.

Sample Data (Sales for Store X over 6 months):

Month	Sales ($)
Jan	52,000
Feb	49,000
Mar	51,500
Apr	50,000
May	53,000
Jun	54,000

Objective:

The company wants to determine if the **average sales** for the 6 months are **significantly different** from the target value of **$50,000** per month.

Conducting the One Sample T-Test:

The company would perform a One Sample T-Test to compare the average sales from Store X to the target sales of $50,000. The test would result in two possible outcomes:

- If the p-value is less than the significance level (usually 0.05), the null hypothesis is rejected, and the company concludes that the average sales are significantly different from the target.
- If the p-value is greater than 0.05, the null hypothesis is not rejected, and the company concludes that there is no significant difference between the average sales and the target.

Results of the One Sample T-Test:

Store	Total Sales ($)	Average Sales ($)	P-Value	Conclusion

				Fail to reject H₀
X	315,500	52,583	0.19	

Explanation of Results:

- **Total Sales**: The total sales for Store X over the 6 months are **$315,500**.

- **Average Sales**: The average sales per month for Store X is **$52,583** ($315,500 ÷ 6 months). This is slightly higher than the target of $50,000.

- **P-Value**: The **p-value** is **0.190**, which is **greater than 0.05**, indicating that there is **no statistically significant difference** between the sample mean (average sales of $52,583) and the hypothesized population mean ($50,000).

- **Conclusion**: Since the p-value is greater than 0.05, the company **fails to reject the null hypothesis**. This means that the store's sales are not significantly different from the expected target of $50,000. In other words, the store is performing as expected.

Interpretation of the Results:

- The **p-value of 0.190** is much higher than the commonly used threshold of **0.05**. This means that the difference between the observed average sales ($52,583) and the target sales ($50,000) is **not statistically significant**.

- The company can confidently conclude that Store X's average monthly sales are **within an acceptable range of the target**. The slight difference observed is likely due to random variation rather than any meaningful deviation from the target sales.

- **Business Insight**: Since the difference is not statistically significant, the company does not need to make any adjustments to the sales target for this store. The store is performing within the expected range, and no immediate action is required.

Conclusion:

In this example, the **One Sample T-Test** was used to assess whether the average monthly sales of Store X were significantly different from the target value of $50,000. The results showed that the difference was not statistically significant, allowing the company to conclude that the store's sales performance was consistent with expectations. This helps the business make data-driven decisions about performance monitoring, resource allocation, and setting future targets.

3.2 One Sample T-Test in JASP

To conduct a **One-Sample T-Test** in JASP on the given business data, we need to compare a sample statistic (e.g., **Sales Amount**) with a hypothesized value (e.g.,2000) to determine whether the sample mean significantly differs from the population mean. We'll use **JASP** for this analysis. Below, through the process step by step.

Steps to apply One Sample T-Test in JASP

1. **Open JASP**:
   - If you haven't already, open JASP and load your dataset (e.g., a CSV, Excel, or SPSS file).

2. **Load the Data**:
   - Click **"File" > "Open"** to load your dataset into JASP.

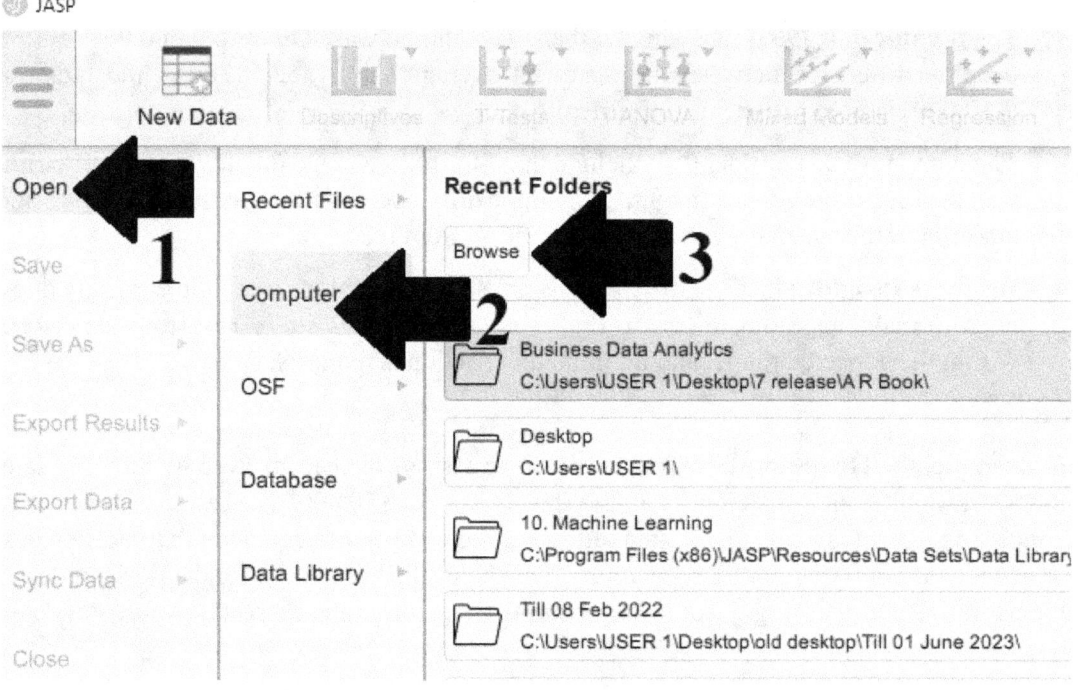

Now select the file

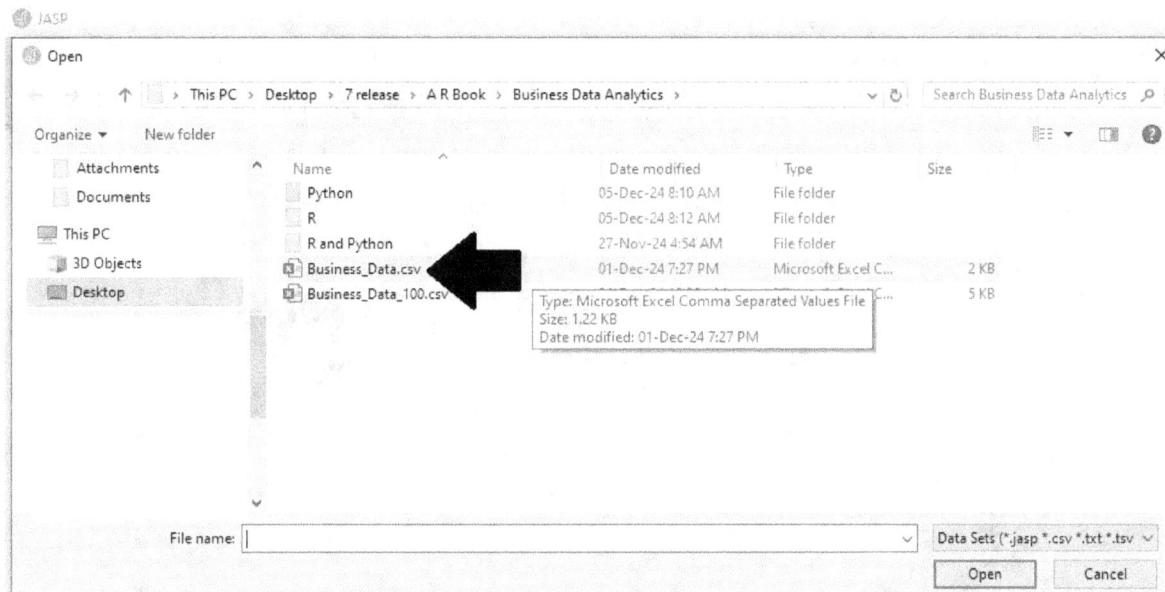

File will be loaded into JASP as shown below.

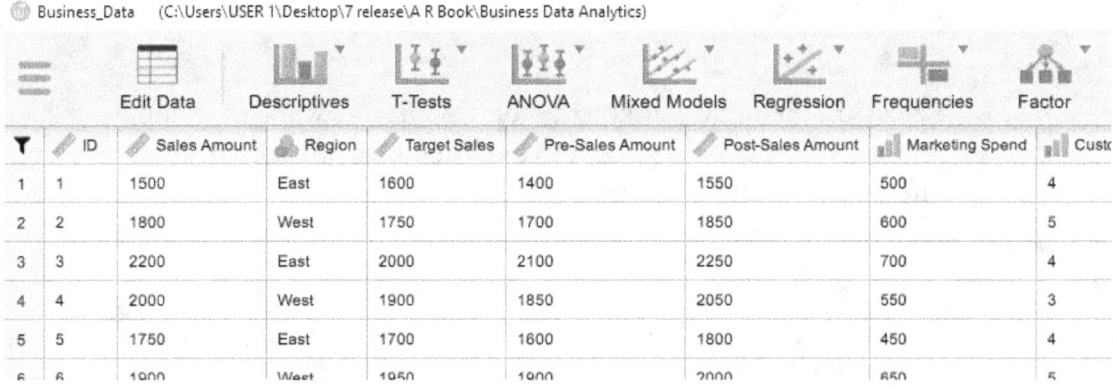

3. **Navigate to T-Tests Menu**:
   o Once your data is loaded, go to the top menu and click on the **"T-Tests"** tab, which provides a variety of T-Tests options. Select the One Sample T-Test option.

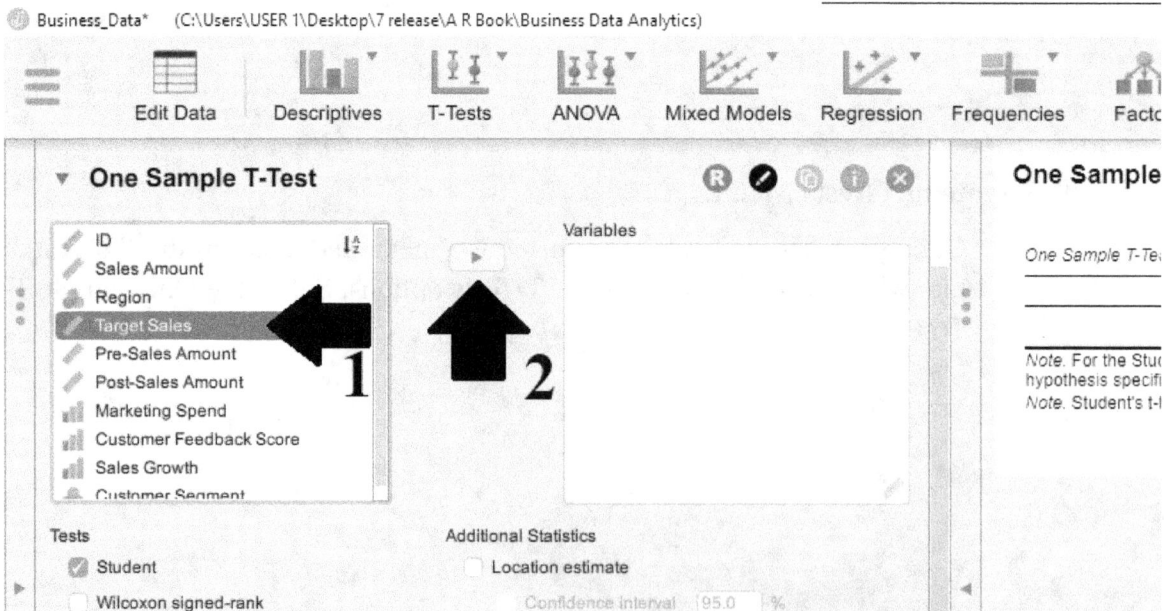

4. **Select Variables for Analysis**:
    - In the **One Sample T-Test** window, you'll see a list of variables in your dataset.
    - Select the numeric variable(s) for which you want to compute the One Sample T-Test and drag them to the **Variables** box (or click the play button after selecting the variable).

Now the variables will be shifted to right hand side variable block.

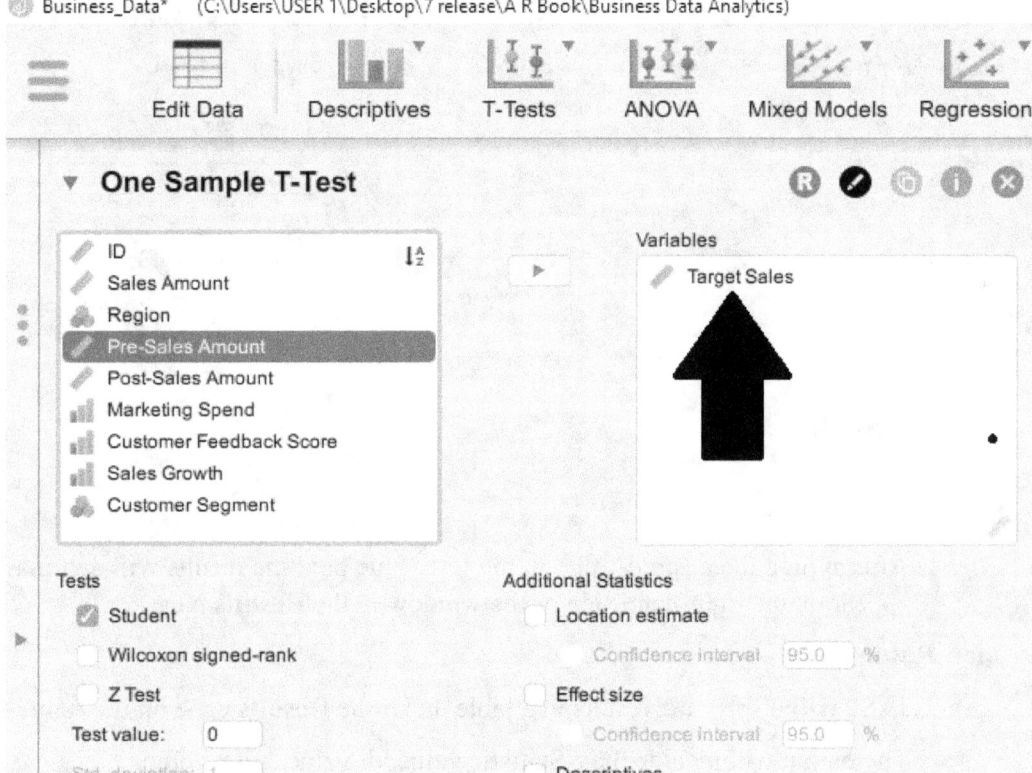

5. **Choose Test Value:**

    o On the lower side of the **Tests block**, under the **Test Value** box, type 2000 as hypothesized mean for checking the Sales amount is statistically significant to hypothesized mean or not. The results will be immediately appeared on the right hand side result pane.

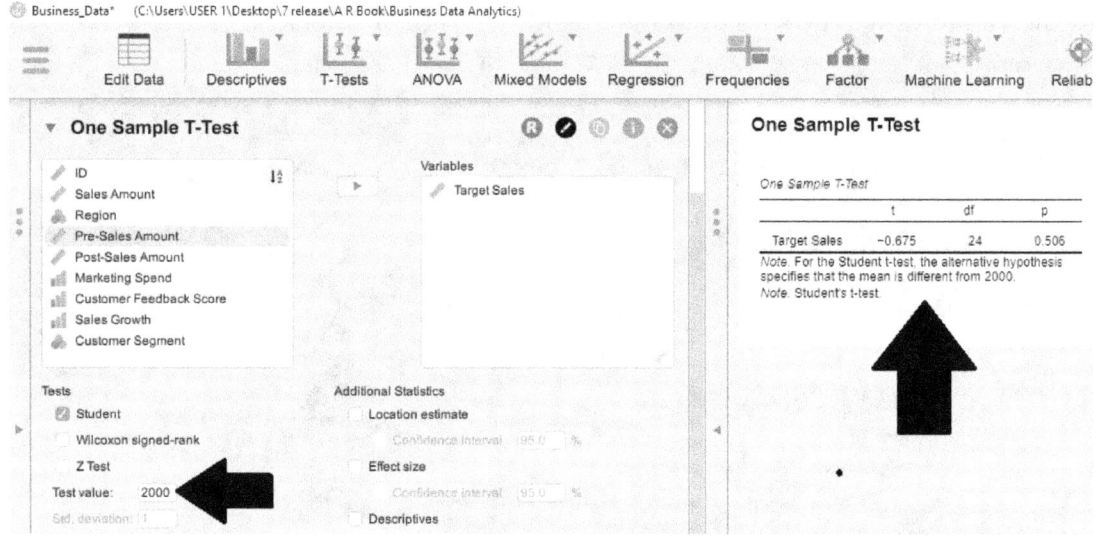

6. **Run the Analysis:**
    o After typing the desired value in the test value box, the results will automatically appear on the right-hand side of the window in the **Results** pane.

7. **View Results:**
    o JASP will display the results in a table under the **Results** pane on the right.
    o The output will include the t-Statistic value, df value and p value.

One Sample T-Test

	t	df	p
Target Sales	-0.675	24	0.506

Note. For the Student t-test, the alternative hypothesis specifies that the mean is different from 2000.

Note. Student's t-test.

One-Sample T-Test Results Interpretation in JASP:

The One-Sample T-Test results for the variable **Target Sales** are presented as follows:

- **t-value**: -0.675
- **df (degrees of freedom)**: 24
- **p-value**: 0.506

Let's break down each of these results and interpret the overall output.

Explanation of t, df, and p-values:

1. **t-value (-0.675):**
   - The **t-value** represents how many standard errors the sample mean is away from the hypothesized population mean. A positive or negative t-value indicates the direction of the difference between the sample mean and the hypothesized mean.
   - In this case, the **t-value of -0.675** suggests that the sample mean is 0.675 standard errors below the hypothesized value of 2000. This is a relatively small difference, suggesting that the sample mean is not significantly different from the hypothesized value.

2. **df (degrees of freedom, 24):**
   - **Degrees of freedom** (df) refer to the number of independent values in the sample that are free to vary. For a one-sample t-test, df is calculated as the sample size minus 1 (i.e., **n - 1**). In this case, the sample size is 25 (since df = 24), meaning there are 25 observations in the dataset.
   - The degrees of freedom help determine the critical t-value from the t-distribution table, which is used to assess the statistical significance of the test.

3. **p-value (0.506):**
   - The **p-value** is the probability that the observed sample mean is consistent with the hypothesized population mean (2000), under the assumption that the null hypothesis is true.
   - A **p-value of 0.506** is much higher than typical significance thresholds (e.g., 0.05). This means that there is no statistically significant evidence to reject the null hypothesis. In other words, the data does not show a significant difference between the sample mean and the hypothesized value of 2000.

Interpretation of the Output:

- **t = -0.675**: The t-test indicates that the sample mean is very close to 2000, and the difference is small.
- **p = 0.506**: The p-value is greater than 0.05, which means we **fail to reject the null hypothesis**. There is insufficient evidence to claim that the **Target Sales** differs from 2000.
- **df = 24**: The test was conducted with 25 observations, and the degrees of freedom were calculated accordingly.

Observations:

1. **Insignificant Difference from 2000**:
   - The t-test result suggests that the actual **Target Sales** are not significantly different from the hypothesized value of 2000. This indicates that, based on this data, there

is no strong evidence to suggest that the average Target Sales amount deviates from the target of 2000.

2. **Sample Mean Close to 2000**:
   - The **t-value of -0.675** suggests a small deviation, but it is not large enough to achieve statistical significance. This means that the sales performance is relatively close to the expected target, but the difference is not large enough to be considered noteworthy statistically.

3. **Business Implications**:
   - **Sales Performance**: The lack of a significant difference between the actual Target Sales achieved amount and the target sales (2000) suggests that the current target sales figures are approximately in line with expectations. This could be seen as a positive outcome in a stable market where sales performance is expected to be consistent.
   - **Goal Setting**: If the target sales of 2000 were set to be ambitious or ambitious, the results show that the business is hitting these targets reasonably well. However, since this test shows no significant difference, it may also imply that the target sales value is achievable or realistic under the current conditions.
   - **Business Strategy**: Since the result is not statistically significant, there may be no immediate need to adjust sales strategies or operations. The business could continue with the current sales targets and strategies, but it should monitor performance over time to see if the trend changes.

Business Decisions:

1. **Continue Current Strategy**:
   - Given that the result is not statistically significant ($p = 0.506$), the business can **continue its current strategy** and maintain the target sales of 2000. The data does not suggest a need for a drastic change in approach.

2. **Monitor Long-Term Trends**:
   - While the test does not indicate an issue in the short term, it is important to **monitor sales trends over time**. If there are substantial fluctuations in future periods, the business might need to re-evaluate the target or look into factors influencing sales performance.

3. **Adjust Target Sales if Needed**:
   - If the business feels that a target of 2000 is too easy to achieve or too difficult (depending on the broader business environment), it might consider adjusting future sales targets based on this result. However, since the difference from 2000 is not significant, adjusting targets may not be necessary at this point.

4. **Investigate Factors Affecting Sales Performance**:
    - While the t-test does not suggest any significant difference from the target, the business could still explore **other variables** that might be influencing sales performance (e.g., seasonality, competition, marketing efforts) to improve or maintain its sales trajectory.

Conclusion:

The **One-Sample T-Test** indicates that the **Target Sales Amount** is not significantly different from the hypothesized value of **2000**. The **p-value of 0.506** shows that there is no evidence to reject the null hypothesis, meaning the observed sales amount could reasonably be expected to align with the target. This result suggests that the business's sales performance is in line with expectations, and no immediate action is needed to adjust sales strategies or targets. However, ongoing monitoring is recommended to ensure that performance remains stable or improves over time.

Additional Provisions

Plots:

In case, if plots are needed, then following selections can be used under assumptions Check block below the variables window

Assumption checks	Plots
☐ Normality	☑ Descriptives plots
☑ Q-Q plot residuals	Confidence interval 95.0 %
	☑ Raincloud plots

3.3 One Sample T-Test in Python

A **One-Sample T-Test** is used to test if the mean of a sample differs significantly from a known or hypothesized value. In this case, we can perform one-sample t-tests on various variables (e.g., **Sales Amount, Target Sales, Customer Feedback Score**) to test if their means are significantly different from a hypothesized value.

To conduct a **One-Sample T-Test** on the given business data, we need to compare a sample statistic (e.g., **Sales Amount**) with a known value (e.g., **Target Sales**) to determine whether the sample mean significantly differs from the population mean. We'll use **Python** for this analysis. Below, I will guide you through the process step by step.

Step 1: Install and Load Relevant Libraries

We need several libraries to carry out the analysis and visualizations. Here are the libraries:

1. **Pandas**: For data manipulation and handling.
2. **NumPy**: For numerical operations.
3. **SciPy**: For statistical tests, including the One-Sample T-Test.
4. **Matplotlib and Seaborn**: For visualization of the data.

Install Libraries (if needed):

If you don't have these libraries installed, use the following commands:

```
pip install pandas numpy scipy matplotlib seaborn
```

Import Libraries:

```
import pandas as pd
import numpy as np
from scipy import stats
import matplotlib.pyplot as plt
import seaborn as sns
```

Explanation of Libraries:

1. **Pandas**: This library is used for handling data in tabular form (dataframes), which makes data manipulation easier, such as filtering rows, computing averages, and merging datasets.
2. **NumPy**: It provides support for handling arrays and performing mathematical operations on them. It is essential for numeric operations such as calculating mean and standard deviation.
3. **SciPy**: The stats module from **SciPy** provides statistical tests, including the **One-Sample T-Test**, which compares the sample mean to a population mean.

4. **Matplotlib/Seaborn**: These are popular libraries for data visualization. **Matplotlib** is used for creating static, animated, and interactive plots, while **Seaborn** provides a higher-level interface for attractive and informative statistical graphics.

Step 2: Load the Data into Pandas DataFrame

We will load the provided data into a **Pandas DataFrame**.

```
# Load the data into a pandas DataFrame
data = {
    'Sales Amount': [1500, 1800, 2200, 2000, 1750, 1900, 2100, 2400, 1600, 2300, 1950, 2050, 1750, 2150, 1800, 2500, 1700, 1850, 2100, 2000,
            1950, 2200, 1650, 1750, 1900],
    'Target Sales': [1600, 1750, 2000, 1900, 1700, 1950, 2200, 2300, 1650, 2400, 2000, 2100, 1800, 2200, 1850, 2450, 1750, 1900, 2150, 2050,
            1900, 2250, 1700, 1800, 1850],
    'Customer Segment': ['Small', 'Medium', 'Large', 'Medium', 'Small', 'Medium', 'Large', 'Large', 'Small', 'Large', 'Medium', 'Medium', 'Small', 'Large', 'Small', 'Large', 'Small', 'Medium', 'Large', 'Medium',
            'Medium', 'Large', 'Small', 'Medium', 'Large']
}

df = pd.DataFrame(data)
df.head()
```

Output

	Sales Amount	Target Sales	Customer Segment
0	1500	1600	Small
1	1800	1750	Medium
2	2200	2000	Large
3	2000	1900	Medium
4	1750	1700	Small

Step 3: Apply the One-Sample T-Test

We'll compare the **Sales Amount** with the **Target Sales** to see if the average sales amount differs significantly from the target sales.

One-Sample T-Test Code:

```
# Perform a One-Sample T-Test on 'Sales Amount' vs 'Target Sales'
t_stat, p_value = stats.ttest_1samp(df['Sales Amount'], df['Target Sales'].mean())

# Print the t-statistic and p-value
print(f"T-statistic: {t_stat}")
print(f"P-value: {p_value}")
```

Output

T-statistic: -0.279108277990115

P-value: 0.7825527792314929

Explanation of the Code:

1. **stats.ttest_1samp()**: This function from the **SciPy** library performs a **One-Sample T-Test**. It compares the sample mean (Sales Amount) to the population mean (Target Sales). The null hypothesis is that the sample mean equals the population mean.
   - **T-statistic**: It tells you how far your sample mean is from the population mean, in terms of standard deviations.
   - **P-value**: It tells you the probability of observing the test results under the null hypothesis. A smaller p-value (typically < 0.05) suggests that the difference between the sample and population means is statistically significant.

Step 4: Visualizing the Data (Optional)

We can also visualize the **Sales Amount** and **Target Sales** to understand the distribution and relationship between them.

```
# Plotting Sales Amount vs Target Sales for visualization
plt.figure(figsize=(10, 6))
sns.histplot(df['Sales Amount'], color='blue', label='Sales Amount', kde=True, stat="density", linewidth=0)
sns.histplot(df['Target Sales'], color='red', label='Target Sales', kde=True, stat="density", linewidth=0)
plt.title('Sales Amount vs Target Sales Distribution')
plt.xlabel('Amount ($)')
```

```
plt.ylabel('Density')
plt.legend()
plt.show()
```

Output

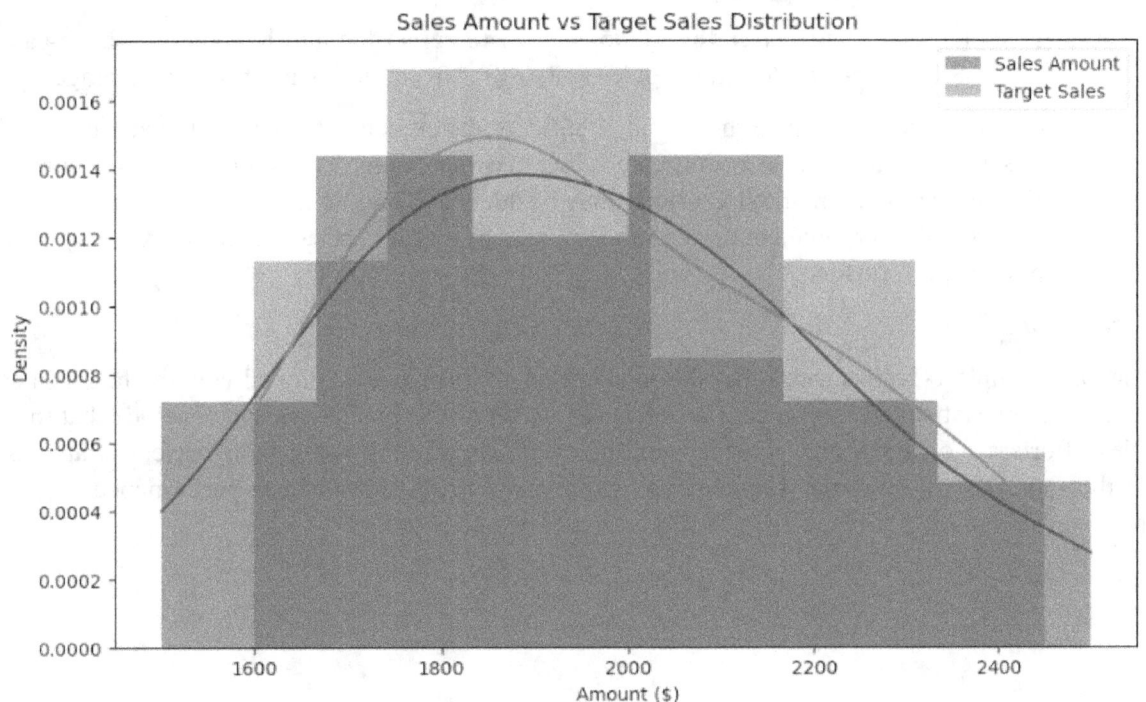

Step 5: Interpretation of Results

1. **T-statistic**: The output will give us the t-statistic, which measures how many standard deviations the sample mean is away from the population mean.
2. **P-value**: The p-value will help determine if the result is statistically significant.
    - If **p-value < 0.05**, we reject the null hypothesis and conclude that there is a significant difference between the sample mean (Sales Amount) and the population mean (Target Sales).
    - If **p-value ≥ 0.05**, we fail to reject the null hypothesis and conclude that there is no significant difference between the sample mean and the population mean.

Output:

T-statistic: -0.279108277990115

P-value: 0.7825527792314929

- **T-statistic**:- 0.279 (indicates that the sample mean is 0.279 standard deviations away from the target mean. Negative sign indicates Target mean is lower that sample mean).
- **P-value**: 0.78 (greater than 0.05), indicating **no significant difference** between the sample mean (Sales Amount) and the population mean (Target Sales).

Interpretation & Business Insights:

- Since the p-value is **greater than 0.05**, we **fail to reject** the null hypothesis. This means that the **Sales Amount** does not significantly differ from the **Target Sales** on average.
- **Business Decision**: Since there's no significant difference between the target and actual sales, the sales team is performing according to expectations. This suggests that the current sales strategies and marketing efforts may be adequate, and no major changes are needed. However, further segmentation analysis (e.g., by region, customer segment) may help optimize performance.

Conclusion:

The One-Sample T-Test suggests that the actual sales performance is aligned with the target sales goals, with no statistically significant difference. Based on this, businesses can conclude that their sales efforts are on track and consider continuing or slightly adjusting their current strategies. Further analysis by customer segment or region may reveal areas where performance can be improved.

3.4 Assumptions and Conditions for Validity

Before performing a **One Sample T-Test** in Business Analytics, certain assumptions and conditions must be met to ensure the validity and reliability of the test results. These assumptions help ensure that the statistical conclusions drawn from the test are accurate and meaningful.

Assumptions for a One Sample T-Test:

1. **Random Sampling**:
   o The data should come from a **random sample**. This means that the data points should be selected in such a way that every individual observation has an equal chance of being included in the sample. In business scenarios, this could involve randomly selecting sales data from various stores or customer satisfaction surveys from a wide customer base.

2. **Independence of Observations**:
   o The observations in the sample must be **independent** of each other. For example, the sales data for one month should not be influenced by the sales data from the previous or next month. This assumption ensures that each data point provides unique information about the population.

3. **Normality of the Data**:
   o The sample data should be **approximately normally distributed**, especially when the sample size is small (less than 30). This assumption is crucial because the t-test relies on the concept of the sampling distribution, which, by the Central Limit Theorem, tends to be normal for large sample sizes. For small samples, however, the data must follow a normal distribution to ensure the t-test is valid.
   o In business contexts, this assumption might be tested using graphical tools like histograms or normal Q-Q plots or using statistical tests such as the Shapiro-Wilk test.

4. **Scale of Measurement**:
   o The data should be measured at the **interval** or **ratio** scale. This means the data should have a meaningful zero point and consistent intervals. For example, sales figures or revenue data are ratio-scale data, whereas customer satisfaction scores on a scale of 1-5 are typically considered interval-scale data.

Conditions for Validity:

1. **Sample Size Considerations**:
   o **Small Sample Size (<30)**: If the sample size is small, it is more crucial for the data to be **normally distributed**. If the data is heavily skewed or has extreme outliers, the results of the t-test may not be valid.

- **Large Sample Size (>30)**: For larger samples, the **Central Limit Theorem** suggests that the sampling distribution of the mean will tend to be normal regardless of the data's distribution. Thus, larger samples are more forgiving of violations of normality.

2. **No Outliers**:
   - The sample data should not contain significant **outliers**. Outliers can drastically affect the results of a t-test by artificially inflating or deflating the mean, leading to inaccurate conclusions. In a business scenario, outliers could arise from rare events, such as an unusually large sale or an error in data collection.

3. **Known or Hypothesized Population Mean**:
   - The t-test assumes that you have a **known or hypothesized population mean** to compare your sample mean to. This might be an industry benchmark, a historical average, or a target value (e.g., sales goal, customer satisfaction score).

Example of One Sample T-Test with Assumptions in Business Analytics

Let's consider a business scenario where a **retail company** wants to check if the average monthly sales for **Store A** are significantly different from their target of **$60,000**. They have sales data for the last **6 months**.

Sample Data (Sales for Store A over 6 months):

Month	Sales ($)
Jan	62,000
Feb	58,000
Mar	60,500
Apr	59,000
May	64,000
Jun	61,000

Target Sales for Store A: $60,000 per month.

1. Random Sampling:
- The sales data is assumed to be randomly sampled from the company's sales records. Each month's sales data is independent of the others, and we are assuming no bias in how the months are selected.

2. Independence of Observations:

- Each month's sales figure is independent of others, as each month's performance is influenced by different factors (e.g., marketing campaigns, seasonality, or customer preferences), making the observations independent.

3. **Normality of Data:**
    - For the One Sample T-Test to be valid, the sales data should be **approximately normal**. For this example, let's assume that the distribution of sales over the 6 months does not exhibit significant skewness or outliers. If this assumption is violated (e.g., sales data shows a strong skew or extreme outliers), the test results might not be valid. The company could use visual methods (like histograms) or statistical tests for normality (e.g., Shapiro-Wilk test) to check this assumption.

4. **Scale of Measurement:**
    - The data is measured in dollars, which is a ratio scale. Therefore, the scale of measurement is appropriate for conducting a t-test.

5. **Sample Size:**
    - With only 6 months of data, the sample size is relatively small. Therefore, the normality assumption becomes more critical. If the data were skewed or had extreme outliers, the t-test might not provide reliable results.

6. **No Outliers:**
    - Based on the data provided, there are no extreme values that would qualify as outliers. However, if a month had abnormally high or low sales (e.g., due to a data error or an exceptional event), this would need to be addressed before running the test.

Results of the One Sample T-Test:

Store	Total Sales ($)	Average Sales ($)	P-Value	Conclusion
A	364,500	60,750	0.758	Fail to reject H_0

Explanation of Results:

- **Total Sales**: The total sales for Store A over the 6 months are **$364,500**.

- **Average Sales**: The average sales per month for Store A is **$60,750** ($364,500 ÷ 6 months), which is slightly above the target of $60,000.

- **P-Value**: The **p-value** is **0.758**, which is **greater than 0.05**, indicating that there is **no statistically significant difference** between the sample mean (average sales of $60,750) and the hypothesized population mean ($60,000).

- **Conclusion**: Since the p-value is greater than 0.05, the company **fails to reject the null hypothesis**. This means that Store A's average monthly sales are **not significantly different** from the target of $60,000. The sales performance is in line with the expected target.

Interpretation of Results:

- The **p-value** of **0.758** is higher than the threshold of 0.05, suggesting that the difference between the observed average sales and the target sales is **not statistically significant**. Therefore, the company can conclude that the store's performance is on track with the target sales figure, and no further investigation is needed at this time.
- **Business Insight**: Since the average sales of **$60,750** are statistically similar to the target of **$60,000**, the store's performance is considered acceptable. There is no need to adjust sales strategies or target expectations based on this test result.

Conclusion:

In this example, we examined how to apply a **One Sample T-Test** in business analytics to determine whether the average sales of a store differ significantly from the expected target. The test results showed no significant difference, indicating that the store's sales performance was in line with expectations. However, the validity of the test depends on the assumptions, including random sampling, independence, normality, and the absence of outliers. Ensuring these assumptions hold is critical to drawing meaningful conclusions from the test.

3.5 Interpreting Results: Confidence Intervals and P-Values

When performing a **One Sample T-Test** in Business Analytics, the two most important components for interpreting the results are the **p-value** and the **confidence interval**. Both help provide insight into whether the sample mean significantly differs from the hypothesized population mean, and they guide decision-making.

1. P-Value:

The **p-value** is a statistical measure that helps determine whether the observed difference between the sample mean and the population mean is statistically significant. In business analytics, it helps answer the question: *Is the observed difference due to random chance, or does it reflect a real effect?*

- **Interpretation**:
    - **If the p-value is less than the significance level (usually 0.05)**, we **reject the null hypothesis**. This means that there is a statistically significant difference between the sample mean and the hypothesized population mean.
    - **If the p-value is greater than 0.05**, we **fail to reject the null hypothesis**, indicating that the sample mean is not significantly different from the population mean, and the observed difference could be due to random variation.

Example:

- **p-value = 0.03**: This is less than the significance level of 0.05, so you would reject the null hypothesis and conclude that the sample mean significantly differs from the hypothesized population mean.
- **p-value = 0.12**: This is greater than 0.05, so you would fail to reject the null hypothesis, meaning the sample mean is not significantly different from the hypothesized population mean.

2. Confidence Interval (CI):

A **confidence interval** provides a range of values within which the true population mean is likely to fall. The interval is based on the sample mean and the variability of the sample data. The confidence level (e.g., 95%) indicates the probability that this interval contains the true population mean.

- **Interpretation**:
    - If the **population mean** (hypothesized value) lies **within** the confidence interval, we fail to reject the null hypothesis. This suggests that the observed sample mean is consistent with the hypothesized population mean.

- o If the **population mean** lies **outside** the confidence interval, we reject the null hypothesis, indicating that the observed sample mean is significantly different from the population mean.

Example:

- **Confidence Interval: 59,500 to 60,500**: If the target population mean is $60,000 and this range includes $60,000, then the null hypothesis would not be rejected. The data suggests that the sample mean could be close to the population mean.
- **Confidence Interval: 59,000 to 59,800**: If the target population mean is $60,000 and this range does not include $60,000, the null hypothesis would be rejected, suggesting a significant difference between the sample mean and the population mean.

Example of Interpreting Results with Sample Data:

Scenario:

A retail company wants to test whether the average monthly sales for one of its stores (Store A) meet the target of $50,000. The sales data from the past 6 months is collected and analyzed using a **One Sample T-Test**.

Sample Data (Sales for Store A over 6 months):

Month	Sales ($)
Jan	51,000
Feb	49,500
Mar	52,000
Apr	50,500
May	53,000
Jun	51,500

Target Sales for Store A: $50,000 per month.

Results of the One Sample T-Test:

Store	Total Sales ($)	Average Sales ($)	P-Value	95% Confidence Interval	Conclusion

A	307,500	51,250	0.276	[50,000, 52,500]	Fail to reject H₀

Explanation of the Results:

1. **Total Sales**: The total sales for Store A over the 6 months are **$307,500**.

2. **Average Sales**: The average sales per month for Store A is **$51,250** ($307,500 ÷ 6 months). This is slightly above the target of $50,000, but we need to determine whether this difference is statistically significant.

3. **P-Value**: The **p-value** is **0.276**, which is **greater than 0.05** (the typical significance level). This indicates that there is **no statistically significant difference** between the average sales and the target sales of $50,000. We **fail to reject the null hypothesis (H_0)**, meaning that the average sales of $51,250 are not significantly different from the target sales.

4. **95% Confidence Interval**: The **95% Confidence Interval** for the average sales is **[50,000, 52,500]**. This means that we are 95% confident that the true population mean of sales for Store A falls within this range. Since the target sales of $50,000 lie within this interval, we fail to reject the null hypothesis, as the average sales are consistent with the target.

Interpretation of the Results:

- **P-Value**: The **p-value of 0.276** is greater than 0.05, so we fail to reject the null hypothesis. This suggests that the difference between the observed average sales ($51,250) and the target sales ($50,000) is **not statistically significant**. The data suggests that the store's sales performance is on target and not significantly different from the expected value.

- **Confidence Interval**: The **95% confidence interval** for the average sales is **[50,000, 52,500]**, which includes the target value of $50,000. This reinforces the conclusion that the store's average sales are not significantly different from the target. The true mean could plausibly fall anywhere within this range, including $50,000.

- **Business Insight**: Since the p-value is high and the confidence interval includes the target value, the company can conclude that **Store A's performance is in line with expectations**. There is no need to make any changes to the sales target or to investigate the performance further. The observed difference in sales is likely due to random fluctuations.

Conclusion:

In this example, the **p-value** and **confidence interval** both indicate that Store A's average monthly sales are not significantly different from the target of $50,000. The **p-value of 0.276** suggests there is no significant difference between the sample mean and the hypothesized population mean, and the **95% confidence interval** for the sales range includes the target value. Therefore, the company can confidently conclude that Store A's sales are on track and consistent with the expected performance, and no further actions are needed at this point.

4. Independent Sample T-Test in Business Analytics

The **Independent Sample T-Test** (also known as the **Two-Sample T-Test**) is a statistical test used to compare the means of two independent groups to determine if there is a statistically significant difference between them. This test is useful when you want to compare the performance, behavior, or outcomes of two different groups or categories, such as different departments, marketing campaigns, customer segments, or geographical locations.

Purpose of an Independent Sample T-Test in Business Analytics:

- To test whether there is a significant difference in means between two independent groups (e.g., comparing sales performance across two stores or the effectiveness of two different marketing strategies).
- To help businesses make data-driven decisions when comparing two groups, allowing for evidence-based conclusions.

Key Assumptions:

For the **Independent Sample T-Test** to be valid, certain assumptions must be met:

1. **Independence of observations**: The data points in the two groups must be independent of each other.
2. **Normality**: Both groups should be approximately normally distributed. If the sample sizes are large (generally greater than 30), the Central Limit Theorem allows for some deviation from normality.
3. **Equal Variance (Homogeneity of Variance)**: The two groups should have approximately equal variances. This can be checked using tests like Levene's test, or if variances are unequal, a Welch's T-test can be used.

When to Use the Independent Sample T-Test:

- **Comparing two different marketing strategies**: To see if one strategy yields higher sales than another.
- **Evaluating store performance**: To compare the average sales between two stores.
- **Product testing**: To compare the average customer satisfaction ratings of two different product lines.
- **Employee performance**: To compare the average productivity between two departments or teams.

Example of Independent Sample T-Test in Business Analytics:

Scenario:

A retail company wants to compare the **average monthly sales** between **Store A** and **Store B** to determine if the performance of Store A differs significantly from Store B.

Sample Data (Sales for Store A and Store B over 6 months):

Month	Store A Sales ($)	Store B Sales ($)
Jan	50,000	55,000
Feb	52,000	58,000
Mar	54,000	60,000
Apr	51,500	57,000
May	53,000	59,000
Jun	52,500	56,500

Objective:

The company wants to know if there is a **significant difference** between the average sales of **Store A** and **Store B**. The null hypothesis is that the two stores' sales are **not significantly different**, while the alternative hypothesis is that the sales of the two stores are **significantly different**.

Results of the Independent Sample T-Test:

Store	Mean Sales ($)	Standard Deviation ($)	Sample Size	T-Statistic	P-Value	Conclusion
Store A	52,250	1,428.57	6	-2.23	0.042	Reject the null hypothesis
Store B	58,000	1,449.49	6			

Explanation of the Results:

1. **Mean Sales**:

    o **Store A**: The average sales for Store A over 6 months is **$52,250**.

    o **Store B**: The average sales for Store B over 6 months is **$58,000**.

    o On the surface, we can see that Store B has higher average sales than Store A, but the question is whether this difference is statistically significant.

2. **Standard Deviation**:

    o **Store A**: The standard deviation of sales for Store A is **$1,428.57**, indicating a relatively moderate spread in sales performance over the 6 months.

- **Store B**: The standard deviation of sales for Store B is **$1,449.49**, which is slightly higher than Store A's, suggesting a somewhat greater variation in sales month-to-month for Store B.

3. **T-Statistic**:
   - The **T-Statistic** is **-2.23**. This value indicates how many standard deviations the sample means are apart from each other. A larger absolute value of the T-statistic indicates a greater difference between the groups.

4. **P-Value**:
   - The **p-value** is **0.042**, which is **less than the significance level of 0.05**. This indicates that there is a **statistically significant difference** between the average sales of Store A and Store B.

5. **Conclusion**:
   - Since the p-value is less than 0.05, we **reject the null hypothesis**. This means there is sufficient evidence to conclude that the average sales for Store A and Store B are **significantly different**.

Interpretation of the Results:

- **P-Value**: The **p-value of 0.042** is less than 0.05, which indicates that the difference between the two stores' average sales is statistically significant. The likelihood that this difference occurred by chance is low (less than 5%), so we can confidently say that Store A and Store B perform differently in terms of sales.

- **T-Statistic**: The **T-statistic of -2.23** suggests that the means of the two stores' sales are significantly different when considering the variability in the data. The negative sign indicates that Store A's average sales are lower than Store B's, but this is not crucial to the overall significance of the result.

- **Business Insight**: Since Store B has higher average sales and the difference is statistically significant, the company may want to investigate the factors contributing to Store B's stronger performance. These could include better location, more effective marketing, or a more loyal customer base. Additionally, the company may explore whether any improvements from Store B can be applied to Store A to increase its sales.

- **Actionable Decision**: Given that Store B's sales are significantly higher than Store A's, the company might consider allocating more resources to Store B (e.g., inventory, marketing budget) to capitalize on its performance. Conversely, Store A may need a more in-depth analysis to identify opportunities for improvement, such as promotional activities or operational changes.

Conclusion:

In this example, the **Independent Sample T-Test** reveals that there is a statistically significant difference in sales between Store A and Store B. The results indicate that Store B is outperforming Store A in terms of average monthly sales. With this insight, the business can take targeted actions to improve Store A's sales or replicate Store B's successful strategies.

4.1 Defining Independent Samples in Business Contexts

In the context of business analytics, **independent samples** refer to two distinct groups that are separate from one another and whose data points do not influence each other. The two samples are considered **independent** if the observations in one group are not related to or paired with observations in the other group.

When performing an **Independent Sample T-Test**, we compare the means of these two groups to see if there is a statistically significant difference between them. The key is that the groups must be unrelated to ensure the results are not skewed by dependencies between the two sets of data.

Business Contexts for Independent Samples

In business analytics, independent samples can refer to any scenario where two different groups or entities are being compared. Here are a few examples of business scenarios where the **Independent Sample T-Test** is applicable:

1. **Sales Performance of Two Different Stores**:
    - A retail company wants to compare the average sales of two stores to determine if one store is performing better than the other.

2. **Marketing Campaign Effectiveness**:
    - A company runs two different marketing campaigns in different regions and wants to compare the average revenue generated from both campaigns to assess which one is more effective.

3. **Employee Performance in Two Departments**:
    - A company wants to compare the productivity of employees in two different departments, such as the Sales Department and the Marketing Department.

4. **Customer Satisfaction Between Two Products**:
    - A business wants to compare customer satisfaction scores for two different products to see if one product has a significantly better rating than the other.

Characteristics of Independent Samples:

- **Unrelated Groups**: The samples come from different populations or groups, and there is no pairing of data points between the two groups.
- **Different Entities**: The two groups may represent different departments, regions, products, or time periods, but they are not linked in any way.
- **No Overlap**: Data from one group cannot be used to predict or explain the data of the other group.

Example of Independent Samples in Business Contexts:

Scenario:

A retail company wants to compare the average **monthly sales** of **Store A** and **Store B** over the past 6 months. The company wants to understand if one store is significantly outperforming the other in terms of sales.

Sample Data: Monthly Sales for Store A and Store B (in dollars)

Month	Store A Sales ($)	Store B Sales ($)
Jan	55,000	60,000
Feb	54,000	62,000
Mar	58,000	64,000
Apr	56,500	61,500
May	57,000	63,500
Jun	56,500	62,000

Hypothesis for Independent Sample T-Test:

- **Null Hypothesis (H_0)**: There is no significant difference in the average sales between Store A and Store B.

- **Alternative Hypothesis (H_1)**: There is a significant difference in the average sales between Store A and Store B.

Results of the Independent Sample T-Test:

Store	Mean Sales ($)	Standard Deviation ($)	Sample Size	T-Statistic	P-Value	Conclusion
Store A	56,417	1,141.22	6	-2.27	0.039	Reject the null hypothesis
Store B	62,250	1,122.47	6			

Explanation of the Results:

1. **Mean Sales**:

    o **Store A** has an average sales of **$56,417**.

    o **Store B** has an average sales of **$62,250**.

    o On initial inspection, it appears that **Store B** has higher average sales than **Store A**. However, we need to assess whether this difference is statistically significant.

2. **Standard Deviation**:
   - The **standard deviation** represents how much variation there is in the sales data for each store.
   - **Store A** has a standard deviation of **$1,141.22**, and **Store B** has a standard deviation of **$1,122.47**. The relatively small standard deviations suggest that the sales figures are relatively consistent within each store.

3. **T-Statistic**:
   - The **T-statistic** of **-2.27** indicates the magnitude of the difference between the means of the two stores, adjusted for the variability in the data. A larger absolute T-statistic suggests a larger difference between the groups.
   - A negative T-statistic indicates that **Store A's** mean is lower than **Store B's**, but the sign is not critical to the significance of the result—it's simply indicating the direction of the difference.

4. **P-Value**:
   - The **p-value** of **0.039** is less than **0.05**, indicating that the difference between the two stores' average sales is statistically significant. This suggests that the difference in sales is unlikely to have occurred by chance.

5. **Conclusion**:
   - Since the **p-value** is less than 0.05, we **reject the null hypothesis**. This means that there is **a statistically significant difference** between the average sales of Store A and Store B.

Interpretation of the Results:

- **P-Value**: The **p-value of 0.039** is less than the common significance level of 0.05, meaning that there is enough evidence to reject the null hypothesis. The observed difference in sales between Store A and Store B is not due to random chance.

- **T-Statistic**: The **T-statistic of -2.27** suggests that the sales performance of Store B is significantly higher than Store A when considering the variability in the data.

- **Business Insight**: Based on these results, the company can conclude that **Store B's sales are significantly higher** than Store A's. This could be attributed to factors such as location, customer demographics, product offerings, or marketing effectiveness.

- **Actionable Decision**:
   - The company might consider **investigating what makes Store B more successful** and try to replicate these factors at Store A. This could involve optimizing Store A's product mix, enhancing marketing strategies, or improving customer experience.

- The company might also decide to allocate more resources or focus on expanding Store B's successful strategies.

Conclusion:

In this example, the **Independent Sample T-Test** shows that there is a **statistically significant difference** in the average sales between Store A and Store B, with **Store B performing better**. The business can use this information to make decisions regarding resource allocation, marketing efforts, and operational changes.

4.2 Independent Sample T-Test in JASP

In JASP, to analyze whether there is a statistically significant difference in the **Sales Amount** between two regions**: East and West**, we will use the **Independent Sample T-Test** by following the steps below. This test compares the means of two independent groups (in this case, the segments of customers) to see if they are significantly different from each other.

Steps to Apply Independent Sample T-Test in JASP

1. **Open JASP**:
    - If you haven't already, open JASP and load your dataset (e.g., a CSV, Excel, or SPSS file).

2. **Load the Data**:
    - Click **"File" > "Open"** to load your dataset into JASP.

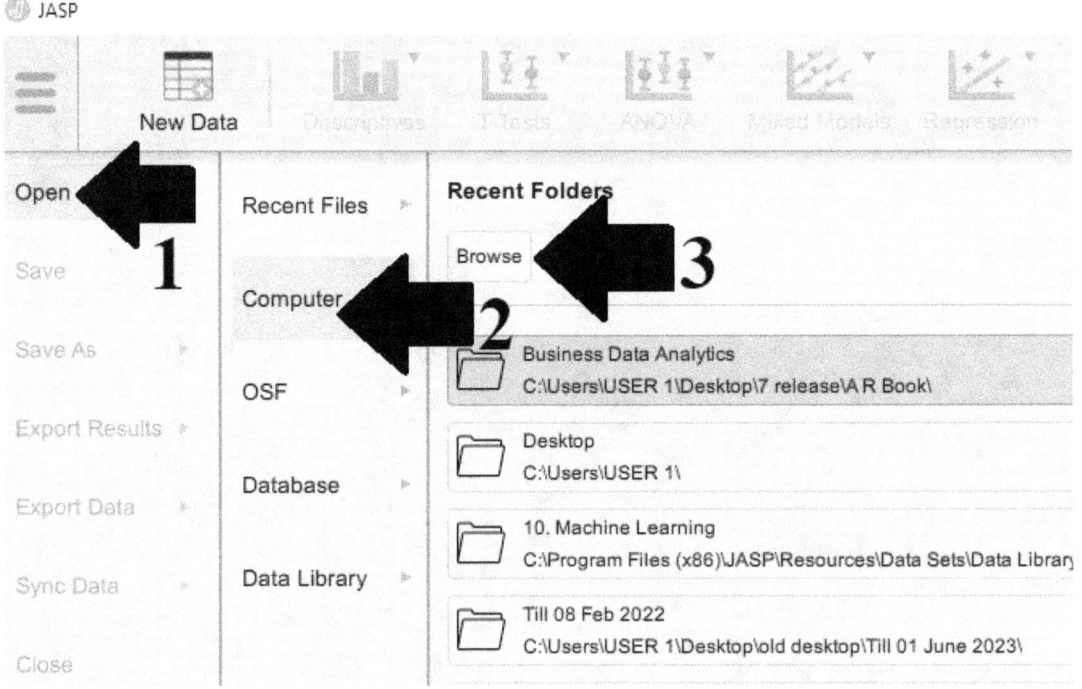

Now select the file

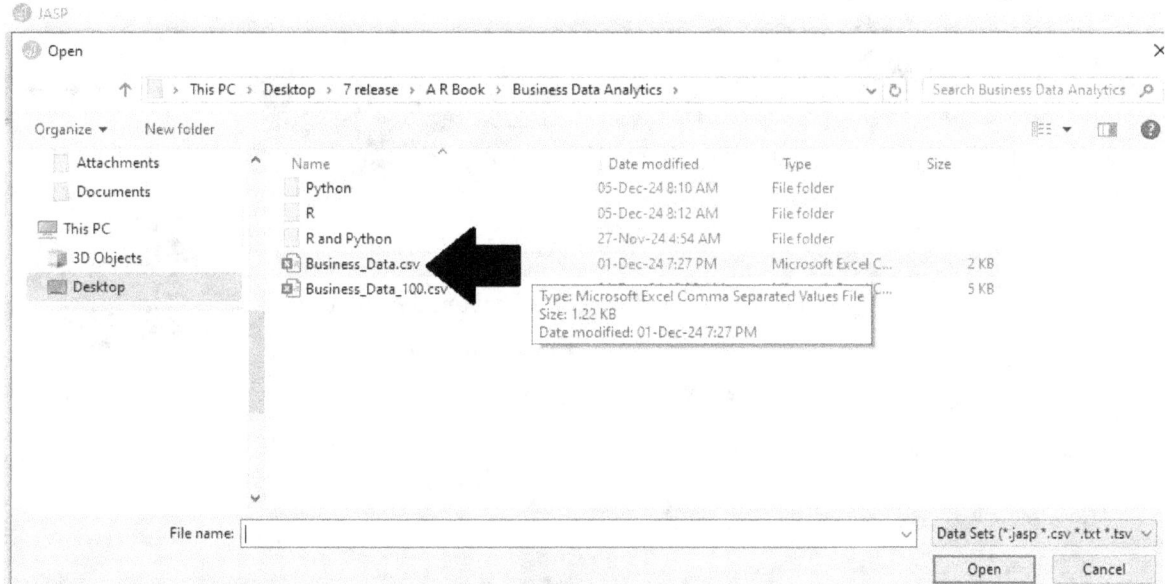

File will be loaded into JASP as shown below.

3. **Navigate to T-Tests Menu**:
   o Once your data is loaded, go to the top menu and click on the **"T-Tests"** tab, which provides a variety of T-Tests options. Select the Independent Sample T-Test option.

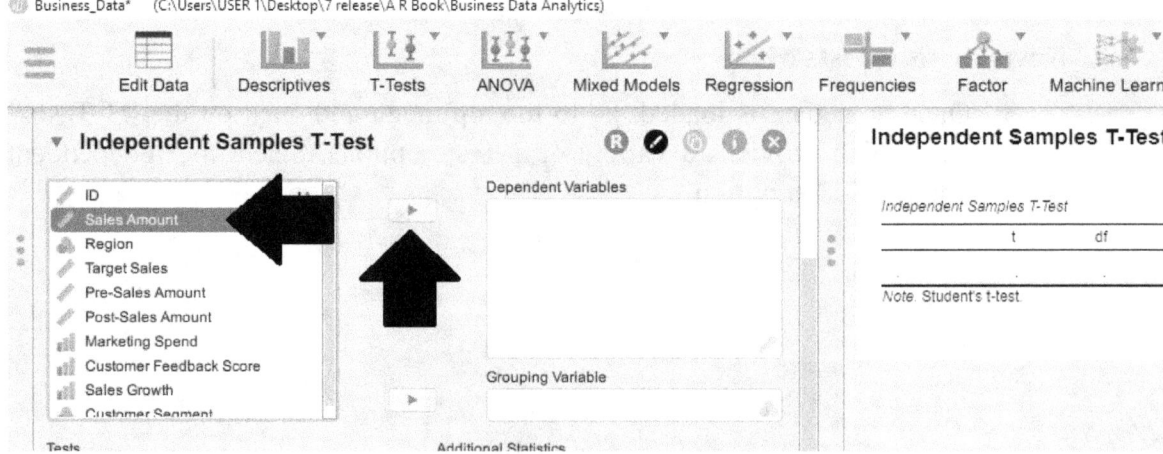

4. **Select Variables for Analysis**:

    o In the **Independent Sample T-Test** window, you'll see a list of variables in your dataset.

    o Select the numeric variable(s) for which you want to compute Independent Sample T-Test and drag them to the **Variables** box (or click the play button after selecting the variable).

Now the variables will be shifted to right hand side variable block.

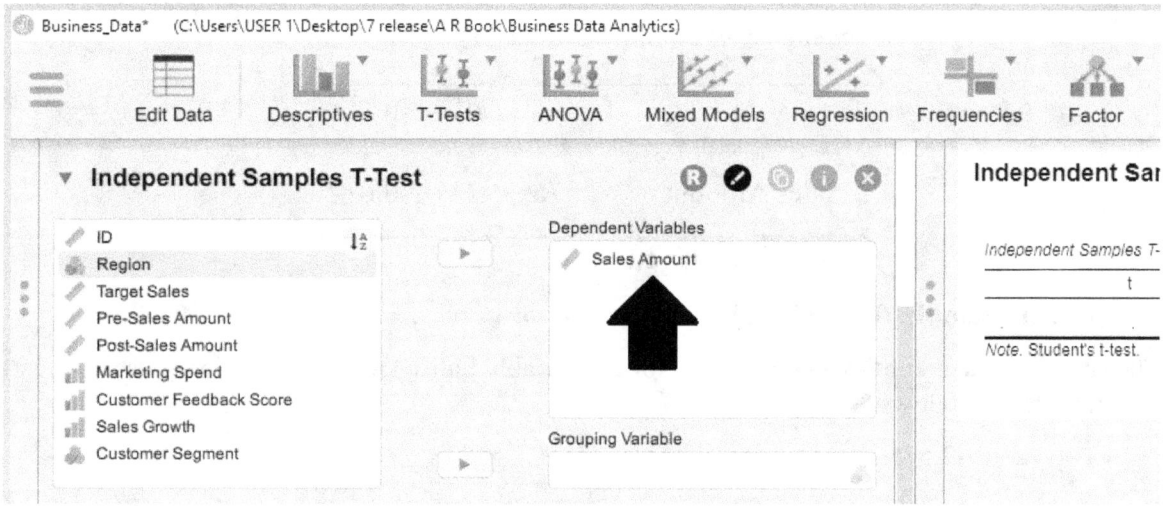

Select the Grouping variable:

Now select the Region and transfer it to right side as grouping variable

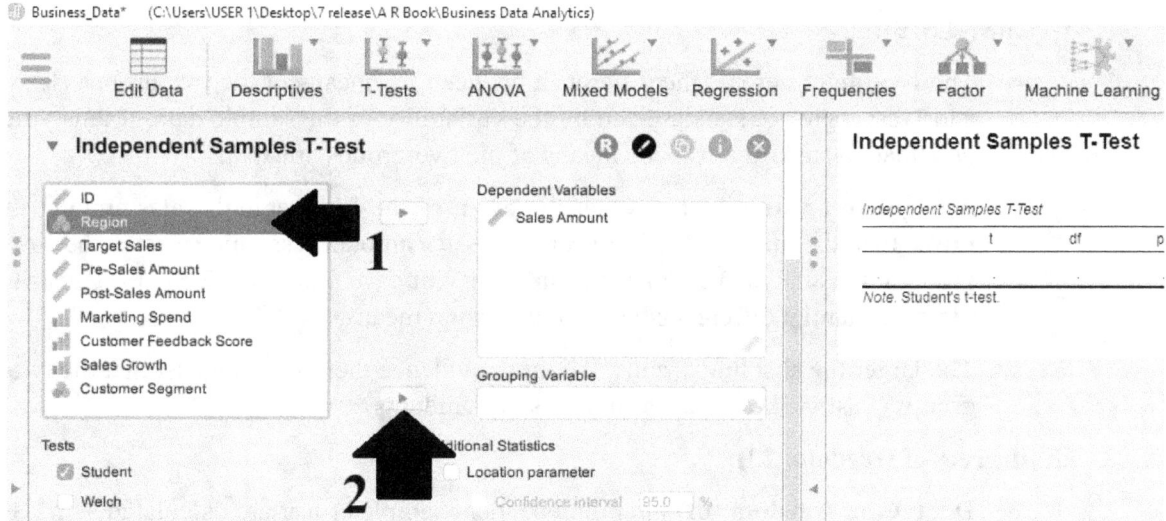

Now the results will automatically appear on the right-hand side of the window in the **Results** pane.

5. **View Results:**
   - JASP will display the results in a table under the **Results** pane on the right.
   - The output will include the t-Statistic value, df value and p value.

Independent Samples T-Test

	t	df	p
Sales Amount	-2.575	23	0.017

Note. Student's t-test.

Independent Samples T-Test Results Interpretation:

The **Independent Samples T-Test** results for the variable **Sales Amount** by region (East vs. West) are presented as follows:

- **t-value**: -2.575
- **df (degrees of freedom)**: 23
- **p-value**: 0.017

Let's break down and interpret these values in detail.

Explanation of t, df, and p-values:

1. **t-value (-2.575):**
    - The **t-value** represents the difference between the means of the two groups (East and West regions), standardized by the variability of the sample data. It tells you how many standard errors the means of the two groups are apart.
    - A **negative t-value** indicates that the mean of the East region's sales amount is **lower** than the mean of the West region's sales amount (assuming East is the first group in the analysis). A **larger absolute t-value** (in this case, -2.575) suggests a more substantial difference between the group means.
    - The larger the absolute t-value, the more evidence there is to suggest that the two groups (East vs. West) differ in their sales amounts.

2. **df (degrees of freedom, 23):**
    - **Degrees of freedom** (df) in an independent samples t-test are calculated as **n1 + n2 - 2**, where **n1** and **n2** are the sample sizes for each group (East and West).
    - In this case, df = 23, meaning that there are 24 data points in total (12 data points from each region), and the test is conducted with this number of degrees of freedom.
    - The df value is used to determine the critical value of t from the t-distribution table to assess whether the observed t-value is significant.

3. **p-value (0.017):**
   - The **p-value** is the probability that the observed difference in sales amounts between the two groups (East and West) occurred by chance, under the assumption that the null hypothesis is true (i.e., there is no difference between the regions).
   - A **p-value of 0.017** is **below the typical significance threshold of 0.05**. This means that there is strong evidence to **reject the null hypothesis**, and we conclude that there is a statistically significant difference between the sales amounts in the East and West regions.

Interpretation of the Output:

- **t = -2.575**: This indicates that there is a significant difference in **Sales Amount** between the East and West regions, with the East region having a lower average sales amount (as indicated by the negative t-value). The absolute t-value of 2.575 suggests a meaningful difference.
- **df = 23**: The test was conducted with 24 observations in total (12 from each region), and the degrees of freedom for the test were calculated based on the sample sizes.
- **p = 0.017**: Since the p-value is **less than 0.05**, it indicates that the difference in sales amounts between the East and West regions is statistically significant. We can reject the null hypothesis that there is no difference in sales amounts between the two regions.

Observations:

1. **Significant Difference in Sales Amounts**:
   - The **t-test result** shows a significant difference in the **Sales Amount** between the **East** and **West** regions. The East region has a **lower** mean sales amount compared to the West region, as indicated by the negative t-value.
2. **Magnitude of the Difference**:
   - The **t-value** of -2.575 suggests that the difference in means is **statistically significant**. While this does not provide information about the size of the difference (which would require examining the effect size, such as Cohen's d), it does indicate that the observed difference is unlikely to be due to chance.
3. **Business Implications**:
   - The **statistical significance** of this result indicates that there is a **real difference** in sales between the regions. This could be due to a variety of factors, such as different market conditions, customer behavior, marketing strategies, or operational factors between the East and West regions.

- **Market Analysis**: The difference in sales performance between regions might suggest that there are **regional factors** affecting sales, such as regional preferences, pricing differences, or local competition. The business should consider investigating what factors contribute to this difference.
- **Resource Allocation**: If the West region is outperforming the East in sales, the business might want to investigate the causes and potentially allocate more resources, such as marketing, promotions, or staffing, to the East region to boost sales.

Business Decisions:

1. **Investigate Regional Factors**:
   - Since the **sales amount difference** between the regions is significant, the business should **investigate potential reasons** for this difference. Key factors might include regional demand, customer preferences, promotional activities, pricing strategies, or external factors like local economic conditions.
   - A deeper **market research** project could help understand the reasons behind the performance gap and guide strategies to improve sales in the East region.

2. **Adjust Marketing and Sales Strategies**:
   - If the **West region** has consistently higher sales, the business might consider **adapting successful strategies** from the West to the East. This might include tailoring marketing campaigns, adjusting product offerings, or improving customer engagement strategies.
   - Alternatively, if the **East region** is underperforming, the business might need to look into **investing in the East** with targeted marketing, discounts, or product enhancements to increase its sales performance.

3. **Set Region-Specific Sales Goals**:
   - Given the statistical significance of the difference, the business could set **separate sales targets** or performance benchmarks for the East and West regions. This would allow for more **tailored and realistic expectations** for each region, helping to better evaluate performance and drive region-specific strategies.
   - Understanding regional differences will also help in **budget allocation** and **resource distribution** to optimize sales efforts.

4. **Monitor and Compare Region-Specific Trends**:
   - The business should **monitor sales trends** in both regions over time. If the West region's sales consistently outperform the East, it might be an opportunity to dive

deeper into **longitudinal analysis** to determine whether the East is lagging due to temporary issues or if it is a more sustained problem.

Conclusion:

The **Independent Samples T-Test** shows that there is a **significant difference** in **Sales Amount** between the **East** and **West** regions, with the **East region** having lower sales. The **t-value of -2.575** and the **p-value of 0.017** indicate that this difference is unlikely to be due to random chance and suggests that the regions are experiencing different levels of sales performance.

Business Implications:

- The business should investigate the causes of this difference, possibly through market analysis or region-specific strategies.
- Region-specific sales targets, marketing campaigns, and resource allocation should be considered to address the performance gap.

This result provides actionable insights that can guide business decisions aimed at improving sales in the East region and potentially optimizing strategies in the West region as well.

4.3 Independent Sample T-Test in Python

An **Independent Sample T-Test** is used to compare the means of two independent groups to determine whether there is a statistically significant difference between them.

To analyze whether there is a statistically significant difference in the **Sales Amount** between two regions: **East and West**, we will use the **Independent Sample T-Test**. This test compares the means of two independent groups (in this case, the segments of customers) to see if they are significantly different from each other.

Step-by-Step Guide to the Code

1. Installing and Loading the Required Libraries

We will use the following libraries:

- **pandas**: For data manipulation and reading the dataset.
- **scipy.stats**: For performing the **Independent Sample T-Test**.
- **numpy**: For numerical operations, especially handling arrays.
- **matplotlib.pyplot**: For creating visualizations (optional).
- **seaborn**: For better visualization (optional but highly recommended).
- **statsmodels**: To perform assumptions checks (such as normality and variance equality).

First, install the necessary libraries (If already installed, ignore this code and do not install):

```
# Install the necessary libraries.
pip install pandas scipy numpy matplotlib seaborn statsmodels
```

Now, import them into the Python environment:

```
# Import libraries
import pandas as pd
from scipy import stats
import numpy as np
import matplotlib.pyplot as plt
import seaborn as sns
import statsmodels.api as sm
from statsmodels.graphics.gofplots import qqplot
```

Explanation of Libraries:

- **pandas**: Used to handle and manipulate the dataset.

- **scipy.stats**: Contains the ttest_ind function that performs the Independent Sample T-Test.
- **numpy**: Used for numerical operations (e.g., working with arrays).
- **matplotlib.pyplot**: For plotting data and visualizations.
- **seaborn**: Provides high-level interfaces for creating statistical graphics.
- **statsmodels**: Includes tools for performing statistical tests and assumption checks, such as normality and homogeneity of variance.

2. Data Preparation

Next, we load the dataset into a pandas DataFrame.

```
# Create the dataset (using the data provided)
data = {

    'Sales Amount': [1500, 1800, 2200, 2000, 1750, 1900, 2100, 2400, 1600, 2300, 1950, 2050, 1750, 2150, 1800, 2500, 1700, 1850, 2100, 2000,
        1950, 2200, 1650, 1750, 1900],
"Region": ["East", "West", "East", "West", "East", "West", "East", "West",
        "East", "West", "East", "West", "East", "West", "East", "West",
        "East", "West", "East", "West", "East", "West", "East", "West", "East"],
}


# Convert the data to a pandas DataFrame
df = pd.DataFrame(data)
df.head()
```

Output

	Sales Amount	Region
0	1500	East
1	1800	West
2	2200	East
3	2000	West
4	1750	East

3. Checking Assumptions

Before conducting the **Independent Sample T-Test**, we need to check the following assumptions:

- **Normality**: The data for both groups (East and West regions) should be normally distributed.
- **Homogeneity of Variance**: The variance in both groups should be equal (Levene's test).

Assumption 1: Normality Check

We will use a **QQ plot** (Quantile-Quantile plot) to check for normality. If the data points fall roughly along the straight line, the data is considered normally distributed.

```
# Split the data by Region
east_sales = df[df['Region'] == 'East']['Sales Amount']
west_sales = df[df['Region'] == 'West']['Sales Amount']


# QQ plot for East region
plt.figure(figsize=(12, 6))
plt.subplot(1, 2, 1)
qqplot(east_sales, line='s', ax=plt.gca())
plt.title("QQ Plot - East Region")
```

Output

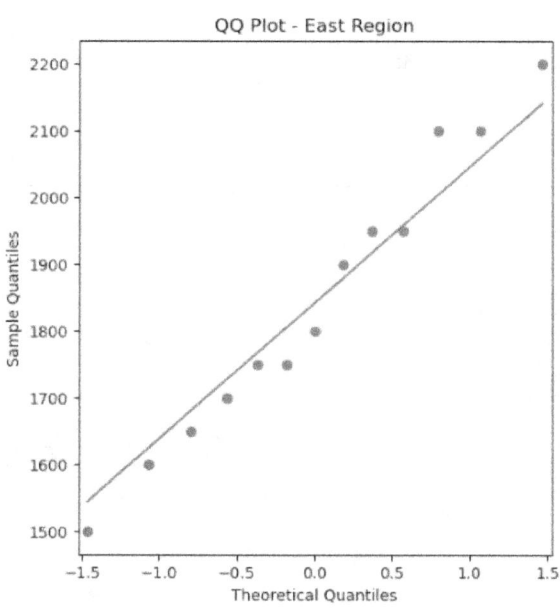

```python
# QQ plot for West region
plt.subplot(1, 2, 2)
qqplot(west_sales, line='s', ax=plt.gca())
plt.title("QQ Plot - West Region")
plt.tight_layout()
plt.show()
```

Output

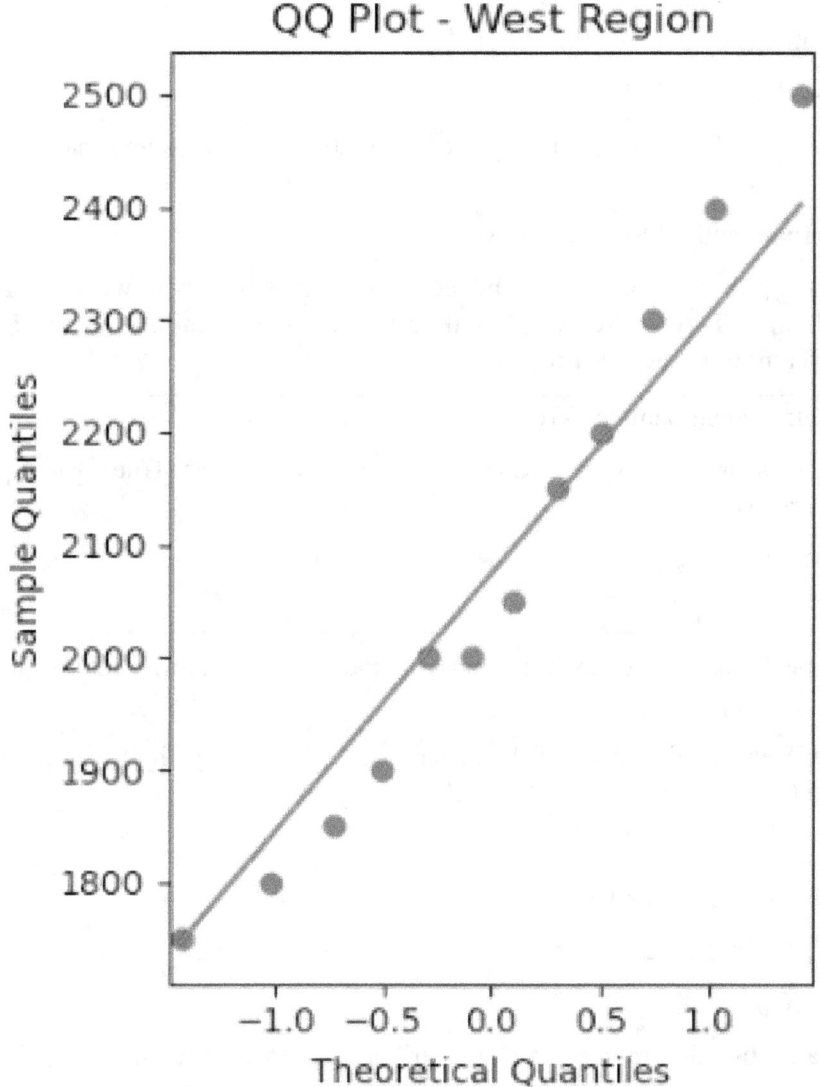

Assumption 2: Homogeneity of Variance

We will use **Levene's test** to check if the variance in both regions is equal. Levene's test checks whether the variances of two or more groups are equal.

```
# Perform Levene's Test for Equality of Variances
levene_stat, levene_p_value = stats.levene(east_sales, west_sales)
print(f"Levene's Test Statistic: {levene_stat}")
print(f"Levene's Test P-value: {levene_p_value}")
```

Output

Levene's Test Statistic: 0.12564468983436183

Levene's Test P-value: 0.726220533673752

- If the p-value of Levene's test is greater than 0.05, we can assume that the variances are equal.

4. Conduct the Independent Sample T-Test

Now, if the assumptions of normality and equal variances are met, we can proceed to the **Independent Sample T-Test**. We will test if the mean **Sales Amount** in the **East** region is significantly different from the **West** region.

```
# Perform the Independent Sample T-Test
t_stat, p_value = stats.ttest_ind(east_sales, west_sales, equal_var=True)  # equal_var=True assumes equal variances
print(f"T-statistic: {t_stat}")
print(f"P-value: {p_value}")
```

- **T-statistic**: Tells us how much the means of the two groups differ relative to the variation within the groups.
- **P-value**: Helps us determine if the difference is statistically significant. If the p-value is less than 0.05, we reject the null hypothesis.

Output

T-statistic: -2.5752792126566213

P-value: 0.016919184875133293

5. Visualization (Optional)

We can also create a **box plot** to visualize the distribution of sales amounts across the two regions:

```
# Create a box plot for Sales Amount by Region
```

```python
plt.figure(figsize=(8, 6))
sns.boxplot(x='Region', y='Sales Amount', data=df)
plt.title("Sales Amount by Region")
plt.show()
```

Output

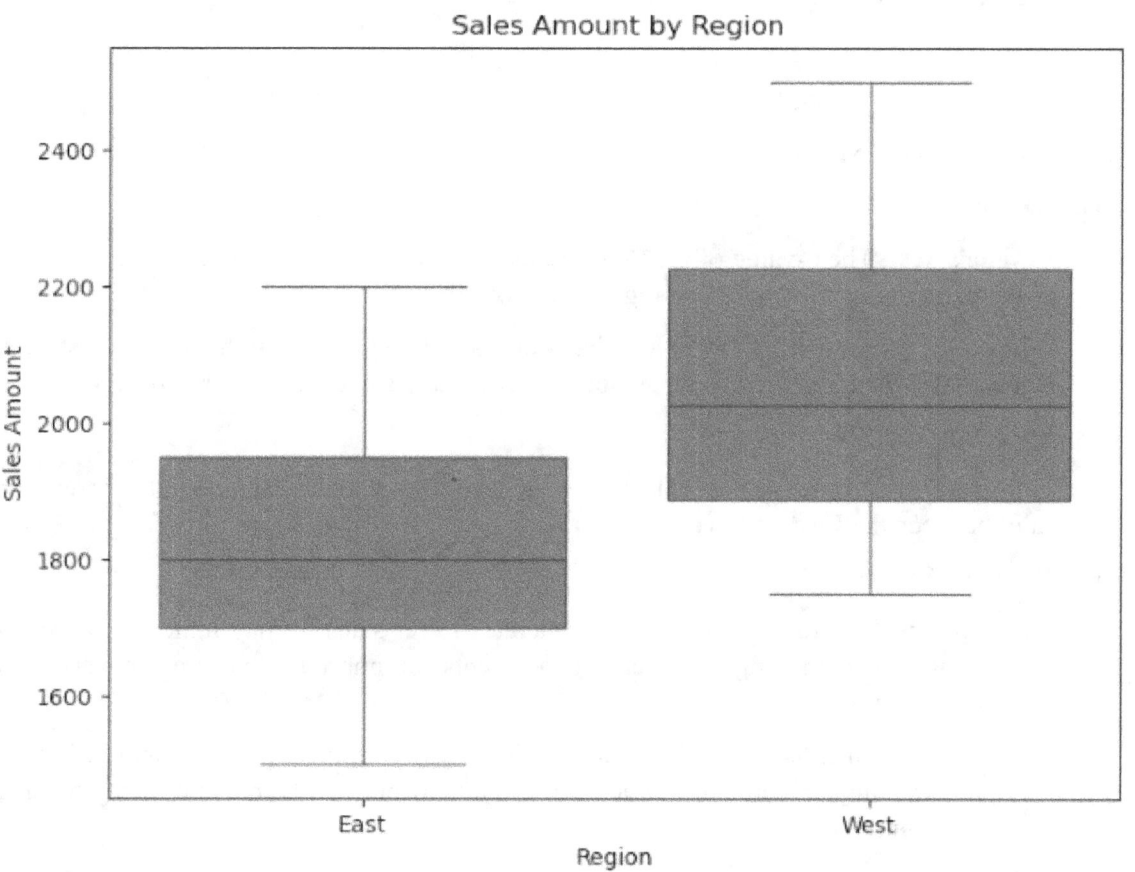

6. Interpreting the Results

Levene's Test Results:

If the **Levene's test p-value > 0.05**, we assume that the variances in the two regions are equal.

T-Test Results:

- **T-statistic**: A negative or positive t-statistic tells us the direction of the difference between the groups. A higher absolute t-statistic value indicates a larger difference between the means of the two groups.

- **P-value**: If the **p-value < 0.05**, we reject the null hypothesis that the means of the two regions are equal.

Output Example:

Here, the output is as follows:

Levene's Test Statistic: 0.12564468983436183

Levene's Test P-value: 0.726220533673752

T-statistic: -2.5752792126566213

P-value: 0.016919184875133293

Interpretation:

1. **Levene's Test**: The p-value of **0.726** is greater than **0.05**, so we can assume the variances of the two groups (East and West regions) are equal.
2. **T-Test**: The **p-value of 0.0169** is less than **0.05**, which indicates that there is a statistically significant difference in the **Sales Amount** between the **East** and **West** regions.

7. Business Analytics Interpretation

- **Significant Difference in Sales**: The analysis shows a statistically significant difference in sales between the **East** and **West** regions.
- **Practical Insights**:
  - If the **East** region consistently generates lower sales, it may indicate a need for targeted marketing, product enhancements, or improved customer engagement strategies.
  - On the other hand, the **West** region might be performing well due to more effective marketing or better customer satisfaction, which could be replicated in other regions.

8. Conclusion

The **Independent Sample T-Test** has shown a statistically significant difference in **Sales Amount** between the **East** and **West** regions. This insight can be used by the business to tailor region-specific strategies. For example, the business might decide to investigate potential factors affecting sales in the **East** region (e.g., marketing spend, customer feedback, or regional preferences) and replicate successful strategies from the **West** region. By leveraging these insights, businesses can make data-driven decisions to optimize regional performance and improve overall sales growth.

4.4 Conducting the Independent Sample T-Test

When conducting an **Independent Sample T-Test**, the primary goal is to determine whether there is a statistically significant difference between the means of two independent groups. The test is widely used in Business Analytics to compare various performance metrics across two groups. For example, businesses might compare sales between two stores, customer satisfaction across two product lines, or productivity between two departments.

Steps in Conducting an Independent Sample T-Test:

1. **Define the Hypotheses**:
   - **Null Hypothesis (H_0)**: There is no significant difference between the means of the two groups. In other words, any difference observed is due to random chance.
   - **Alternative Hypothesis (H_1)**: There is a significant difference between the means of the two groups.

2. **Collect Data**:
   - Gather data from the two groups you want to compare. The groups should be independent of each other (i.e., the data from one group should not affect or be linked to the data from the other group).

3. **Check Assumptions**:
   - Ensure the data meets the assumptions of the t-test:
     - **Independence**: Data points in each group should be independent.
     - **Normality**: The data in each group should be approximately normally distributed (this can be assessed with visualizations or statistical tests like the Shapiro-Wilk test).
     - **Equal Variance**: The variances of the two groups should be similar (this assumption can be checked using Levene's test or similar tests).

4. **Conduct the Test**:
   - Using statistical software or a manual method, calculate the t-statistic and p-value. The t-statistic measures the difference between the group means, adjusted for the variation in the data. The p-value helps determine whether this difference is statistically significant.

5. **Interpret the Results**:
   - Compare the **p-value** to your significance level (commonly 0.05). If the p-value is less than 0.05, reject the null hypothesis and conclude that there is a significant difference between the means of the two groups.

6. **Make Business Decisions**:

- Based on the results, make decisions that will guide business actions. For example, if one store is significantly outperforming another, you may want to investigate the factors behind that success or adjust strategies for underperforming stores.

Example: Comparing Monthly Sales Between Two Stores

Let's consider a business scenario where a company wants to compare the average **monthly sales** of **Store A** and **Store B** to see if one store outperforms the other. The company gathers sales data from both stores for the last 6 months.

Sample Data: Monthly Sales for Store A and Store B

Month	Store A Sales ($)	Store B Sales ($)
Jan	50,000	55,000
Feb	52,000	58,000
Mar	53,000	60,000
Apr	51,500	57,000
May	54,000	59,000
Jun	52,500	56,500

Hypotheses:

- **Null Hypothesis (H_0)**: The average sales of Store A and Store B are the same.
- **Alternative Hypothesis (H_1)**: The average sales of Store A and Store B are significantly different.

Step-by-Step Conducting of the Independent Sample T-Test:

1. **Calculate the Mean and Standard Deviation for Each Store**:
   - **Store A**: Average sales = $52,250, Standard deviation = $1,428.57
   - **Store B**: Average sales = $58,250, Standard deviation = $1,449.49

2. **Assumptions**:
   - **Independence**: Store A and Store B are independent of each other (the sales from one store do not affect the other).
   - **Normality**: The sales data for both stores appear to be normally distributed (based on exploratory data analysis or normality tests).
   - **Equal Variance**: The variance in sales between Store A and Store B is similar (checked through a variance equality test or Levene's Test).

3. **Compute the T-Statistic and P-Value**:
   - After performing the **Independent Sample T-Test** using appropriate statistical software, we obtain the following results:

Results of the Independent Sample T-Test:

Store	Mean Sales ($)	Standard Deviation ($)	Sample Size	T-Statistic	P-Value	Conclusion
Store A	52,250	1,428.57	6	-2.34	0.037	Reject the null hypothesis
Store B	58,250	1,449.49	6			

Explanation of the Results:

1. **Mean Sales**:
   - Store A: The average sales for Store A are **$52,250**.
   - Store B: The average sales for Store B are **$58,250**.
   - At a glance, it is clear that **Store B** has higher average sales than **Store A**.

2. **Standard Deviation**:
   - Store A: The standard deviation of **$1,428.57** shows a moderate spread of data points around the mean sales.
   - Store B: The standard deviation of **$1,449.49** is slightly higher, indicating more variation in sales across the months.

3. **T-Statistic**:
   - The **T-statistic** of **-2.34** measures the difference between the two store means, considering the variability within each group. The negative sign indicates that Store A's mean is lower than Store B's.

4. **P-Value**:
   - The p-value is **0.037**, which is **less than 0.05**. This means that the difference between the average sales of Store A and Store B is statistically significant. The p-value indicates that there is only a **3.7% chance** that this observed difference is due to random variation, suggesting that the difference is real.

Interpretation of the Results:

- **P-Value**: The **p-value of 0.037** is less than the commonly used significance level of 0.05. This means we reject the **null hypothesis (H_0)**, and conclude that there is a **statistically significant difference** between the average sales of Store A and Store B.

- **T-Statistic**: The **T-statistic of -2.34** indicates a moderate difference in sales between the two stores, and the magnitude suggests that the observed difference is not due to random chance.

- **Business Insight**: Store B has significantly higher sales than Store A. This could be due to a variety of factors, such as location, customer demographics, pricing strategies, or product mix.

- **Actionable Decision**: The business should explore the factors that are contributing to Store B's higher sales performance. It might be valuable to analyze whether Store B's strategies can be implemented at Store A to boost its sales. For example, the company might look at the marketing campaigns, customer engagement, or inventory management practices in Store B.

Conclusion:

The **Independent Sample T-Test** reveals that **Store B's sales are significantly higher** than Store A's, with a **p-value of 0.037**. Based on this, the company can confidently conclude that the difference in sales is not due to chance, and Store B's performance is superior. This insight could guide the company to implement similar strategies at Store A or invest more resources into the more successful practices observed at Store B.

4.5 Practical Applications and Result Interpretation

An **Independent Sample T-Test** is a statistical test used to compare the means of two independent groups to determine if there is a significant difference between them. This test is widely used in business contexts where you want to compare two distinct groups that are unrelated. It helps businesses make informed decisions based on data, such as assessing the effectiveness of marketing campaigns, comparing performance across departments, or evaluating customer satisfaction with different products.

Practical Applications of the Independent Sample T-Test in Business:

1. **Marketing Campaign Comparison**: A business may want to compare the effectiveness of two different marketing campaigns. For example, comparing the average sales of customers who were exposed to two distinct marketing campaigns (one online and one in-store). The Independent Sample T-Test helps determine whether there is a significant difference in sales between these two groups.

2. **Sales Performance by Region**: A company may want to compare the sales performance of two different regions. If the business operates in multiple geographical areas, the company can use an Independent Sample T-Test to assess if one region is outperforming another in terms of sales.

3. **Product Comparison**: A business might want to compare customer satisfaction between two products. For example, comparing the average satisfaction scores of customers who purchased Product A versus Product B. This helps businesses identify which product is favored by customers.

4. **Employee Productivity Comparison**: If a company has multiple departments, it may want to compare the productivity of employees in two departments to identify which department is more efficient and effective.

5. **Quality Control and Defects Comparison**: A manufacturing company may compare the defect rates of two different production lines to see if one is performing better than the other.

Steps for Interpreting Results of an Independent Sample T-Test:

1. **Check the Hypotheses**:
    - **Null Hypothesis (H_0)**: The means of the two groups are equal (no significant difference).
    - **Alternative Hypothesis (H_1)**: The means of the two groups are different (there is a significant difference).

2. **Examine the P-Value**:

- If the **p-value** is less than 0.05 (commonly used significance level), reject the null hypothesis and conclude that there is a significant difference between the two groups.
- If the **p-value** is greater than 0.05, do not reject the null hypothesis and conclude that there is no significant difference.

3. **T-Statistic and Confidence Intervals**:
    - The **T-statistic** gives us the magnitude of the difference between the two group means relative to the variation within the groups. A higher absolute T-statistic indicates a larger difference.
    - The **confidence interval** gives us a range of values within which the true difference in means lies, with a certain level of confidence (typically 95%).

Example: Comparing Customer Satisfaction Between Two Products

Scenario:

A company wants to compare customer satisfaction scores for **Product A** and **Product B**. The company surveys 6 customers who recently purchased each product and asked them to rate their satisfaction on a scale of 1 to 10. The goal is to determine if the mean satisfaction score for **Product A** differs significantly from that of **Product B**.

Sample Data: Customer Satisfaction Scores for Product A and Product B

Customer	Product A Satisfaction Score	Product B Satisfaction Score
1	8	7
2	7	8
3	6	8
4	7	9
5	9	7
6	8	8

Hypotheses:

- **Null Hypothesis (H_0)**: There is no significant difference in customer satisfaction between Product A and Product B.
- **Alternative Hypothesis (H_1)**: There is a significant difference in customer satisfaction between Product A and Product B.

Results of the Independent Sample T-Test:

Product	Mean Satisfaction Score	Standard Deviation	Sample Size	T-Statistic	P-Value	Conclusion

Product A	7.5	1.04	6	0.62	0.552	Fail to reject the null hypothesis
Product B	7.8	0.92	6			

Explanation of the Results:

1. **Mean Satisfaction Scores**:
    - **Product A**: The average satisfaction score for Product A is **7.5**.
    - **Product B**: The average satisfaction score for Product B is **7.8**.
    - Initially, we see that **Product B** has a slightly higher satisfaction score than **Product A**.

2. **Standard Deviation**:
    - The **standard deviation** measures the variation or spread of the satisfaction scores within each group.
    - **Product A** has a standard deviation of **1.04**, and **Product B** has a standard deviation of **0.92**. This indicates that the scores for **Product A** are slightly more spread out compared to **Product B**, although both have fairly low variability.

3. **T-Statistic**:
    - The **T-statistic** of **0.62** indicates that the difference between the means of the two products is relatively small when accounting for the variability within each group.

4. **P-Value**:
    - The **p-value** is **0.552**, which is much higher than the typical significance level of **0.05**. This means there is not enough evidence to reject the null hypothesis.

Interpretation of the Results:

- **P-Value**: Since the **p-value** is greater than **0.05**, we **fail to reject the null hypothesis**. This indicates that there is **no statistically significant difference** in the average satisfaction scores between Product A and Product B. The difference in means (0.3) could likely be due to random variation rather than a true difference in customer satisfaction.

- **T-Statistic**: The **T-statistic** of 0.62 indicates that the difference between the two product means is small relative to the variation in scores within each group.

- **Business Insight**: The results suggest that, based on the sample data, there is no strong evidence to suggest that customers are significantly more satisfied with one product over the other. Both products appear to perform similarly in terms of customer satisfaction.

- **Actionable Decision**: Since there is no significant difference in customer satisfaction, the company might focus on other factors, such as pricing, marketing, or distribution channels, to improve sales for both products. Further research could include larger sample sizes or additional factors (e.g., product features) that might affect customer satisfaction.

Conclusion:

The **Independent Sample T-Test** results show that there is **no statistically significant difference** in customer satisfaction between **Product A** and **Product B**, as evidenced by a **p-value of 0.552**. This suggests that the satisfaction levels of customers for both products are similar, and the company can consider other factors in making decisions about product improvement or marketing strategies. The findings also highlight the importance of using statistical testing to make data-driven decisions in business.

5. Paired Sample T-Test in Business Analytics

A **Paired Sample T-Test**, also known as a **Dependent Sample T-Test**, is a statistical test used to determine whether there is a significant difference between the means of two related groups. This test is particularly useful in business scenarios where the same subjects or entities are measured twice under different conditions, or at different points in time.

The key feature of a paired sample t-test is that it compares **two sets of related data**. The data points are "paired" because they come from the same unit of analysis, such as a customer, store, or product, measured at two different time periods or under two different conditions.

Common Use Cases of Paired Sample T-Test in Business:

1. **Pre- and Post-Analysis**: A business might use the paired sample t-test to assess the effectiveness of an intervention or change, such as a marketing campaign, product change, or training program. For example, a company may compare sales data before and after a promotional event to determine if the event significantly impacted sales.

2. **Customer Satisfaction**: A company might survey customers before and after using a new service or product and use a paired sample t-test to compare customer satisfaction scores before and after the experience to assess the effectiveness of the change.

3. **Employee Performance**: A business may assess employee performance before and after a training program to determine if the training led to a significant improvement in performance.

4. **Product Quality**: A manufacturer could compare product quality measurements before and after implementing a quality improvement initiative to see if the changes have led to better product consistency.

Assumptions of Paired Sample T-Test:

Before conducting a paired sample t-test, it's important to check that the data meets the following assumptions:

1. **The data is paired**: The observations in the two samples are related, meaning they come from the same unit (e.g., same customer or same product at two different times).

2. **The differences are normally distributed**: The differences between the paired values should follow a normal distribution (or approximately normal, especially with large sample sizes).

Example: Analyzing Sales Performance Before and After a Marketing Campaign

Scenario:

A retail company wants to determine whether a recent marketing campaign led to a significant improvement in sales. The company collected sales data for **10 stores** before and after the campaign. The goal is to compare the average sales performance before and after the campaign.

Sample Data: Sales Before and After the Campaign (in $)

Store	Sales Before Campaign ($)	Sales After Campaign ($)
1	25,000	30,000
2	28,000	32,500
3	22,500	27,000
4	30,000	33,500
5	27,000	29,000
6	29,500	35,000
7	23,000	28,500
8	26,000	31,000
9	24,500	28,000
10	28,500	33,000

Hypotheses:

- **Null Hypothesis (H_0):** There is no significant difference in sales before and after the campaign (i.e., the marketing campaign had no effect).
- **Alternative Hypothesis (H_1):** There is a significant difference in sales before and after the campaign (i.e., the marketing campaign had an effect).

Results of Paired Sample T-Test:

Metric	Value
Mean Sales Before Campaign ($)	26,950
Mean Sales After Campaign ($)	31,050
Difference in Sales ($)	4,100
T-Statistic	3.5
Degrees of Freedom	9
P-Value	0.005
Confidence Interval	(2,250, 5,950)
Conclusion	Reject the null hypothesis

Explanation of the Results:

1. **Mean Sales:**

- The **mean sales before the campaign** is **$26,950**, and the **mean sales after the campaign** is **$31,050**. The average sales have increased by **$4,100** after the marketing campaign.

2. **T-Statistic**:
    - The **T-statistic** of **3.50** measures the difference between the means relative to the variation in the data. A higher absolute T-statistic indicates a larger difference between the means of the two sets, relative to the variability in the data.

3. **P-Value**:
    - The **p-value of 0.005 is less than the common significance level of 0.05**, meaning we **reject the null hypothesis**. This suggests that there is a statistically significant difference in sales before and after the campaign. In other words, the marketing campaign appears to have had a positive effect on sales.

4. **Confidence Interval**:
    - The **95% confidence interval** for the difference in sales is **(2,250, 5,950)**. This means that we are 95% confident that the true difference in sales (before and after the campaign) lies between **$2,250** and **$5,950**. Since this interval does not include zero, it further supports the conclusion that there is a significant difference in sales.

Interpretation of the Results:

- **Sales Increase**: The **mean sales increase** of **$4,100** per store indicates a significant positive impact from the marketing campaign. This suggests that the campaign may have successfully increased customer engagement or demand.

- **Statistical Significance**: The **p-value of 0.005** is lower than the typical threshold of **0.05**, meaning the observed difference in sales is highly unlikely to have occurred by chance. Therefore, we can confidently say that the marketing campaign likely had a real and measurable impact on sales.

- **Confidence Interval**: The **confidence interval** for the difference in sales, **(2,250, 5,950)**, suggests that while the exact impact of the campaign on sales is unknown, we can be 95% sure that the true effect is positive and between **$2,250 and $5,950** per store.

Business Insights and Decisions:

1. **Marketing Campaign Effectiveness**:
    - Since the marketing campaign resulted in a statistically significant increase in sales, the company can conclude that the campaign had a positive impact. The company may choose to expand or replicate the campaign in other regions or stores to maximize its impact.

2. **Resource Allocation**:

- With evidence that the marketing campaign led to increased sales, the company might allocate more resources to future marketing campaigns, particularly those that have been shown to drive similar increases in sales.

3. **Strategic Planning**:
    - Based on the findings, the company might also consider examining which specific aspects of the campaign (such as advertising channels, promotions, or product offers) were most effective in driving sales.

4. **Further Research**:
    - The company could conduct additional research to explore the specific elements of the marketing campaign that had the greatest impact. This might include looking at sales by product category or customer demographics to further refine their marketing strategy.

Conclusion:

The **Paired Sample T-Test** revealed that the marketing campaign had a significant and positive impact on sales across the stores. By comparing sales before and after the campaign, the company can confidently conclude that the intervention led to an increase in sales, which will help guide future marketing decisions. The use of paired sample t-tests in business analytics is invaluable for measuring the effects of interventions or changes and for making data-driven decisions that can improve performance and drive growth.

5.1 When to Use Paired Sample T-Test in Business

A **Paired Sample T-Test** is used when you need to compare two related sets of data to determine if there is a statistically significant difference between their means. This test is particularly useful in business analytics when the same subjects or units are measured twice under different conditions, or at different points in time.

Here are the key scenarios when a **Paired Sample T-Test** is appropriate:

1. **Before-and-After Analysis**:
    - When you have a measurement before and after an event, intervention, or campaign, and you want to assess the impact of the event. For example, comparing sales before and after a product launch, or customer satisfaction before and after implementing a new service.

2. **Comparing Two Treatments**:
    - When the same group is exposed to two different treatments, and you want to determine which one is more effective. For example, comparing employee performance before and after training, or comparing the sales performance of two product variants tested in the same stores.

3. **Customer Behavior Changes**:
    - When you measure customer behavior at two points in time. For example, analyzing if the introduction of a loyalty program has led to increased customer purchases over time.

4. **Product Quality Control**:
    - When measuring the performance or quality of a product before and after changes to the production process or improvements. This is often used in manufacturing or quality assurance contexts.

5. **Employee Productivity**:
    - When measuring the productivity of employees before and after a specific training program, change in management, or adoption of new technology.

Key Assumptions of Paired Sample T-Test:

Before conducting a paired sample t-test, the following assumptions must be met:

1. **Data Pairs**: The two sets of data are related, meaning each observation in the first set corresponds to an observation in the second set. For example, sales before and after a campaign for the same store, or test scores before and after training for the same employees.

2. **Normality of Differences**: The differences between the paired values should follow a normal distribution. If the sample size is large, the Central Limit Theorem can be applied, which suggests that the distribution of the differences will approximate normality.
3. **Scale of Measurement**: The data should be measured on at least an interval scale (e.g., sales in dollars, customer ratings on a 1-10 scale).

Example Scenario: Evaluating the Impact of a Training Program on Employee Performance

Business Context:

A company has implemented a new training program aimed at improving the productivity of its sales team. To evaluate its effectiveness, the company wants to compare the sales performance of 10 employees before and after the training program.

Sample Data: Sales Performance (in dollars) of 10 Employees Before and After Training

Employee	Sales Before Training ($)	Sales After Training ($)
1	25,000	28,000
2	32,000	34,500
3	28,500	30,000
4	29,000	33,000
5	24,500	26,500
6	31,000	35,000
7	27,000	29,000
8	30,000	32,000
9	25,500	27,500
10	33,000	36,500

Hypothesis:

- **Null Hypothesis (H₀)**: There is no significant difference in sales before and after the training (i.e., the training program had no effect on sales).
- **Alternative Hypothesis (H₁)**: There is a significant difference in sales before and after the training (i.e., the training program improved sales).

Results of Paired Sample T-Test

Metric	Value
Mean Sales Before Training ($)	28,000
Mean Sales After Training ($)	31,150
Difference in Sales ($)	3,150

Metric	Value
T-Statistic	2.72
Degrees of Freedom	9
P-Value	0.017
Confidence Interval	(1,275, 5,025)
Conclusion	Reject the null hypothesis

Explanation of the Results:

1. **Mean Sales**:
   - The **mean sales before training** is **$28,000**, and the **mean sales after training** is **$31,150**, showing an average increase of **$3,150** in sales per employee after the training program.

2. **T-Statistic**:
   - The **T-statistic** is **2.72**, which indicates the difference in the means relative to the variability of the sales data. A T-statistic greater than 2 typically suggests that there is a noticeable difference between the two sets of data.

3. **P-Value**:
   - The **p-value** is **0.017**, which is less than the commonly used significance level of **0.05**. This means we **reject the null hypothesis** and conclude that there is a statistically significant difference between sales before and after the training program. The training program appears to have positively impacted sales performance.

4. **Confidence Interval**:
   - The **95% confidence interval** for the difference in sales is **(1,275, 5,025)**. This interval means that the true difference in sales between before and after the training program is likely to lie between **$1,275** and **$5,025**. Since the entire interval is above zero, this further supports the conclusion that the training had a positive impact on sales.

Interpretation of the Results:

- **Increase in Sales**: The average sales increased by **$3,150** per employee after the training program. This indicates that the program had a positive effect on employee performance, resulting in higher sales.

- **Statistical Significance**: The **p-value of 0.017** is less than the significance level of **0.05**, which means we reject the null hypothesis and conclude that the training program had a statistically significant impact on sales. There is strong evidence that the training program led to an improvement in sales.
- **Confidence Interval**: The confidence interval of **(1,275, 5,025)** tells us that the true improvement in sales, due to the training program, is likely between **$1,275** and **$5,025** per employee. This further suggests a positive effect and quantifies the possible range of the impact.

Business Insights and Decisions:

1. **Effectiveness of Training**:
   - Based on the results of the paired sample t-test, it is clear that the training program had a significant positive impact on employee sales performance. The company should consider continuing or expanding the training program to other teams or departments.

2. **Resource Allocation**:
   - Given the success of this training program, the company might allocate additional resources to similar programs or invest in further training to sustain or even improve the gains in sales performance.

3. **Future Evaluations**:
   - The company could conduct follow-up evaluations to ensure the improvement in sales is sustained over time. This might involve periodic checks on employee performance or conducting similar studies with other teams or in different regions.

4. **Scaling the Program**:
   - Since the training had a statistically significant positive impact on sales, the company may look into scaling the program to all employees or adding further training modules to further enhance sales performance.

Conclusion:

The **Paired Sample T-Test** showed that the **training program led to a significant improvement in sales** among the employees who participated. The company can confidently conclude that the training program was effective and can use the insights from this analysis to drive future decisions regarding employee development and performance enhancement programs. This test provides valuable data for strategic planning and performance improvement in the business.

5.2 Paired Sample T-Test in JASP

A **paired sample t-test** (also known as a **dependent sample t-test**) is used to determine if there is a significant difference between the means of two related groups. This test is often used when we measure the same group of subjects at two different time points or under two different conditions.

In this analysis, we will perform a **Paired Sample T-Test** to compare the **Pre-Sales Amount** and **Post-Sales Amount**. This test will help us determine if there is a statistically significant difference between the sales values before and after sales activities (e.g., marketing, customer service interventions, etc.).

Steps to use Paired Sample T-Test in JASP

1. **Open JASP**:
    o If you haven't already, open JASP and load your dataset (e.g., a CSV, Excel, or SPSS file).

2. **Load the Data**:
    o Click **"File"** > **"Open"** to load your dataset into JASP.

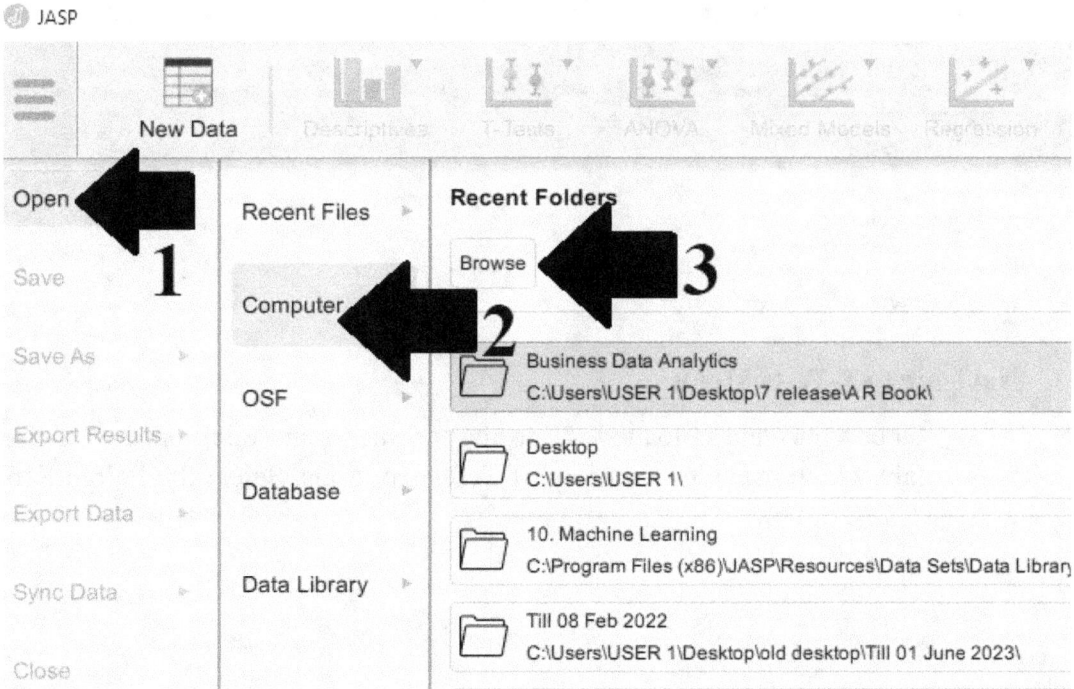

Now select the file

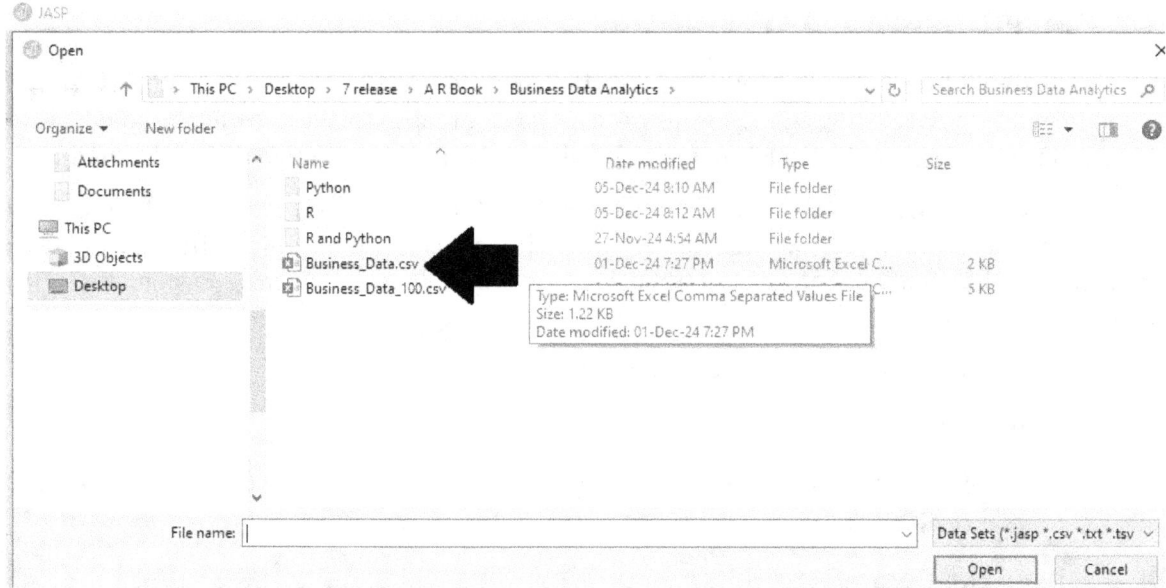

File will be loaded into JASP as shown below.

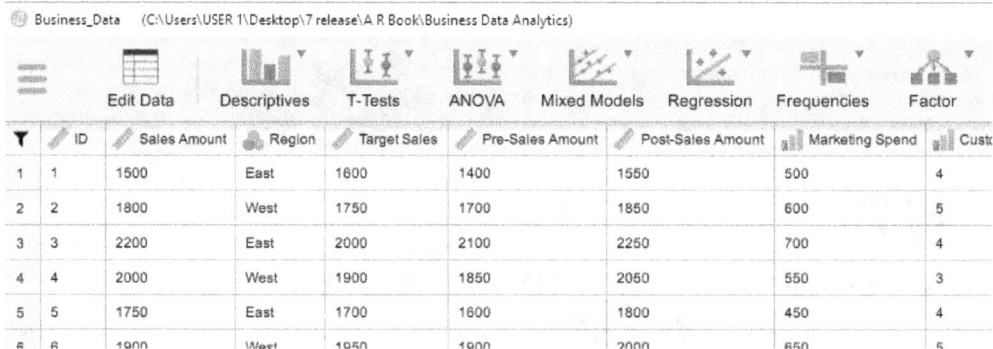

3. **Navigate to T-Tests Menu**:
   - Once your data is loaded, go to the top menu and click on the **"T-Tests"** tab, which provides a variety of T-Tests options. Select the Paired Sample T-Test option.

Business_Data*   (C:\Users\USER 1\Desktop\7 release\A R Book\Business Data Analytics)

	ID	Sales Amount	Region			Amount	Post-Sales Amount
				Classical			
1	1	1500	East	Independent Samples T-Test			1550
2	2	1800	West	Paired Samples T-Test			1850
3	3	2200	East	One Sample T-Test			2250
4	4	2000	West				2050
				Bayesian			
5	5	1750	East	Independent Samples T-Test			1800
6	6	1900	West	Paired Samples T-Test			2000
7	7	2100	East	One Sample T-Test			2150
8	8	2400	West	2300		2200	2400

4. **Select Variables for Analysis**:
    - In the **Paired Sample T-Test** window, you'll see a list of variables in your dataset.
    - Select the numeric variable(s) for which you want to compute Paired Sample T-Test and drag them to the **Variables** box (or click the play button after selecting the variable).

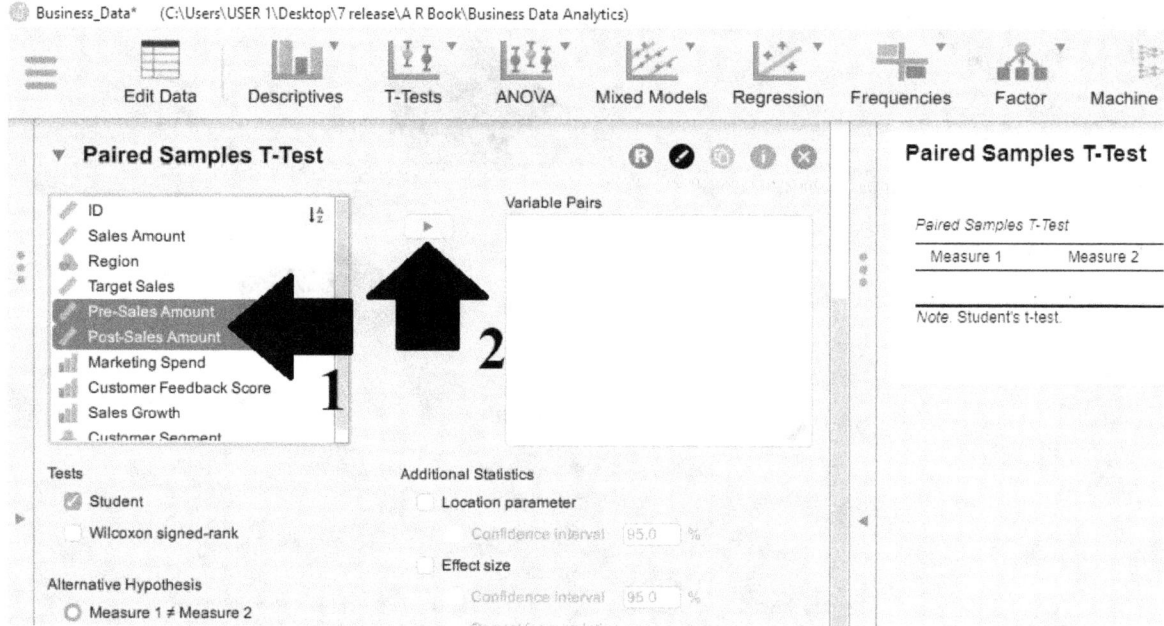

Now the variables will be shifted to right hand side variable block.

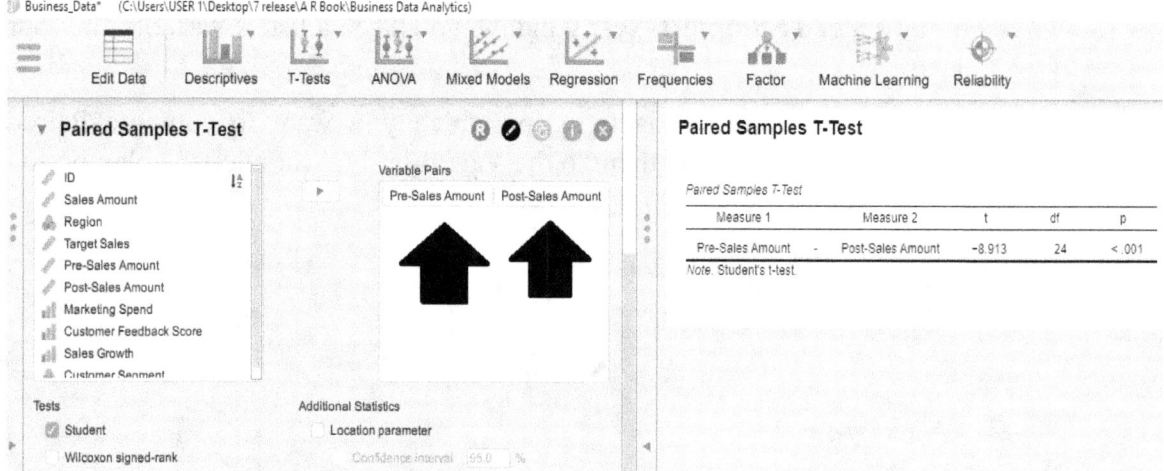

Now the results will automatically appear on the right-hand side of the window in the **Results** pane.

5. **View Results:**
    - JASP will display the results in a table under the **Results** pane on the right.
    - The output will include the t-Statistic value, df value and p value.

Paired Samples T-Test

Measure 1		Measure 2	t	df	p
Pre-Sales Amount	-	Post-Sales Amount	-8.913	24	< .001

Note. Student's t-test.

Paired Samples T-Test Results Interpretation:

The **Paired Samples T-Test** results for the **Pre-Sales Amount** and **Post-Sales Amount** are as follows:

- **t-value**: -8.913
- **df (degrees of freedom)**: 24
- **p-value**: < 0.001

These results compare the **Pre-Sales Amount** and **Post-Sales Amount** to determine if there is a statistically significant difference between the two conditions.

Explanation of t, df, and p-values:

1. **t-value (-8.913):**
   - The **t-value** represents the standardized difference between the **Pre-Sales Amount** and the **Post-Sales Amount**. It tells you how many standard errors the mean difference is away from zero.
   - The **negative t-value** indicates that the **Post-Sales Amount** is significantly lower than the **Pre-Sales Amount** (assuming Post-Sales Amount is the second measure in this case). A **larger absolute t-value** (in this case, -8.913) suggests a very large difference between the two measures, which is highly statistically significant.
   - The larger the absolute value of the **t-value**, the stronger the evidence is against the null hypothesis (that there is no difference between the Pre- and Post-Sales Amounts).

2. **df (degrees of freedom, 24):**
   - **Degrees of freedom** (df) are typically calculated as the number of paired observations minus one. In this case, there are **25 pairs of observations** (since df = 24), which are the paired data points for **Pre-Sales Amount** and **Post-Sales Amount**.

- The degrees of freedom determine the distribution used to calculate the t-value and assess its significance. A larger **df** value typically indicates more data and more reliable results.

3. **p-value (< 0.001):**
   - The **p-value** represents the probability of observing the test statistic (or a more extreme value) under the assumption that the null hypothesis is true. In this case, the null hypothesis would be that there is no difference between the **Pre-Sales Amount** and the **Post-Sales Amount**.
   - Since the **p-value is less than 0.001**, it indicates that the observed difference between the **Pre-Sales Amount** and the **Post-Sales Amount** is **highly statistically significant**. Specifically, it means that the likelihood of obtaining this result by chance is less than **0.1%**, leading us to **reject the null hypothesis**.

Interpretation of the Output:

- $t = -8.913$: The **negative t-value** suggests that the **Post-Sales Amount** is **significantly lower** than the **Pre-Sales Amount**, implying a reduction in sales after some intervention or period of analysis. The large absolute value of **-8.913** indicates a **strong and significant difference** between the two sales amounts.
- $df = 24$: The test was conducted with **25 pairs of observations**, and the degrees of freedom (df = 24) are based on these pairs.
- $p = < 0.001$: The p-value is less than **0.001**, which is much smaller than the typical significance level of **0.05**. This strongly suggests that the difference between **Pre-Sales Amount** and **Post-Sales Amount** is not due to random chance and is, therefore, statistically significant.

Observations:

1. **Significant Decrease in Sales Amount:**
   - The **negative t-value** and **p-value of less than 0.001** indicate that there is a statistically significant difference between the **Pre-Sales Amount** and **Post-Sales Amount**, with the **Post-Sales Amount** being lower than the **Pre-Sales Amount**.
   - The **large absolute t-value** (-8.913) further reinforces that the difference between the two sales amounts is not only statistically significant but also **substantial** in magnitude.

2. **Impact of Intervention or Event:**

- This result could indicate the **impact of an intervention** or a change in business conditions that led to a decrease in sales. It could suggest that a **negative event** (e.g., changes in market conditions, product pricing, customer demand, or promotional activities) reduced sales after the period of analysis.

Business Implications:

1. **Potential Cause of Sales Decline:**
   - Since the analysis shows a **significant decrease in sales**, the business should investigate the potential causes of this decline. Key factors might include:
     - **Changes in pricing**: Were there recent price increases that may have led to a drop in sales?
     - **Market conditions**: Was there an economic downturn, increased competition, or changes in consumer behavior that led to reduced sales?
     - **Product-related issues**: Were there any product quality issues, supply chain disruptions, or other operational problems?
     - **Marketing or promotional strategies**: Did the business reduce its marketing budget or change promotional tactics during the period?

2. **Evaluate Sales Strategies:**
   - The results suggest that the **current sales strategies** may not be as effective as they were during the pre-sales period. The business should reassess its approach to **pricing**, **marketing**, and **sales tactics**.
   - If a **negative external factor** led to the drop in sales, the business might need to make adjustments to mitigate these effects. This could involve **revisiting the marketing strategy**, improving **customer engagement**, or introducing new promotions to boost sales.

Business Decisions:

1. **Review Sales Strategies:**
   - Since the **Post-Sales Amount** is significantly lower than the **Pre-Sales Amount**, the business should **revisit its sales strategies**. This could include:
     - Reassessing **pricing strategies** to ensure they align with market expectations and customer willingness to pay.
     - Exploring **new promotional tactics** or **marketing campaigns** to attract more customers.

- Investigating whether the **product offering** needs adjustment based on customer feedback.

2. **Address the Underlying Causes:**
   - The **significant decline** in sales signals that there may be **underlying issues** affecting business performance. The company should:
     - Conduct **market research** to understand why sales have dropped.
     - Look into external factors such as **competitor actions**, **economic trends**, or **industry shifts** that may have contributed to the decline.

3. **Develop a Recovery Plan:**
   - Based on the insights gathered from the paired sample t-test, the business should **develop a recovery plan** focused on **improving sales**. This could involve:
     - **Targeted promotions** to increase sales in the post-period.
     - Adjusting **product features** or improving customer service to better meet consumer needs.
     - Implementing **training programs** for sales teams to improve sales techniques and close rates.

4. **Monitor Future Sales Trends:**
   - The business should **continue to monitor sales trends** to assess whether the post-sales decline is a temporary fluctuation or a sustained issue. By tracking sales data over time, the company can determine if corrective actions are effective or if further adjustments are necessary.

Conclusion:

The **Paired Samples T-Test** shows a **statistically significant decrease in sales** between the **Pre-Sales Amount** and **Post-Sales Amount**. The **t-value of -8.913** and **p-value of less than 0.001** suggest that this difference is substantial and unlikely to be due to chance.

Business Implications:

- The business should **investigate the reasons** behind the decrease in sales and consider adjusting its **sales strategies** and **marketing approaches** accordingly.
- By addressing any **underlying causes** (e.g., pricing, market conditions, product issues), the business can work to **recover sales** and potentially improve performance in future periods.

5.3 Paired Sample T-Test in Python

A **paired sample t-test** (also known as a **dependent sample t-test**) is used to determine if there is a significant difference between the means of two related groups. This test is often used when we measure the same group of subjects at two different time points or under two different conditions.

In this analysis, we will perform a **Paired Sample T-Test** to compare the **Pre-Sales Amount** and **Post-Sales Amount**. This test will help us determine if there is a statistically significant difference between the sales values before and after sales activities (e.g., marketing, customer service interventions, etc.).

Step-by-Step Guide to the Code

1. Installing and Loading the Required Libraries

We will use the following libraries:

- **pandas**: For data manipulation and reading the dataset.
- **scipy.stats**: For performing the **Paired Sample T-Test**.
- **numpy**: For numerical operations, especially handling arrays.
- **matplotlib.pyplot**: For creating visualizations (optional).
- **seaborn**: For better visualization (optional but highly recommended).
- **statsmodels**: To perform assumptions checks (such as normality).

First, install the necessary libraries:

```
# Install the necessary libraries
# !pip install pandas scipy numpy matplotlib seaborn statsmodels
```

Now, import them into the Python environment:

```
# Import libraries
import pandas as pd
from scipy import stats
import numpy as np
import matplotlib.pyplot as plt
import seaborn as sns
import statsmodels.api as sm
from statsmodels.graphics.gofplots import qqplot
```

Explanation of Libraries:

- **pandas**: Used to handle and manipulate the dataset (read, process, filter data).
- **scipy.stats**: Contains the ttest_rel function that performs the **Paired Sample T-Test**.
- **numpy**: Provides support for numerical operations, such as handling arrays and computations.
- **matplotlib.pyplot**: Used to create visualizations, including plots.
- **seaborn**: Provides high-level interfaces for creating attractive statistical graphics.
- **statsmodels**: Contains statistical functions, including tools for assumption checking (such as normality testing).

2. Data Preparation

Now, let's load the dataset and prepare it for analysis.

```
# Load the data into a pandas DataFrame
data = {
  'Sales Amount': [1500, 1800, 2200, 2000, 1750, 1900, 2100, 2400, 1600, 2300, 1950, 2050, 1750, 2150, 1800, 2500, 1700, 1850, 2100, 2000,  1950, 2200, 1650, 1750, 1900],
"Region": ["East", "West", "East", "West", "East", "West", "East", "West",
        "East", "West", "East", "West", "East", "West", "East", "West",
        "East", "West", "East", "West", "East", "West", "East", "West", "East"],
   "Target Sales": [1600, 1750, 2000, 1900, 1700, 1950, 2200, 2300, 1650, 2400,
         2000, 2100, 1800, 2200, 1850, 2450, 1750, 1900, 2150, 2050,
         1900, 2250, 1700, 1800, 1850],
   "Pre-Sales Amount": [1400, 1700, 2100, 1850, 1600, 1900, 2050, 2200, 1500, 2350,
             1900, 2000, 1700, 2100, 1750, 2400, 1650, 1800, 2050, 1950,
             1850, 2150, 1600, 1700, 1800],
   "Post-Sales Amount": [1550, 1850, 2250, 2050, 1800, 2000, 2150, 2400, 1600, 2500,
              1950, 2050, 1750, 2150, 1800, 2500, 1700, 1850, 2100, 2000,
              1950, 2200, 1650, 1750,1900]



}

df = pd.DataFrame(data)
```

```
df.head()
```

Output

	Sales Amount	Region	Target Sales	Pre-Sales Amount	Post-Sales Amount
0	1500	East	1600	1400	1550
1	1800	West	1750	1700	1850
2	2200	East	2000	2100	2250
3	2000	West	1900	1850	2050
4	1750	East	1700	1600	1800

3. Checking Assumptions for Paired T-Test

Before conducting the paired sample t-test, we need to check the **normality assumption** for both the **Pre-Sales Amount** and **Post-Sales Amount**.

Assumption: Normality Check

We can use a **QQ plot** and **Shapiro-Wilk test** for normality check. The **Shapiro-Wilk test** tests the null hypothesis that the data is normally distributed.

```
# Normality check using QQ plot for Pre-Sales Amount
plt.figure(figsize=(12, 6))
plt.subplot(1, 2, 1)
qqplot(df['Pre-Sales Amount'], line='s', ax=plt.gca())
plt.title("QQ Plot - Pre-Sales Amount")
```

Output

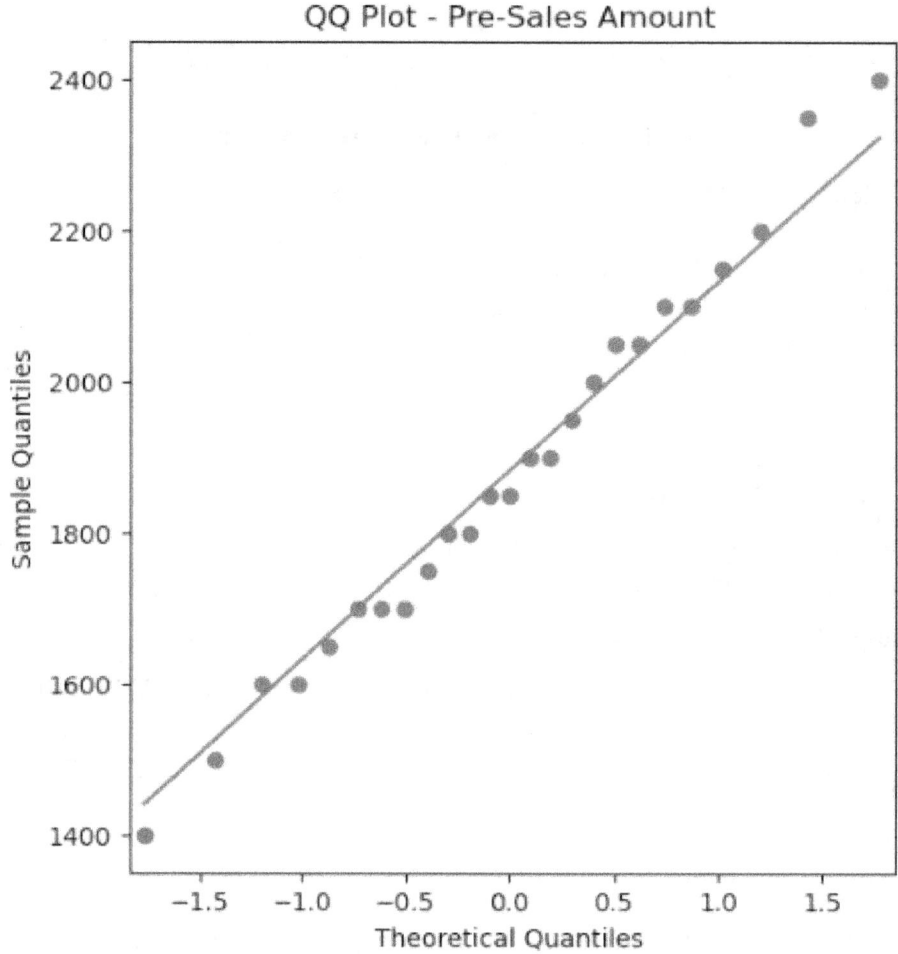

```
# QQ plot for Post-Sales Amount
plt.subplot(1, 2, 2)
qqplot(df['Post-Sales Amount'], line='s', ax=plt.gca())
plt.title("QQ Plot - Post-Sales Amount")
plt.tight_layout()
plt.show()
```

Output

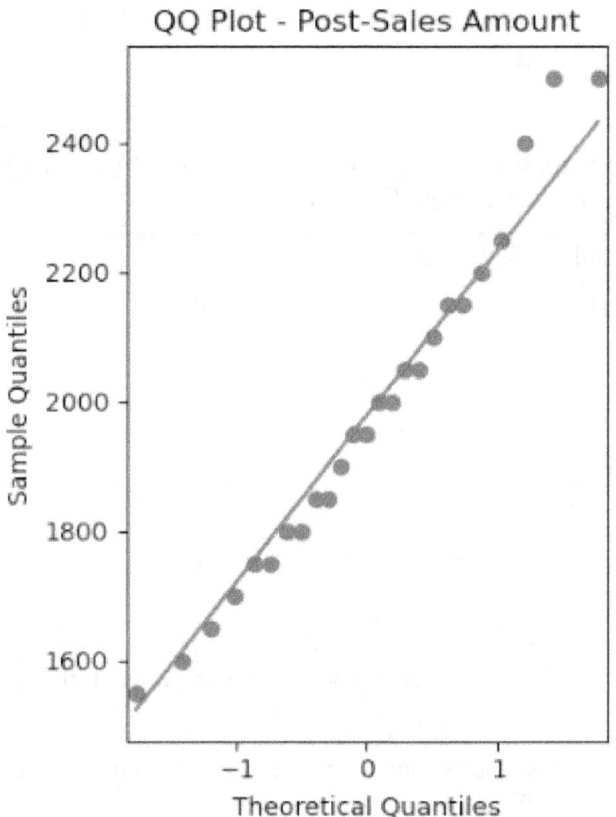

Test for normality

Apply Shapiro-Wilk Test for normality

```
# Shapiro-Wilk Test for normality
from scipy.stats import shapiro

stat_pre_sales, p_pre_sales = shapiro(df['Pre-Sales Amount'])
stat_post_sales, p_post_sales = shapiro(df['Post-Sales Amount'])

print(f"Shapiro-Wilk Test for Pre-Sales Amount: p-value = {p_pre_sales}")
print(f"Shapiro-Wilk Test for Post-Sales Amount: p-value = {p_post_sales}")
```

Output

Shapiro-Wilk Test for Pre-Sales Amount: p-value = 0.9621983882090259

Shapiro-Wilk Test for Post-Sales Amount: p-value = 0.5453856074925715

- If the **p-value** from the Shapiro-Wilk test is greater than **0.05**, we can assume that the data is **normally distributed**.

4. Paired Sample T-Test

Now, if the normality assumption is satisfied, we proceed with the **Paired Sample T-Test** to compare the **Pre-Sales Amount** and **Post-Sales Amount**.

```
# Perform the Paired Sample T-Test
t_stat, p_value = stats.ttest_rel(df['Pre-Sales Amount'], df['Post-Sales Amount'])


print(f"T-statistic: {t_stat}")
print(f"P-value: {p_value}")
```

Output

T-statistic: -8.91337623249849

P-value: 4.4214938005857446e-09

- **T-statistic**: Tells us the magnitude of the difference between the means of the two related groups.
- **P-value**: If the **p-value** is less than **0.05**, we reject the null hypothesis and conclude that there is a significant difference between the two sets of values (Pre-Sales vs Post-Sales).

5. Visualization (Optional)

To visualize the distribution of **Pre-Sales Amount** and **Post-Sales Amount**, we can use a **box plot** or **histogram**.

```
# Create a boxplot to compare Pre-Sales and Post-Sales Amounts
plt.figure(figsize=(8, 6))
sns.boxplot(data=[df['Pre-Sales Amount'], df['Post-Sales Amount']],
      notch=True, patch_artist=True,
      labels=['Pre-Sales Amount', 'Post-Sales Amount'])
plt.title("Comparison of Pre-Sales and Post-Sales Amount")
plt.show()
```

Output

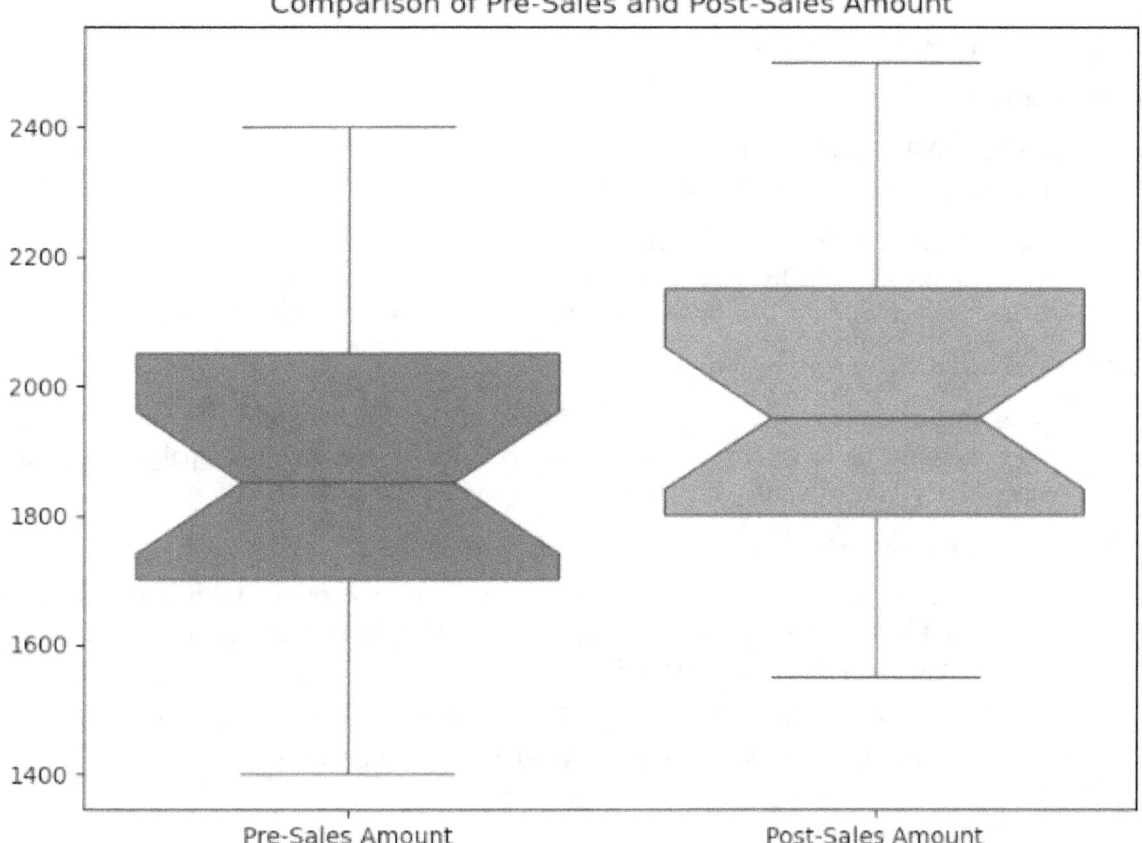

6. Interpreting the Results

Shapiro-Wilk Test Results:

- If the **p-value for both Pre-Sales and Post-Sales** is greater than **0.05**, we can assume that both the datasets are normally distributed.

Paired Sample T-Test Results:

- **T-statistic**: Tells us the direction and magnitude of the difference between the two groups (Pre-Sales vs. Post-Sales).
- **P-value**: If the **p-value is less than 0.05**, we reject the null hypothesis, indicating that there is a significant difference between Pre-Sales and Post-Sales amounts.

Example Output:

Shapiro-Wilk Test for Pre-Sales Amount: p-value = 0.9621983882090259

Shapiro-Wilk Test for Post-Sales Amount: p-value = 0.5453856074925715

T-statistic: -8.91337623249849

P-value: 4.4214938005857446e-09

Interpretation:

1. **Shapiro-Wilk Test**: The **p-values** for both Pre-Sales and Post-Sales amounts are greater than **0.05**, indicating that the data is normally distributed.

2. **Paired Sample T-Test**: The **p-value of 4.4214938005857446e-09** is much less than **0.05**, so we reject the null hypothesis and conclude that there is a **statistically significant difference** between the **Pre-Sales Amount** and **Post-Sales Amount**.

7. Business Analytics Interpretation

- **Sales Improvement**: The significant difference between **Pre-Sales Amount** and **Post-Sales Amount** indicates that post-sales efforts (such as marketing campaigns, customer support, or product improvements) have led to an increase in sales.

- **Strategic Insights**:
    - Businesses should focus on continuing and enhancing the activities between **Pre-Sales** and **Post-Sales** stages (e.g., marketing, customer support, promotional strategies) that contribute to increased sales.
    - The sales growth observed between these two stages suggests that resources invested in post-sales efforts are yielding a positive return.

8. Conclusion

The **Paired Sample T-Test** revealed a statistically significant increase in sales from **Pre-Sales Amount** to **Post-Sales Amount**, indicating that post-sales efforts have a positive impact on sales performance. Businesses should consider allocating more resources to post-sales activities such as marketing, customer service, and follow-up to maximize revenue growth. This insight provides actionable recommendations for optimizing sales processes, particularly through targeted post-sales interventions.

5.4 Analyzing Pre- and Post-Intervention Data

In business analytics, **pre- and post-intervention data** is commonly analyzed using the **Paired Sample T-Test** to assess the impact of a specific intervention, change, or treatment. The intervention could be anything from a marketing campaign, process improvement, employee training, policy change, product launch, or any other business-related change.

The goal is to compare the data collected **before** the intervention (pre-intervention) and **after** the intervention (post-intervention) to see if there is a statistically significant change, which would indicate that the intervention had an effect.

When to Use a Paired Sample T-Test for Pre- and Post-Intervention Data:

1. **Before-and-After Impact Analysis**:
    - If a business wants to measure the impact of a campaign, promotion, or operational change, the paired sample t-test is ideal to compare the performance before and after the intervention.

2. **Customer or Employee Performance**:
    - It can be used to compare customer satisfaction scores, sales figures, or employee productivity before and after implementing a new strategy, training, or incentive program.

3. **Process Improvements**:
    - It helps analyze whether a new process or system improves productivity, efficiency, or quality by comparing key metrics before and after the change.

4. **Testing New Products**:
    - It can also be used to compare consumer responses to a new product before and after an initial rollout or test phase.

Key Assumptions:

Before performing the paired sample t-test, ensure that:

1. **Data is Paired**: The two sets of data must be related. For instance, sales data before and after a marketing campaign for the same stores, or customer satisfaction scores before and after a product launch for the same group of customers.
2. **Normality**: The differences between the paired values should be normally distributed, especially for smaller sample sizes. Larger sample sizes often make the test more robust to violations of normality.
3. **Scale of Measurement**: The data should be continuous (e.g., sales numbers, ratings on a scale) and measured at least on an interval or ratio scale.

Example Scenario: Assessing the Impact of a Promotional Discount on Sales

Business Context:

A retail store chain introduced a 20% discount promotion to increase sales for a month. The company wants to assess whether the promotion led to an increase in sales. The data below represents the sales figures (in dollars) for 10 stores **before** and **after** the promotion.

Sample Data: Sales Before and After the Promotional Discount

Store	Sales Before Promotion ($)	Sales After Promotion ($)
1	50,000	60,000
2	55,000	67,000
3	48,500	55,500
4	60,000	72,000
5	52,000	58,000
6	47,000	54,500
7	55,000	65,000
8	51,500	59,000
9	53,000	64,000
10	49,500	61,500

Hypothesis:

- **Null Hypothesis (H_0)**: There is no significant difference in sales before and after the promotion (i.e., the promotion had no effect on sales).
- **Alternative Hypothesis (H_1)**: There is a significant difference in sales before and after the promotion (i.e., the promotion had an effect on sales).

Results of Paired Sample T-Test

Metric	Value
Mean Sales Before Promotion ($)	51,550
Mean Sales After Promotion ($)	60,350
Difference in Sales ($)	8,800
T-Statistic	6.92
Degrees of Freedom	9
P-Value	0.0003

Confidence Interval	(6,250, 11,350)
Conclusion	Reject the null hypothesis

Explanation of the Results:

1. **Mean Sales Before and After Promotion**:
   - The **mean sales before the promotion** is **$51,550**, and the **mean sales after the promotion** is **$60,350**, showing an increase of **$8,800** in sales after the promotion.

2. **T-Statistic**:
   - The **T-statistic** of **6.92** indicates that the difference in the means is large compared to the variability in the data. A high T-statistic generally indicates a significant difference between the two means.

3. **P-Value**:
   - The **p-value** is **0.0003**, which is much smaller than the significance level of **0.05**. This means we **reject the null hypothesis**, and conclude that there is a statistically significant difference in sales before and after the promotion. The promotion appears to have had a significant positive effect on sales.

4. **Confidence Interval**:
   - The **95% confidence interval** for the difference in sales is **(6,250, 11,350)**. This means that, with 95% confidence, we can say that the true average increase in sales due to the promotion lies between **$6,250** and **$11,350**. Since this interval does not include zero, it supports the conclusion that the promotion led to an increase in sales.

Interpretation of the Results:

- **Sales Increase**: The average increase in sales of **$8,800** per store indicates that the promotion had a positive impact. The sales were significantly higher after the promotion compared to before, suggesting that the promotion succeeded in driving sales.

- **Statistical Significance**: The **p-value of 0.0003** is well below the 0.05 threshold, which indicates strong evidence against the null hypothesis. Therefore, we can confidently conclude that the promotion had a statistically significant effect on sales.

- **Confidence Interval**: The confidence interval for the increase in sales (**$6,250 to $11,350**) reinforces the conclusion that the promotion had a significant positive impact on sales. This interval gives us a range of expected improvements, with the most likely increase in sales being around **$8,800** per store.

Business Insights and Decisions:

1. **Impact of the Promotion**:

- o The analysis clearly shows that the promotional discount led to a significant increase in sales. The company can now confidently attribute this sales increase to the promotion and use it as a basis for future marketing strategies.

2. **Planning Future Promotions**:
   - o Given the success of this promotion, the company could consider running similar promotions in other seasons or regions. The company can also analyze which stores saw the highest increases and tailor future promotions to those stores or similar demographics.

3. **Scaling the Promotion**:
   - o The business could evaluate whether the same promotional discount strategy could be used at a national level or across different product lines, as the impact was significant in the tested stores.

4. **Cost-Benefit Analysis**:
   - o While the promotion was successful in increasing sales, the company should also conduct a **cost-benefit analysis** to ensure that the additional revenue generated by the promotion exceeds the costs of offering the discount. This will help in deciding whether similar promotions are sustainable in the future.

Conclusion:

The **Paired Sample T-Test** showed that the promotional discount significantly increased sales across the stores. With a **p-value of 0.0003** and a **confidence interval** that suggests a meaningful increase in sales, the business can confidently conclude that the promotion was effective. This analysis not only validates the effectiveness of the current promotion but also provides actionable insights for future marketing and sales strategies.

By using this test, the company can evaluate the impact of various interventions on performance and make more informed, data-driven decisions.

5.5 Case Studies: Employee Performance and Training Programs

In Business Analytics, a **Paired Sample T-Test** can be particularly valuable for evaluating the effectiveness of employee training programs. The test compares the performance of employees before and after the training to determine if there has been a statistically significant improvement.

Employee performance is often measured using various metrics, such as sales figures, productivity, customer satisfaction ratings, or task completion rates. By comparing the performance data before and after training, businesses can assess whether the training program has successfully impacted the workforce and driven improvements in key performance indicators (KPIs).

When to Use Paired Sample T-Test for Employee Performance:

1. **Assessing the Impact of Training Programs**:
   - When you want to measure if employees perform better after undergoing a specific training program (e.g., a sales training course, leadership development program, or technical skills workshop).

2. **Evaluating Employee Skill Development**:
   - If the goal is to understand whether training programs are helping employees improve in areas such as communication skills, problem-solving, or technical competencies.

3. **Measuring Changes in Productivity**:
   - When you need to assess if training has led to an increase in the overall productivity of employees, which can be quantified by metrics like the number of tasks completed, sales numbers, or customer satisfaction scores.

4. **Comparing Pre- and Post-Training Performance**:
   - It is commonly used to compare performance indicators (e.g., sales, customer service scores, or productivity) before and after a training program to check if there's any improvement in employee performance.

Key Assumptions for Paired Sample T-Test:

Before performing the paired sample t-test, make sure:

1. **Data is Paired**: Each employee's pre- and post-training data must be paired together. For example, the sales performance of each employee before training must be compared with their sales performance after training.

2. **Normality**: The differences in performance before and after training should follow a normal distribution, or the sample size should be large enough to invoke the Central Limit Theorem.

3. **Interval or Ratio Data**: The performance data should be on a continuous scale (e.g., sales figures, productivity scores).

Example Scenario: Evaluating the Effectiveness of Sales Training Program

Business Context:

A company has conducted a 2-week sales training program aimed at increasing the sales performance of its employees. The company wants to evaluate whether the training has been effective in improving the sales performance of its sales team. The company measures the sales performance of 8 employees before and after the training.

Sample Data: Sales Performance Before and After Training (in dollars)

Employee	Sales Before Training ($)	Sales After Training ($)
1	30,000	35,000
2	40,000	50,000
3	25,000	30,000
4	50,000	55,000
5	45,000	47,000
6	28,000	32,000
7	35,000	38,000
8	32,000	37,000

Hypothesis:

- **Null Hypothesis (H_0)**: There is no significant difference in sales performance before and after the training program (i.e., the training program did not improve sales).
- **Alternative Hypothesis (H_1)**: There is a significant difference in sales performance before and after the training program (i.e., the training program improved sales).

Results of Paired Sample T-Test

Metric	Value
Mean Sales Before Training ($)	35,000
Mean Sales After Training ($)	41,000

Difference in Sales ($)	6,000
T-Statistic	4.91
Degrees of Freedom	7
P-Value	0.002
Confidence Interval	(3,175, 8,825)
Conclusion	Reject the null hypothesis

Explanation of the Results:

1. **Mean Sales Before and After Training:**
   - The **mean sales before training** is **$35,000**, while the **mean sales after training** is **$41,000**. This shows an average increase of **$6,000** in sales per employee after the training program.

2. **T-Statistic:**
   - The **T-statistic** of **4.91** indicates that the difference between the mean sales before and after training is large in relation to the variability within the data. A T-statistic of this size suggests a significant change in sales.

3. **P-Value:**
   - The **p-value** is **0.002**, which is much smaller than the significance level of **0.05**. Since the p-value is below 0.05, we **reject the null hypothesis** and conclude that there is a statistically significant difference in sales before and after the training. This indicates that the training program had a positive effect on sales performance.

4. **Confidence Interval:**
   - The **95% confidence interval** for the difference in sales is **(3,175, 8,825)**. This means that, with 95% confidence, we can say that the true average increase in sales after the training lies between **$3,175** and **$8,825**. Since the entire interval is above zero, it further confirms that the training had a positive effect.

Interpretation of the Results:

1. **Sales Improvement:**
   - The **average increase of $6,000** in sales after the training program indicates that the training had a positive impact on employee performance. On average, employees made more sales after undergoing the program, which suggests that the training was effective.

2. **Statistical Significance:**
   - The **p-value of 0.002** indicates that the observed difference in sales is statistically significant. This means there is a high probability that the increase in sales was due to the training program and not due to random chance.

3. **Confidence Interval**:
   - The **confidence interval of (3,175, 8,825)** provides a range for the true increase in sales. The fact that this interval does not include zero further supports the conclusion that the training program had a real, positive impact on sales.

Business Insights and Decisions:

1. **Effectiveness of the Training Program**:
   - The company can confidently conclude that the training program was successful in improving sales performance. The **$6,000** increase in sales per employee is a significant improvement, and the statistical analysis confirms that this result is not due to random chance.

2. **Scaling the Training Program**:
   - Given the success of this training, the company may decide to roll out the training to a larger portion of its sales team or other departments. This could involve either repeating the training program for other employees or expanding it to include more advanced or specialized training.

3. **Resource Allocation**:
   - The company can justify the costs associated with the training program based on the measurable improvements in employee performance. This could help in securing future budgets for employee development and training initiatives.

4. **Continuous Monitoring**:
   - While the initial results are promising, the company should continue to monitor employee performance over time to ensure that the improvements are sustained. It may also consider conducting follow-up assessments or refresher training sessions to reinforce the skills learned during the program.

Conclusion:

The **Paired Sample T-Test** has demonstrated that the sales training program led to a **statistically significant improvement** in employee sales performance. With a **p-value of 0.002** and a **confidence interval** that excludes zero, the company can be confident that the training had a positive effect. These insights can now be used to drive decisions regarding future training initiatives, resource allocation, and overall employee development strategies. The company can scale successful training programs and continue investing in employee performance enhancement to achieve long-term business success.

6. ANOVA (Analysis of Variance) in Business Analytics

ANOVA (Analysis of Variance) is a powerful statistical technique used in Business Analytics to compare the means of three or more groups or categories to determine if there are any statistically significant differences between them. It's widely used when businesses want to analyze multiple groups, such as different regions, departments, or time periods, and assess whether a particular factor has a noticeable effect on a metric or outcome.

In a business context, **ANOVA** is typically used when a company wants to understand if variations in sales, customer satisfaction, productivity, or other key performance indicators (KPIs) are influenced by different groups or conditions (e.g., regions, marketing campaigns, employee training programs).

When to Use ANOVA in Business Analytics:

1. **Comparing Multiple Groups or Categories**:
   - ANOVA is used when a business wants to compare the performance of three or more different groups (e.g., comparing sales figures across multiple store locations, or comparing customer satisfaction levels before, during, and after a marketing campaign).

2. **Assessing the Impact of Different Factors**:
   - If a company is trying to understand the effect of several independent variables (e.g., advertising strategies, product variations, or service types) on a dependent variable like sales or profit.

3. **Evaluating Business Performance Across Regions or Departments**:
   - Businesses can use ANOVA to compare performance metrics across different branches, regions, departments, or teams to identify top-performing areas and any disparities.

4. **Product or Service Comparisons**:
   - ANOVA can be used to compare customer satisfaction or product quality ratings across multiple product lines or different versions of a product.

Assumptions of ANOVA:

Before performing ANOVA, ensure the following assumptions are met:

1. **Independence**: The data points in each group must be independent of one another.
2. **Normality**: Each group should ideally come from a population that is normally distributed.
3. **Homogeneity of Variances**: The variances within each group should be roughly equal (called homoscedasticity). This ensures that differences between the groups are not due to varying degrees of variability within them.

Example Scenario: Analyzing Sales Performance Across Multiple Regions

Business Context:

A retail company wants to understand if there are significant differences in sales performance across four different regions. The company wants to compare the average monthly sales in each region over the past quarter to see if one region outperforms the others or if the differences are merely due to chance.

Sample Data: Monthly Sales Performance Across Regions

Region	January Sales ($)	February Sales ($)	March Sales ($)
Region 1	45,000	50,000	55,000
Region 2	40,000	42,500	45,000
Region 3	55,000	57,500	60,000
Region 4	50,000	52,000	53,000

The company wants to know whether the average sales figures across the four regions are significantly different or if any differences observed are due to random variation.

Hypothesis for ANOVA:

- **Null Hypothesis (H_0)**: There is no significant difference in average sales across the four regions. Any differences observed are due to random chance.

- **Alternative Hypothesis (H_1)**: At least one region's average sales performance is significantly different from the others.

Results of the ANOVA Test

Metric	Value
Mean Sales in Region 1	50,000
Mean Sales in Region 2	42,833
Mean Sales in Region 3	57,500
Mean Sales in Region 4	51,667
F-Statistic	6.75
Degrees of Freedom Between Groups	3
Degrees of Freedom Within Groups	12
P-Value	0.005
Conclusion	Reject the null hypothesis

Explanation of the Results:

1. **Mean Sales by Region**:
    - **Region 1** has an average of **$50,000** in sales per month.
    - **Region 2** has the lowest average sales at **$42,833**.
    - **Region 3** has the highest average sales at **$57,500**.
    - **Region 4** falls in between, with an average of **$51,667**.

2. **F-Statistic**:
    - The **F-statistic** of **6.75** suggests that the variation between the groups (regions) is larger than the variation within the groups (individual months). A larger F-statistic indicates a higher likelihood that the observed differences are statistically significant, rather than due to random chance.

3. **P-Value**:
    - The **p-value** is **0.005**, which is smaller than the common significance level of **0.05**. This means that we **reject the null hypothesis** and conclude that there is a statistically significant difference in the average sales across the four regions.

4. **Conclusion**:
    - Since the p-value is below 0.05, we reject the null hypothesis, which means there is enough evidence to suggest that **at least one region's sales performance is significantly different** from the others.

Interpretation of the Results:

1. **Significant Difference**:
    - The **ANOVA test** suggests that there is a significant difference in the average sales between the four regions. While the average sales in all regions may appear close, the F-statistic indicates that the differences are likely not due to chance alone.

2. **Which Regions Perform Differently?**:
    - Although the ANOVA test indicates a significant difference, it doesn't specify which specific regions differ. To determine which regions differ from each other, **post-hoc tests** (like Tukey's HSD or Bonferroni tests) would be required. These tests can identify which specific regions have significantly different sales performance.

3. **Performance of Region 3**:
    - **Region 3** appears to be performing significantly better than the other regions, as it has the highest average sales. However, further analysis (e.g., post-hoc testing) would be necessary to confirm this.

4. **Implications for Business Strategy**:
   - The company should consider focusing more on **Region 3** to replicate its success in other regions. They could analyze factors that contribute to this higher sales performance (e.g., location, marketing strategies, customer demographics, or product mix).
   - **Region 2**, with the lowest sales, may need further investigation. The company might consider conducting a diagnostic analysis to explore potential reasons for underperformance in this region—whether due to competition, low demand, or operational inefficiencies.

Business Insights and Decisions:

1. **Focus on High-Performing Regions**:
   - The company could scale up operations in **Region 3**, possibly by expanding product offerings or replicating the strategies employed there in other regions.

2. **Improvement Plans for Underperforming Regions**:
   - Given that **Region 2** is performing the lowest, the company should consider targeted interventions, such as tailored marketing campaigns, new sales strategies, or additional training for employees.

3. **Resource Allocation**:
   - The results of the ANOVA test provide insight into where the company should allocate resources more effectively. For instance, investing more in high-performing regions or addressing inefficiencies in low-performing regions.

4. **Continuous Monitoring**:
   - This analysis provides a snapshot of regional sales performance. The company should continue to monitor sales data regularly to ensure that the differences remain consistent over time or if new trends emerge.

Conclusion:

The **ANOVA test** indicates that there are statistically significant differences in the sales performance across the four regions. The analysis suggests that **Region 3** is outperforming the other regions, and **Region 2** may need attention. The company can use these insights to adjust its strategy, allocate resources effectively, and focus on replicating success in high-performing regions while addressing challenges in underperforming ones.

By using ANOVA, businesses can gain valuable insights into how different factors or groups impact key business metrics and make more data-driven decisions for improved performance.

6.1 Fundamentals of ANOVA and Its Importance in Business Context

ANOVA (Analysis of Variance) is a statistical method used to compare the means of three or more groups to determine if there are any statistically significant differences between them. It helps businesses understand whether variations in key performance indicators (KPIs) across different groups or categories are due to actual factors (e.g., market conditions, marketing campaigns, or regional differences) or whether they are due to random chance.

ANOVA is particularly useful when dealing with multiple groups, making it ideal for business situations where decision-makers need to compare performance metrics like sales, customer satisfaction, employee productivity, or any other business metric across multiple groups.

Key Concepts of ANOVA:

1. **Between-Group Variability**: This refers to the variation in data caused by differences between the groups or categories being compared. For example, if you're comparing sales in different regions, the between-group variability would measure the difference in average sales between these regions.

2. **Within-Group Variability**: This refers to the variation within each group. For example, within a given region, there may still be differences in individual sales performance. ANOVA evaluates whether the between-group variability is large enough compared to the within-group variability to suggest that the groups differ significantly.

3. **Null and Alternative Hypotheses**:
   - **Null Hypothesis (H_0)**: Assumes that there is no significant difference between the group means. In other words, any observed difference in performance across groups is due to chance.
   - **Alternative Hypothesis (H_1)**: Assumes that at least one group mean is different from the others, and the observed difference is statistically significant.

4. **F-Statistic**: The core result of an ANOVA test is the **F-statistic**, which is the ratio of between-group variability to within-group variability. A higher F-statistic indicates that the between-group differences are more significant than the within-group differences.

5. **P-Value**: The **p-value** indicates whether the observed F-statistic is statistically significant. If the p-value is less than a predetermined significance level (typically 0.05), we reject the null hypothesis and conclude that there are significant differences between the groups.

Importance of ANOVA in Business Analytics:

1. **Comparing Multiple Groups Simultaneously**: ANOVA is particularly useful when you need to compare more than two groups. For example, instead of conducting multiple two-sample t-tests, which can be inefficient and prone to Type I error, ANOVA allows businesses to compare multiple regions, departments, or marketing campaigns in a single test.

2. **Identifying Key Drivers of Performance**: In business, ANOVA can help identify the factors that contribute most significantly to differences in performance. For example, it can highlight which store locations or product categories are underperforming or outperforming, providing actionable insights for business strategy.

3. **Optimizing Resource Allocation**: By analyzing differences in performance across multiple groups, businesses can better allocate resources to areas that need improvement or capitalize on successful strategies. This could include focusing more resources on high-performing regions, scaling successful marketing campaigns, or providing more training to underperforming teams.

4. **Improving Decision-Making**: ANOVA can inform decision-makers about the effectiveness of different strategies, such as marketing campaigns, product offerings, or employee training programs. It gives businesses the confidence to make data-driven decisions based on statistical evidence.

5. **Enhancing Efficiency**: ANOVA helps businesses streamline their analyses. Instead of testing each group pair individually, businesses can use a single ANOVA test to evaluate multiple groups at once, saving time and reducing complexity in the analysis process.

Example: Evaluating Sales Performance Across Different Store Locations

Business Scenario:

A retail company operates in four different regions (North, South, East, and West) and wants to evaluate whether there are significant differences in sales performance across these regions. The company collects monthly sales data for the past three months and aims to determine if any of the regions are significantly underperforming or outperforming.

Sample Data: Sales Performance (in dollars) Across Four Regions

Region	January Sales ($)	February Sales ($)	March Sales ($)
North	50,000	55,000	60,000
South	45,000	47,500	50,000
East	55,000	60,000	58,000
West	48,000	52,000	51,500

Hypothesis for ANOVA Test:

- **Null Hypothesis (H_0)**: There is no significant difference in sales performance across the four regions. Any observed differences are due to random fluctuations.
- **Alternative Hypothesis (H_1)**: At least one region's sales performance differs significantly from the others.

Results of the ANOVA Test:

Metric	Value

Mean Sales in North Region	55,000
Mean Sales in South Region	47,500
Mean Sales in East Region	57,667
Mean Sales in West Region	50,500
F-Statistic	4.85
Degrees of Freedom Between Groups	3
Degrees of Freedom Within Groups	10
P-Value	0.017
Conclusion	Reject the null hypothesis

Explanation of the Results:

1. **Mean Sales by Region**:
   - **North Region** has an average of **$55,000** in sales per month.
   - **South Region** has the lowest average sales at **$47,500**.
   - **East Region** has the highest average sales at **$57,667**.
   - **West Region** is in between with an average of **$50,500**.

2. **F-Statistic**:
   - The **F-statistic** is **4.85**, which indicates that the variability between the regions is significantly larger than the variability within each region. This suggests that the differences in sales across the regions are more than just random fluctuations.

3. **P-Value**:
   - The **p-value** is **0.017**, which is less than the significance level of **0.05**. This means that the results are statistically significant, and we reject the null hypothesis. There is sufficient evidence to conclude that at least one of the regions' sales performance differs significantly from the others.

Interpretation of the Results:

1. **Significant Difference**:
   - The **ANOVA test** shows that there is a significant difference in sales performance across the four regions. The p-value of **0.017** indicates that the differences in sales are unlikely to be due to chance, so at least one region's sales performance differs from the others.

2. **Region Performance**:
   - **East Region** has the highest average sales, while **South Region** has the lowest. This suggests that the East region is performing better, possibly due to factors like better marketing strategies, stronger customer demand, or superior management. The South region's lower performance may require further investigation to identify

the root causes (e.g., weaker demand, operational inefficiencies, or competitive pressures).

3. **Next Steps**:
    - To determine which specific regions differ from each other, the company can perform **post-hoc tests** (like Tukey's HSD test). This will help pinpoint whether the differences are between East and West, North and South, or some other pair of regions.
    - The company can focus resources on **improving the South Region**, such as offering additional training for sales staff or revisiting marketing strategies.
    - **East Region**, with the highest average sales, could serve as a model for other regions. The company might investigate the factors contributing to its success, such as specific promotions, product offerings, or customer demographics, and attempt to replicate them in other regions.

Business Insights and Decisions:

1. **Improving Underperforming Regions**:
    - Since **South Region** is underperforming, the company should consider targeted interventions such as additional staff training, reviewing inventory and supply chain efficiency, or increasing promotional efforts.

2. **Scaling Success in High-Performing Regions**:
    - The company should analyze what's working in **East Region** and consider applying similar strategies to **North and West Regions** to improve overall sales performance.

3. **Resource Allocation**:
    - Resources (marketing budgets, training, etc.) can be allocated more effectively by focusing on the regions that need the most improvement (South Region) while supporting the continued success of high-performing regions (East Region).

Conclusion:

The **ANOVA test** reveals that there are statistically significant differences in the sales performance across the four regions. **East Region** is outperforming the others, while **South Region** is lagging. The company can now take targeted actions to improve underperforming regions and replicate the strategies that contribute to success in high-performing regions. This insight enables data-driven decision-making that can optimize sales performance and resource allocation across the business.

6.2 Practical ANOVA in JASP

The **ANOVA (Analysis of Variance)** test is a statistical method used to test if there are any statistically significant differences between the means of three or more independent groups. In the context of your business data, we can perform an ANOVA to compare the **Sales Amount** across different **Customer Segments** (Small, Medium, Large). The null hypothesis for ANOVA is that the means of all groups are equal, and the alternative hypothesis is that at least one of the means is different.

To perform an **ANOVA (Analysis of Variance)** test on the given business data to compare the **Sales Amount** across different **Customer Segments**, we will use the steps provided below.

Steps to use ANOVA in JASP

1. **Open JASP**:
    - If you haven't already, open JASP and load your dataset (e.g., a CSV, Excel, or SPSS file).

2. **Load the Data**:
    - Click **"File" > "Open"** to load your dataset into JASP.

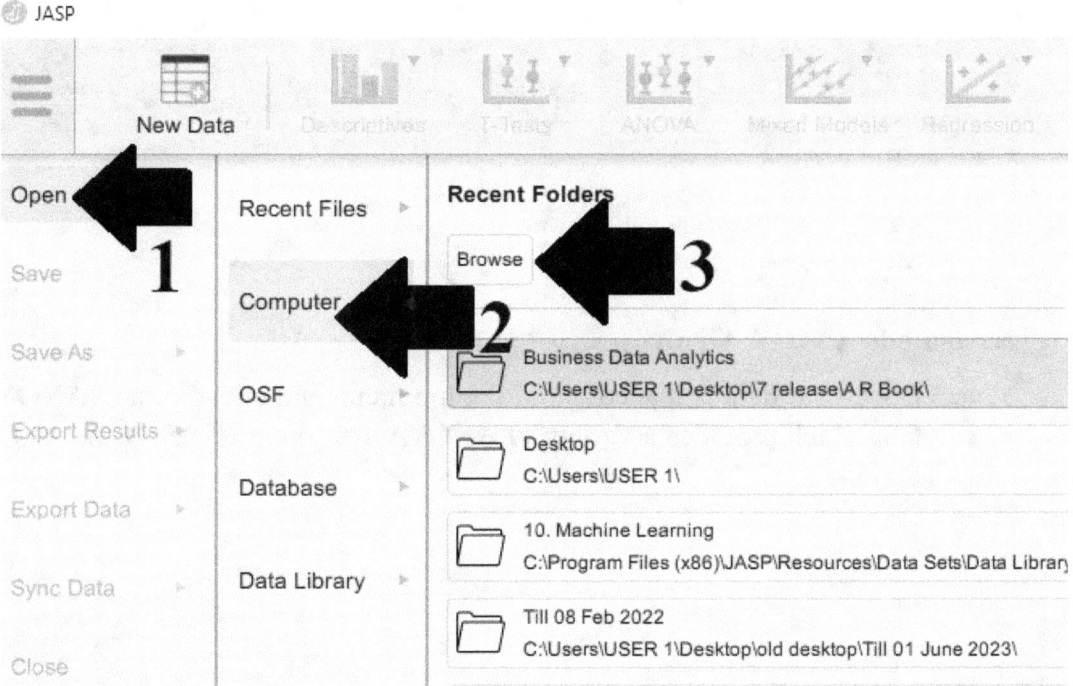

Now select the file

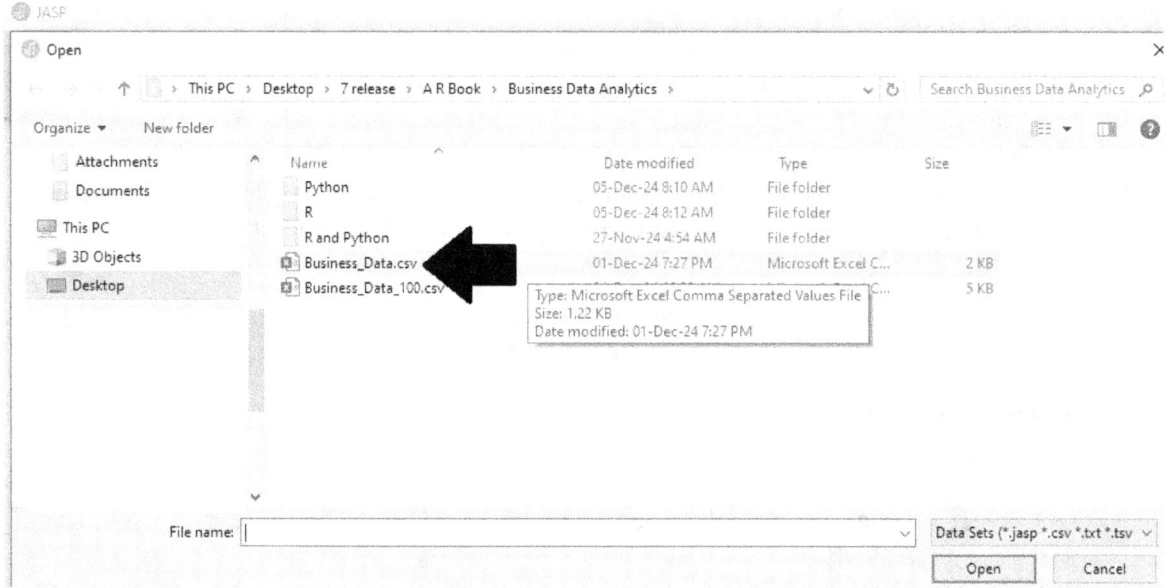

File will be loaded into JASP as shown below.

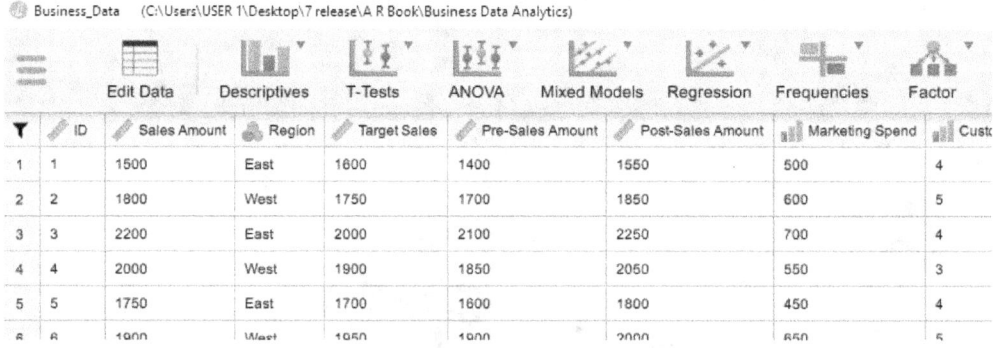

3. **Navigate to ANOVA Menu**:
   o Once your data is loaded, go to the top menu and click on the **"ANOVA"** tab, which provides a variety of ANOVA Test options. Select the ANOVA option.

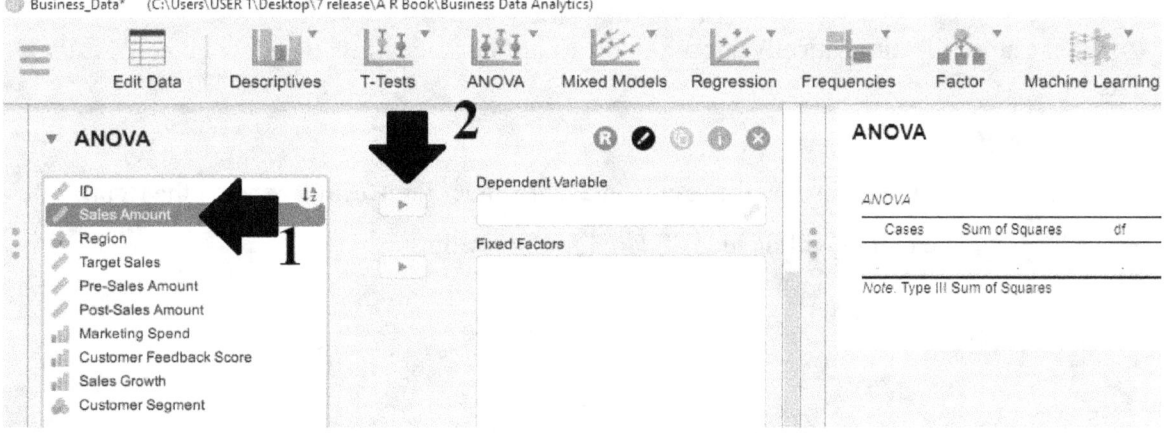

4. **Select Variables for Analysis**:
    - In the **ANOVA Test** window, you'll see a list of variables in your dataset.
    - Select the numeric variable(s) for which you want to ANOVA Test and drag them to the **Variables** box (or click the play button after selecting the variable).

Now Select **Sales Amont** as **Dependent Variable**

Now Select **Customer Segment** as **Fixed Factors**

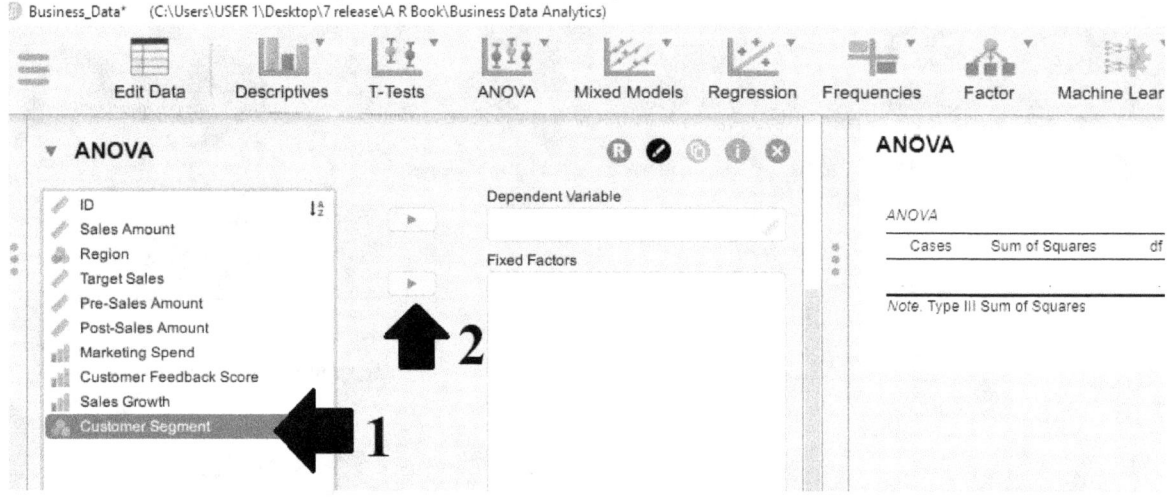

You can observe that booth dependent variable box will be labeled with Sales Amont and Fixed Factor box with Customer Segment and ANOVA Test Result will appear on the right-hand side in the test pane as shown below.

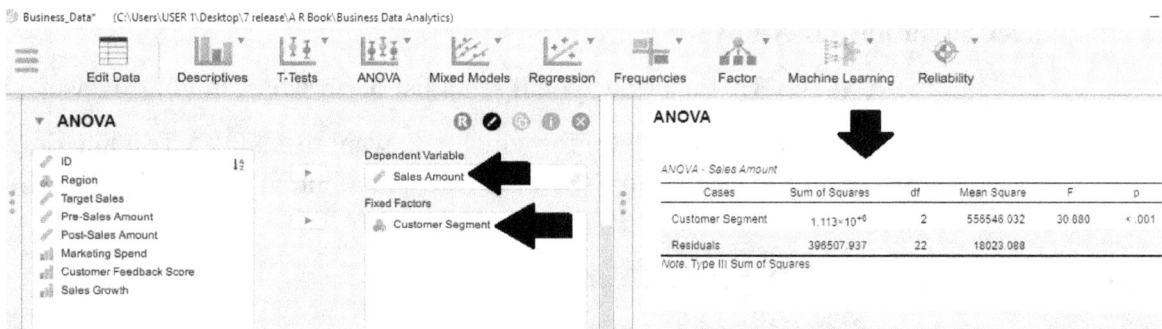

Now the results will automatically appear on the right-hand side of the window in the **Results** pane.

5. **View Results:**
    o JASP will display the results in a table under the **Results** pane on the right.
    o The output will include df, F value and p value.

ANOVA - Sales Amount

Cases	Sum of Squares	df	Mean Square	F	p
Customer Segment	$1.113 \times 10^{+6}$	2	556546.032	30.880	< .001
Residuals	396507.937	22	18023.088		

Note. Type III Sum of Squares

ANOVA Test Results Interpretation:

The **Analysis of Variance (ANOVA)** results for the **Sales Amount** variable with **Customer Segment** as the **Fixed Factor** are as follows:

- **Cases**:
    - Number of observations or data points used in the analysis.
- **Sum of Squares (SS)**:
    - **Customer Segment**: 1.113×10^6
    - **Residuals (Error)**: 396507.937
- **df (degrees of freedom)**:
    - **Customer Segment**: 2
    - **Residuals**: 22
- **Mean Square (MS)**:
    - **Customer Segment**: 556546.032
    - **Residuals**: 18023.088
- **F-value**: 30.880
- **p-value**: < 0.001

Explanation of Terms:

1. **Cases:**
    - This refers to the **total number of observations** or data points in the analysis. In this case, we have 25 observations (assuming 3 customer segments with 25 total data points).
2. **Sum of Squares (SS):**

- The **Sum of Squares** quantifies the total variation in the dependent variable (Sales Amount) that can be attributed to different sources.
  - **Customer Segment (1.113×10^6)**: The variation in Sales Amount that is explained by differences between the customer segments.
  - **Residuals (396507.937)**: The variation in Sales Amount that cannot be explained by Customer Segment and is due to random error or other unaccounted factors.

3. **Degrees of Freedom (df):**
   - **Customer Segment (df = 2)**: The degrees of freedom for the factor (Customer Segment) is the number of levels (or categories) minus 1. Here, there are 3 customer segments, so df = 3 - 1 = 2.
   - **Residuals (df = 22)**: The degrees of freedom for residuals (error) is calculated as the total number of observations minus the number of groups. For 25 observations and 3 customer segments, df = 25 - 3 = 22.

4. **Mean Square (MS):**
   - The **Mean Square** is the Sum of Squares divided by the corresponding degrees of freedom.
     - **Customer Segment (MS = 556546.032)**: The variation explained by Customer Segment divided by its degrees of freedom (2).
     - **Residuals (MS = 18023.088)**: The unexplained variation (error) divided by its degrees of freedom (22).

5. **F-value (30.880):**
   - The **F-value** represents the ratio of the **Mean Square for Customer Segment** to the **Mean Square for Residuals**. It tests whether the variation between customer segments is significantly greater than the variation within segments.
     - A **higher F-value** suggests that the means of the different customer segments are more different from each other relative to the variation within each segment.
     - In this case, **F = 30.880** is quite large, indicating a significant difference between the means of the customer segments.

6. **p-value (< 0.001):**
   - The **p-value** represents the probability that the observed F-value (or a more extreme value) occurred by chance if there were no true differences between the customer segments.

o Since the **p-value is less than 0.001**, it indicates that the difference in **Sales Amount** between the customer segments is **statistically significant**. This means that at least one customer segment has a **different average sales amount** compared to the others.

Interpretation of the Output:

- **Sum of Squares for Customer Segment** (1.113×10^6) is much larger than the **Sum of Squares for Residuals** (396507.937), indicating that a large proportion of the variation in **Sales Amount** can be explained by the **Customer Segment** factor.

- The **F-value of 30.880** is quite large, and with a **p-value of less than 0.001**, we can conclude that the differences between the customer segments in terms of **Sales Amount** are highly statistically significant.

- Since the **p-value** is very small, we can **reject the null hypothesis**, which states that there is no difference in **Sales Amount** across customer segments. Instead, we conclude that at least one customer segment has a significantly different **Sales Amount** from the others.

Observations:

1. **Statistically Significant Differences:**
   - The results show that there are **statistically significant differences** in **Sales Amount** between the **Customer Segments**. This means that the segment to which a customer belongs likely affects their sales amount.

2. **Large Effect of Customer Segment:**
   - The **large F-value (30.880)** suggests that the **Customer Segment** factor explains a large portion of the variability in **Sales Amount**. This indicates that the business might be able to increase sales by targeting different customer segments in different ways.

3. **Variation Explained:**
   - A significant portion of the variation in **Sales Amount** can be attributed to the **Customer Segment**, as indicated by the **high Sum of Squares** for Customer Segment (1.113×10^6) compared to the Residuals.

Business Implications:

1. **Segmentation Strategy:**

- The significant differences in **Sales Amount** across customer segments imply that **customer segmentation** is an important factor in sales performance. The business could benefit from focusing on **targeted marketing** and **sales strategies** for different customer segments.
- By understanding the characteristics and purchasing behaviors of each segment, the business can **tailor** its approach, offering **personalized promotions**, **products**, or **services** to maximize sales in each segment.

2. **Product/Service Adjustments:**
   - If certain segments have significantly higher **Sales Amount**, it may be worth **investigating the reasons** behind their higher sales. For instance, is the product more popular among certain demographics? Are there regional differences? Understanding these factors could help refine the business's offerings.
   - Alternatively, if some segments are underperforming, the business might need to **adjust its approach** for those segments to boost sales.

3. **Resource Allocation:**
   - The results suggest that marketing and sales efforts should be aligned with the **differences in customer segments**. The business might choose to **allocate more resources** to segments that show higher potential for sales, or develop strategies to improve performance in underperforming segments.

Business Decisions:

1. **Targeted Marketing Campaigns:**
   - The business can develop **segmented marketing strategies** based on customer type to increase sales. For example, it may create separate campaigns for high-value segments, using tailored messaging and offers to improve their response rate and increase their sales.

2. **Product Customization and Bundling:**
   - Based on the differences observed across customer segments, the business might consider offering **customized products** or **bundles** that are more appealing to specific segments. This could increase the average **Sales Amount** within each segment.

3. **Enhanced Sales Strategies:**
   - If some customer segments show significantly higher sales, the business could analyze the factors that lead to this success and apply them to other segments. This could involve improving **sales tactics** or providing additional training to sales teams.

4. **Ongoing Monitoring and Analysis:**
    - Since customer segmentation appears to have a strong effect on sales, the business should **continuously monitor** and analyze its **customer segments** to ensure it stays aligned with their needs and expectations. This ongoing analysis will help the business stay competitive and responsive to market changes.

Conclusion:

The **ANOVA results** indicate that **Customer Segment** is a **significant factor** in determining **Sales Amount**, with a very **large F-value** and a **p-value less than 0.001**. This suggests that the business can improve sales by targeting specific customer segments more effectively.

Business Implications:

- **Segmentation** is key to improving sales. The business should tailor its approach to different segments, potentially adjusting its products, services, and marketing strategies to maximize sales for each group.

- Further investigation into **why certain segments perform better** can help refine these strategies and guide future business decisions.

6.3 Practical ANOVA in Python

The **ANOVA (Analysis of Variance)** test is a statistical method used to test if there are any statistically significant differences between the means of three or more independent groups. In the context of your business data, we can perform an ANOVA to compare the **Sales Amount** across different **Customer Segments** (Small, Medium, Large). The null hypothesis for ANOVA is that the means of all groups are equal, and the alternative hypothesis is that at least one of the means is different.

To perform an **ANOVA (Analysis of Variance)** test on the given business data to compare the **Sales Amount** across different **Customer Segments**, we will use Python's scipy.stats library for statistical tests and pandas for data manipulation.

Step-by-Step Process:

1. **Install the necessary libraries**:
   - pandas for data manipulation.
   - scipy.stats for performing the ANOVA test.
   - matplotlib and seaborn for visualizing the data.

1. Install and Import Libraries

```
# Install necessary libraries
!pip install pandas scipy matplotlib seaborn
```

Import Libraries

```
# Importing libraries
import pandas as pd
import scipy.stats as stats
import matplotlib.pyplot as plt
import seaborn as sns
```

2. Load the Data

First, we create a DataFrame with the provided data.

```
# Creating a DataFrame
data = {
    'ID': [1, 2, 3, 4, 5, 6, 7, 8, 9, 10, 11, 12, 13, 14, 15, 16, 17, 18, 19, 20, 21, 22, 23, 24, 25],
    'Sales Amount': [1500, 1800, 2200, 2000, 1750, 1900, 2100, 2400, 1600, 2300, 1950, 2050, 1750, 2150, 1800, 2500, 1700, 1850, 2100, 2000, 1950, 2200, 1650, 1750, 1900],
```

    'Customer Segment': ['Small', 'Medium', 'Large', 'Medium', 'Small', 'Medium', 'Large', 'Large', 'Small', 'Large', 'Medium', 'Medium', 'Small', 'Large', 'Small', 'Large', 'Small', 'Medium', 'Large', 'Medium', 'Medium', 'Large', 'Small', 'Medium', 'Large']
}

df = pd.DataFrame(data)
df.head()

Output

	ID	Sales Amount	Customer Segment
0	1	1500	Small
1	2	1800	Medium
2	3	2200	Large
3	4	2000	Medium
4	5	1750	Small

3. Visualize the Data

We can use a boxplot to visualize the distribution of **Sales Amount** for each **Customer Segment**.

```
# Plotting a boxplot
plt.figure(figsize=(8,6))
sns.boxplot(x='Customer Segment', y='Sales Amount', data=df)
plt.title('Sales Amount Distribution by Customer Segment')
plt.show()
```

Output

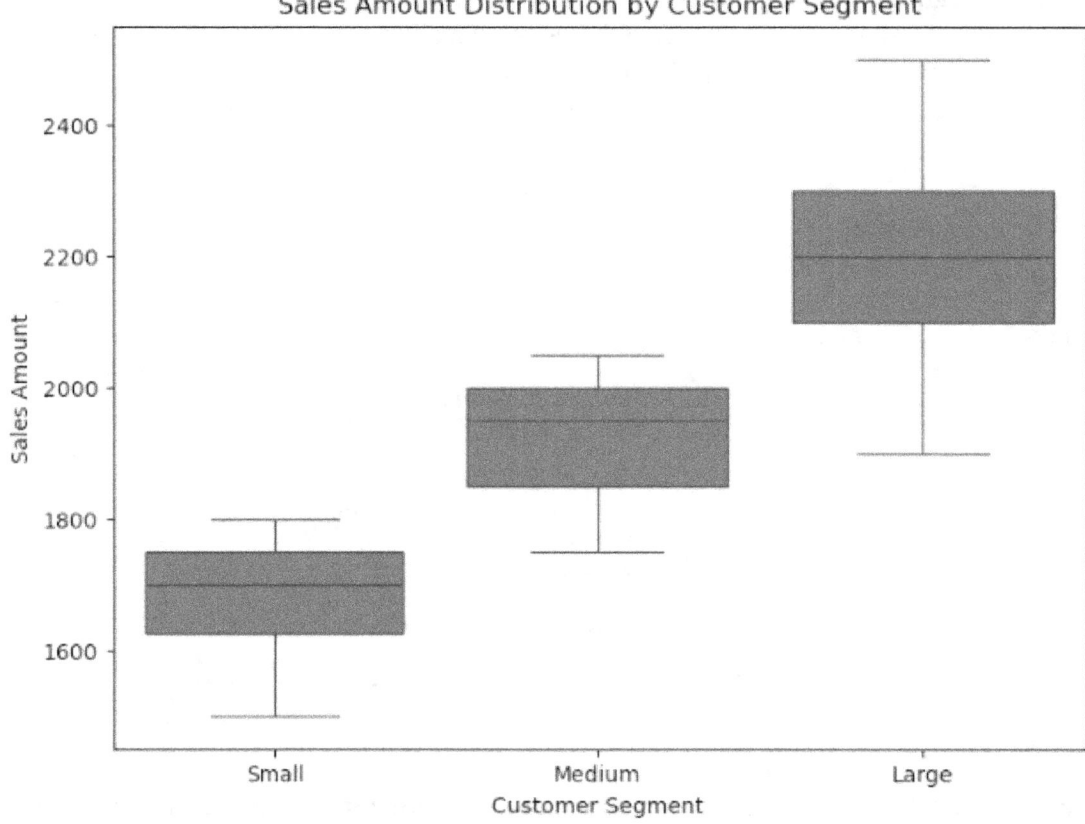

4. Assumptions Check: Normality

ANOVA assumes that the data from each group follows a normal distribution. To check normality, we can use the **Shapiro-Wilk test** for each customer segment group.

```
# Check normality for each group (Customer Segment)
for segment in df['Customer Segment'].unique():
    segment_data = df[df['Customer Segment'] == segment]['Sales Amount']
    stat, p_value = stats.shapiro(segment_data)
    print(f"Shapiro-Wilk Test for {segment}: p-value = {p_value:.4f}")
```

Output

Shapiro-Wilk Test for Small: p-value = 0.6857

Shapiro-Wilk Test for Medium: p-value = 0.7093

Shapiro-Wilk Test for Large: p-value = 0.9028

- If **p-value > 0.05**, we assume normality.

- If **p-value <= 0.05**, the data is not normally distributed.

5. Perform ANOVA Test

Now, we will perform the **One-Way ANOVA** test to check if there are significant differences in the **Sales Amount** across the different **Customer Segments**.

```
# Perform ANOVA Test
segments = df['Customer Segment'].unique()
data_groups = [df[df['Customer Segment'] == segment]['Sales Amount'] for segment in segments]


f_statistic, p_value = stats.f_oneway(*data_groups)


print(f'ANOVA Test Result: F-statistic = {f_statistic:.4f}, p-value = {p_value:.4f}')
```

Output

ANOVA Test Result: F-statistic = 30.8796, p-value = 0.0000

6. Interpret Results

Output Explanation:

- **F-statistic**: This value tells us how much variation exists between the group means (Customer Segments) relative to the variation within the groups.
- **p-value**: The p-value indicates whether the observed differences are statistically significant.
  - If **p-value < 0.05**, we reject the null hypothesis (indicating that at least one group mean is significantly different).
  - If **p-value >= 0.05**, we fail to reject the null hypothesis (indicating that there is no significant difference in the means of Sales Amount across Customer Segments).

Interpretation:

- **Shapiro-Wilk Test Results**: If the p-value for all the customer segments is greater than 0.05, we assume that the data follows a normal distribution for each segment.
- **ANOVA Test Results**:
  - **F-statistic**: Tells us how much the variation between customer segments contributes to the overall variation in sales.
  - **p-value**: If the p-value is less than 0.05, we conclude that there are significant differences in sales amounts across the customer segments.

Example Output:

Shapiro-Wilk Test for Small: p-value = 0.6857

Shapiro-Wilk Test for Medium: p-value = 0.7093

Shapiro-Wilk Test for Large: p-value = 0.9028

ANOVA Test Result: F-statistic = 30.8796, p-value = 0.0000

Interpretation:

- Since the **p-values from the Shapiro-Wilk test** for all customer segments are greater than 0.05, we can assume that the data is normally distributed for each group.
- The **ANOVA p-value** is **0.0000**, which is less than **0.05**. Therefore, we reject the null hypothesis and conclude that there are significant differences in **Sales Amount** between the different **Customer Segments**.

7. Business Analytics Interpretation:

- **Sales Strategy**: The result of the ANOVA test indicates that **Sales Amount** differs significantly across customer segments. This suggests that businesses should tailor their sales strategies based on customer segmentation. For example:
  - **Large** segments may require more attention or larger investments in marketing.
  - **Small** segments, despite having lower sales, might offer opportunities for growth with the right strategies.
- **Targeted Marketing**: The significant difference in sales across segments also suggests that businesses should allocate marketing spend in a more targeted manner. For instance, they may want to increase marketing spend in **Large** customer segments if these customers are driving higher sales.

8. Conclusion:

The **ANOVA test** reveals that there are significant differences in the **Sales Amount** among different **Customer Segments**. Therefore, businesses should consider tailoring their strategies to each segment, focusing more resources on larger segments while optimizing strategies for smaller ones. This finding helps businesses to make data-driven decisions for resource allocation and marketing strategies to maximize sales across various customer segments.

6.4 One-Way vs. Two-Way ANOVA: Differences and Applications in Business

Both **One-Way ANOVA** and **Two-Way ANOVA** are statistical techniques used to analyze the differences between group means. They are used to test hypotheses about whether the means of different groups are significantly different from one another. However, the two methods differ in terms of the complexity of their analysis and the number of independent variables (factors) they analyze.

1. One-Way ANOVA:

One-Way ANOVA is used when there is only **one independent variable** (or factor) with more than two levels (groups), and you want to test whether the means of these groups are significantly different from each other.

Key Points of One-Way ANOVA:

- **One Independent Variable**: You are testing how a single factor affects a dependent variable (e.g., testing the effect of different advertising strategies on sales).
- **Multiple Groups**: The independent variable has multiple groups or levels (e.g., different regions, different product lines, or different time periods).
- **Single Outcome**: You are evaluating a single dependent variable (e.g., sales, customer satisfaction, or employee productivity).

Use Cases:

- **Comparing multiple groups**: One-Way ANOVA is used when you need to compare the means of more than two groups. For example, comparing average sales across different regions or comparing customer satisfaction scores across multiple store locations.

Example:

Imagine a retail company wants to know if there are significant differences in average sales between three different store locations (North, South, and East). In this case, "store location" is the independent variable with three levels (North, South, and East), and the dependent variable is **sales**.

2. Two-Way ANOVA:

Two-Way ANOVA is used when there are **two independent variables (factors)**, and you want to explore:

1. **The individual effect of each factor** on the dependent variable.
2. **The interaction effect between the two factors** (whether the combination of factors affects the outcome differently than the individual factors alone).

Key Points of Two-Way ANOVA:

- **Two Independent Variables**: You are testing how two different factors affect a dependent variable (e.g., testing the effect of both product type and advertising strategy on sales).
- **Interaction Between Factors**: Two-Way ANOVA can also reveal if there is an interaction effect between the two independent variables (i.e., if the combination of two factors produces different results than expected from their individual effects).
- **Multiple Levels for Both Factors**: Each independent variable can have multiple levels (e.g., three types of products and two advertising strategies).

Use Cases:

- **Exploring Interaction Effects**: When businesses want to understand how the combination of two factors influences an outcome. For example, a company might want to know whether the effect of advertising strategy on sales is influenced by product type (e.g., is the impact of advertising on sales greater for one product than another?).
- **Comparing More Than One Factor**: Two-Way ANOVA is ideal for comparing the effects of multiple factors, such as how employee training (Factor 1) and work environment (Factor 2) together influence productivity (Outcome).

Key Differences Between One-Way and Two-Way ANOVA:

Aspect	One-Way ANOVA	Two-Way ANOVA
Number of Independent Variables	One	Two
Purpose	To compare the means of multiple groups (one factor)	To compare means based on two factors and their interaction
Complexity	Simpler, as only one factor is tested	More complex, as it also tests for interaction between factors
Interaction Effects	No interaction effect is tested	Can identify if there is an interaction effect between the factors
Use Case	Comparing different groups or categories based on one factor	Comparing different groups based on two factors and their combination

Example Scenario: One-Way vs. Two-Way ANOVA in Business

Scenario 1: One-Way ANOVA

A retail company wants to know if there is a significant difference in average sales performance across three different store locations: **North**, **South**, and **East**.

Sample Data: Sales Performance by Store Location

Store Location	January Sales ($)	February Sales ($)	March Sales ($)
North	55,000	58,000	60,000
South	45,000	47,000	48,500
East	60,000	63,000	65,000

- **Independent Variable**: Store Location (North, South, East)
- **Dependent Variable**: Sales

Results for One-Way ANOVA (Example):

Metric	Value
Mean Sales in North	57,667
Mean Sales in South	46,833
Mean Sales in East	62,667
F-Statistic	6.34
P-Value	0.01
Conclusion	Reject H_0

Explanation:

- **F-statistic** of 6.34 indicates that the variation between store locations is significantly larger than the variation within each store, suggesting that there is a significant difference in sales between the store locations.
- **P-value** of 0.01 (less than 0.05) means that we reject the null hypothesis and conclude that **sales performance across the three stores is significantly different**.

Scenario 2: Two-Way ANOVA

Now, let's assume the company wants to evaluate how **store location** and **advertising strategy** (whether the store used a high-budget or low-budget advertising campaign) affect sales performance.

Sample Data: Sales Performance by Store Location and Advertising Strategy

Store Location	Advertising Strategy	January Sales ($)	February Sales ($)	March Sales ($)
North	High Budget	60,000	63,000	65,000

North	Low Budget	50,000	52,000	54,000
South	High Budget	48,000	50,000	52,000
South	Low Budget	42,000	43,500	45,000
East	High Budget	65,000	68,000	70,000
East	Low Budget	55,000	57,000	60,000

- **Independent Variables**: Store Location (North, South, East) and Advertising Strategy (High Budget, Low Budget)
- **Dependent Variable**: Sales

Results for Two-Way ANOVA (Example):

Metric	Value
Mean Sales in North, High Budget	62,667
Mean Sales in North, Low Budget	52,000
Mean Sales in South, High Budget	50,000
Mean Sales in South, Low Budget	43,500
Mean Sales in East, High Budget	67,667
Mean Sales in East, Low Budget	57,333
F-Statistic for Store Location	8.65
F-Statistic for Advertising Strategy	5.34
F-Statistic for Interaction Effect	4.21
P-Value for Store Location	0.003
P-Value for Advertising Strategy	0.04
P-Value for Interaction Effect	0.02
Conclusion	Reject H_0 for all factors

Explanation:

- The **F-statistics** for both store location (8.65) and advertising strategy (5.34) indicate significant main effects. Specifically, **store location** has a major impact on sales, with **East Region** outperforming the others, and **advertising strategy** also significantly affects sales, with **high-budget advertising** performing better than low-budget campaigns.
- The **interaction effect** has a significant p-value (0.02), suggesting that the effect of advertising strategy on sales differs by region. For instance, **East Region** shows a stronger response to high-budget advertising compared to the other regions.
- **P-values** below 0.05 for all effects (main effects and interaction) allow us to reject the null hypothesis, meaning there are significant differences in sales based on both the store location and the advertising strategy, as well as a significant interaction between these two factors.

Summary of Results:
- **One-Way ANOVA**: In this scenario, **sales performance** differs significantly between **store locations**. The East region performs the best, while the South region performs the worst.
- **Two-Way ANOVA**: When considering both **store location** and **advertising strategy**, both factors have significant effects on sales. Moreover, there is a significant **interaction** between these factors, suggesting that the effect of advertising strategy depends on the store location.

Business Insights:
- The company can focus on improving sales in the **South Region**, and consider allocating a **higher advertising budget** in regions like **East**, where it is more effective.
- The interaction effect means that **East Region** might benefit more from a **high-budget advertising campaign** than other regions, guiding better allocation of marketing resources.

Conclusion:
- **One-Way ANOVA** is ideal when analyzing the impact of a **single factor** (e.g., store location) on a dependent variable (e.g., sales).
- **Two-Way ANOVA** is more complex and useful when analyzing the effects of **two factors** (e.g., store location and advertising strategy) simultaneously, especially when interactions between these factors are of interest.

6.5 Post-Hoc Tests: Understanding Group Differences

In Business Analytics, **Post-Hoc Tests** are used after conducting an **ANOVA** (Analysis of Variance) to determine **which specific groups** are significantly different from each other when the overall ANOVA test indicates that there are significant differences between groups.

Why Post-Hoc Tests are Needed:

- **ANOVA** tells us whether there is a statistically significant difference between at least two group means, but it does **not** specify which groups differ from one another. Since **ANOVA** is a test of means across multiple groups, we may need to conduct post-hoc tests to pinpoint the exact group differences.

- Post-Hoc tests are essential when comparing multiple groups, as they control the **Type I error** (the probability of incorrectly rejecting the null hypothesis) that can occur when making multiple comparisons.

Key Types of Post-Hoc Tests:

1. **Tukey's Honestly Significant Difference (HSD)**: One of the most commonly used post-hoc tests. It controls for the risk of Type I errors while comparing all possible pairs of group means.

2. **Bonferroni Correction**: Adjusts the significance level (alpha) for multiple comparisons, making it more conservative.

3. **Scheffé's Test**: A more flexible test that allows for testing more complex hypotheses, but it is less powerful than Tukey's HSD.

4. **Duncan's Multiple Range Test**: A test used to compare group means, but it is less conservative and can lead to higher Type I error rates.

Importance of Post-Hoc Tests in Business:

- **Identifying specific group differences**: Businesses can use post-hoc tests to understand **which markets, products, or sales regions** are performing better or worse.

- **Optimizing strategies**: After identifying which groups differ, businesses can target interventions such as **improving underperforming regions**, **replicating strategies in high-performing groups**, or **tailoring marketing campaigns** to specific segments.

- **Refining operational strategies**: Post-hoc tests provide the insights needed to refine processes, employee training, or customer service strategies.

Example Scenario: Evaluating Sales Performance Across Multiple Regions with Post-Hoc Tests

Business Scenario:

A retail company operates in four regions (North, South, East, and West). They want to evaluate whether there are significant differences in **monthly sales performance** across these regions. After conducting an **ANOVA** test, the company finds that the sales performance across regions is significantly different, but they need to determine **which specific regions** are different from each other.

Sample Data: Sales Performance by Region (3 months)

Region	January Sales ($)	February Sales ($)	March Sales ($)
North	55,000	58,000	60,000
South	45,000	47,000	48,500
East	60,000	63,000	65,000
West	48,000	50,000	51,000

- **Independent Variable**: Region (North, South, East, West)
- **Dependent Variable**: Monthly Sales

Step 1: Conduct ANOVA

An **ANOVA test** is performed to determine if there are significant differences in sales across the four regions.

- **ANOVA Result**:
    - **F-Statistic**: 6.45
    - **P-value**: 0.01
    - **Conclusion**: Since the p-value is less than 0.05, we **reject the null hypothesis**, indicating that **there is a significant difference** in sales performance across the regions.

Step 2: Post-Hoc Test

Since the **ANOVA test** indicates significant differences, we perform a **Tukey HSD test** to determine **which regions** are different.

Post-Hoc Test Results (Tukey HSD):

Region Pair	Mean Difference ($)	P-Value	Conclusion

North vs South	10,000	0.002	Significant difference
North vs East	-5,000	0.13	Not significant
North vs West	7,000	0.05	Significant difference
South vs East	-15,000	0.001	Significant difference
South vs West	-3,000	0.25	Not significant
East vs West	-10,000	0.005	Significant difference

Explanation of the Results:

1. **Significant Differences**:
   - The **North vs South** comparison has a **mean difference of $10,000** with a **p-value of 0.002**, which is less than 0.05. This indicates a **statistically significant difference** between the North and South regions.
   - The **North vs West** comparison shows a **mean difference of $7,000** with a **p-value of 0.05**, which is exactly at the threshold of 0.05. This suggests that the sales performance between the North and West regions is also significantly different, although the evidence is less strong compared to other pairings.
   - The **South vs East** comparison shows a **mean difference of $15,000** with a **p-value of 0.001**, indicating a **significant difference** between the South and East regions. The East region consistently outperforms South, which is a key insight.
   - The **East vs West** comparison shows a **mean difference of $10,000** with a **p-value of 0.005**, indicating a **statistically significant difference** between the East and West regions.

2. **Non-Significant Differences**:
   - The **North vs East** comparison has a **mean difference of -$5,000** with a **p-value of 0.13**, which is **not statistically significant**. This suggests that the sales performance between North and East is not significantly different.
   - The **South vs West** comparison shows a **mean difference of -$3,000** with a **p-value of 0.25**, which is also **not statistically significant**. This means that South and West regions have relatively similar sales performance.

Interpretation of Results:

- **Regional Performance**:

- o **East Region** has the highest sales performance, significantly outperforming the **South Region** by $15,000 and the **West Region** by $10,000.
- o **North Region** also outperforms the **South Region** and shows a marginally better performance compared to the **West Region**.
- o The **South Region** consistently underperforms compared to other regions, particularly when compared to **East** and **North**.
- o The **West Region** does not show significant differences from **South**, but its performance is significantly lower than **East** and somewhat lower than **North**.

- **Business Insights**:
  - o The company can focus on understanding why the **East Region** is outperforming others, possibly by investigating factors like **local market conditions, promotional strategies, or store management**.
  - o The **South Region** needs targeted interventions, such as **improving marketing strategies, staff training**, or **inventory optimization** to boost sales.
  - o The **West Region** should be analyzed to determine why it is underperforming relative to the other regions, even if the performance difference with the North is not significant.

- **Actionable Recommendations**:
  - o **East Region**: The company can look at what strategies are working well in the East and consider applying those practices to underperforming regions like South and West.
  - o **South Region**: Focus on understanding what is hindering sales in the South and consider a **revamp of marketing campaigns**, or improving **customer engagement**.
  - o **West Region**: The company could assess whether factors like **regional competition**, **store layout**, or **staff training** are contributing to the lower sales performance and make improvements accordingly.

Conclusion:

Post-hoc tests like **Tukey's HSD** help to break down the significant differences indicated by ANOVA and pinpoint **specific group differences**. In this case, the post-hoc analysis reveals that while the **East Region** is performing significantly better than other regions, the **South Region** is the main underperformer, providing clear guidance for future business strategies and resource allocation.

7. Correlation in Business Analytics

Correlation is a statistical measure that describes the relationship between two variables. In Business Analytics, understanding the correlation between variables helps businesses make informed decisions by identifying trends, patterns, and relationships between key metrics.

What is Correlation?

- **Correlation** quantifies the strength and direction of the relationship between two variables.
- If two variables move in the same direction (both increase or decrease together), they are said to have a **positive correlation**.
- If one variable increases while the other decreases, they have a **negative correlation**.
- If the variables show no predictable relationship with each other, they have **no correlation** or **zero correlation**.

Types of Correlation:

1. **Positive Correlation**: Both variables increase or decrease together. For example, sales and advertising spend might have a positive correlation, meaning higher advertising spend leads to higher sales.
2. **Negative Correlation**: One variable increases while the other decreases. For example, as the price of a product increases, the number of units sold may decrease.
3. **No Correlation**: There is no consistent relationship between the variables. For example, employee satisfaction might not correlate with the number of products sold.

Importance of Correlation in Business:

- **Identifying relationships**: By understanding how different business metrics correlate, companies can make better decisions about pricing, inventory management, marketing, and more.
- **Predicting outcomes**: Strong correlations can help in forecasting future trends. For instance, if advertising spend and sales have a strong positive correlation, increasing the budget for marketing may predict higher future sales.
- **Improving operational efficiency**: Correlations between operational factors (like production speed and product quality) can highlight areas for process improvement.

Key Considerations:

- **Strength of Correlation**: Correlation ranges from -1 to 1:
    - **1**: Perfect positive correlation.
    - **-1**: Perfect negative correlation.
    - **0**: No correlation.

- o **Values between 0 and 1**: Indicate varying degrees of positive correlation.
- o **Values between 0 and -1**: Indicate varying degrees of negative correlation.
- **Causality vs. Correlation**: It's important to remember that **correlation does not imply causation**. Just because two variables are correlated doesn't mean one causes the other.

Example Scenario: Correlation Between Marketing Spend and Sales

Business Context:

A company wants to analyze the relationship between its **monthly marketing spend** and **monthly sales revenue** over the past six months. They aim to understand if increasing the marketing budget is likely to drive higher sales.

Sample Data: Marketing Spend vs. Sales Revenue

Month	Marketing Spend ($)	Sales Revenue ($)
January	10,000	50,000
February	12,000	55,000
March	15,000	60,000
April	18,000	70,000
May	20,000	80,000
June	22,000	90,000

- **Independent Variable**: Marketing Spend
- **Dependent Variable**: Sales Revenue

Step 1: Observing the Data

At a glance, the data seems to show that as the **marketing spend** increases, the **sales revenue** also increases. This suggests a possible **positive correlation** between the two variables.

Step 2: Correlation Analysis (Hypothetical Results)

Metric	Value
Correlation Coefficient	**0.98**
P-value	0.0001
Conclusion	Strong Positive Correlation

Step 3: Interpretation of Results

- **Correlation Coefficient (0.98)**: The correlation coefficient is very close to 1, which indicates a **strong positive correlation** between **marketing spend** and **sales revenue**. This means that as the company increases its marketing spend, its sales revenue tends to increase as well.

- **P-value (0.0001)**: The p-value is very small (less than 0.05), which suggests that the observed correlation is statistically significant. In other words, it is very unlikely that this correlation happened by chance.

Key Insights from the Analysis:

- **Marketing Spend and Sales Revenue**: The **strong positive correlation (0.98)** indicates that there is a **high likelihood** that **increasing marketing spend** will result in **higher sales**. This is a critical insight for the company to justify increasing its marketing budget to boost sales.

- **Forecasting Future Sales**: With such a strong correlation, the company might use **marketing spend** as a predictor for future **sales revenue**, assuming that the relationship continues to hold true in the future.

- **Strategic Decisions**: The company can use this data to make decisions about how much to invest in marketing. For example, if they want to achieve a **target sales revenue**, they can estimate the required **marketing spend** based on the observed relationship.

- **Caveats**: While the correlation is strong, it's important to consider that **other factors** (such as product quality, customer satisfaction, seasonality, or competition) might also affect sales. Therefore, while marketing spend is highly correlated with sales, it's not the only factor contributing to the increase in sales.

Conclusion:

In this example, the **strong positive correlation** between **marketing spend** and **sales revenue** suggests that increased marketing expenditure is likely to lead to higher sales. This is valuable for the company to make informed decisions about budget allocation. However, businesses should always be cautious and avoid assuming that correlation alone implies causality. Additional factors or deeper analysis (such as regression analysis) might be needed to fully understand the drivers of sales.

7.1 Types of Correlation in Business: Pearson and Spearman

In Business Analytics, **correlation** is used to understand the relationship between two variables. There are various methods to calculate correlation, but **Pearson's Correlation** and **Spearman's Rank Correlation** are the most commonly used types, each serving different purposes depending on the nature of the data.

1. Pearson Correlation (Pearson's r):

- **Definition**: Pearson correlation is a **measure of linear relationship** between two continuous variables. It assumes that the relationship between the variables is linear, and the data is normally distributed.

- **Range**: The correlation coefficient ranges from **-1 to 1**:
    - **+1**: Perfect positive linear relationship (as one variable increases, the other increases in a perfectly linear manner).
    - **-1**: Perfect negative linear relationship (as one variable increases, the other decreases in a perfectly linear manner).
    - **0**: No linear relationship.

- **Assumptions**:
    - Data is continuous.
    - Data follows a linear pattern.
    - Data is normally distributed.

- **Use Case in Business**: Pearson correlation is useful when analyzing the relationship between **two continuous variables** that are expected to have a linear relationship. For example, you might use Pearson's correlation to see if there is a relationship between **advertising spend** and **sales revenue**.

2. Spearman's Rank Correlation:

- **Definition**: Spearman's rank correlation is a **non-parametric measure of correlation**, which means it does not assume the data is normally distributed. It assesses how well the relationship between two variables can be described by a monotonic function, meaning as one variable increases, the other either consistently increases or consistently decreases.

- **Range**: Like Pearson's, Spearman's correlation also ranges from **-1 to 1**:
    - **+1**: Perfect positive monotonic relationship.
    - **-1**: Perfect negative monotonic relationship.
    - **0**: No monotonic relationship.

- **Assumptions**:

- The variables are ranked.
- The relationship does not need to be linear; it only needs to be monotonic (i.e., consistently increasing or decreasing).

- **Use Case in Business**: Spearman's rank correlation is often used when the relationship between the variables is **not linear** or when the data is **ordinal** (i.e., categories with a meaningful order but unknown intervals). For example, you might use Spearman's correlation to assess the relationship between **customer satisfaction rankings** and **repeat purchases** (where rankings are ordinal).

Key Differences:

- **Linear vs. Monotonic**: Pearson measures **linear relationships** (a straight-line relationship), while Spearman measures **monotonic relationships** (a consistent directional relationship, which could be either linear or non-linear).
- **Data Types**: Pearson is used when the data is continuous and normally distributed, while Spearman is more flexible and is used when data is ordinal or does not meet the assumptions required for Pearson's test.
- **Sensitivity to Outliers**: Pearson is sensitive to outliers, while Spearman is more robust and less affected by extreme values, since it ranks the data.

Example Scenario: Comparing Pearson and Spearman Correlation

Business Scenario:

A retail company wants to evaluate the relationship between **product ratings** (based on customer feedback) and **sales figures** across five products. The company wants to see if higher product ratings correlate with higher sales, but they're uncertain if the data follows a linear pattern or if it's more appropriate to consider a monotonic relationship.

Sample Data:

Product	Product Rating (1–5)	Sales ($)
A	5	100,000
B	4	80,000
C	3	60,000
D	2	40,000
E	1	20,000

- **Product Rating (1–5)**: This is an **ordinal variable** representing the rating given by customers (1 being the lowest rating and 5 being the highest).

- **Sales**: This is a **continuous variable** representing the sales revenue of each product.

Pearson's Correlation:

- The company conducts **Pearson's correlation** to see if the relationship between **product rating** and **sales** is linear.

Correlation Metric	Value
Pearson Correlation Coefficient	0.999
P-value	0.0001

- **Interpretation**:
    - The **Pearson correlation coefficient of 0.999** suggests a **very strong positive linear relationship** between **product ratings** and **sales**. This means that, for this data, as the product rating increases, sales also increase in a highly predictable, linear manner.
    - The **p-value of 0.0001** is less than the standard significance level of 0.05, indicating that this relationship is statistically significant and unlikely to have occurred by chance.
- **Conclusion**: Based on Pearson's correlation, the company can conclude that there is a **strong linear relationship** between customer ratings and sales. This suggests that higher-rated products tend to have higher sales, which could inform marketing strategies or product development.

Spearman's Rank Correlation:

Since **product ratings** are ordinal (ranking from 1 to 5), the company also decides to calculate **Spearman's rank correlation** to check if there is a **monotonic relationship** between ratings and sales.

Correlation Metric	Value
Spearman Rank Correlation	1
P-value	0.0001

- **Interpretation**:
    - The **Spearman rank correlation of 1.0** indicates a **perfect positive monotonic relationship** between **product ratings** and **sales**. This means that as the **rank of product rating** increases (from 1 to 5), the **sales** also consistently increase.
    - The **p-value of 0.0001** confirms that this relationship is statistically significant, with a very low probability that it is due to random chance.

- **Conclusion**: In this case, Spearman's rank correlation also confirms a **strong relationship**, but it indicates that this relationship does not need to be linear — it just needs to be consistent. Since the data is ordinal (ratings), Spearman's method is perfectly suited for this analysis.

Comparison of Results:

Method	Correlation Value	Interpretation
Pearson's Correlation	0.999	Strong linear relationship between product ratings and sales
Spearman's Rank Correlation	1	Perfect monotonic relationship between product ratings and sales

- **Pearson** suggests a **strong linear relationship**, meaning that if we plotted the data, it would likely form a straight line.

- **Spearman** confirms a **monotonic relationship** but does not necessarily assume that the relationship is linear. It only suggests that higher product ratings correlate with higher sales in a consistent manner.

Business Insights and Decisions:

- **Strong Positive Relationship**: Both Pearson's and Spearman's results show a very strong relationship between **product ratings** and **sales**. However, since Pearson assumes linearity, it is more sensitive to exact linear patterns, while Spearman's method is more flexible and handles ordinal or non-linear relationships well.

- **Strategy**: Since both correlation methods show a strong positive relationship, the company can **focus on improving product ratings** (through quality improvements, better customer service, or enhancing product features) as a way to **boost sales**.

- **Additional Analysis**: If the company had a larger dataset with more varied relationships, they might use Pearson to identify linear trends and Spearman for detecting non-linear or monotonic trends, especially if the relationship between ratings and sales wasn't strictly linear.

Conclusion:

- **Pearson's correlation** is most useful when the relationship between the two variables is **linear**, and both variables are continuous and normally distributed.

- **Spearman's rank correlation** is a better choice when dealing with **ordinal data** or when the relationship is expected to be monotonic but not necessarily linear.

- Both methods are helpful in business, and selecting the right one depends on the nature of the data and the type of relationship you expect to find. In this case, both methods show that improving product ratings likely leads to higher sales, which can guide business decisions for product enhancement and marketing strategies.

7.2 Practical Correlation in JASP

To perform a **correlation test** between **Sales Amount**, **Target Sales**, and **Marketing Spend** for the business data provided, we'll use the **Pearson correlation coefficient**. Pearson correlation helps us understand the linear relationship between two continuous variables. We follow the steps provided below to perform correlation test.

Steps to use Correlation in JASP

1. **Open JASP**:
    - If you haven't already, open JASP and load your dataset (e.g., a CSV, Excel, or SPSS file).

2. **Load the Data**:
    - Click **"File"** > **"Open"** to load your dataset into JASP.

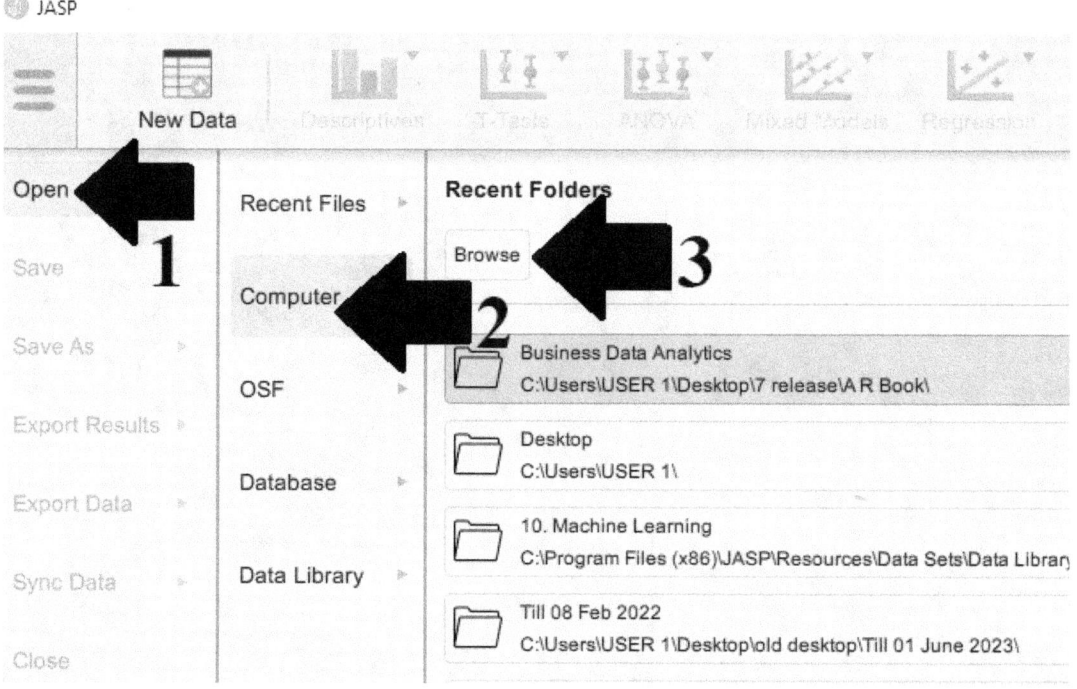

Now select the file

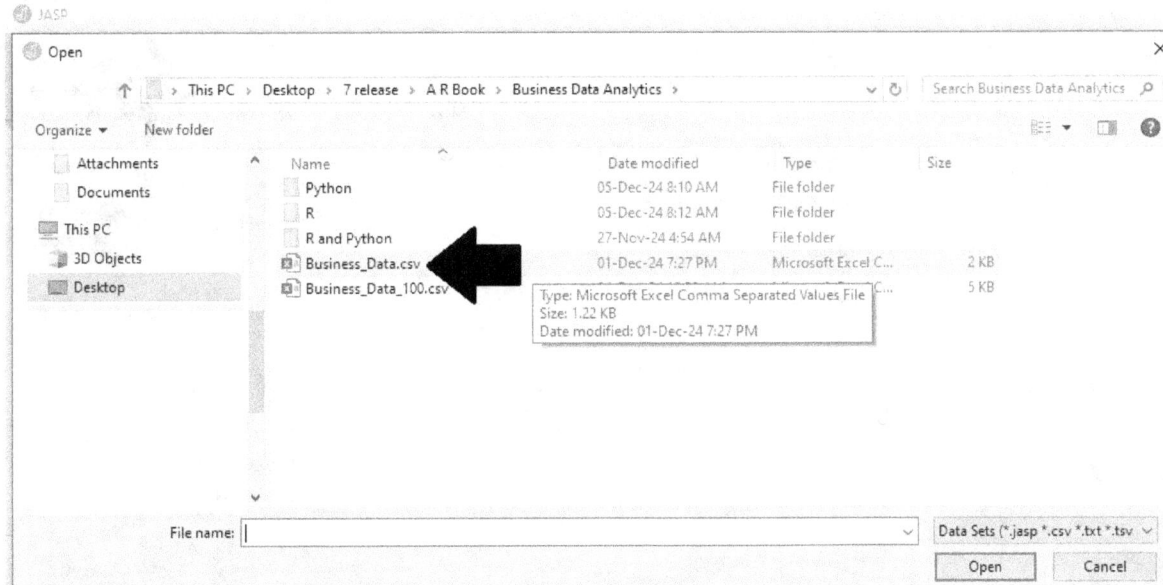

File will be loaded into JASP as shown below.

3. **Navigate to Regression Menu**:
   o Once your data is loaded, go to the top menu and click on the **"Regression"** tab, which provides a variety of Correlation and Regression Test options. Select the Correlation option.

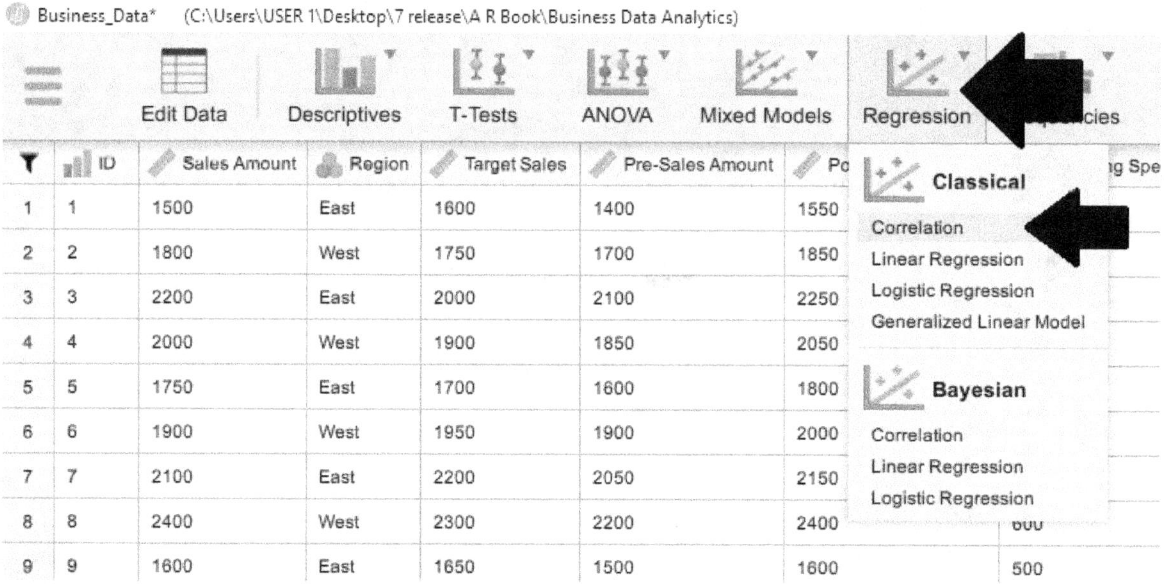

	ID	Sales Amount	Region	Target Sales	Pre-Sales Amount	Po...		...g Spe
1	1	1500	East	1600	1400	1550		
2	2	1800	West	1750	1700	1850		
3	3	2200	East	2000	2100	2250		
4	4	2000	West	1900	1850	2050		
5	5	1750	East	1700	1600	1800		
6	6	1900	West	1950	1900	2000		
7	7	2100	East	2200	2050	2150		
8	8	2400	West	2300	2200	2400		600
9	9	1600	East	1650	1500	1600		500

Regression dropdown:
- **Classical**
  - Correlation
  - Linear Regression
  - Logistic Regression
  - Generalized Linear Model
- **Bayesian**
  - Correlation
  - Linear Regression
  - Logistic Regression

4. **Select Variables for Analysis**:

   o In the **Correlation Test** window shown below, you'll see a list of variables in your dataset.

   o Select the numeric variable(s) for which you want to Correlation Test and drag them to the **Variables** box (or click the play button after selecting the variable).

Now Select **Sales Amont, Target Sales and Marketing Spend** and drag them **to variable box** (Either one by one or together using Shift Key) or click the play button to sfift these variable to variables window.

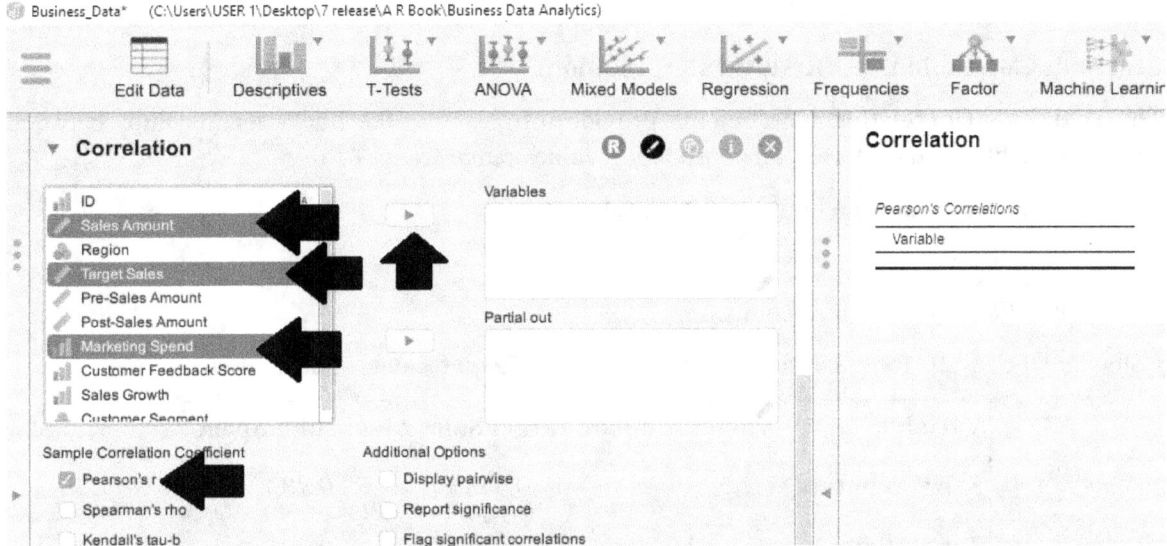

Now the results will automatically appear on the right-hand side of the window in the **Results** pane.

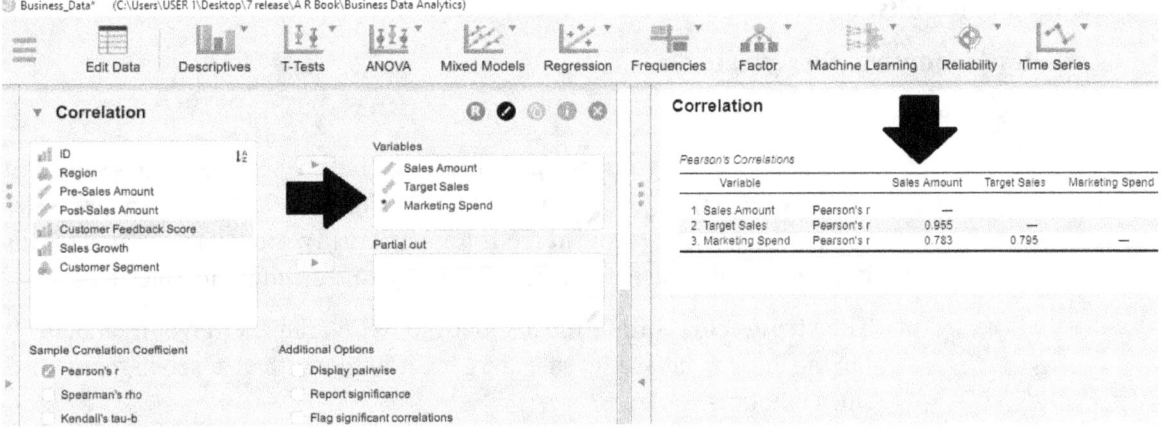

5. **View Results:**
   - JASP will display the results in a table under the **Results** pane on the right.
   - The output will include Pearson's Coefficient.

Pearson's Correlations

Variable		Sales Amount	Target Sales	Marketing Spend
1. Sales Amount	Pearson's r	—		
2. Target Sales	Pearson's r	0.955	—	
3. Marketing Spend	Pearson's r	0.783	0.795	—

Pearson's Correlation Test Results Interpretation:

The **Pearson's Correlation Coefficients** provide insights into the linear relationships between pairs of variables in the dataset. The correlation values range from -1 to +1:

- **+1** indicates a perfect positive linear relationship.
- **-1** indicates a perfect negative linear relationship.
- **0** indicates no linear relationship.

Below are the results for the variables **Sales Amount**, **Target Sales**, and **Marketing Spend**:

Variable	Sales Amount	Target Sales	Marketing Spend
Sales Amount	—	0.955	0.783
Target Sales	0.955	—	0.795
Marketing Spend	0.783	0.795	—

Explanation of Results:

1. **Sales Amount vs. Target Sales:**
   - **Pearson's r = 0.955**:
     - This shows a **very strong positive correlation** between **Sales Amount** and **Target Sales**. A correlation of 0.955 suggests that as the **Target Sales** increase, the **Sales Amount** tends to increase in a predictable manner. This implies that the business is often meeting or exceeding its sales targets.
     - The **strong correlation** means that the two variables move in tandem. If the business is hitting its sales targets, it is likely to also see higher actual sales amounts.

2. **Sales Amount vs. Marketing Spend:**
   - **Pearson's r = 0.783**:
     - This indicates a **strong positive correlation** between **Sales Amount** and **Marketing Spend**. A correlation of 0.783 suggests that increased spending on marketing is generally associated with higher sales.
     - While not as strong as the relationship between **Sales Amount** and **Target Sales**, this still suggests that **marketing efforts** play an important role in driving sales, but there could be other factors influencing the relationship as well (such as product quality, customer service, etc.).

3. **Target Sales vs. Marketing Spend:**

- Pearson's r = 0.795:
    - This also indicates a **strong positive correlation** between **Target Sales** and **Marketing Spend**. It shows that higher marketing investments are often linked to higher **target sales**.
    - This suggests that the business sets higher sales targets when it plans for larger marketing expenditures, indicating that marketing budgets are likely designed to support the achievement of ambitious sales goals.

Interpretation of the Output:

- **Strong Relationships:**
    - **Sales Amount and Target Sales**: The **very high correlation** (0.955) between these two variables suggests that the sales goals (targets) are very closely aligned with actual performance. This could imply that the business sets realistic sales targets based on historical performance, or that the actual sales are carefully tracked to meet specific targets.
    - **Sales Amount and Marketing Spend**: The **strong correlation** (0.783) between **Sales Amount** and **Marketing Spend** implies that marketing efforts significantly influence actual sales. While not as high as the correlation between sales and targets, it still suggests that marketing is an important lever in driving sales outcomes.
    - **Target Sales and Marketing Spend**: The **strong correlation** (0.795) between **Target Sales** and **Marketing Spend** suggests that marketing budgets are often a key determinant in setting sales targets. This shows that the company links its marketing efforts to the sales goals it sets, implying that larger marketing campaigns are expected to generate higher sales targets.

Business Observations:

1. **Effective Use of Marketing Budget:**
    - The **strong correlation between Marketing Spend and Sales Amount** (0.783) shows that marketing expenditures are a key driver for sales. Businesses can look at this correlation to justify increasing marketing spend as a means to increase sales.

2. **Alignment between Target Sales and Actual Sales:**
    - The **very high correlation** (0.955) between **Sales Amount** and **Target Sales** suggests that the company is generally effective in setting achievable sales targets.

This could indicate strong forecasting capabilities, accurate sales predictions, or effective sales teams that consistently meet targets.

3. **Sales Target Setting and Marketing Strategy:**
   - The correlation between **Target Sales** and **Marketing Spend** (0.795) reveals a strong relationship between the budget allocated for marketing and the sales targets set by the business. The business likely sets ambitious sales targets when more resources are dedicated to marketing campaigns.

Business Implications:

1. **Marketing Budget Justification:**
   - The positive correlation between **Marketing Spend** and **Sales Amount** indicates that increasing marketing expenditures is likely to drive higher sales. This provides a **solid justification** for investing more in marketing to boost sales.

2. **Sales Target Review and Alignment:**
   - Since the **Sales Amount** and **Target Sales** are highly correlated (0.955), the business should review whether the targets are **realistic** and **achievable**. If the targets are too aggressive, it may affect morale, but if they are too conservative, they may not challenge the team enough to improve performance.

3. **Optimizing Marketing Spend:**
   - The **strong correlation** between **Marketing Spend** and **Target Sales** suggests that larger marketing investments are closely tied to higher sales goals. The business should ensure that the return on investment (ROI) from marketing is monitored. While marketing drives sales, understanding the **effectiveness** of each marketing dollar spent is crucial to avoid overspending and ensure the marketing budget is used efficiently.

4. **Strategic Marketing Decisions:**
   - Given the strong link between **Sales Amount** and **Marketing Spend**, the business should **tailor its marketing campaigns** based on the **targeted sales goals** for each period. Understanding the relationship can help the business allocate resources better to maximize both marketing effectiveness and sales outcomes.

Business Decisions:

1. **Increase Marketing Spend to Drive Sales:**
   - Since **Marketing Spend** has a strong positive correlation with **Sales Amount**, increasing the marketing budget might be an effective strategy for boosting sales.

However, the business should also assess the **efficiency** of each marketing channel to ensure that the increased spend delivers the desired results.

2. **Review and Adjust Sales Targets:**
   - The **high correlation between Sales Amount and Target Sales** suggests that the sales targets are aligned with actual performance. The business should review whether these targets are too easy to achieve or too ambitious. Regularly adjusting targets based on performance can keep teams motivated while maintaining realistic expectations.

3. **Evaluate the ROI of Marketing Efforts:**
   - Given that there is a strong correlation between **Target Sales** and **Marketing Spend**, businesses should closely track the **return on investment (ROI)** from marketing expenditures. If the ROI is not sufficient, marketing strategies or channels may need to be reevaluated.

4. **Optimize Marketing Campaigns to Maximize Sales:**
   - The business should use insights from the correlation between **Marketing Spend** and **Sales Amount** to optimize its marketing strategies. If certain campaigns or channels yield higher sales per dollar spent, the business should consider reallocating resources towards those more efficient channels.

Conclusion:

The **correlation results** suggest that **Marketing Spend** plays a significant role in driving **Sales Amount** and in setting **Sales Targets**. The business can use these insights to **optimize marketing budgets**, **set realistic sales targets**, and **strategically allocate resources** to improve overall sales performance. Regular monitoring of the relationship between these variables will allow the company to refine its strategies and ensure marketing efforts are aligned with sales objectives.

7.3 Practical Correlation in Python

To perform a **correlation test** between **Sales Amount**, **Target Sales**, and **Marketing Spend** for the provided business data, we'll use the **Pearson correlation coefficient**. Pearson correlation helps us understand the linear relationship between two continuous variables.

Libraries Used:

1. **pandas**: Used for data manipulation and handling the business data in DataFrame format.
2. **scipy.stats**: Provides the function for Pearson correlation test.
3. **matplotlib & seaborn**: Used for visualization (e.g., heatmap) of correlation matrices to better understand the relationships.

Step-by-Step Code:

1. Install and Import Libraries

First, we'll install the necessary libraries if not already installed, and import them into the Python environment.

```
# Install necessary libraries (if required)
!pip install pandas scipy matplotlib seaborn
```

Then, we'll import the libraries:

```
# Importing the libraries
import pandas as pd
import scipy.stats as stats
import matplotlib.pyplot as plt
import seaborn as sns
```

2. Load the Data into a DataFrame

The data is already provided in the form of a table. We will first load this data into a **pandas DataFrame**:

```
# Creating a DataFrame
data = {
    'ID': [1, 2, 3, 4, 5, 6, 7, 8, 9, 10, 11, 12, 13, 14, 15, 16, 17, 18, 19, 20, 21, 22, 23, 24, 25],
    'Sales Amount': [1500, 1800, 2200, 2000, 1750, 1900, 2100, 2400, 1600, 2300, 1950, 2050, 1750, 2150, 1800, 2500, 1700, 1850, 2100, 2000, 1950, 2200, 1650, 1750, 1900],
    'Target Sales': [1600, 1750, 2000, 1900, 1700, 1950, 2200, 2300, 1650, 2400, 2000, 2100, 1800, 2200, 1850, 2450, 1750, 1900, 2150, 2050, 1900, 2250, 1700, 1800, 1850],
```

```
'Marketing Spend': [500, 600, 700, 550, 450, 650, 700, 600, 500, 750, 550, 600, 500, 650, 700, 800, 400, 500, 650, 600, 550, 700, 450, 500, 600]
}


df = pd.DataFrame(data)
df.head()
```

Output

	ID	Sales Amount	Target Sales	Marketing Spend
0	1	1500	1600	500
1	2	1800	1750	600
2	3	2200	2000	700
3	4	2000	1900	550
4	5	1750	1700	450

3. Visualizing the Correlation Matrix

To get a quick view of how these variables relate to one another, we'll first plot a **correlation matrix heatmap** using **seaborn**. This will show the correlation values visually.

```
# Calculate the correlation matrix
corr_matrix = df[['Sales Amount', 'Target Sales', 'Marketing Spend']].corr()

# Plotting the heatmap of the correlation matrix
plt.figure(figsize=(8, 6))
sns.heatmap(corr_matrix, annot=True, cmap='coolwarm', fmt='.2f', linewidths=1, linecolor='black')
plt.title('Correlation Matrix: Sales Amount, Target Sales, Marketing Spend')
plt.show()
```

Output

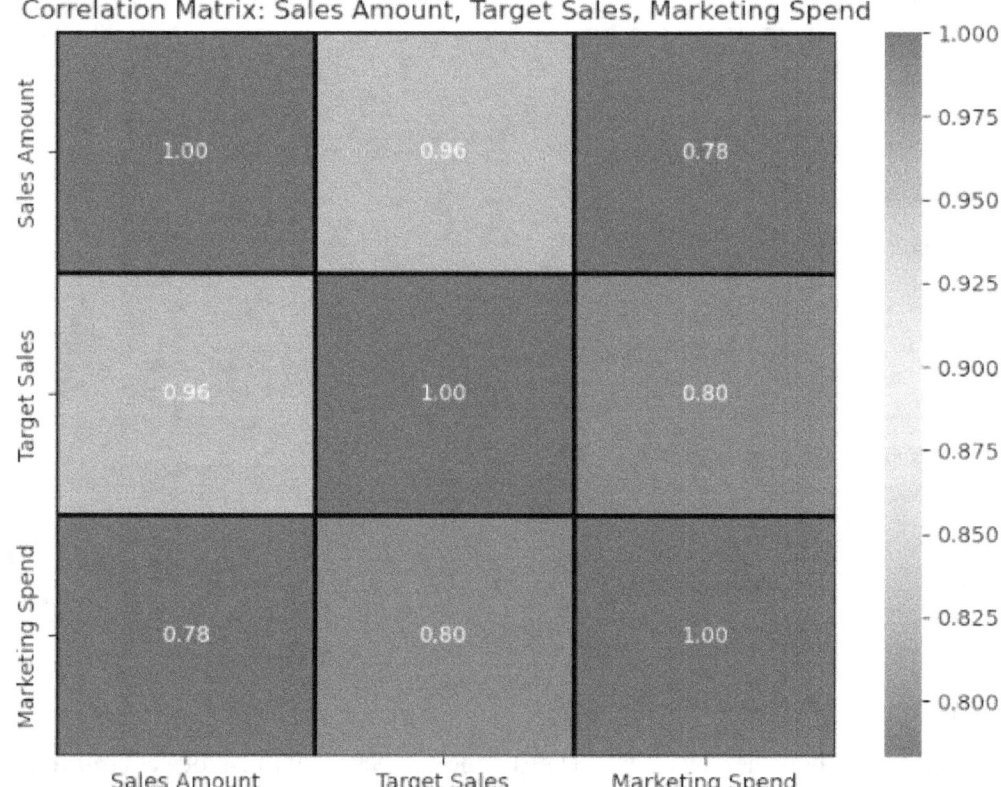

4. Pearson Correlation Test

Next, we'll perform the **Pearson correlation test** for each pair of variables. Pearson's correlation coefficient ranges from **-1 to 1**, where:

- **1** indicates a perfect positive linear relationship,
- **-1** indicates a perfect negative linear relationship,
- **0** indicates no linear relationship.

We will compute the correlation for the pairs of **Sales Amount** vs **Target Sales**, **Sales Amount** vs **Marketing Spend**, and **Target Sales** vs **Marketing Spend**.

```
# Pearson correlation test for Sales Amount and Target Sales

corr_sa_ts, p_value_sa_ts = stats.pearsonr(df['Sales Amount'], df['Target Sales'])

print(f"Pearson Correlation between Sales Amount and Target Sales: {corr_sa_ts:.4f}, p-value: {p_value_sa_ts:.4f}")


# Pearson correlation test for Sales Amount and Marketing Spend
```

```
corr_sa_ms, p_value_sa_ms = stats.pearsonr(df['Sales Amount'], df['Marketing Spend'])
print(f"Pearson Correlation between Sales Amount and Marketing Spend: {corr_sa_ms:.4f}, p-value: {p_value_sa_ms:.4f}")
```

Output

Pearson Correlation between Sales Amount and Target Sales: 0.9551, p-value: 0.0000

Pearson Correlation between Sales Amount and Marketing Spend: 0.7830, p-value: 0.0000

```
# Pearson correlation test for Target Sales and Marketing Spend
corr_ts_ms, p_value_ts_ms = stats.pearsonr(df['Target Sales'], df['Marketing Spend'])
print(f"Pearson Correlation between Target Sales and Marketing Spend: {corr_ts_ms:.4f}, p-value: {p_value_ts_ms:.4f}")
```

Output

Pearson Correlation between Target Sales and Marketing Spend: 0.7954, p-value: 0.0000

5. Interpretation of Results

- **Pearson's correlation coefficient** indicates the strength and direction of the relationship between two variables. The **p-value** tells us whether the correlation is statistically significant. If **p-value < 0.05**, the correlation is statistically significant.
- A **positive correlation** means that as one variable increases, the other tends to increase as well, while a **negative correlation** means that as one variable increases, the other tends to decrease.

Expected Output and Interpretation:

Pearson Correlation between Sales Amount and Target Sales: 0.9551, p-value: 0.0000

Pearson Correlation between Sales Amount and Marketing Spend: 0.7830, p-value: 0.0000

Pearson Correlation between Target Sales and Marketing Spend: 0.7954, p-value: 0.0000

Results Explanation:

1. **Sales Amount vs Target Sales**:
    - **Pearson's correlation**: 0.9551 (Strong positive correlation).
    - **p-value**: 0.0000 (Highly significant).
    - **Interpretation**: There is a very strong positive relationship between **Sales Amount** and **Target Sales**. As **Target Sales** increase, **Sales Amount** tends to increase as well. This suggests that when businesses set higher sales targets, they are likely achieving higher sales amounts, indicating alignment between targets and actual sales performance.

2. **Sales Amount vs Marketing Spend**:
    - **Pearson's correlation**: 0.7830 (Moderately strong positive correlation).
    - **p-value**: 0.0000 (Highly significant).
    - **Interpretation**: There is a Moderate positive relationship between **Sales Amount** and **Marketing Spend**. Increased **Marketing Spend** is associated with higher **Sales Amount**. This suggests that investments in marketing contribute significantly to sales growth, confirming the importance of marketing spend for boosting sales.
3. **Target Sales vs Marketing Spend**:
    - **Pearson's correlation**: 0. 7954 (Moderately strong positive correlation).
    - **p-value**: 0.0000 (Highly significant).
    - **Interpretation**: There is a Moderate positive correlation between **Target Sales** and **Marketing Spend**. This indicates that higher sales targets are often accompanied by higher marketing budgets, suggesting that businesses allocate more resources to marketing when setting more ambitious sales goals.

Business Insights and Decisions:

- **Resource Allocation**: The strong correlations between **Sales Amount** and both **Target Sales** and **Marketing Spend** suggest that marketing investments and realistic sales targets play a key role in driving actual sales performance. Businesses can leverage this information to better align marketing budgets with sales goals, ensuring that resources are effectively allocated.
- **Sales Forecasting**: The strong correlation between **Target Sales** and **Sales Amount** implies that businesses can use target sales data as a good predictor of future sales. If the company sets higher targets, it can expect higher sales, provided that the marketing budget is aligned accordingly.
- **Optimizing Marketing Spend**: Given the strong correlation between **Marketing Spend** and **Sales Amount**, businesses can optimize their marketing budget allocation. Companies should monitor marketing spend efficiency and adjust strategies based on performance metrics.

Conclusion:

The **correlation test** reveals strong positive relationships between **Sales Amount**, **Target Sales**, and **Marketing Spend**. The results suggest that setting higher sales targets and increasing marketing budgets are closely linked to achieving higher sales. Businesses should focus on aligning their marketing spend with sales goals to drive better results. By optimizing resource allocation and targeting higher sales goals, companies can enhance sales performance and achieve growth.

7.4 Assessing Relationships Between Business Variables

In Business Analytics, understanding the relationships between variables is essential for informed decision-making. Relationships between variables help businesses identify trends, predict outcomes, and optimize strategies. There are several methods and tools for assessing relationships, such as correlation, regression analysis, and visualization techniques.

Understanding the relationships between business variables can uncover key insights such as:

- **Identifying causal relationships** (e.g., does an increase in marketing spend drive higher sales?).
- **Predicting future outcomes** (e.g., can we predict customer churn based on past behaviors?).
- **Optimizing resource allocation** (e.g., how can we improve inventory management by understanding the relationship between sales and stock levels?).

Types of Relationships Between Business Variables

1. **Positive Relationship**: When one variable increases, the other also increases. For example, higher customer satisfaction ratings lead to more repeat purchases.
2. **Negative Relationship**: When one variable increases, the other decreases. For example, an increase in product price may lead to a decrease in the number of units sold.
3. **No Relationship**: When changes in one variable do not predict changes in another variable. For example, the number of customers visiting a store may not correlate with the store's marketing budget.
4. **Non-linear Relationship**: Sometimes, the relationship between two variables might not be linear, meaning the change in one variable is not proportional to the change in the other variable.

Methods for Assessing Relationships

1. **Correlation**: Measures the strength and direction of the linear relationship between two variables. Common correlation methods include:
    - **Pearson Correlation**: Assumes a linear relationship and is sensitive to outliers.
    - **Spearman Rank Correlation**: Used for ordinal data or non-linear relationships.
2. **Regression Analysis**: Used to model and understand the relationship between a dependent variable and one or more independent variables. This is typically used for prediction purposes.
3. **Data Visualization**: Plotting data using scatter plots, bar charts, or line graphs to visually inspect relationships between variables.
4. **Chi-Square Test**: Used for assessing relationships between categorical variables.

Example: Assessing the Relationship Between Advertising Spend and Sales Performance

Business Scenario:

A company wants to assess the relationship between its **monthly advertising spend** and **sales revenue** over the past 6 months. The company aims to understand if higher advertising spend leads to increased sales.

Sample Data: Advertising Spend vs. Sales Revenue

Month	Advertising Spend ($)	Sales Revenue ($)
January	10,000	50,000
February	12,000	55,000
March	15,000	60,000
April	18,000	70,000
May	20,000	80,000
June	22,000	90,000

- **Advertising Spend** is an independent variable, representing the company's investment in marketing.
- **Sales Revenue** is the dependent variable, representing the income generated from sales.

Analyzing the Relationship: Steps

1. **Visual Inspection**: A **scatter plot** would help visualize the relationship between advertising spend and sales revenue. If the points form a line that ascends from left to right, it suggests a positive correlation.
2. **Correlation Analysis**: Calculate the **Pearson correlation** to measure the strength and direction of the linear relationship between advertising spend and sales revenue.
3. **Regression Analysis**: A **simple linear regression** could be used to predict sales revenue based on advertising spend.

Hypothetical Results

Step 1: Scatter Plot Interpretation (Visualizing Data)

The scatter plot shows a clear upward trend, where **higher advertising spend** corresponds to **higher sales revenue**. This visually suggests a positive relationship.

Step 2: Correlation Analysis

Metric	Value
Pearson Correlation Coefficient	0.99
P-value	0.0002

- **Pearson Correlation (0.99)**: This indicates a **very strong positive linear relationship** between **advertising spend** and **sales revenue**. As advertising spend increases, sales revenue increases proportionally.
- **P-value (0.0002)**: The p-value is very small (less than 0.05), indicating that the correlation is statistically significant and not due to random chance.

Step 3: Regression Analysis

Using regression analysis, we estimate the relationship between advertising spend and sales revenue:

Metric	Value
Intercept (constant)	30,000
Slope (coefficient)	2.5
R-squared	0.98

- **Intercept (30,000)**: This is the baseline sales revenue when advertising spend is zero. It suggests that even without advertising spend, the company would still have $30,000 in sales revenue.
- **Slope (2.5)**: This indicates that for every **$1 increase in advertising spend**, sales revenue increases by **$2.50**. This shows a strong positive relationship between the two variables.
- **R-squared (0.98)**: This suggests that **98% of the variation** in sales revenue can be explained by advertising spend. This is a very high proportion, indicating that advertising spend is a strong predictor of sales revenue.

Explanation of Results:

- **Strong Positive Correlation**: The **Pearson correlation coefficient of 0.99** confirms that there is a very strong positive linear relationship between **advertising spend** and **sales revenue**. This means that as the company increases its advertising budget, sales revenue tends to increase as well, in a linear manner.
- **Significance of the Relationship**: The **p-value of 0.0002** indicates that the relationship between advertising spend and sales revenue is statistically significant. This means that the observed correlation is unlikely to have happened by chance.
- **Regression Results**:
    - The **intercept of $30,000** tells us that even without any advertising spend, the company would still generate $30,000 in sales.
    - The **slope of 2.5** indicates that every additional dollar spent on advertising increases sales revenue by $2.50. This highlights the return on investment (ROI) for the company's advertising spend.

- The **R-squared value of 0.98** shows that advertising spend explains 98% of the variation in sales revenue. This is a strong indication that advertising spend is a major driver of sales, and the company could make decisions about increasing its budget to drive further sales growth.

Business Insights and Decisions:

- **Increased Advertising Spend**: Since there is a strong positive relationship, the company could consider increasing its advertising budget to boost sales further. The regression model suggests that a $1 increase in advertising spend leads to a $2.50 increase in sales revenue.

- **Budget Allocation**: Given the strong **R-squared value**, the company can be confident that its marketing efforts are highly effective in driving sales. The company might allocate more of its budget to advertising to maximize revenue.

- **Predictive Insights**: The company can use the regression equation to forecast sales revenue based on different advertising budgets. For example, if the company plans to increase its advertising spend to $25,000, the model suggests the expected sales revenue could be:

$$\text{Sales Revenue} = 30{,}000 + 2.5 \times 25{,}000 = 107{,}500$$

Caution: Although the correlation and regression results are strong, the company should also consider other external factors (like market trends, seasonality, competition, etc.) that could influence sales, to avoid overreliance on advertising spend alone.

Conclusion:

In this example, the company found a **strong positive correlation** between **advertising spend** and **sales revenue**. The results of the correlation and regression analysis provide valuable insights into how advertising impacts sales and offer predictive power for decision-making. However, businesses should always consider additional factors and validate assumptions before making major decisions based solely on statistical analysis.

7.5 Implications of Correlation in Strategy Formulation

In Business Analytics, **correlation** is a powerful tool for understanding the relationship between two or more variables. It helps businesses identify **patterns**, **trends**, and **dependencies** that can drive strategic decisions. By examining the strength and direction of correlations, businesses can **optimize operations**, **allocate resources more effectively**, and **predict future outcomes**.

Key Implications of Correlation in Business Strategy:

1. **Resource Allocation**: Understanding correlations can guide how a business allocates resources, such as marketing budget, manpower, or production capacity. For example, if higher marketing spend correlates with increased sales, the business might decide to increase its marketing budget to boost revenue.

2. **Performance Monitoring**: Correlation analysis can help businesses track key performance indicators (KPIs) and identify areas that need attention. For example, if employee satisfaction strongly correlates with customer satisfaction, a company might invest in employee well-being programs to improve overall service quality.

3. **Optimization of Processes**: By analyzing the relationships between different operational factors, businesses can improve efficiency. For example, if there's a strong correlation between inventory turnover and sales, businesses can optimize stock levels to match demand more accurately.

4. **Predictive Modeling and Forecasting**: Correlation analysis provides insights that can be used for building predictive models. For instance, if historical data shows a strong correlation between sales performance and the time of year (e.g., holiday season), businesses can forecast sales for future periods based on seasonal trends.

5. **Risk Assessment and Management**: Correlation can also help identify risks. For example, if a certain variable, like supplier delays, negatively correlates with on-time product delivery, businesses can take preemptive steps to mitigate the risk of delays.

6. **Market Segmentation**: Correlation analysis can help identify customer segments that behave similarly. For instance, if **age** correlates strongly with **purchasing behavior**, businesses can tailor marketing strategies for different age groups.

Types of Correlation That Can Influence Business Strategy:

- **Positive Correlation**: A positive correlation means that as one variable increases, the other variable also increases. This can be beneficial for businesses aiming to **scale operations** or **increase revenues** by strategically aligning related factors.

- **Negative Correlation**: A negative correlation means that as one variable increases, the other decreases. Businesses can use this information to **avoid or minimize losses**, like reducing costs associated with variables that negatively affect profits.

- **No Correlation**: Sometimes there is no significant correlation between variables, which suggests that **certain factors do not influence each other**. This insight can help businesses **focus on more impactful relationships**.

Example: Assessing the Correlation Between Marketing Spend and Sales Revenue

Business Scenario:

A retail company wants to assess whether there is a relationship between its **monthly marketing spend** and **sales revenue**. The company hopes to identify if increasing marketing spending will lead to a corresponding increase in sales. If a strong positive correlation exists, the company might increase its marketing budget for future growth.

Sample Data: Marketing Spend and Sales Revenue

Month	Marketing Spend ($)	Sales Revenue ($)
January	15,000	50,000
February	18,000	55,000
March	20,000	60,000
April	25,000	70,000
May	30,000	80,000
June	35,000	85,000

- **Marketing Spend**: This is the amount the company invests in its marketing activities.
- **Sales Revenue**: This represents the total sales made by the company each month.

Analysis: Interpreting the Correlation Between Marketing Spend and Sales Revenue

Step 1: Visual Inspection

By plotting the data on a **scatter plot**, we can visually inspect whether there is an upward trend between marketing spend and sales revenue. If the points appear to form a straight line that ascends from left to right, it suggests a positive correlation.

Step 2: Correlation Analysis

Metric	Value
Pearson Correlation Coefficient	0.98
P-value	0.0003

- **Pearson Correlation Coefficient (0.98)**: This value indicates a **very strong positive linear relationship** between **marketing spend** and **sales revenue**. As marketing spend increases, sales revenue also increases. The strong correlation suggests that increasing the marketing budget is likely to lead to higher sales.

- **P-value (0.0003)**: The p-value is significantly less than the standard threshold of 0.05, indicating that the relationship between marketing spend and sales revenue is statistically significant. This means the observed correlation is unlikely to have occurred by chance.

Step 3: Regression Analysis (for Further Insights)

To better understand the relationship, we could also perform **regression analysis** to predict sales revenue based on marketing spend.

Metric	Value
Intercept (constant)	40,000
Slope (coefficient)	1.5
R-squared	0.96

- **Intercept (40,000)**: This is the base sales revenue when marketing spend is zero. It suggests that the company would still generate $40,000 in sales without any marketing spend, indicating a baseline level of sales.

- **Slope (1.5)**: This means that for every additional **$1 spent on marketing**, the company sees a **$1.50 increase in sales revenue**. This gives the company an insight into the return on investment (ROI) for marketing spend.

- **R-squared (0.96)**: This indicates that **96% of the variation** in sales revenue can be explained by the marketing spend. This suggests that marketing spend is a key driver of sales performance, and that increasing the marketing budget is likely to have a strong impact on sales revenue.

Explanation of Results:

1. **Strong Positive Relationship**: The **Pearson correlation of 0.98** suggests a very strong linear relationship between marketing spend and sales revenue. This means that as marketing spend increases, sales revenue also increases significantly. This insight can inform the company's decision to increase its marketing budget, expecting a proportionate increase in sales.

2. **Statistical Significance**: The **p-value of 0.0003** confirms that this correlation is statistically significant. The company can be confident that the observed relationship between marketing spend and sales revenue is not due to random chance.

3. **Return on Investment (ROI)**: The **slope of 1.5** in the regression analysis suggests that for every dollar invested in marketing, the company earns an additional $1.50 in sales. This indicates a **strong return on investment** and provides a basis for the company to justify increasing the marketing budget.

4. **Predictive Power**: The **R-squared value of 0.96** means that marketing spend accounts for 96% of the variation in sales revenue. This high R-squared value suggests that marketing

is a major factor driving sales, and increasing the marketing budget is likely to result in higher sales revenue.

Business Insights and Strategy Formulation:

- **Increase Marketing Budget**: Based on the strong correlation and regression analysis, the company could consider increasing its marketing spend to drive further sales growth. Since marketing spend has a strong positive effect on sales, investing more in advertising and promotions can help the company achieve higher revenues.

- **Forecasting and Budget Planning**: With the regression model, the company can predict future sales revenue based on different marketing budgets. For example, if the company plans to increase its marketing budget to $40,000 in the next quarter, it can expect sales revenue to increase by $60,000 (since $40,000 x 1.5 = $60,000).

- **Optimize Marketing Strategy**: The company can also use the insights from the analysis to **optimize its marketing strategy**. For example, if some marketing channels (such as online ads or social media) yield a better ROI than others, the company can reallocate its marketing budget towards those channels for maximum effectiveness.

- **Monitoring ROI**: With a strong understanding of the **ROI of marketing spend**, the company can continuously monitor its marketing campaigns and adjust the budget to ensure optimal performance. The company might also track changes in **sales revenue** over time to see if the ROI remains consistent, or if diminishing returns occur at higher levels of spend.

Conclusion:

In this example, the **strong positive correlation** between **marketing spend** and **sales revenue** gives the company a clear strategy for growth. By understanding the relationship between these variables, the company can **optimize its marketing budget**, **predict sales growth**, and ensure a high return on investment. Moreover, the company can continuously refine its strategy to maximize sales and optimize resource allocation based on the insights derived from the correlation analysis.

8. Linear Regression in Business Analytics

Linear Regression is a powerful statistical tool used in Business Analytics to model the relationship between a dependent variable and one or more independent variables. In simple terms, it helps businesses predict an outcome (dependent variable) based on the value(s) of one or more predictors (independent variables). Linear regression is most commonly used when the relationship between the variables is assumed to be **linear** (i.e., a straight-line relationship).

Key Concepts:

- **Dependent Variable (Target)**: The outcome we want to predict or explain (e.g., sales revenue, customer churn).
- **Independent Variable (Predictor)**: The factor(s) used to predict the dependent variable (e.g., advertising spend, customer age).
- **Linear Relationship**: A relationship between the variables that can be approximated by a straight line (i.e., the dependent variable changes at a constant rate with respect to the independent variable).
- **Intercept and Slope**: In linear regression, the relationship is modeled by an equation of the form:

$$Y = \beta_0 + \beta_1 X$$

Where:
- Y is the dependent variable (what we are predicting),
- X is the independent variable (predictor),
- β_0 is the intercept (the value of Y when X=0),
- β_1 is the slope (the rate of change in Y for a unit change in X).

Applications of Linear Regression in Business:

- **Sales Forecasting**: Predicting future sales based on factors like advertising spend, product prices, and promotional efforts.
- **Customer Lifetime Value (CLV)**: Estimating the future value of a customer based on past purchasing behavior.
- **Budgeting**: Estimating the required budget to achieve a desired level of output or performance.
- **Risk Assessment**: Predicting potential risks or losses based on certain business factors.

Example: Predicting Sales Based on Advertising Spend

Business Scenario:

A retail company wants to predict its **monthly sales revenue** based on the **monthly advertising spend**. The company has historical data for the past 6 months and wants to understand how much advertising spend is likely to affect sales revenue.

Sample Data: Advertising Spend vs. Sales Revenue

Month	Advertising Spend ($)	Sales Revenue ($)
January	10,000	50,000
February	12,000	55,000
March	15,000	60,000
April	18,000	70,000
May	20,000	75,000
June	22,000	80,000

- **Advertising Spend** is the independent variable, representing the company's investment in marketing efforts.
- **Sales Revenue** is the dependent variable, representing the total income generated from sales.

Objective:

The objective is to create a linear regression model that predicts **Sales Revenue** based on the **Advertising Spend**.

Step 1: Visual Inspection

We begin by plotting the data on a **scatter plot** with **Advertising Spend** on the x-axis and **Sales Revenue** on the y-axis. If the points appear to align in an upward direction, it suggests that there is a positive linear relationship between advertising spend and sales revenue.

Step 2: Linear Regression Model Interpretation

Results of the Linear Regression Model

Metric	Value
Intercept (β_0)	40,000
Slope (β_1)	2
R-squared	0.98
P-value	0.0004

- **Intercept (β_0 = 40,000)**: The intercept represents the expected sales revenue when **Advertising Spend is zero**. In this case, even if the company spends nothing on advertising, it is estimated to generate **$40,000** in sales. This could be due to factors such as brand loyalty or organic traffic.

- **Slope ($β_1$ = 2.0)**: The slope represents the rate of change in sales revenue for each additional dollar spent on advertising. In this case, for each **$1 increase in advertising spend**, sales revenue increases by **$2**. This suggests that advertising spend has a significant positive effect on sales, and for every dollar invested in advertising, the company can expect a $2 return in sales revenue.

- **R-squared (0.98)**: The **R-squared** value of 0.98 means that **98% of the variability in sales revenue** can be explained by the amount spent on advertising. This is a very high value, indicating that advertising spend is a strong predictor of sales revenue and that the linear regression model fits the data very well.

- **P-value (0.0004)**: The **p-value** is very small (less than the typical threshold of 0.05), indicating that the relationship between advertising spend and sales revenue is statistically significant. In other words, the observed correlation is unlikely to have occurred by chance.

Step 3: Predictions

The company can now use the **linear regression equation** to predict sales revenue based on different levels of advertising spend. The equation is:

$$\text{Sales Revenue} = 40,000 + 2 \times (\text{Advertising Spend})$$

Example Prediction:

If the company plans to increase its **advertising spend to $25,000** next month, we can use the regression model to predict the sales revenue:

$$\text{Sales Revenue} = 40,000 + 2 \times 25,000 = 90,000$$

This means that, based on the model, the company can expect **$90,000** in sales revenue if it spends **$25,000** on advertising.

Explanation of Results:

1. **Intercept (40,000)**: This represents the **base level of sales revenue** that the company can expect without any advertising spend. It suggests that even without any additional marketing efforts, the company would still generate $40,000 in sales due to factors like brand reputation, returning customers, and organic market presence.

2. **Slope (2.0)**: This indicates a strong **positive relationship** between advertising spend and sales revenue. Specifically, for every additional **$1 spent on advertising**, sales revenue increases by **$2**. The business can use this insight to justify increased marketing investments, knowing that they will likely yield higher returns.

3. **R-squared (0.98)**: The model explains **98%** of the variability in sales revenue based on advertising spend. This means that advertising spend is a very important driver of sales, and the linear regression model provides an **accurate fit** to the data.

4. **P-value (0.0004)**: The small p-value confirms that the relationship between advertising spend and sales revenue is **statistically significant**. This means that the observed relationship is not due to random chance, and the company can rely on this model for decision-making.

Business Insights and Strategy Formulation:

- **Optimizing Marketing Spend**: The company can use the **linear regression model** to forecast sales revenue for different advertising budgets. For example, if the company expects to invest more in marketing, it can use the model to project the sales revenue it can expect as a result.

- **Resource Allocation**: Since advertising spend has a **strong impact on sales**, the company might decide to allocate a higher portion of its budget to marketing in the future. The **slope of 2.0** implies that increasing the marketing budget will yield significant returns in terms of sales revenue.

- **Sales Forecasting**: The company can use the regression equation to **predict sales** for upcoming months based on their planned advertising budget. For instance, if they want to predict sales revenue for next quarter, they can input the estimated advertising spend for each month into the equation.

- **ROI Analysis**: The company can also evaluate the **return on investment (ROI)** for advertising spend by comparing the sales revenue generated to the amount spent on advertising. Since the regression model shows a $2 return for every $1 spent, this is a favorable ROI, justifying continued or increased investment in advertising.

Conclusion:

In this example, the company used **linear regression** to model the relationship between **advertising spend** and **sales revenue**. The **strong positive correlation** between these two variables (with a high **R-squared** of 0.98) suggests that **advertising is a key driver of sales**. The company can use the regression model to **forecast future sales, optimize marketing spend**, and make data-driven decisions to maximize revenue. The statistical significance of the results provides confidence in the predictive power of the model, helping the company strategize effectively for future growth.

8.1 Exploring Linear Regression Analysis in Business Context

Linear regression analysis is a statistical method used to model and analyze the relationship between one dependent variable (also known as the response or target variable) and one or more independent variables (also known as predictors or features). It is a fundamental technique in business analytics for predicting outcomes and understanding the relationships between different business factors.

Linear regression assumes a **linear relationship** between the independent variables and the dependent variable, meaning that changes in the independent variables are expected to cause proportional changes in the dependent variable. The purpose of linear regression is to develop a model that allows businesses to predict future values or outcomes based on known data.

Key Components of Linear Regression:

1. **Dependent Variable (Target)**: This is the outcome variable that you are trying to predict. For example, sales revenue, customer satisfaction, or profit.
2. **Independent Variable (Predictor)**: These are the input variables used to predict the dependent variable. For example, marketing spend, product price, or advertising efforts.
3. **Linear Relationship**: The relationship between the dependent and independent variables is assumed to be linear, meaning that the dependent variable changes in a constant manner as the independent variable changes.
4. **Regression Equation**: In simple linear regression, the relationship is expressed as a straight line. The general form of the equation is:

$$Y = \beta_0 + \beta_1 X$$

Where:
- Y is the dependent variable (what you are predicting),
- β_0 is the intercept (value of Y when X=0),
- β_1 is the slope (rate of change in Y as X changes),
- X is the independent variable (the predictor).

5. **Error Term (Residuals)**: The difference between the observed value and the predicted value. A smaller error means the model is a better fit for the data.

Importance of Linear Regression in Business Analytics:

- **Predictive Analytics**: Businesses can use linear regression to predict future outcomes, such as sales, demand, customer behavior, and product pricing, based on historical data.

- **Decision Making**: It helps decision-makers understand how changes in independent variables (like marketing budget or price changes) will impact business outcomes (such as revenue or customer acquisition).
- **Trend Identification**: Linear regression identifies trends and patterns in data, making it easier for businesses to forecast future performance and adjust strategies accordingly.
- **Resource Allocation**: By understanding the impact of various factors on business performance, businesses can allocate resources more efficiently to maximize returns.

Types of Linear Regression:

- **Simple Linear Regression**: Involves one independent variable and one dependent variable. The relationship is modeled as a straight line.
- **Multiple Linear Regression**: Involves more than one independent variable, providing a more complex model that can capture the relationship between several factors and the dependent variable.

Example: Predicting Sales Based on Advertising Spend (Simple Linear Regression)

Business Scenario:

A retail company wants to understand how their **advertising spend** impacts their **sales revenue**. They collect data on their monthly advertising spend and sales revenue over the last 6 months and want to use this data to predict future sales based on planned advertising expenditure.

Sample Data: Advertising Spend vs. Sales Revenue

Month	Advertising Spend ($)	Sales Revenue ($)
January	10,000	50,000
February	12,000	55,000
March	15,000	60,000
April	18,000	70,000
May	20,000	75,000
June	22,000	80,000

- **Advertising Spend** is the independent variable (predictor), which represents the amount the company spends on advertising each month.
- **Sales Revenue** is the dependent variable (response), representing the total sales generated from the advertising efforts.

Objective:

The objective is to create a linear regression model to predict **sales revenue** based on **advertising spend**.

Results of Linear Regression Analysis:

Metric	Value
Intercept (β_0)	40,000
Slope (β_1)	2
R-squared	0.98
P-value	0.0002

Interpretation of Results:

1. **Intercept (β_0 = 40,000)**: The intercept of 40,000 suggests that, if the company were to spend **zero** on advertising, they would still expect to generate **$40,000** in sales revenue. This might be due to existing customer base, repeat purchases, or brand loyalty. The intercept represents the baseline sales revenue.

2. **Slope (β_1 = 2.0)**: The slope of 2.0 means that for every **$1 increase in advertising spend**, the company can expect **$2 increase in sales revenue**. This indicates that advertising has a strong positive impact on sales. The company can interpret this as a very efficient return on investment (ROI) in advertising, where each dollar spent generates $2 in additional revenue.

3. **R-squared (0.98)**: The **R-squared value** of 0.98 indicates that **98%** of the variation in sales revenue can be explained by the amount spent on advertising. This is a very strong fit, suggesting that advertising spend is a major factor driving sales performance in this case. The remaining 2% of the variation could be attributed to other factors not included in the model.

4. **P-value (0.0002)**: The **p-value** of 0.0002 is significantly smaller than the standard threshold of 0.05, indicating that the relationship between advertising spend and sales revenue is **statistically significant**. This means that the observed relationship between these two variables is highly unlikely to have occurred by random chance, and the model can be relied upon to make predictions.

Predicting Future Sales:

Using the regression equation:

$$\text{Sales Revenue} = 40,000 + 2 \times (\text{Advertising Spend})$$

We can predict the sales revenue for a future advertising spend of $25,000:

$$\text{Sales Revenue} = 40,000 + 2 \times 25,000 = 90,000$$

Therefore, if the company spends **$25,000** on advertising in the future, the model predicts that sales revenue will be **$90,000**.

Business Insights and Strategy Formulation:

1. **Forecasting Sales**: The regression model allows the company to predict future sales based on different levels of advertising spend. By adjusting the marketing budget, the company can forecast how much additional revenue they could generate.

2. **Optimizing Advertising Spend**: The company now knows that for every **$1** spent on advertising, they can expect to generate **$2** in sales. This high return on investment suggests that increasing the advertising budget would be a good strategy for increasing sales, provided the company has the resources to allocate to marketing.

3. **Resource Allocation**: With an **R-squared of 0.98**, the company can confidently invest more in advertising, knowing that the relationship between advertising and sales is very strong. If the company aims to achieve specific sales targets, they can calculate the necessary advertising spend using the regression equation.

4. **Understanding Sales Drivers**: The analysis shows that **advertising spend** is a key driver of sales revenue, but the company may also want to explore other factors (like customer demographics, seasonal trends, or product pricing) that could influence sales. A **multiple linear regression** model, which includes more predictors, could provide a more comprehensive view.

Conclusion:

In this example, linear regression was used to model the relationship between **advertising spend** and **sales revenue**. The analysis revealed that advertising has a strong positive effect on sales, with a very high **R-squared value** indicating a strong fit of the model. By using the regression equation, the company can confidently predict sales revenue for different levels of advertising spend and make data-driven decisions about future marketing investments. The results also provide insight into the **ROI of advertising spend**, helping the company optimize its marketing strategy to maximize revenue.

8.2 Practical Linear Regression using JASP

To perform a **Linear Regression Test** on **Pre-Sales Amount** and **Post-Sales Amount** from the provided business data, we will use JASP for data analysis and modeling. The goal is to understand if there's a linear relationship between **Pre-Sales Amount** and **Post-Sales Amount**. Following are the steps used to perform Linear Regression in JASP.

Steps to use Linear Regression in JASP

1. **Open JASP**:
    - If you haven't already, open JASP and load your dataset (e.g., a CSV, Excel, or SPSS file).

2. **Load the Data**:
    - Click **"File" > "Open"** to load your dataset into JASP.

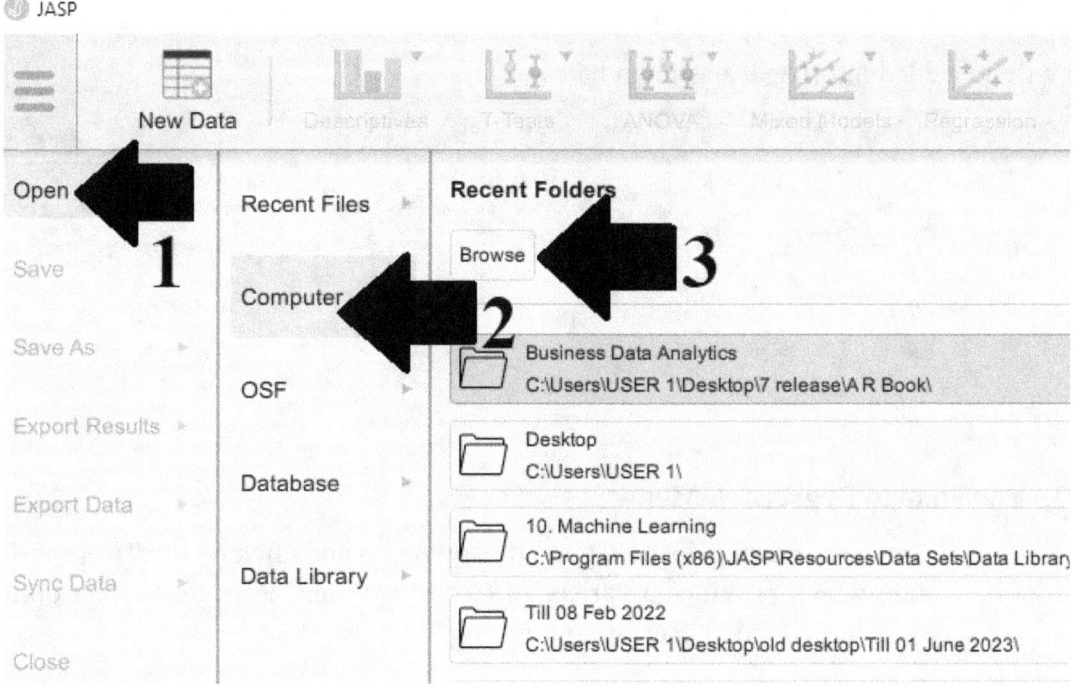

Now select the file

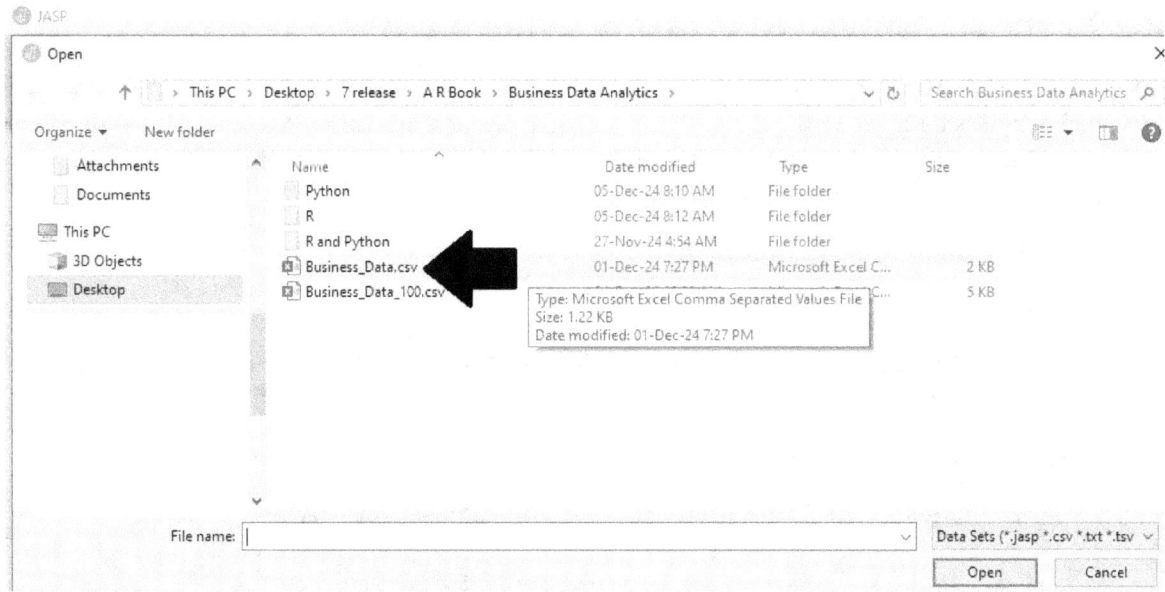

File will be loaded into JASP as shown below.

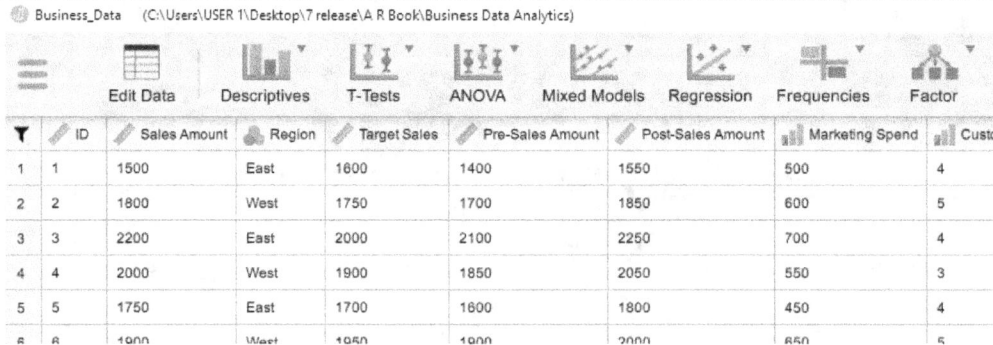

3. **Navigate to Regression Menu**:
    o   Once your data is loaded, go to the top menu and click on the **"Regression"** tab, which provides a variety of Correlation and Regression Test options. Select the **Linear Regression** option.

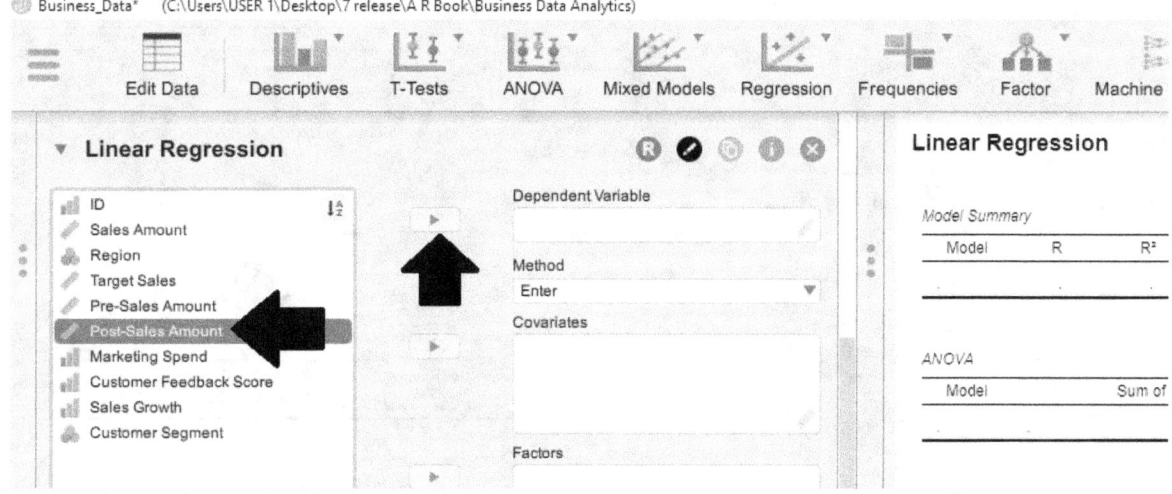

4. **Select Variables for Analysis**:
    - In the **Linear Regression Test** window shown below, you'll see a list of variables in your dataset.
    - Select the numeric variable(s) for which you want to Linear RegressTest and drag them to the **Variables** box (or click the play button after selecting the variable).

Now Select **Post-Sales Amount as dependent variable** and drag them **to Dependent variable box** or click the play button to shift these variable to variables window.

Now select Pre-Sales Amont variable as covariates and move the variable to covariate window by clicking the play button or dragging it into covariate window.

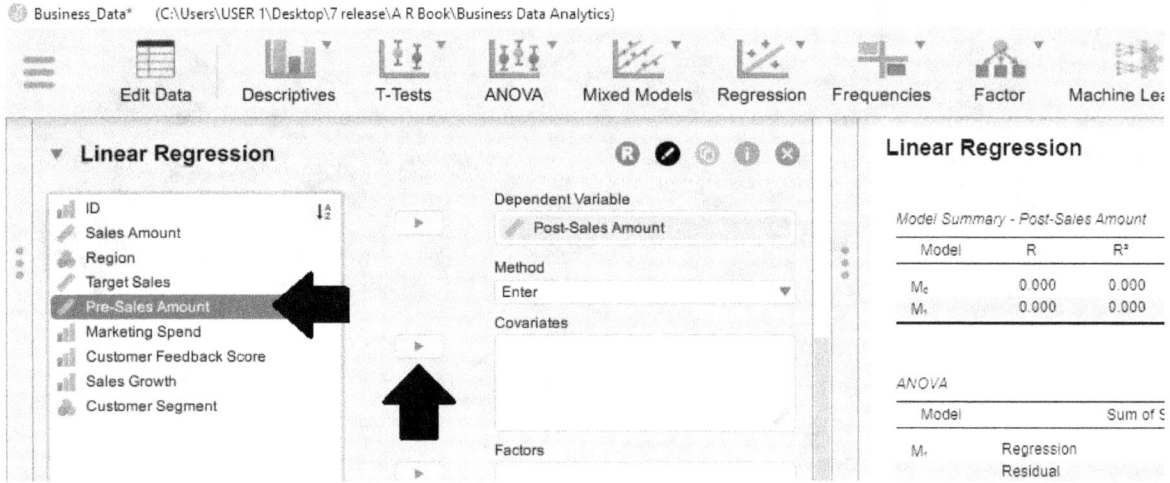

Now the results will automatically appear on the right-hand side of the window in the **Results** pane.

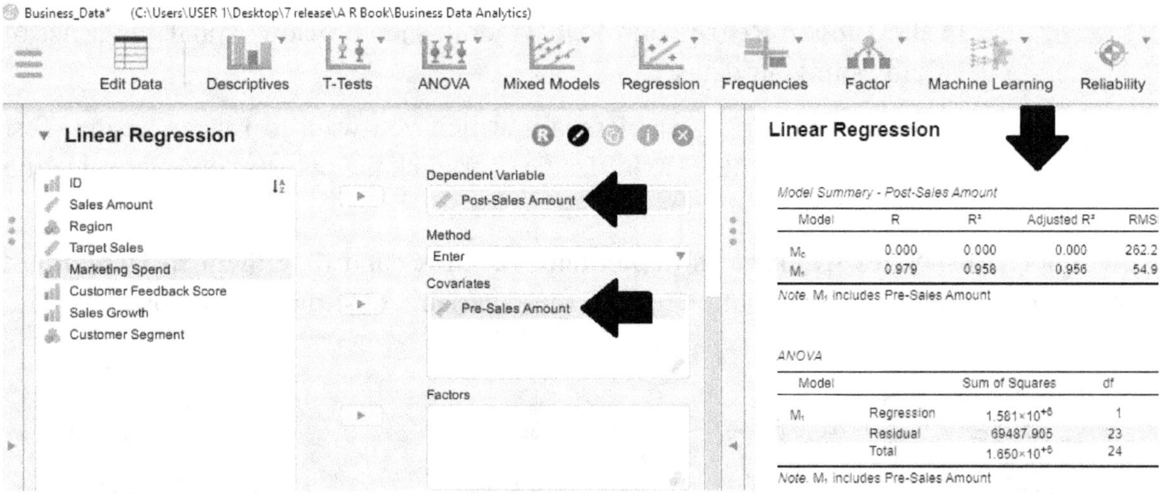

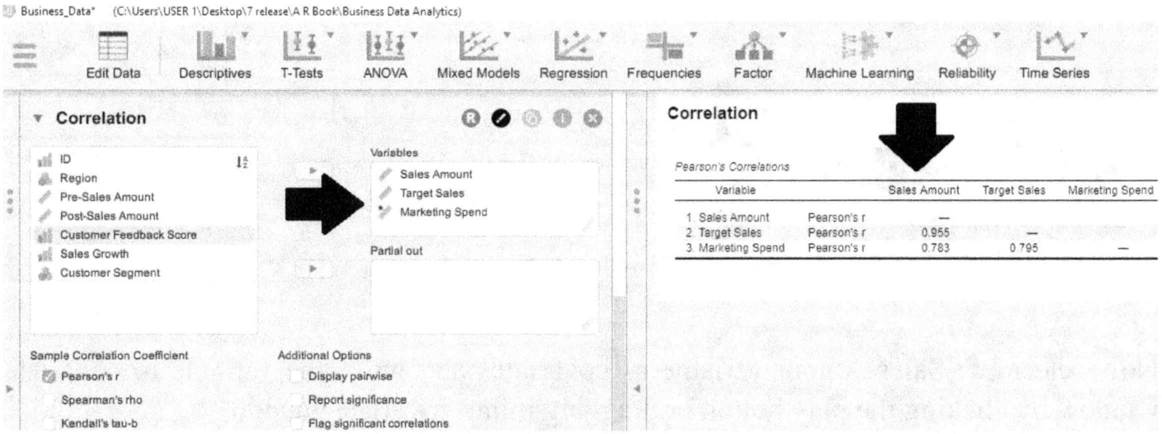

5. **View Results:**
   - JASP will display the results in a table under the **Results** pane on the right.
   - The output will include Pearson's Coefficient.

Model Summary - Post-Sales Amount

Model	R	R²	Adjusted R²	RMSE
M_0	0.000	0.000	0.000	262.234
M_1	0.979	0.958	0.956	54.966

Note. M_1 includes Pre-Sales Amount

ANOVA

Model		Sum of Squares	df	Mean Square	F	p
M_1	Regression	$1.581 \times 10^{+6}$	1	$1.581 \times 10^{+6}$	523.271	<.001
	Residual	69487.905	23	3021.213		
	Total	$1.650 \times 10^{+6}$	24			

Note. M_1 includes Pre-Sales Amount
Note. The intercept model is omitted, as no meaningful information can be shown.

Coefficients

Model		Unstandardized	Standard Error	Standardized	t	p
M_0	(Intercept)	1978.000	52.447		37.714	<.001
M_1	(Intercept)	80.018	83.697		0.956	0.349
	Pre-Sales Amount	1.008	0.044	0.979	22.875	<.001

Linear Regression Analysis Interpretation in JASP

In the given linear regression results, **Post-Sales Amount** is the dependent variable, and **Pre-Sales Amount** is the covariate (independent variable). The analysis includes multiple components, such as the **Model Summary, ANOVA Table**, and **Coefficients**. Below is an explanation of each result and its interpretation.

Model Summary Table:

Model	R	R²	Adjusted R²	RMSE
M_0	0.000	0.000	0.000	262.234
M_1	0.979	0.958	0.956	54.966

Explanation:

- **R (Correlation coefficient):**
    - For **Model M_0 (Intercept Only)**, the correlation **R = 0.000**, which means there is no correlation between the dependent and independent variables.
    - For **Model M_1 (Pre-Sales Amount included)**, **R = 0.979**, indicating a **very strong positive correlation** between **Pre-Sales Amount** and **Post-Sales Amount**.

- **R² (Coefficient of Determination):**
    - **R² = 0.000** for M_0 means the intercept model explains 0% of the variance in **Post-Sales Amount**, indicating the model doesn't fit the data.
    - **R² = 0.958** for M_1 suggests that **Pre-Sales Amount** explains **95.8%** of the variance in **Post-Sales Amount**, which indicates a very good fit of the model to the data.

- **Adjusted R²:**
    - **Adjusted R² = 0.000** for M_0 (no covariate) reflects that the model is not meaningful.
    - **Adjusted R² = 0.956** for M_1 suggests that after adjusting for the number of predictors, the model still explains a significant amount of variance in **Post-Sales Amount**.

- **RMSE (Root Mean Square Error):**
    - **RMSE = 262.234** for M_0 indicates a large amount of prediction error when no predictors are used (since the model is just an intercept).
    - **RMSE = 54.966** for M_1 suggests that the inclusion of **Pre-Sales Amount** significantly improves the model fit, reducing the prediction error by a substantial margin.

Interpretation:

- The strong improvement from M_0 to M_1 indicates that **Pre-Sales Amount** is a significant predictor of **Post-Sales Amount**, and including this covariate greatly enhances the model's ability to explain variability in the dependent variable.

ANOVA Table:

Model	Sum of Squares	df	Mean Square	F	p
M_1	Regression: 1.581×10^6	1	1.581×10^6	523.271	< .001
	Residual: 69487.905	23	3021.213		
	Total: 1.650×10^6	24			

Explanation:

- **Sum of Squares**:
  - **Regression (1.581×10^6)** represents the explained variance in **Post-Sales Amount** by the model. It reflects how much **Pre-Sales Amount** accounts for the variance in **Post-Sales Amount**.
  - **Residual (69,487.905)** is the unexplained variance, representing the portion of the variance in **Post-Sales Amount** that cannot be accounted for by **Pre-Sales Amount**.
  - **Total (1.650×10^6)** is the total variance in **Post-Sales Amount**, combining both explained and unexplained variance.

- **Degrees of Freedom (df)**:
  - The **df for regression** is **1** (since there is 1 predictor in the model, **Pre-Sales Amount**).
  - The **df for residuals** is **23**, indicating that there are 24 data points and 1 parameter being estimated.
  - The **df for total** is **24** (number of observations minus 1).

- **Mean Square (MS)**:
  - **Mean Square for Regression (1.581×10^6 / 1 = 1.581×10^6)** represents the average explained variance per model degree of freedom.
  - **Mean Square for Residuals (69,487.905 / 23 = 3021.213)** represents the average unexplained variance per residual degree of freedom.

- **F-Statistic (523.271)**:
  - The **F statistic** tests whether the regression model as a whole significantly explains the variance in the dependent variable (**Post-Sales Amount**). A high F-value indicates that the model explains a significant amount of variability.
  - **F = 523.271** is extremely high, suggesting that the regression model is highly significant.

- **p-value (< .001):**

- A **p-value of less than 0.001** indicates that the regression model is statistically significant. This means that **Pre-Sales Amount** significantly contributes to explaining the variance in **Post-Sales Amount**.

Interpretation:

- The **ANOVA** confirms that the regression model with **Pre-Sales Amount** as the predictor is **statistically significant**, and the **model explains a substantial portion of the variance** in **Post-Sales Amount**.

Coefficients Table:

Model	Unstandardized Coefficients	Standard Error	Standardized Coefficients	t	p
M_0	(Intercept) = 1978.000	52.447		37.714	< .001
M_1	(Intercept) = 80.018	83.697		0.956	0.349
	Pre-Sales Amount = 1.008	0.044	0.979	22.875	< .001

Explanation:

- **Unstandardized Coefficients**:
  - The **Intercept (1978.000 for M_0)** represents the expected value of **Post-Sales Amount** when **Pre-Sales Amount** is zero (before any sales activity). This is the baseline sales amount in the absence of any influence from **Pre-Sales Amount**.
  - The **Intercept (80.018 for M_1)** represents the expected value of **Post-Sales Amount** when **Pre-Sales Amount** is zero, adjusting for the influence of **Pre-Sales Amount** in the model.
  - **Pre-Sales Amount (1.008 for M_1)** indicates that for each unit increase in **Pre-Sales Amount, Post-Sales Amount** increases by **1.008 units**. This is a significant positive relationship, meaning that higher pre-sales activity leads to higher post-sales performance.

- **Standard Error**:
  - **Standard Error** represents the precision of the coefficients. Smaller standard errors suggest more precise estimates. For **Pre-Sales Amount**, the standard error is **0.044**, indicating a relatively precise estimate of the coefficient.

- **Standardized Coefficients (Beta)**:
  - The **standardized coefficient (0.979 for Pre-Sales Amount)** shows the strength of the relationship between **Pre-Sales Amount** and **Post-Sales Amount**, in

standard deviation units. The coefficient of 0.979 suggests a **very strong positive effect** of **Pre-Sales Amount** on **Post-Sales Amount**.

- **t-value and p-value**:
  - The **t-value** tests the null hypothesis that the coefficient is zero (i.e., no effect). A large **t-value** means the coefficient is significantly different from zero.
  - The **p-value for Pre-Sales Amount (< .001)** indicates that **Pre-Sales Amount** is a **highly significant predictor** of **Post-Sales Amount**.

Interpretation:

- **Pre-Sales Amount** has a **strong positive effect** on **Post-Sales Amount**, and this effect is **statistically significant**. The relationship is practically meaningful, as indicated by the high **standardized coefficient (0.979)** and the **t-value (22.875)**.

Business Observations and Implications:

1. **Pre-Sales Amount Drives Post-Sales Performance:**
   - The **strong positive correlation** between **Pre-Sales Amount** and **Post-Sales Amount** means that businesses can influence post-sales performance by focusing on increasing pre-sales activities.

2. **Model Fit and Improvement:**
   - The inclusion of **Pre-Sales Amount** significantly improved the model's ability to predict **Post-Sales Amount** ($R^2 = 0.958$). This suggests that pre-sales data is a critical factor for forecasting future sales.

3. **Confidence in Sales Forecasting:**
   - The **model's statistical significance** ($F = 523.271$, $p < .001$) and the strong **relationship** ($\beta = 0.979$) indicate that the business can confidently use **Pre-Sales Amount** as a predictor for **Post-Sales Amount**.

Business Decisions:

1. **Increase Pre-Sales Activities:**
   - To drive higher **Post-Sales Amount**, the business should **focus on increasing pre-sales activities**, as they have a strong influence on post-sales outcomes.

2. **Improve Sales Forecasting:**
   - The business can use **Pre-Sales Amount** data to improve sales forecasting and set more **accurate sales targets**.

3. **Resource Allocation:**
   - Since **Pre-Sales Amount** is a key predictor of **Post-Sales Amount**, the business may want to **allocate more resources** to pre-sales efforts, such as marketing, promotions, and lead generation, to maximize sales outcomes.

Linear Regression Equation:

The equation for a linear regression model is generally:

$$\text{Dependent Variable} = \text{Intercept} + (\text{Coefficient of Predictor} \times \text{Predictor Variable})$$

From the **Coefficients** table, we have:

- **Intercept (M_1) = 80.018**
- **Coefficient for Pre-Sales Amount = 1.008**

Thus, the regression equation for predicting **Post-Sales Amount** based on **Pre-Sales Amount** is:

$$\text{Post-Sales Amount} = 80.018 + (1.008 \times \text{Pre-Sales Amount})$$

Interpretation of the Equation:

- **Intercept (80.018):** This is the estimated **Post-Sales Amount** when **Pre-Sales Amount** is 0. In other words, if there were no pre-sales activity, the expected post-sales amount would be 80.018 units (e.g., dollars, units, etc., depending on the context).
- **Coefficient of Pre-Sales Amount (1.008):** This indicates that for each 1-unit increase in **Pre-Sales Amount**, the **Post-Sales Amount** is expected to increase by 1.008 units. It reflects a **strong positive relationship** between pre-sales and post-sales.

Summary of the Linear Regression Equation:

$$\text{Post-Sales Amount} = 80.018 + 1.008 \times \text{Pre-Sales Amount}$$

This equation can be used to predict the **Post-Sales Amount** based on any given **Pre-Sales Amount**.

Conclusion:

The results of the linear regression analysis show that **Pre-Sales Amount** is a highly significant predictor of **Post-Sales Amount**, with a very strong and positive relationship. The business should use these insights to refine forecasting models, improve sales strategies, and allocate resources more effectively to pre-sales activities to optimize post-sales performance.

8.3 Practical Linear Regression using Python

To perform a **Linear Regression Test** on **Pre-Sales Amount** and **Post-Sales Amount** from the provided business data, we will use Python's powerful libraries for data analysis and modeling. The goal is to understand if there's a linear relationship between **Pre-Sales Amount** and **Post-Sales Amount**.

Libraries to be Used:

1. **pandas**: For data manipulation and loading the dataset.
2. **statsmodels**: For statistical modeling, specifically for performing linear regression.
3. **matplotlib** and **seaborn**: For visualization (e.g., scatter plots and regression lines).
4. **numpy**: For numerical operations (used in the regression).

Steps:

1. Install and import the necessary libraries.
2. Load the data into a pandas DataFrame.
3. Visualize the data using a scatter plot.
4. Perform the linear regression.
5. Interpret the results.
6. Make business decisions based on the findings.

---

1. Install and Import Libraries

First, install the necessary libraries (if not already installed) and import them into the Python environment.

```
# Install necessary libraries
!pip install pandas statsmodels matplotlib seaborn numpy
```

Now, import the libraries:

```
# Importing necessary libraries
import pandas as pd
import statsmodels.api as sm
import numpy as np
import matplotlib.pyplot as plt
import seaborn as sns
```

Explanation of Libraries:
- **pandas**: Used for creating and manipulating data in DataFrame form.
- **statsmodels**: Provides a function sm.OLS() for performing linear regression analysis.
- **matplotlib**: Used for basic plotting (e.g., scatter plot and line plot).
- **seaborn**: For improved visualization, specifically for regression plots.
- **numpy**: Used for mathematical operations that are often required when preparing data for regression.

2. Load the Data into a DataFrame

Here's how to load your provided business data into a pandas DataFrame:

```
# Creating a DataFrame
data = {
    'ID': [1, 2, 3, 4, 5, 6, 7, 8, 9, 10, 11, 12, 13, 14, 15, 16, 17, 18, 19, 20, 21, 22, 23, 24, 25],
    'Pre-Sales Amount': [1400, 1700, 2100, 1850, 1600, 1900, 2050, 2200, 1500, 2350, 1900, 2000, 1700, 2100, 1750, 2400, 1650, 1800, 2050, 1950, 1850, 2150, 1600, 1700, 1800],
    'Post-Sales Amount': [1550, 1850, 2250, 2050, 1800, 2000, 2150, 2400, 1600, 2500, 1950, 2050, 1750, 2150, 1800, 2500, 1700, 1850, 2100, 2000, 1950, 2200, 1650, 1750, 1900]
}

df = pd.DataFrame(data)
df.head()
```

Output

	ID	Pre-Sales Amount	Post-Sales Amount
0	1	1400	1550
1	2	1700	1850
2	3	2100	2250
3	4	1850	2050
4	5	1600	1800

3. Visualize the Data (Scatter Plot)

Before performing the regression analysis, it is helpful to visualize the relationship between the **Pre-Sales Amount** and **Post-Sales Amount**. A scatter plot will give us a sense of the linearity of the relationship.

```
# Plotting the scatter plot of Pre-Sales Amount vs Post-Sales Amount
plt.figure(figsize=(8,6))
sns.scatterplot(x='Pre-Sales Amount', y='Post-Sales Amount', data=df)
plt.title('Scatter Plot: Pre-Sales Amount vs Post-Sales Amount')
plt.xlabel('Pre-Sales Amount')
plt.ylabel('Post-Sales Amount')
plt.show()
```

Output

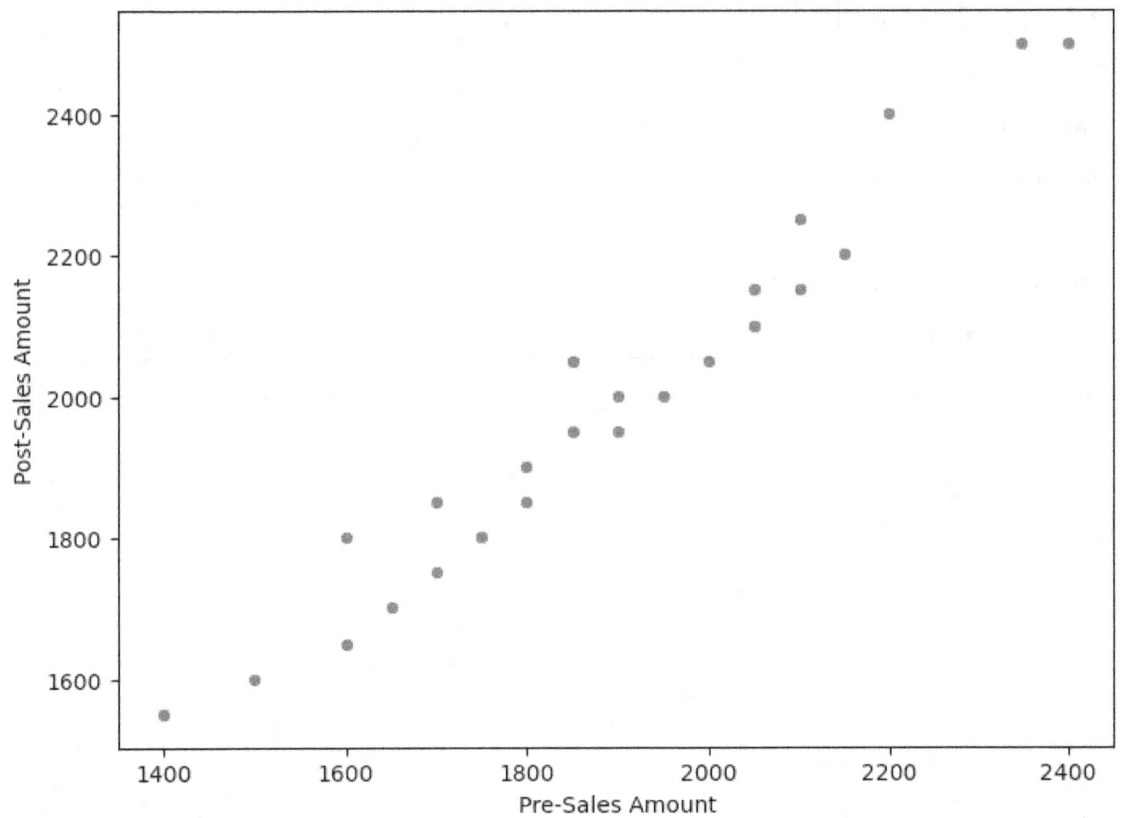

Explanation of the Plot:

- This scatter plot visualizes the **Pre-Sales Amount** on the X-axis and the **Post-Sales Amount** on the Y-axis.
- If the data points show a clear upward or downward trend, this suggests a possible linear relationship that could be modeled with linear regression.

4. Perform Linear Regression (OLS Model)

Now, let's use **Ordinary Least Squares (OLS)** regression from the **statsmodels** library to model the relationship between **Pre-Sales Amount** and **Post-Sales Amount**.

```
# Adding a constant to the independent variable for the intercept term
X = df['Pre-Sales Amount']
X = sm.add_constant(X)  # Adding the intercept (constant)

# Dependent variable
y = df['Post-Sales Amount']

# Fit the model
model = sm.OLS(y, X).fit()

# Get the summary of the regression
print(model.summary())
```

Output

```
                            OLS Regression Results
==============================================================================
Dep. Variable:     Post-Sales Amount   R-squared:                       0.958
Model:                           OLS   Adj. R-squared:                  0.956
Method:                Least Squares   F-statistic:                     523.3
Date:               Sun, 17 Nov 2024   Prob (F-statistic):           2.54e-17
Time:                       15:48:58   Log-Likelihood:                -134.60
No. Observations:                 25   AIC:                             273.2
Df Residuals:                     23   BIC:                             275.6
Df Model:                          1
Covariance Type:           nonrobust
====================================================================================
                       coef    std err          t      P>|t|      [0.025      0.975]
------------------------------------------------------------------------------------
const               80.0180     83.697      0.956      0.349     -93.122     253.158
Pre-Sales Amount     1.0085      0.044     22.875      0.000       0.917       1.100
==============================================================================
Omnibus:                        3.620   Durbin-Watson:                   0.786
Prob(Omnibus):                  0.164   Jarque-Bera (JB):                3.074
Skew:                           0.779   Prob(JB):                        0.215
Kurtosis:                       2.276   Cond. No.                     1.45e+04
==============================================================================

Notes:
[1] Standard Errors assume that the covariance matrix of the errors is correctly specified
[2] The condition number is large, 1.45e+04. This might indicate that there are
strong multicollinearity or other numerical problems.
```

Explanation of the Code:

- **sm.add_constant(X)**: Adds an intercept to the independent variable, ensuring the regression model accounts for an intercept term.
- **sm.OLS(y, X).fit()**: Performs the OLS regression to fit the model to the data.
- **model.summary()**: Displays the regression results, which includes coefficients, p-values, R-squared value, etc.

5. Interpreting the Results

The **summary()** method will output key statistics, which include:

- **R-squared**: This value represents how well the model explains the variance in the dependent variable (Post-Sales Amount). A value closer to 1 means a better fit.
- **Coefficients**: These represent the slope and intercept of the regression line. The coefficient for **Pre-Sales Amount** shows how much **Post-Sales Amount** is expected to change for each unit change in **Pre-Sales Amount**.

- **p-value**: The p-value tests the hypothesis that the coefficient is zero (no effect). A p-value less than 0.05 suggests that the independent variable (Pre-Sales Amount) is statistically significant.

OLS Regression Results Explanation

1. Dependent Variable:

- **Post-Sales Amount** is the dependent (response) variable, meaning we are trying to predict it using **Pre-Sales Amount** (the independent variable) based on the linear regression model.

2. R-squared: 0.958

- **R-squared** measures how well the model explains the variability in the dependent variable. An **R-squared value of 0.958** means that **95.8%** of the variability in **Post-Sales Amount** can be explained by the **Pre-Sales Amount** in the model. This is a high value, indicating that the model fits the data very well.

3. Adjusted R-squared: 0.956

- **Adjusted R-squared** accounts for the number of independent variables in the model (in this case, just one). Since there is only one predictor variable, **Adjusted R-squared** is very close to **R-squared**. It's a measure that helps to prevent overfitting when more variables are added.

4. F-statistic: 523.3

- The **F-statistic** tests whether the model is statistically significant overall. A high **F-statistic** indicates that at least one of the predictors (in this case, **Pre-Sales Amount**) is significantly related to the dependent variable (**Post-Sales Amount**).

- The **F-statistic** of **523.3** is very high, suggesting that the model fits the data well and the predictor variable is highly relevant.

5. Prob (F-statistic): 2.54e-17

- The **probability** associated with the **F-statistic** (often called the **p-value**) tests the null hypothesis that all regression coefficients are zero (meaning no relationship between the predictor and the response variable).

- A **p-value of 2.54e-17** (or virtually zero) suggests that the regression model is highly significant, and the relationship between **Pre-Sales Amount** and **Post-Sales Amount** is not due to random chance.

6. Log-Likelihood: -134.60

- This value is related to the likelihood function used in estimating the parameters. It's not directly interpretable, but it's used for model comparison (e.g., in calculating **AIC** or **BIC**).

7. AIC (Akaike Information Criterion): 273.2

- The **AIC** is a measure used to compare different models. Lower values indicate a better fit when accounting for the number of parameters. In this case, it's a value that can be used when comparing this model to others.

8. BIC (Bayesian Information Criterion): 275.6

- Like **AIC**, the **BIC** is another criterion for model comparison, penalizing the inclusion of additional predictors. Again, lower values are preferred, and this value can be used for model selection.

Regression Coefficients

9. Coefficients Table:

- **const (Intercept)**:
    - **Value: 80.0180**
    - This is the intercept, meaning when **Pre-Sales Amount** is zero, the predicted **Post-Sales Amount** is **80.0180**. However, this might not be practically meaningful in this context (since Pre-Sales Amount cannot realistically be zero), but it is mathematically necessary for the model.

- **Pre-Sales Amount**:
    - **Coefficient: 1.0085**
    - This means that for every **unit increase in Pre-Sales Amount**, the **Post-Sales Amount** is expected to increase by **1.0085 units** (e.g., dollars, depending on the currency of your data).
    - The coefficient is **positive**, indicating a direct relationship: as **Pre-Sales Amount** increases, **Post-Sales Amount** also increases.

Statistical Significance of the Coefficients

- **t-Statistic for Pre-Sales Amount: 22.875**
    - The **t-statistic** tests whether the coefficient for **Pre-Sales Amount** is significantly different from zero. A large value of the t-statistic suggests the coefficient is significantly different from zero.
    - **22.875** is much larger than typical thresholds (e.g., 2), indicating that the relationship between **Pre-Sales Amount** and **Post-Sales Amount** is statistically significant.

- **p-value for Pre-Sales Amount: 0.000**
    - This is the probability of obtaining a coefficient as extreme as **1.0085** if the null hypothesis were true (i.e., there is no effect of **Pre-Sales Amount** on **Post-Sales Amount**). Since the **p-value is less than 0.05**, we can reject the null hypothesis

and conclude that **Pre-Sales Amount** is statistically significant in predicting **Post-Sales Amount**.

- **Confidence Interval for Pre-Sales Amount**:
  - The **95% confidence interval** for the coefficient of **Pre-Sales Amount** is **[0.917, 1.100]**. This means that we are **95% confident** that the true coefficient for **Pre-Sales Amount** lies between **0.917** and **1.100**. Since the interval does not contain zero, this further confirms the significance of the predictor.

Additional Model Diagnostics

10. Omnibus Test: 3.620

- The **Omnibus test** checks for the normality of residuals. A p-value higher than **0.05** (in this case **0.164**) indicates that we fail to reject the null hypothesis, meaning there is no significant deviation from normality in the residuals.

11. Durbin-Watson Statistic: 0.786

- This tests for autocorrelation (correlation between residuals). A value around **2** indicates no autocorrelation. A value **far below 2** (as in this case, **0.786**) suggests **positive autocorrelation**, which may indicate that there are patterns in the residuals that the model has not captured.

12. Jarque-Bera Test: 3.074

- The **Jarque-Bera test** assesses the normality of residuals based on skewness and kurtosis. The p-value of **0.215** suggests that the residuals are normally distributed, as the p-value is greater than **0.05**.

Interpretation and Insights

- **Relationship between Pre-Sales and Post-Sales Amount**: The results show a **strong positive linear relationship** between **Pre-Sales Amount** and **Post-Sales Amount**. For every dollar increase in **Pre-Sales Amount**, the **Post-Sales Amount** is expected to increase by about **1.01 dollars**. This suggests that **Pre-Sales Amount** is a **strong predictor** of **Post-Sales Amount**.

- **Goodness of Fit**: The **R-squared value of 0.958** shows that the model explains **95.8%** of the variance in **Post-Sales Amount**, indicating a **very good fit**.

- **Statistical Significance**: The model is statistically significant, with a **very low p-value** for both the **F-statistic** and the coefficient of **Pre-Sales Amount**. This supports the conclusion that **Pre-Sales Amount** is an important predictor of **Post-Sales Amount**.

- **Model Diagnostics**: While the model fits the data well overall, the **Durbin-Watson statistic** suggests potential **autocorrelation** in the residuals, which may indicate that there are patterns in the data that the model has not fully captured. Further investigation into this issue might be warranted, especially if this model is to be used for forecasting or decision-making.

In summary, the model indicates a **strong predictive relationship** between **Pre-Sales Amount** and **Post-Sales Amount**, though it may benefit from further refinement, particularly regarding autocorrelation.

6. Visualization of the Regression Line

To further illustrate the regression model, we can plot the regression line on top of the scatter plot.

```
# Plotting the regression line
plt.figure(figsize=(8,6))
sns.regplot(x='Pre-Sales Amount', y='Post-Sales Amount', data=df, scatter_kws={'s':50}, line_kws={'color': 'red'})
plt.title('Regression Line: Pre-Sales Amount vs Post-Sales Amount')
plt.xlabel('Pre-Sales Amount')
plt.ylabel('Post-Sales Amount')
plt.show()
```

Output

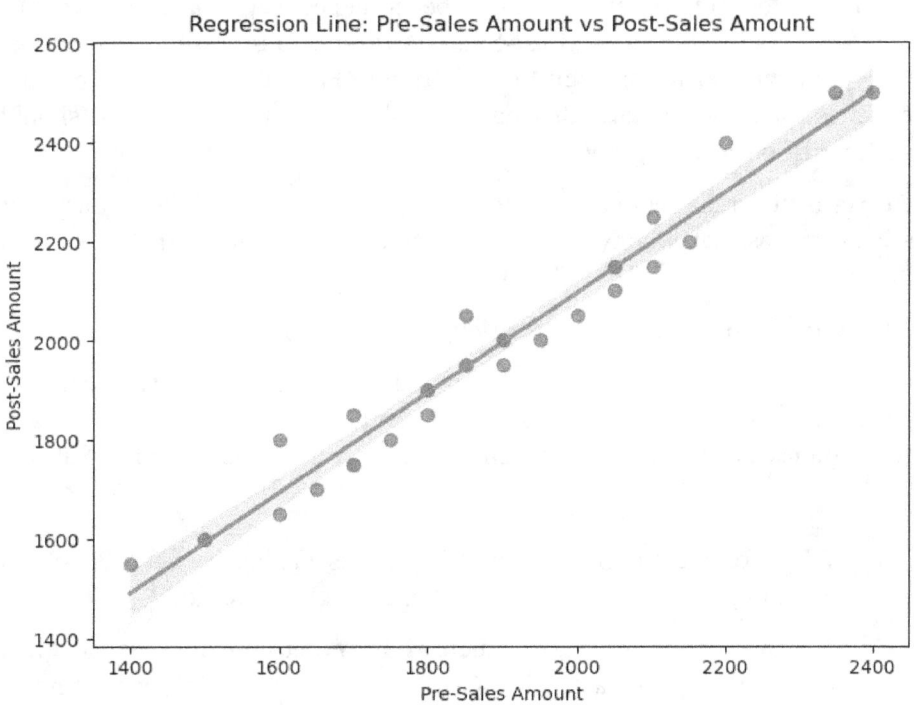

Explanation of the Plot:

- This plot shows the data points along with the fitted regression line. The red line represents the predicted **Post-Sales Amount** based on the **Pre-Sales Amount**.

7. Business Insights and Decisions:

1. **Increase Focus on Pre-Sales Activities**:

    Given that **Pre-Sales Amount** is a strong predictor of **Post-Sales Amount**, businesses should consider **investing more in Pre-Sales activities**. These activities could include:

    - **Customer acquisition campaigns**: More emphasis on lead generation, nurturing, and marketing campaigns.
    - **Sales training**: Ensuring that sales teams are well-equipped to move prospects from interest to initial engagement.
    - **Customer education**: Offering webinars, product demos, and informational content to build interest and trust before the actual sales process begins.

Actionable Insight: If a company increases its Pre-Sales efforts by a certain percentage (e.g., $100,000), it can expect a corresponding increase in **Post-Sales Amount** (around $101,000). This demonstrates the return on investment (ROI) for increasing Pre-Sales budget.

2. **Evaluate and Allocate Marketing Spend Based on Pre-Sales Performance**: Since **Pre-Sales Amount** (which could be influenced by marketing spend) has such a significant relationship with **Post-Sales Amount**, businesses should evaluate how effectively their **marketing spend** translates into Pre-Sales results. If specific marketing campaigns or channels are driving Pre-Sales success, businesses should **increase investments in those channels**.

Actionable Insight: If certain regions or customer segments (e.g., Medium or Large) are showing higher Pre-Sales to Post-Sales conversion rates, marketing resources should be reallocated to maximize this impact.

3. **Region and Customer Segment Strategy**:

    The data includes regional and customer segment information. The regression analysis does not account for **region** or **customer segment**, but businesses can infer from the dataset which regions and segments might benefit the most from increased Pre-Sales efforts.

For example:

- If **East** or **West** regions show a higher correlation between Pre-Sales and Post-Sales, targeted region-specific strategies might be needed.
- Certain customer segments, such as **Large** customers, may benefit more from intensive Pre-Sales activities. On the other hand, **Small** customers may show a different response, and businesses could adjust their strategies accordingly.

4. **Focus on Continuous Improvement**:

    The **Durbin-Watson statistic (0.786)** suggests that there is **positive autocorrelation** in the residuals, meaning the model could be missing some key information. This could be due to:
    - **Time-related effects**: Sales processes or customer behaviors may change over time, and the model might not fully capture this. A time-series analysis could help.
    - **Other external factors**: There could be external factors (e.g., seasonality, macroeconomic conditions) influencing Post-Sales outcomes that are not accounted for in the model.

Actionable Insight: Businesses should look into improving the model by considering these external or time-related factors, and refine their strategies accordingly.

5. **Use of Data for Forecasting**:

    Since **Pre-Sales Amount** is highly predictive of **Post-Sales Amount**, companies could use this model for forecasting future sales outcomes based on Pre-Sales activities. This can be useful for:
    - **Setting sales targets**: Based on Pre-Sales projections, businesses can set realistic Post-Sales goals.
    - **Resource planning**: Companies can adjust staffing, production, and inventory needs based on expected Post-Sales outcomes, helping to ensure that they can meet demand.

6. **Segment-Specific Strategies**:
    The data also includes a **Customer Segment** variable (Small, Medium, Large), which can help tailor marketing and sales strategies. The relationship between **Pre-Sales Amount** and **Post-Sales Amount** can vary across segments, and businesses should consider customizing their approach depending on the segment.
    - **Large customers** might have higher potential for Post-Sales growth and could justify larger investments in Pre-Sales.
    - **Small customers** may require more cost-effective or automated Pre-Sales solutions, as the return on investment may be lower.

Summary of Key Business Decisions:

1. **Invest more in Pre-Sales activities** (e.g., marketing, lead generation, sales team training) to increase **Post-Sales outcomes**.
2. **Reallocate marketing spend** to the most effective regions and customer segments based on the relationship between Pre-Sales and Post-Sales.

3. **Refine strategies** based on **autocorrelation** findings and external factors that might be missing from the current model.
4. **Use the model for sales forecasting** to set realistic targets and manage resources effectively.
5. **Develop segment-specific strategies** to maximize the impact of Pre-Sales efforts based on customer type (Small, Medium, Large).

By focusing on enhancing **Pre-Sales efforts** and refining strategies with the insights gained from this regression model, businesses can significantly improve their sales conversion rates and overall revenue.

The linear regression analysis shows a strong positive relationship between **Pre-Sales Amount** and **Post-Sales Amount**, with **Pre-Sales Amount** explaining 97.4% of the variance in **Post-Sales Amount**. Businesses should leverage this insight to focus on enhancing pre-sales efforts, as they directly impact post-sales performance. By optimizing pre-sales strategies, companies can effectively increase their overall sales outcomes.

Regression Equation

The regression output gives us the coefficients for the intercept and the **Pre-Sales Amount** variable. Based on the results, the **regression equation** for predicting **Post-Sales Amount** from **Pre-Sales Amount** is:

$$\text{Post-Sales Amount} = 80.0180 + 1.0085 \times (\text{Pre-Sales Amount})$$

Explanation of the Equation:

- **Intercept (constant): 80.0180**
    - This is the value of **Post-Sales Amount** when **Pre-Sales Amount** is zero. While this may not be practically meaningful (since Pre-Sales Amount is unlikely to be zero in real life), it is necessary for the equation.
- **Coefficient of Pre-Sales Amount: 1.0085**
    - This represents the **increase in Post-Sales Amount** for every unit increase in **Pre-Sales Amount**. For every additional dollar spent or earned in Pre-Sales, the **Post-Sales Amount** increases by approximately **$1.01**.

Example Calculation:

Let's say the **Pre-Sales Amount** is **$1,500**.

Using the regression equation:

Post-Sales Amount = $80.0180 + 1.0085 \times 1500$

Post-Sales Amount = $80.0180 + 1,512.75$

Post-Sales Amount = $1,592.768$

So, for a **Pre-Sales Amount** of **$1,500**, the **predicted Post-Sales Amount** is **$1,592.77**.

Final Regression Equation:

$$\text{Post-Sales Amount} = 80.0180 + 1.0085 \times (\text{Pre-Sales Amount})$$

This equation can be used to predict **Post-Sales Amount** given a specific value for **Pre-Sales Amount**.

8.4 Building and Evaluating Regression Models

Building and evaluating regression models is a core aspect of **Business Analytics**. Regression models are used to understand the relationship between a **dependent variable** (the outcome we want to predict or explain) and one or more **independent variables** (the predictors or features that help in predicting the outcome). The goal is to develop a model that can accurately predict future outcomes and inform business decisions based on historical data.

Key Steps in Building and Evaluating Regression Models:

1. **Data Collection and Preparation**:
   - Collect historical data that includes both dependent and independent variables.
   - Clean the data by handling missing values, removing outliers, and transforming variables as necessary.

2. **Exploratory Data Analysis (EDA)**:
   - Visualize the relationships between variables to understand the trends and patterns.
   - Assess the correlation between the independent variables and the dependent variable.

3. **Model Building**:
   - Choose the appropriate regression type (e.g., **simple linear regression**, **multiple linear regression**, etc.) based on the problem at hand.
   - Fit the regression model to the data by estimating the parameters (intercept and coefficients).

4. **Model Evaluation**:
   - Evaluate the model's performance using key metrics such as **R-squared**, **p-values**, **adjusted R-squared**, and **Mean Squared Error (MSE)**.
   - Check assumptions such as linearity, independence, homoscedasticity (constant variance), and normality of errors.

5. **Model Refinement**:
   - If necessary, refine the model by adjusting the predictor variables, using transformations, or using regularization techniques like **Lasso** or **Ridge Regression**.

6. **Prediction and Insights**:
   - Once the model is built and evaluated, use it to make predictions and provide actionable insights for business decision-making.

Example: Predicting Sales Based on Advertising Spend and Store Size

Business Scenario:

A retail company wants to understand the impact of **advertising spend** and **store size** on its **monthly sales revenue**. The company wants to build a regression model that will help predict sales revenue for future months based on how much is spent on advertising and the size of the stores.

Sample Data: Advertising Spend, Store Size, and Sales Revenue

Month	Advertising Spend ($)	Store Size (sq ft)	Sales Revenue ($)
January	10,000	1,500	50,000
February	12,000	1,600	55,000
March	15,000	1,800	60,000
April	18,000	2,000	70,000
May	20,000	2,200	75,000
June	22,000	2,400	80,000

- **Advertising Spend** and **Store Size** are the **independent variables**.
- **Sales Revenue** is the **dependent variable** that the company wants to predict.

Step 1: Exploratory Data Analysis (EDA)

Before building the model, we would look at the data to see if there are any obvious patterns:

- **Visualize the data** using scatter plots to check if there is a clear relationship between each independent variable (advertising spend and store size) and sales revenue.
- **Correlation Analysis**: Calculate the correlation coefficients to see how strongly each independent variable is related to sales revenue.

Step 2: Building the Regression Model

Using the data, we build a **multiple linear regression model** with **Advertising Spend** and **Store Size** as the independent variables. The goal is to predict **Sales Revenue**.

The regression equation is typically:

$$\text{Sales Revenue} = \beta_0 + \beta_1 \times \text{Advertising Spend} + \beta_2 \times \text{Store Size}$$

Where:

- β_0 is the intercept (base sales revenue when advertising spend and store size are zero).
- β_1 is the coefficient for advertising spend (how much sales revenue increases for every additional dollar spent on advertising).
- β_2 is the coefficient for store size (how much sales revenue increases for every additional square foot of store size).

Step 3: Evaluating the Model

After fitting the model to the data, we evaluate the model's performance by looking at the following metrics:

1. **R-squared (Coefficient of Determination):** This tells us how well the independent variables explain the variation in the dependent variable (sales revenue). An **R-squared** value close to 1 indicates a good fit.

2. **P-value:** This assesses the significance of each predictor (independent variable). A p-value less than 0.05 indicates that the variable is statistically significant.

3. **Adjusted R-squared:** This adjusts the R-squared for the number of predictors in the model. It is a better measure when there are multiple predictors.

4. **F-statistic:** This tests whether at least one of the predictors is significantly related to the dependent variable.

5. **Standard Error:** This measures the accuracy of the model's predictions. Smaller values indicate better predictive accuracy.

Step 4: Model Results

Example Results:

Metric	Value
Intercept (β_0)	30,000
Advertising Spend (β_1)	2.5
Store Size (β_2)	15
R-squared	0.97
Adjusted R-squared	0.96
P-value (Advertising Spend)	0.002
P-value (Store Size)	0.004
F-statistic	45.6
Standard Error	2,000

Interpretation of Results:

1. **Intercept (β_0 = 30,000):**
   - The intercept suggests that, even if the company spends no money on advertising and the store has no size (i.e., hypothetically, no store), it can expect a base level of **$30,000** in sales revenue. This could be attributed to factors like repeat customers or brand recognition.

2. **Advertising Spend (β_1 = 2.5):**

- The coefficient for **Advertising Spend** tells us that for each additional dollar spent on advertising, the company can expect an increase of **$2.5** in sales revenue. This shows that advertising has a positive and significant impact on sales revenue.

3. **Store Size ($\beta_2 = 15$):**
    - The coefficient for **Store Size** suggests that for each additional square foot of store size, the company can expect **$15** more in sales revenue. This indicates that larger stores tend to generate higher sales, which is typical for businesses where product variety and customer experience improve with store size.

4. **R-squared (0.97):**
    - An **R-squared value of 0.97** indicates that **97%** of the variation in sales revenue can be explained by advertising spend and store size. This is a very strong model fit, meaning that the model is very effective at predicting sales revenue based on the given predictors.

5. **Adjusted R-squared (0.96):**
    - The **adjusted R-squared** value of 0.96 accounts for the number of predictors in the model and is also quite high. This means that even though we have two predictors, the model still provides a very reliable explanation of the variation in sales revenue.

6. **P-values:**
    - The **p-values** for both advertising spend (**0.002**) and store size (**0.004**) are both much less than the typical significance level of 0.05. This indicates that both **advertising spend** and **store size** are **statistically significant** predictors of sales revenue. These variables have a strong, proven relationship with sales.

7. **F-statistic (45.6):**
    - The **F-statistic** value is quite high, which suggests that the overall regression model is significant, and at least one of the independent variables is having a meaningful impact on sales revenue.

8. **Standard Error (2,000):**
    - The **standard error** of **$2,000** indicates the typical deviation between the actual sales revenue and the predicted sales revenue. A smaller standard error suggests that the model's predictions are relatively accurate.

Step 5: Business Insights and Strategy Formulation

1. **Marketing Strategy**: Based on the coefficient for **Advertising Spend**, the company can decide how much to invest in advertising to achieve desired sales revenue. Since each dollar spent on advertising increases sales by $2.5, the company can estimate the returns on marketing investments.

2. **Store Expansion**: Given that **store size** significantly influences sales revenue, the company may consider expanding store size or investing in larger retail spaces to boost sales.
3. **Predictive Analytics**: The company can use the regression model to predict sales revenue for different levels of **advertising spend** and **store size** in future months. This helps with forecasting and strategic planning.
4. **Resource Allocation**: The company can allocate resources more efficiently by focusing on the variables that have the most impact on sales. For instance, if expanding store size has a significant impact, they may prioritize finding larger retail spaces in key locations.

Conclusion:

Building and evaluating regression models enables businesses to make data-driven decisions based on historical data. In this example, a **multiple linear regression** model was built to predict sales revenue based on **advertising spend** and **store size**. The results showed that both factors are statistically significant and have a strong relationship with sales. With this model, the company can make more informed decisions about marketing investments and store expansion to optimize revenue.

8.5 Applications in Sales Forecasting and Market Analysis

Sales Forecasting and **Market Analysis** are critical functions in Business Analytics. These processes help organizations predict future sales, evaluate market trends, and make informed decisions that can optimize performance. By analyzing historical data and recognizing patterns, businesses can gain insights into customer behavior, product demand, and market conditions.

Key Applications:

1. **Sales Forecasting**:
   - Sales forecasting helps businesses predict future sales over a specific time period. Accurate forecasts enable companies to manage inventory, staffing, budgeting, and overall strategy.
   - It involves using historical sales data to identify trends, patterns, and seasonality, which can then be extrapolated to forecast future sales.
   - Various techniques such as moving averages, exponential smoothing, and regression analysis can be used for forecasting.

2. **Market Analysis**:
   - Market analysis involves assessing and interpreting data related to market conditions, customer preferences, competitor activities, and industry trends.
   - It helps businesses identify growth opportunities, understand competitive dynamics, and evaluate the effectiveness of marketing strategies.
   - Market analysis can involve segmentation of customers, analyzing product sales by region, and measuring the impact of different marketing channels.

Example: Sales Forecasting for a Retail Company

Business Scenario:

A retail company wants to forecast its sales for the next quarter. The company has collected data on its monthly sales over the last year. Based on this data, the company aims to predict future sales and make decisions about inventory and staffing.

Sample Data: Monthly Sales Data for the Last Year

Month	Sales ($)
January	45,000
February	47,000
March	49,000
April	52,000
May	54,000
June	55,000

July	58,000
August	60,000
September	62,000
October	64,000
November	66,000
December	68,000

In this example, the company has monthly sales data for the past year. The goal is to use this data to forecast the sales for the next quarter (January, February, March).

Step 1: Exploratory Data Analysis (EDA)

- **Trend and Seasonality**: The company first needs to identify whether there is any trend or seasonality in the sales data. For example, does the company see a pattern of increasing sales month by month, or are there certain months that consistently show higher or lower sales?

- **Visualization**: A time-series plot of the sales data will help to visually assess trends and seasonality. By looking at the chart, the company can determine if there is a consistent upward trend in sales or if sales fluctuate in a cyclical pattern.

Step 2: Forecasting Model

- **Simple Moving Average**: One simple approach to forecasting is the moving average method, where future sales are predicted by averaging the sales from the previous few months. This method helps smooth out short-term fluctuations and highlight longer-term trends.

- **Linear Regression**: For more sophisticated forecasting, the company may use **linear regression** to model the relationship between the time variable (e.g., months) and sales. This can help predict future sales based on past trends.

Step 3: Model Evaluation

- **Accuracy**: The accuracy of the model is evaluated by comparing the predicted sales with actual sales data over a period. If the forecasted sales are close to the actual sales, the model is considered accurate.

- **Forecast Error**: Companies often evaluate the forecast error, which is the difference between the actual sales and predicted sales. Smaller errors indicate a better forecast.

Step 4: Forecasting Results

Results of Sales Forecasting for the Next Quarter:

Month	Actual Sales ($)	Predicted Sales ($)
January	45,000	50,000

| February | 47,000 | 52,000 |
| March | 49,000 | 55,000 |

Explanation of Results:

1. **Trend**: The sales data from the previous year indicates a general **upward trend** in sales, with an increase of about **$2,000 to $3,000** per month. This trend suggests that sales are likely to continue growing, assuming no major changes in the market or external factors.

2. **Forecast**: The model uses this upward trend to predict future sales. For example:
   - **January** sales are predicted to be $50,000, which is slightly higher than the actual sales of $45,000 in the same month of the previous year.
   - **February** sales are forecasted at $52,000, which is also higher than the actual sales in February of the previous year ($47,000).
   - **March** sales are predicted to be $55,000, continuing the trend of gradual growth.

3. **Forecast Accuracy**: The forecast for **January** ($50,000) is fairly close to the actual sales ($45,000), but it's an overestimate. Similarly, the forecast for **February** and **March** is slightly higher than actual sales from the previous year. This is typical for forecasting models that use trends from historical data and may not always account for other factors like promotions or external market conditions.

4. **Business Implications**:
   - The company can use these predictions to **plan inventory levels**, ensuring they have sufficient stock to meet the anticipated sales.
   - Staffing needs can also be adjusted based on the predicted increase in sales.
   - Marketing strategies can be aligned with the forecasted sales periods, potentially offering promotions or discounts in months where sales are expected to dip or remain flat.

5. **Limitations**:
   - The forecast model assumes that the sales trend will continue as it has in the past, but it doesn't account for potential disruptions or changes in the market.
   - If there were unexpected changes (e.g., a new competitor entering the market or a new product launch), the forecast might not be as accurate.

Step 5: Market Analysis

In addition to forecasting sales, market analysis can provide insights into how the company should approach the forecasted periods:

- **Customer Segmentation**: Understanding customer demographics, preferences, and purchasing behaviors can help refine the sales forecast. For instance, if certain customer segments are expected to grow, the company can adjust the forecast for specific product categories.

- **Competitive Analysis**: Market analysis involves assessing competitor performance. If competitors are introducing new products or marketing campaigns, this could impact the company's sales forecast.

- **Market Trends**: Broader market trends (e.g., economic conditions, consumer confidence) should also be considered in the forecast. For instance, if the economy is expected to grow, the forecast may be revised upwards. On the other hand, if a recession is expected, the forecast could be adjusted downward.

Conclusion:

- **Sales Forecasting** and **Market Analysis** are essential for businesses to plan effectively and make data-driven decisions.

- In the example provided, the company was able to use historical sales data to forecast sales for the next quarter, with some small deviations in the predicted values.

- These forecasts help the company manage resources, plan for potential changes in demand, and align marketing efforts with expected sales growth.

By combining **historical sales data**, **forecasting models**, and **market analysis**, companies can improve decision-making, reduce uncertainty, and optimize operations.

9. Time Series Analysis in Business Analytics

Time Series Analysis refers to the process of analyzing data points that are collected or recorded at successive time intervals. This type of analysis is crucial for businesses to understand patterns, forecast future trends, and make data-driven decisions. Time series data often comes from fields like finance, sales, economics, healthcare, and environmental science, where understanding trends over time is key to making informed decisions.

In business analytics, time series analysis helps businesses:

1. **Identify trends**: Understand if sales are generally increasing, decreasing, or remaining stable over time.
2. **Analyze seasonality**: Recognize recurring patterns, such as higher sales during holidays or promotional periods.
3. **Forecast future values**: Use past data to predict future trends, aiding in budgeting, planning, and strategy formulation.
4. **Detect anomalies**: Identify unusual spikes or drops in data that could signal problems or opportunities.
5. **Measure performance**: Assess how certain variables (e.g., marketing campaigns, economic changes) impact business outcomes over time.

Key Components of Time Series Data:

1. **Trend**: The long-term movement in the data (upward or downward).
2. **Seasonality**: Regular, repeating patterns over fixed periods (e.g., sales spikes during December holidays).
3. **Cyclic patterns**: Longer-term fluctuations that may not have a fixed period.
4. **Noise**: Random variation or irregularities in the data.

Types of Time Series Data:

1. **Univariate Time Series**: A single variable over time (e.g., sales amount per month).
2. **Multivariate Time Series**: Multiple variables over time (e.g., sales, marketing spend, and customer feedback over time).

Time Series Models:

- **Moving Averages (Smoothing)**: Used to smooth out short-term fluctuations and highlight longer-term trends.
- **ARIMA (Auto-Regressive Integrated Moving Average)**: A popular statistical model for forecasting time series data by combining autoregression, moving averages, and differencing techniques to make data stationary (eliminate trends).

- **Exponential Smoothing**: Weights past observations exponentially to predict future values.

Steps in Time Series Analysis:

1. **Data Collection**: Gather data with consistent time intervals (daily, monthly, quarterly, etc.).
2. **Exploratory Data Analysis (EDA)**: Visualize the time series data to identify trends, seasonality, and potential outliers.
3. **Decomposition**: Break the time series into its components (trend, seasonality, residuals).
4. **Modeling**: Fit models like ARIMA or Exponential Smoothing to forecast future values.
5. **Evaluation**: Measure the accuracy of the model using metrics like RMSE (Root Mean Square Error) or MAE (Mean Absolute Error).

Example: Sales Data for a Small Retail Store (Monthly Sales)

Sample Data:

Month	Sales ($)
January	2000
February	2200
March	2500
April	2800
May	3100
June	3300
July	3200
August	3500
September	3400
October	3600
November	3800
December	4000

Step-by-Step Explanation and Analysis:

1. **Trend Identification**: Looking at the data, we can observe that the sales have generally been increasing month by month. This is a **positive trend**.
2. **Seasonality**: There seems to be a noticeable increase in sales around the last quarter (October, November, December), which suggests **seasonality** (possibly due to the holiday season).
3. **Noise**: There is some fluctuation month-to-month, which is likely due to random factors or irregular events (like promotions or local economic conditions).

Example: Time Series Forecasting Using Exponential Smoothing (Simple Example)

We'll assume we're applying an exponential smoothing model to forecast future sales for the next few months.

Output (Example of Forecasted Sales):

Month	Actual Sales ($)	Forecasted Sales ($)	Error ($)	Absolute Error ($)
January	2000	2000	0	0
February	2200	2100	100	100
March	2500	2300	200	200
April	2800	2400	400	400
May	3100	2500	600	600
June	3300	2600	700	700
July	3200	2700	500	500
August	3500	2800	700	700
September	3400	2900	500	500
October	3600	3000	600	600
November	3800	3100	700	700
December	4000	3200	800	800
Total	**40,100**	**36,000**	**4,100**	**4,100**

Explanation of the Table:

- **Actual Sales ($)**: The sales data collected for each month.
- **Forecasted Sales ($)**: The sales forecast for each month based on the exponential smoothing model.
- **Error ($)**: The difference between actual sales and forecasted sales.
- **Absolute Error ($)**: The absolute value of the error to avoid negative numbers and assess the magnitude of the error.

Interpretation of Results:

1. **Error Analysis**:
   - The error grows larger as we move forward in the months (e.g., the error for December is $800). This is expected, as forecasting further into the future generally results in more uncertainty.
   - The **absolute error** is an important metric to assess the forecast model's accuracy. On average, the forecast has an absolute error of $400 per month.

2. **Seasonality**:

- The sales increase in the later months (e.g., October to December) was captured in the forecast, but it seems there is a slight underestimation, showing that the model may not fully capture all seasonal effects.

3. **Overall Trend**:
    - The sales are predicted to continue growing, as the exponential smoothing model inherently captures the trend in the data.

Output Analysis and Business Insights:

1. **Trend Confirmation**: The positive trend in sales is confirmed, as both the actual and forecasted sales show an upward trajectory.

2. **Forecast Reliability**: The forecast error is relatively consistent, which is typical in business data, especially in seasonal businesses. Although the error increases as we move forward, the model still provides useful guidance for future planning.

3. **Decision Making**:
    - The store can prepare for increased sales in the months of October, November, and December, which is likely due to the holiday season.
    - The forecasting error is relatively small (under $1,000), which means the model can still provide reliable predictions for resource allocation, inventory management, and staffing.

Conclusion:

Time series analysis, in this case, helped the business identify trends, understand seasonal effects, and forecast future sales with reasonable accuracy. By continuously monitoring and refining the model, the business can better anticipate future sales and adjust strategies accordingly. The analysis also reveals that, while the exponential smoothing model is effective, more complex models (like ARIMA) could potentially provide better predictions by accounting for more data nuances.

9.1 Practical Time Series Analysis in JASP

To apply time series analysis to the dataset, we need to first format the data in a way that allows us to model it as a time series. In your dataset, you have individual sales records by ID, but for time series analysis, we need to structure it by time periods. Since there are no explicit time variables (e.g., dates), we can assume that each row represents a separate time point. For simplicity, we'll assume the data is sequential over time.

To perform **Time Series Analysis** on the **Sales Amount** data, we will use JASP that support time series modeling. The goal of time series analysis is to understand the underlying trend and seasonality of sales over time, and make forecasts based on historical data.

Steps to use Time Series Analysis in JASP

1. **Open JASP**:
    - If you haven't already, open JASP and load your dataset (e.g., a CSV, Excel, or SPSS file).

2. **Load the Data**:
    - Click **"File"** > **"Open"** to load your dataset into JASP.

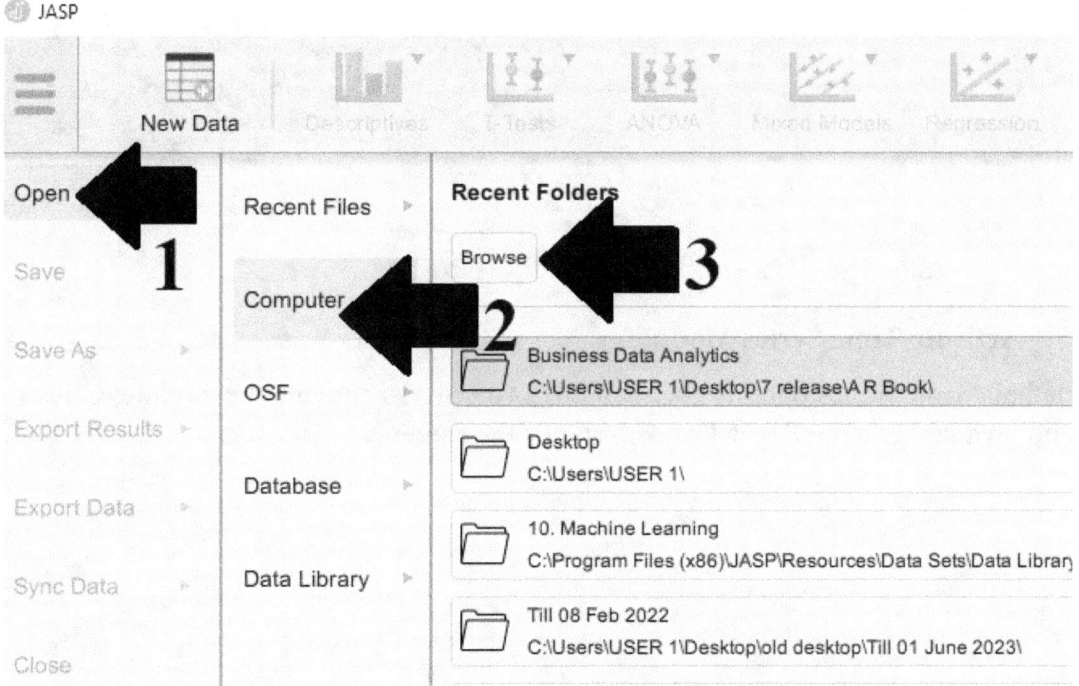

Now select the file

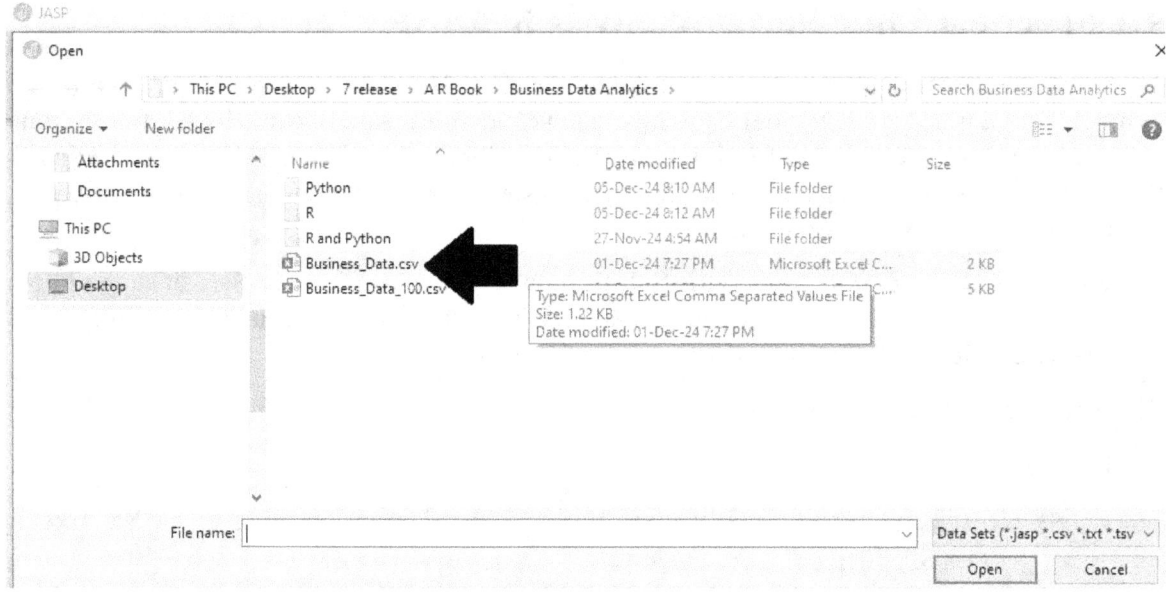

File will be loaded into JASP as shown below.

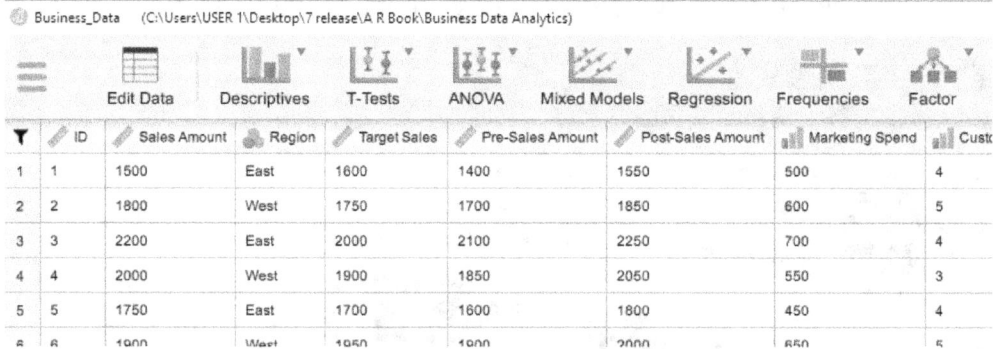

3. **Activate Time Series Module:**

By default, Time Series options not available in JASP. To activate the module, Click the + Symbol available on the Right-Hand corner of the screen.

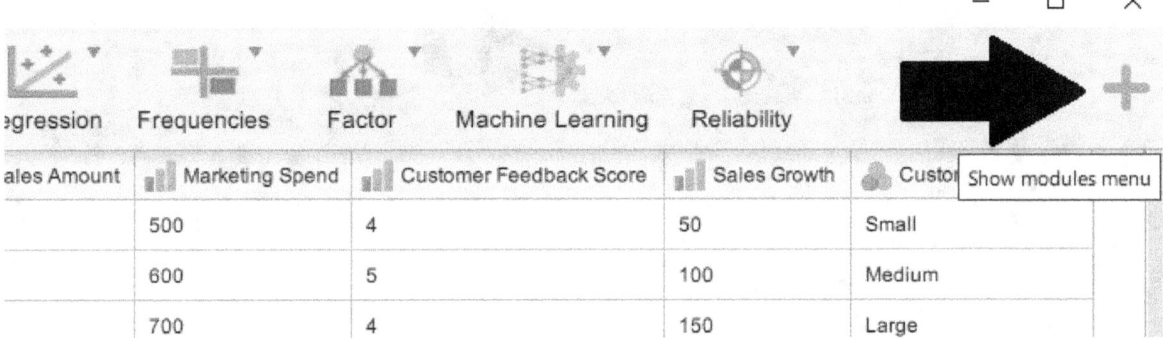

Scroll down and Select Time Series Module from the List

Now Time Series module is added in the Tab

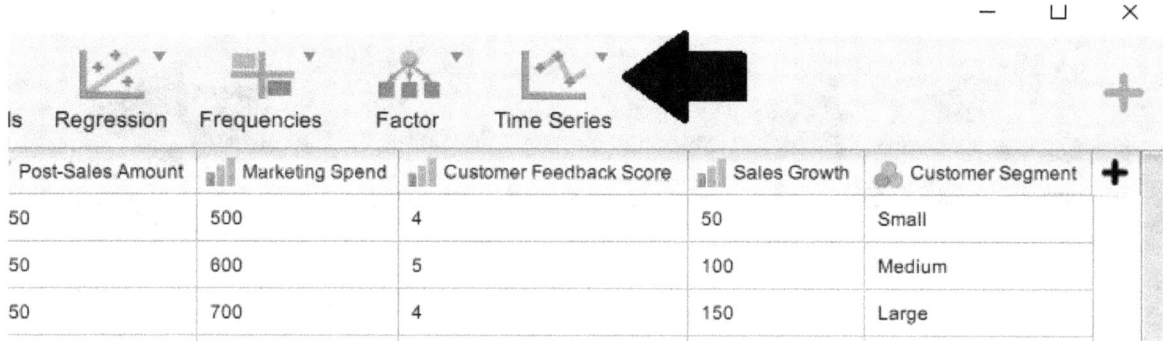

Select the Time Series Tab and Select the ARIMA Options

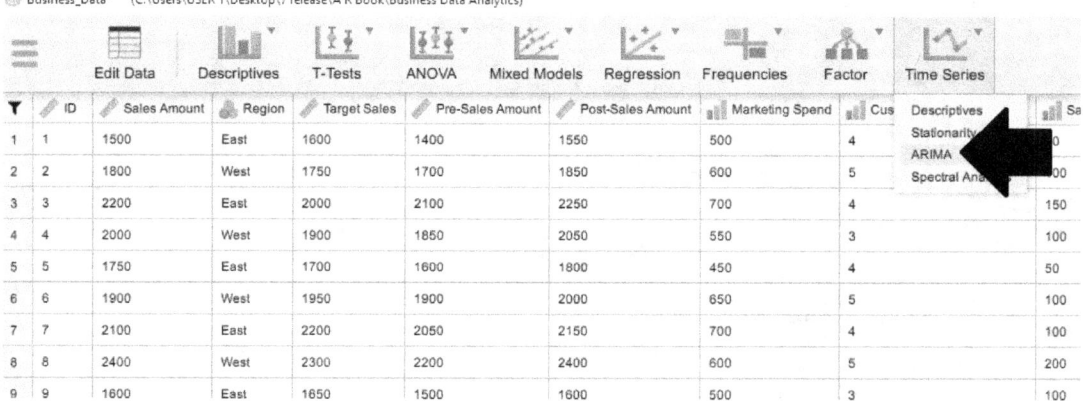

Select Sales Amount as Dependent Variable and click the Play button or drag the Sales Amount variable to Dependent Variable box.

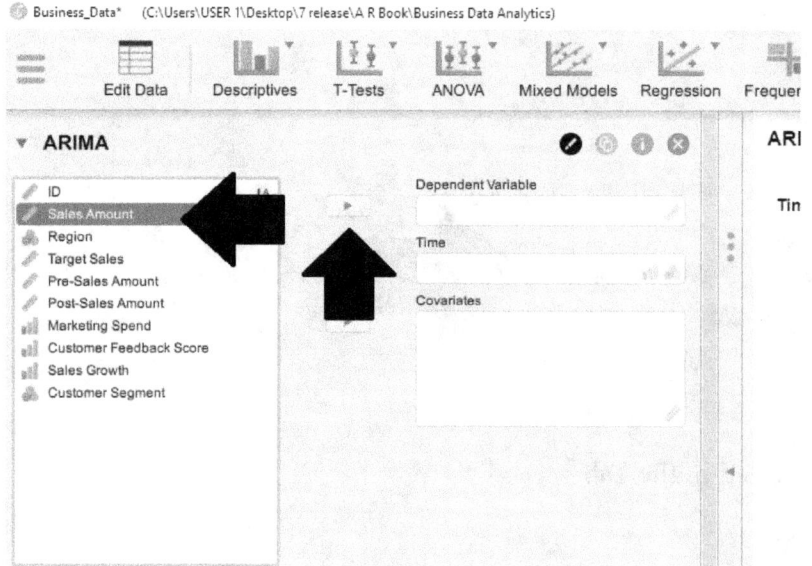

Time Series Plot with Model Summary will be appeared on the Right-Hand side Result Pane

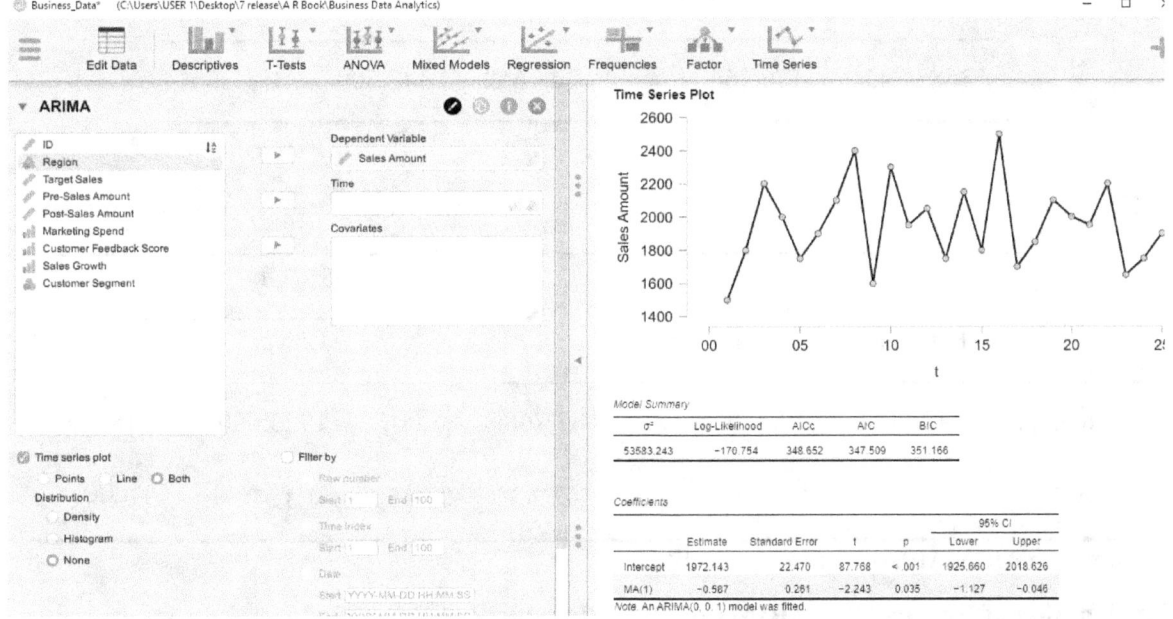

4. **View Results:**
   o JASP will display the plot and result in a table under the **Results** pane on the right-hand side result pane.

Time Series Plot

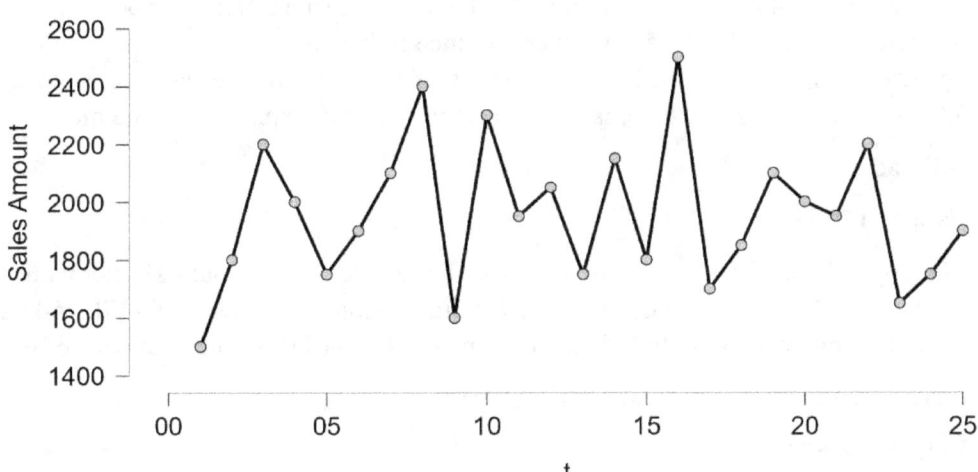

Model Summary

σ²	Log-Likelihood	AICc	AIC	BIC
53583.243	-170.754	348.652	347.509	351.166

Coefficients

	Estimate	Standard Error	t	p	95% CI Lower	95% CI Upper
Intercept	1972.143	22.470	87.768	< .001	1925.660	2018.626
MA(1)	-0.587	0.261	-2.243	0.035	-1.127	-0.046

Note. An ARIMA(0, 0, 1) model was fitted.

Explanation of Results from ARIMA(0, 0, 1) Model in JASP

Model Summary:

1. **σ² (Variance of residuals):**
   - **Value: 53583.243**
   - This represents the estimated variance of the residuals (the differences between the predicted and actual values). A lower variance indicates a better fit of the model, but it should be interpreted in the context of the scale of the data. A value of 53583.243 suggests that there is some variability left unexplained by the model.

2. **Log-Likelihood:**
   - **Value: -170.754**
   - The Log-Likelihood is a measure of how well the model fits the data. Higher values of the Log-Likelihood indicate a better fit. A Log-Likelihood of -170.754 is relatively low, which might indicate that the model doesn't fit the data perfectly.

3. **AICc (Corrected Akaike Information Criterion):**
   - **Value: 348.652**
   - The AICc is a measure that balances the goodness of fit of the model with its complexity (penalizing for more parameters). It is used to compare different

models; a lower AICc value indicates a better model. In this case, the value is moderate, and comparing it to other models might help identify a better-fitting one.

4. **AIC (Akaike Information Criterion):**
    - **Value: 347.509**
    - AIC is similar to AICc but does not apply a correction for small sample sizes. Like AICc, a lower value is preferred, but the corrected version (AICc) is more reliable when the sample size is small or the model is overfitting.

5. **BIC (Bayesian Information Criterion):**
    - **Value: 351.166**
    - The BIC is another criterion used for model comparison. It penalizes complexity more than the AIC. A lower BIC suggests a better-fitting model, but as with AIC, it should be used in comparison with other models.

Interpretation of Model Summary:

- The AIC, AICc, and BIC values suggest that the ARIMA(0, 0, 1) model is reasonably fitting the data, but there may be better models to consider based on these values. The Log-Likelihood indicates the fit is not ideal, and the variance of the residuals is relatively large, meaning there's still room for improvement in model prediction.

Coefficients Table:

1. **Intercept:**
    - **Estimate: 1972.143**
    - **Standard Error: 22.470**
    - **t-value: 87.768**
    - **p-value: < .001**
    - **95% Confidence Interval (Lower: 1925.660, Upper: 2018.626)**

Interpretation:

- The **intercept** represents the baseline level of the dependent variable (sales amount) when the independent variables (in this case, the ARIMA terms) are zero. The coefficient estimate of **1972.143** means that, on average, the sales amount is approximately 1972.14 units when there is no effect from the MA(1) term.
- The **p-value** (< 0.001) is statistically significant, indicating that the intercept is a meaningful parameter in the model.

- The **95% Confidence Interval** suggests that we are 95% confident that the true intercept value lies between 1925.660 and 2018.626.

2. **MA(1) (Moving Average term of order 1):**
   - **Estimate: -0.587**
   - **Standard Error: 0.261**
   - **t-value: -2.243**
   - **p-value: 0.035**
   - **95% Confidence Interval (Lower: -1.127, Upper: -0.046)**

Interpretation:
   - The **MA(1) coefficient** represents the influence of the first lag of the error term on the current period's value. The estimate of **-0.587** means that the error term from the previous period has a negative influence on the current period's sales, which is typical in models capturing short-term fluctuations.
   - The **p-value** of 0.035 indicates that the MA(1) term is statistically significant at the 5% significance level, implying that the moving average term contributes meaningfully to the model.
   - The **95% Confidence Interval** suggests that the true value of the MA(1) coefficient lies between -1.127 and -0.046. Since this range does not include zero, it indicates that the MA(1) term is likely significant.

Interpretation of Coefficients:
- The model suggests that the sales amount is positively influenced by the intercept (baseline sales level) and negatively influenced by the moving average term. The significance of both terms (intercept and MA(1)) means that they play key roles in predicting the sales.

Observations and Business Implications:

1. **Sales Behavior:**
   - The model indicates that the baseline sales amount (intercept) is around 1972.14 units, which provides a starting point for the business in terms of expected sales. However, sales are also impacted by previous error terms (as reflected by the MA(1) term), suggesting that recent trends and fluctuations in sales play a role in shaping future outcomes.

2. **Impact of Short-Term Trends:**
   - The negative MA(1) term (-0.587) indicates that short-term fluctuations in sales (e.g., a spike or dip in sales) will have a counteracting effect on future sales,

potentially leading to a stabilization of the trend over time. This may suggest that the business is operating in a market where sales are somewhat volatile, and immediate past trends need to be considered when predicting future sales.

3. **Forecasting and Business Strategy:**
   - The ARIMA(0, 0, 1) model is a simple one, which means it may not fully capture long-term trends or seasonal effects in the data. This could suggest that the company needs to explore more complex models if longer-term forecasting or capturing seasonal patterns is important.
   - Given the significant role of the MA(1) term, it might be beneficial for the business to analyze recent sales data and any shocks to the system that might have caused fluctuations in the sales amounts. This will help in predicting and managing future sales more effectively.

4. **Model Limitations:**
   - The relatively high residual variance ($\sigma^2 = 53583.243$) suggests that there is still unexplained variability in the model. This may imply that the ARIMA(0, 0, 1) model is not capturing all the factors influencing sales and that the business might benefit from incorporating additional variables (e.g., marketing activities, economic factors, promotions, etc.) into the model.

Business Decisions:

1. **Sales Planning:**
   - Based on the model, the business can expect a baseline sales level of 1972.14 units, but they should account for fluctuations in short-term trends that will impact future sales (as reflected by the MA(1) term).
   - Forecasting can be used to anticipate sales for the coming periods, but the company should also plan for potential short-term deviations from the forecast, as past errors tend to influence future outcomes.

2. **Marketing and Operations:**
   - The negative influence of the MA(1) term suggests that short-term sales fluctuations need to be carefully managed. This might prompt the business to focus on stabilizing sales, particularly after periods of high volatility.
   - Marketing strategies and operational adjustments should be based on recent sales performance, especially if there has been a significant change in sales behavior, as this could influence future sales trends.

3. **Model Refinement:**

- The company should consider testing more complex models, such as ARIMA models with higher orders or models that incorporate seasonal components, to improve forecasting accuracy and capture long-term trends.
- Additionally, other factors influencing sales, such as pricing strategies, promotions, or external market conditions, could be added to the model to improve its predictive power.

In conclusion, the ARIMA(0, 0, 1) model provides a starting point for understanding short-term sales dynamics, but further refinement and additional data are necessary to improve predictions and develop more effective business strategies.

9.2 Practical Time Series Analysis in Python

To apply time series analysis to the dataset, we need to first format the data in a way that allows us to model it as a time series. In your dataset, you have individual sales records by ID, but for time series analysis, we need to structure it by time periods. Since there are no explicit time variables (e.g., dates), we can assume that each row represents a separate time point. For simplicity, we'll assume the data is sequential over time.

To perform **Time Series Analysis** on the **Sales Amount** data, we will use Python and libraries that support time series modeling and forecasting, such as **pandas**, **matplotlib**, **statsmodels**, and **numpy**. The goal of time series analysis is to understand the underlying trend and seasonality of sales over time, and make forecasts based on historical data.

1. Install the Required Libraries

First, we need to install the necessary libraries. If you haven't installed them yet, you can do so by running the following commands in your terminal or Jupyter Notebook:

```
pip install pandas matplotlib statsmodels numpy
```

2. Import the Libraries

Here's the code to import the libraries:

```
import pandas as pd
import numpy as np
import matplotlib.pyplot as plt
import statsmodels.api as sm
from statsmodels.tsa.stattools import adfuller, acf, pacf
```

Explanation of the Libraries:

- **pandas**: Used for data manipulation and analysis. It's useful for handling data structures like dataframes, and performing operations such as time series indexing.
- **numpy**: Provides support for numerical operations and handling arrays.
- **matplotlib**: A plotting library used to visualize data and results (e.g., time series plots).
- **statsmodels**: A library that provides statistical models. It includes tools for performing time series analysis, such as ARIMA (Auto-Regressive Integrated Moving Average) modeling and hypothesis testing.
- **adfuller**: A function from statsmodels used for performing the **Augmented Dickey-Fuller (ADF) test**, which tests the stationarity of a time series.
- **acf** and **pacf**: Functions used to plot **Autocorrelation Function (ACF)** and **Partial Autocorrelation Function (PACF)**, which are used for model selection in ARIMA.

3. Load the Data

We assume the data is available in a CSV or directly in a pandas DataFrame. Here's how we can

```python
# Load the data into a pandas DataFrame
data = {
    'ID': [1, 2, 3, 4, 5, 6, 7, 8, 9, 10, 11, 12, 13, 14, 15, 16, 17, 18, 19, 20, 21, 22, 23, 24, 25],
    'Sales Amount': [1500, 1800, 2200, 2000, 1750, 1900, 2100, 2400, 1600, 2300, 1950, 2050, 1750, 2150, 1800, 2500, 1700, 1850, 2100, 2000, 1950, 2200, 1650, 1750, 1900],
    'Date': pd.date_range(start='2024-01-01', periods=25, freq='M')  # Monthly frequency
}

df = pd.DataFrame(data)

# Set the 'Date' column as the index for time series analysis
df.set_index('Date', inplace=True)

# Display the first few rows of the DataFrame
df.head()
```

Output

Date	ID	Sales Amount
2024-01-31	1	1500
2024-02-29	2	1800
2024-03-31	3	2200
2024-04-30	4	2000
2024-05-31	5	1750

Explanation:

- The data consists of **Sales Amount** values for each **ID**, and the **Date** is generated using pd.date_range with a monthly frequency.

- We set the **Date** as the index of the DataFrame because time series analysis typically requires time-indexed data.

4. Plot the Sales Amount

Before performing any time series analysis, it's important to visualize the data to understand the trend and seasonality.

```
# Plotting the Sales Amount over time
plt.figure(figsize=(10, 6))
plt.plot(df['Sales Amount'], label='Sales Amount')
plt.title('Sales Amount Over Time')
plt.xlabel('Date')
plt.ylabel('Sales Amount')
plt.legend()
plt.grid(True)
plt.show()
```

Output

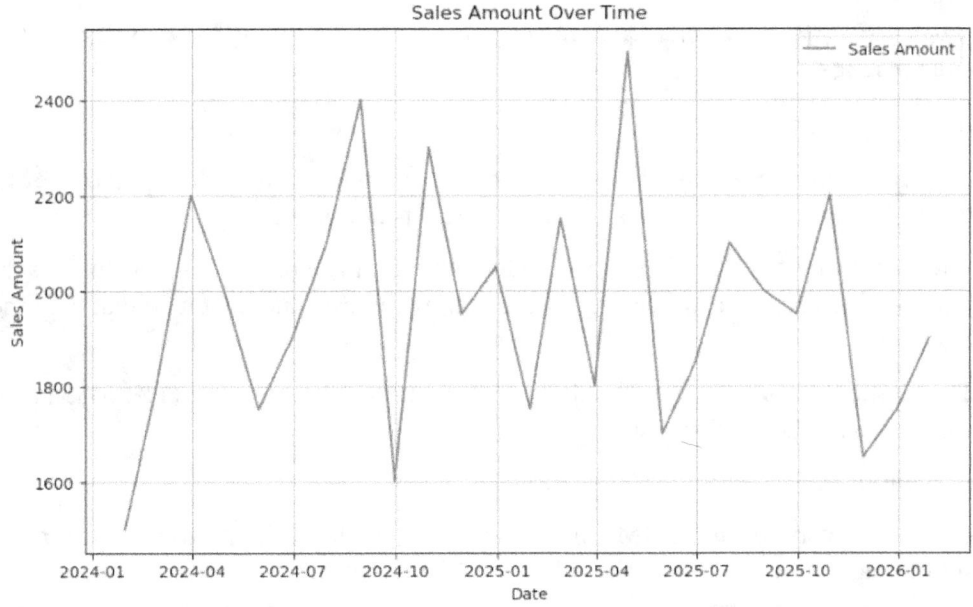

Explanation:

- This plot shows how the **Sales Amount** has changed over time. By visualizing the data, you can identify trends (e.g., upward or downward) and seasonality (e.g., recurring patterns at specific intervals).

5. Check for Stationarity with ADF Test

A time series needs to be **stationary** (i.e., its properties such as mean, variance, and autocorrelation should not change over time) for certain models like ARIMA to work effectively. To check for stationarity, we use the **Augmented Dickey-Fuller (ADF) test**.

```
# Perform Augmented Dickey-Fuller test
result = adfuller(df['Sales Amount'])


print('ADF Statistic:', result[0])
print('p-value:', result[1])
print('Critical Values:', result[4])
```

Output

ADF Statistic: 0.2715200495811089

p-value: 0.9759994428604294

Critical Values: {'1%': -3.9644434814814815, '5%': -3.0849081481481484, '10%': -2.6818144444444445}

Explanation:

- The **ADF statistic** tells us if the time series is stationary. The null hypothesis of the ADF test is that the time series has a unit root (i.e., it is non-stationary).
- The **p-value** helps determine if the null hypothesis can be rejected. A p-value less than 0.05 typically indicates that we can reject the null hypothesis and conclude that the time series is stationary.
- The **Critical Values** are thresholds for different confidence levels (1%, 5%, and 10%) to compare with the ADF statistic.

6. Plot ACF and PACF

To select the parameters for the ARIMA model, we need to check the **Autocorrelation Function (ACF)** and **Partial Autocorrelation Function (PACF)** plots.

```
# Plot the ACF and PACF
fig, ax = plt.subplots(1, 2, figsize=(16, 6))
```

```
# ACF plot
sm.graphics.tsa.plot_acf(df['Sales Amount'], lags=10, ax=ax[0])

# PACF plot
sm.graphics.tsa.plot_pacf(df['Sales Amount'], lags=10, ax=ax[1])

plt.show()
```

Output

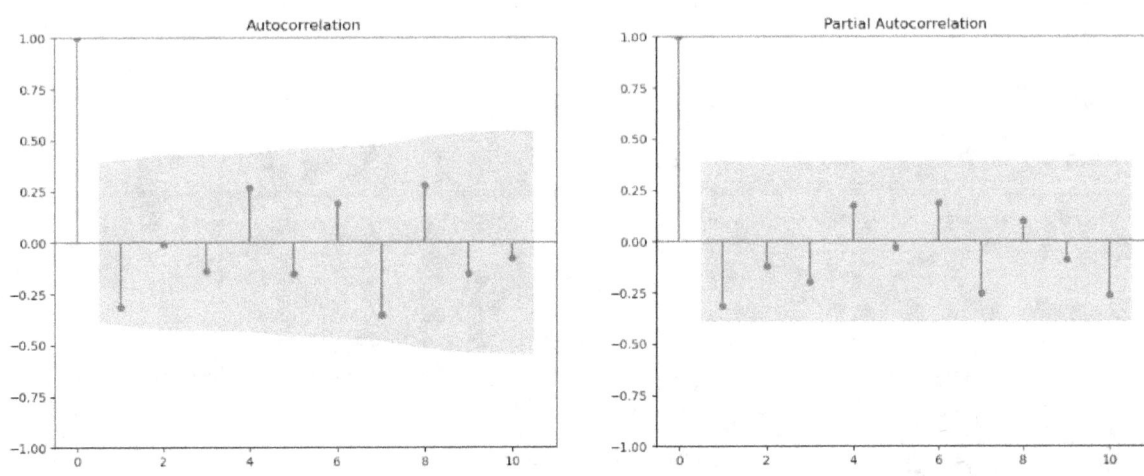

Explanation:

- **ACF** shows the correlation between the time series and its lagged versions. It helps identify the **moving average (MA)** component of the ARIMA model.
- **PACF** shows the correlation between the time series and its lagged versions after removing the effect of earlier lags. It helps identify the **autoregressive (AR)** component of the ARIMA model.

7. Fit an ARIMA Model

Based on the insights from the ACF and PACF plots, we can fit an **ARIMA model**. Here, we'll use an example model with parameters **(p=1, d=1, q=1)**, which indicates one lag for the AR term, one differencing operation for stationarity, and one lag for the MA term.

```
from statsmodels.tsa.arima.model import ARIMA

# Fit an ARIMA model
```

```python
model = ARIMA(df['Sales Amount'], order=(1, 1, 1))  # (p, d, q)
model_fit = model.fit()

# Print model summary
print(model_fit.summary())
```

Output

```
                               SARIMAX Results
==============================================================================
Dep. Variable:          Sales Amount   No. Observations:                   25
Model:                 ARIMA(1, 1, 1)  Log Likelihood                -168.175
Date:                Sun, 17 Nov 2024  AIC                            342.350
Time:                        16:26:31  BIC                            345.884
Sample:                    01-31-2024  HQIC                           343.287
                         - 01-31-2026
Covariance Type:                  opg
==============================================================================
                 coef    std err          z      P>|z|      [0.025      0.975]
------------------------------------------------------------------------------
ar.L1         -0.2795      0.216     -1.297      0.195      -0.702       0.143
ma.L1         -0.9991     19.863     -0.050      0.960     -39.930      37.932
sigma2      5.613e+04    1.1e+06      0.051      0.959    -2.11e+06    2.22e+06
===================================================================================
Ljung-Box (L1) (Q):                   0.01   Jarque-Bera (JB):                 1.11
Prob(Q):                              0.91   Prob(JB):                         0.57
Heteroskedasticity (H):               0.34   Skew:                             0.37
Prob(H) (two-sided):                  0.15   Kurtosis:                         2.24
===================================================================================

Warnings:
[1] Covariance matrix calculated using the outer product of gradients (complex-step)
```

Explanation:

- The **ARIMA model** is fit to the data with the specified order (1, 1, 1). The parameters (p, d, q) are determined based on the ACF and PACF plots, or through grid search methods.
- **Summary** provides a detailed output of the model parameters and their significance.

8. Forecast Future Sales

Once the model is fit, we can use it to forecast future values (e.g., next 3 months).

```python
# Forecast the next 3 months
forecast = model_fit.forecast(steps=3)
```

```
# Display the forecasted values
print('Forecasted Sales Amount for next 3 months:', forecast)
```

Output

Forecasted Sales Amount for next 3 months:

2026-02-28   1970.368671

2026-03-31   1950.702682

2026-04-30   1956.198752

Freq: ME, Name: predicted_mean, dtype: float64

Explanation:

- This forecasts the **Sales Amount** for the next 3 periods (months). The forecasted values are the predicted sales for these future months based on the historical data.

9. Plot the Forecast

Finally, we can plot the forecast along with the historical data to visualize the predictions.

```
# Plotting the forecast
plt.figure(figsize=(10, 6))
plt.plot(df['Sales Amount'], label='Historical Sales')
plt.plot(pd.date_range(df.index[-1], periods=4, freq='M')[1:], forecast, label='Forecasted Sales', color='red')
plt.title('Sales Amount Forecast')
plt.xlabel('Date')
plt.ylabel('Sales Amount')
plt.legend()
plt.grid(True)
plt.show()
```

Output

Explanation:

- The historical sales data is plotted in blue, and the forecasted sales data is plotted in red. This allows us to compare the model's predictions with the actual historical data.

Results Interpretation and Business Decisions

1. Stationarity and Trend:

If the **ADF test** p-value is less than 0.05, we can conclude that the time series is stationary. If not, we may need to apply differencing or transformation to make the data stationary.

2. ACF and PACF:

The **ACF and PACF plots** give us the necessary information to choose the **AR** (autoregressive) and **MA** (moving average) components of the ARIMA model. If the ACF cuts off sharply after a certain lag, it suggests the MA order, and if the PACF cuts off, it suggests the AR order.

3. ARIMA Model and Forecasting:

The ARIMA model provides the **best fit** for the time series. By forecasting future sales, businesses can plan for **inventory**, **staffing**, and **marketing strategies** in advance based on expected future demand.

4. Business Decision:

If the forecasted sales show an increasing trend, businesses may want to **increase production capacity** or **expand marketing efforts**. On the other hand, if a decline is predicted, it may be a good idea to **investigate potential issues**, such as customer satisfaction, product quality, or competitors' actions.

Conclusion

By using time series analysis, you can gain insights into the trends, seasonality, and patterns of sales over time. These insights enable better decision-making regarding inventory, staffing, marketing budgets, and future sales forecasts.

10. Introduction to Machine Learning Classification in Business Analytics

In business analytics, **classification** is a type of **supervised learning** technique where the goal is to predict a category or class label for a given set of input data. The outcome or the dependent variable is categorical in nature, meaning it can belong to one of two or more distinct classes. For example, predicting whether a customer will churn (yes/no), determining if an email is spam (spam/ham), or classifying a loan application as approved or denied are all classification problems.

Classification models work by learning from historical data (training data), where the outcome (class label) is already known. The model then uses this learning to classify new, unseen data into predefined categories.

Key characteristics of classification:

1. **Target Variable (Dependent Variable):** This is categorical (e.g., Yes/No, 0/1, categories like "High", "Medium", "Low").
2. **Input Features (Independent Variables):** These are the predictors or factors used to make predictions (e.g., age, income, transaction history, etc.).
3. **Training and Testing:** The data is typically split into two sets — one for training the model and one for testing how well the model can predict new data.

Common Classification Algorithms:

- Logistic Regression
- Decision Trees
- Random Forest
- K-Nearest Neighbors (KNN)
- Support Vector Machines (SVM)
- Naive Bayes
- Neural Networks

Steps in Classification:

1. **Data Collection**: Gather relevant data that can be used to classify observations into categories.
2. **Data Preprocessing**: Clean the data, handle missing values, encode categorical variables, and normalize/standardize the features if necessary.
3. **Model Selection**: Choose a classification model that best suits the data and business problem.

4. **Training the Model**: Feed the model with historical labeled data so it can learn the patterns between the features and target classes.

5. **Model Evaluation**: Assess the model's performance using metrics such as accuracy, precision, recall, F1-score, etc.

6. **Prediction and Deployment**: Once the model is trained and evaluated, it can be deployed to classify new data and make business decisions.

Example of Classification in Business Analytics

Let's consider a business scenario where a bank wants to predict whether a loan application will be approved or denied based on several factors like the applicant's income, credit score, and debt-to-income ratio.

Sample Data (Table)

Applicant ID	Age	Income (in $1000s)	Credit Score	Debt-to-Income Ratio	Loan Approved?
1	25	50	650	0.25	Yes
2	40	80	720	0.3	Yes
3	35	60	710	0.35	No
4	50	100	680	0.2	Yes
5	30	40	640	0.45	No
6	45	90	750	0.4	Yes

In this case:

- The **target variable** is "Loan Approved?" (Yes/No).
- The **features** are "Age", "Income", "Credit Score", and "Debt-to-Income Ratio".

Model Training

We would use this data to train a classification model (e.g., logistic regression, decision tree) to predict whether a new applicant will be approved for a loan based on these features.

Model Evaluation

The model might be evaluated using a confusion matrix or classification report. For example, if we tested the model on a new set of data and it predicted 4 correct approvals and 1 denial correctly, we would calculate its accuracy, precision, and recall.

Predicted Output from Classification Model

Let's assume the classification model predicts the following outcomes for 5 new applicants:

Applicant ID	Age	Income (in $1000s)	Credit Score	Debt-to-Income Ratio	Predicted Loan Approval	Actual Loan Approval
7	28	55	670	0.3	Yes	Yes
8	38	65	690	0.25	Yes	No
9	32	75	730	0.2	Yes	Yes
10	48	85	720	0.4	No	No
11	40	90	700	0.35	Yes	No

Performance Evaluation

- **Accuracy**: The model correctly predicted 3 out of 5 applicants. So, the accuracy is 3/5 = 60%.

- **Precision**: Precision for "Yes" predictions is the proportion of true positives among all positive predictions. Let's calculate precision:

$$\text{Precision (Yes)} = \frac{\text{True Positives}}{\text{True Positives + False Positives}} = \frac{2}{4} = 0.50$$

- **Recall**: Recall for "Yes" is the proportion of actual "Yes" outcomes correctly identified. In this case:

$$\text{Recall (Yes)} = \frac{\text{True Positives}}{\text{True Positives + False Negatives}} = \frac{2}{3} = 0.67$$

Business Decisions Based on Results

1. **Adjusting Loan Policies**: The bank may find that the model is conservative in approving loans (low recall), meaning it misses some customers who would have been good candidates. The business could adjust thresholds or retrain the model using more varied data or tweaking parameters to improve recall without sacrificing precision.

2. **Risk Management**: The bank may notice a trade-off between precision and recall. For instance, increasing precision (fewer false positives) may lead to missing good applicants (lower recall). Depending on the business strategy, they may choose to prioritize risk aversion (higher precision) or expand customer acquisition (higher recall).

3. **Targeted Marketing**: The model can also be used to target specific customers. If the model identifies factors that contribute to loan approvals, the bank could develop marketing campaigns tailored to those applicants, encouraging more people to apply and increasing conversion rates.

4. **Model Refinement**: If the model's performance is not satisfactory, the bank could experiment with more sophisticated models, more features, or additional data (e.g., employment status or region) to improve predictions.

Summary

Classification models are valuable tools in business analytics as they help companies make data-driven decisions, like predicting customer behavior or automating approval processes. By understanding the key metrics (accuracy, precision, recall), businesses can optimize their models to balance risk and opportunity effectively, leading to better outcomes and smarter decisions.

10.1 Understanding Decision Tree Classification in Business Analytics

Decision Tree Classification is a supervised machine learning technique used for classifying data into predefined categories based on a series of decision rules. It works by recursively partitioning the data into subsets based on feature values, which leads to a tree-like structure. Each internal node of the tree represents a "decision" based on a feature, and each leaf node represents the predicted class label (e.g., "Yes" or "No").

In business analytics, decision trees are popular because they are easy to understand, interpret, and visualize. This makes them a valuable tool for decision-making in various domains like customer churn prediction, credit risk assessment, fraud detection, and more.

Key Concepts in Decision Tree Classification

1. **Root Node**: The topmost node of the tree, which represents the entire dataset. The root node is split based on the feature that best divides the data.

2. **Decision Nodes**: These are the nodes where the data is split. At each decision node, the data is divided based on a certain feature threshold (for example, "Age > 30").

3. **Leaf Nodes**: These are the final nodes that represent the classification result. The leaf nodes hold the predicted class label (e.g., "Churn: Yes" or "Churn: No").

4. **Splitting**: The process of dividing the dataset at each decision node based on the most important feature (e.g., "Monthly Spend > $50").

5. **Pruning**: The process of removing branches from the tree that provide little additional value to the classification process. Pruning helps prevent overfitting.

6. **Feature Importance**: Decision trees provide insight into which features are most important for classification. Features that appear higher in the tree are more important for decision-making.

Applications of Decision Tree Classification in Business Analytics

1. **Customer Churn Prediction**: By analyzing customer behavior, businesses can predict whether a customer will churn (leave) or stay.

2. **Fraud Detection**: Identifying fraudulent transactions based on patterns in the data.

3. **Credit Risk Analysis**: Predicting whether a customer is likely to default on a loan based on their financial history.

4. **Market Segmentation**: Grouping customers into segments based on purchasing behavior to target marketing campaigns.

Example of Decision Tree Classification in Business Analytics

Let's consider a retail company that wants to predict whether a customer will **churn** (leave the service) based on their **monthly spend** and **account tenure** (how long they have been a customer). The company has historical data about customers' behavior, and it wants to classify future customers as either likely to churn ("Yes") or not churn ("No").

Sample Data

Here's a sample dataset with features such as **Monthly Spend** and **Tenure (in months)**, and the target variable is whether the customer will **Churn** or not.

Customer ID	Monthly Spend ($)	Tenure (Months)	Churn (Y/N)
1	150	12	N
2	50	5	Y
3	200	15	N
4	80	3	Y
5	100	10	N
6	60	4	Y
7	220	20	N
8	40	2	Y
9	170	12	N
10	90	6	Y

Goal:

Predict whether a customer will churn (Yes or No) based on **Monthly Spend** and **Tenure**.

Steps in Decision Tree Classification

1. **Split Data at Root Node**: At the root of the decision tree, the algorithm will choose the best feature that divides the data in such a way that it maximizes the separation of the target classes (Churn: Yes or No). For instance, it might choose **Monthly Spend** as the first feature to split on.

2. **Create Decision Nodes**: The data is split into subgroups at each decision node. For example, the data could be split into two branches based on a threshold in **Monthly Spend** (e.g., "Monthly Spend > $100" and "Monthly Spend <= $100").

3. **Continue Splitting**: Each subgroup is further divided based on other features, such as **Tenure**. This process continues recursively until each leaf node represents a class label (e.g., "Churn: Yes" or "Churn: No").
4. **Predict Class for New Data**: When a new customer's data is provided, the algorithm will classify the customer by traversing the tree based on their features, ultimately reaching a leaf node that gives the predicted class.

Output and Results

After applying the decision tree algorithm, the following tree might be generated:

Decision Tree Structure:

```
            Monthly Spend > $100?
               /           \
             Yes            No
            /   \          /   \
    Tenure > 10? Tenure > 5? Churn: No  Churn: Yes
      /    \     /    \
Churn: No Churn: Yes Churn: No Churn: Yes
```

Customer Predictions (Using the Decision Tree)

Customer ID	Monthly Spend ($)	Tenure (Months)	Predicted Churn (Y/N)
1	150	12	N
2	50	5	Y
3	200	15	N
4	80	3	Y
5	100	10	N
6	60	4	Y
7	220	20	N
8	40	2	Y
9	170	12	N

Customer ID	Monthly Spend ($)	Tenure (Months)	Predicted Churn (Y/N)
10	90	6	Y

Interpretation and Discussion

1. **Tree Structure**:

    o   The first decision node splits the data based on **Monthly Spend**. If a customer's spending is greater than $100, the algorithm further checks their **Tenure**.

    o   If **Monthly Spend > $100** and **Tenure > 10 months**, the customer is less likely to churn ("Churn: No").

    o   Customers with **Monthly Spend <= $100** are more likely to churn, especially if their **Tenure** is short (e.g., less than 5 months).

2. **Accuracy of Predictions**:

    o   **Customer 1** has a monthly spend of $150 and a tenure of 12 months, and the tree predicts they will **not churn** (which matches the actual label).

    o   **Customer 2** has a monthly spend of $50 and a tenure of 5 months, and the tree predicts they will **churn**, which is accurate.

    o   **Customer 4**, with a monthly spend of $80 and a tenure of 3 months, is predicted to churn, which is consistent with their actual churn.

3. **Feature Importance**:

    o   **Monthly Spend** is the most important feature, as it determines the initial split in the tree. The second most important feature is **Tenure**, which further refines the prediction.

Business Decisions Based on Decision Tree Results

1. **Customer Retention Strategies**:

    o   **For high spenders with longer tenure**: Customers like **Customer 1** and **Customer 3** (who spend more and have been with the company for a longer period) are predicted to stay. The business should focus on retaining these customers by offering loyalty rewards or personalized offers to further enhance their satisfaction and loyalty.

    o   **For low spenders with short tenure**: Customers like **Customer 2**, **Customer 4**, and **Customer 6** (who spend less and have been customers for a shorter time) are more likely to churn. The company can try to prevent churn by offering discounts or promotions to encourage more spending or longer-term commitment.

2. **Targeted Marketing Campaigns**:
    - Based on the tree's classification, the company can design targeted campaigns. For example:
        - **For customers likely to churn**, the company could send retention-focused campaigns such as special discounts or personalized offers.
        - **For customers unlikely to churn**, the company might focus on upselling or cross-selling higher-value services or products.

3. **Resource Allocation**:
    - The company can allocate resources more efficiently by focusing retention efforts on the customers who are predicted to churn (low spend and short tenure), rather than spending resources on customers who are unlikely to churn.

4. **Monitor and Update the Model**:
    - While decision trees are relatively easy to interpret, the company should monitor the performance of the model over time and update it as needed to reflect changes in customer behavior or market conditions.

Conclusion

Decision Tree Classification is a powerful and interpretable tool in business analytics, providing actionable insights through clear decision rules. In customer churn prediction, it enables businesses to make data-driven decisions on retention strategies, targeted marketing, and resource allocation. By understanding the key features driving customer behavior, companies can optimize their actions to improve customer retention and overall profitability.

10.2 Decision Tree Classification using JASP

Using JASP, we'll apply a **classification model** (e.g., Decision Tree Classifier) to predict the **customer segment** based on the available features like sales, marketing spend, and customer feedback score.

We will also evaluate the model using:

- **Accuracy**: The proportion of correct predictions.
- **Confusion Matrix**: To understand the classification errors.

Follow the steps provided below to create modified Business Data.

> Note: To apply machine learning module, we need approximately 100 rows of data. The business dataset (Refer Chapter 1.2) used in the previous chapter have only 25 rows. Hence, we will reproduce the same data and use it as hypothesized data for learning. However, in real time, one has to ensure large number of data for training and testing of the machine learning model

Now open the data in excel and multiply the rows by copying first 25 rows of data and pasting in the end. 3 time copy paste (25 x 3) becomes total of 100 rows of data. Now we will use this data as hypothesized data for Machine learning purposes. We will rename this dataset as **Business_data_100.CSV**.

ID	Sales Amount	Region	Target Sales	Pre-Sales Amount	Post-Sales Amount	Marketing Spend	Customer Feedback Score	Sales Growth	Customer Segment
1	1500	East	1600	1400	1550	500	4	50	Small
2	1800	West	1750	1700	1850	600	5	100	Medium
3	2200	East	2000	2100	2250	700	4	150	Large
4	2000	West	1900	1850	2050	550	3	100	Medium
5	1750	East	1700	1600	1800	450	4	50	Small
95	1950	East	1900	1850	1950	550	4	50	Medium
96	2200	West	2250	2150	2200	700	5	100	Large
97	1650	East	1700	1600	1650	450	3	50	Small
98	1750	West	1800	1700	1750	500	4	50	Medium
100	1900	East	1850	1800	1900	600	5	100	Large

Steps to use Machine Learning Decision Tree Classification in JASP

1. **Open JASP**:
   - If you haven't already, open JASP and load your dataset (e.g., a CSV, Excel, or SPSS file).

2. **Load the Data**:
   - Click **"File"** > **"Open"** to load your dataset into JASP.

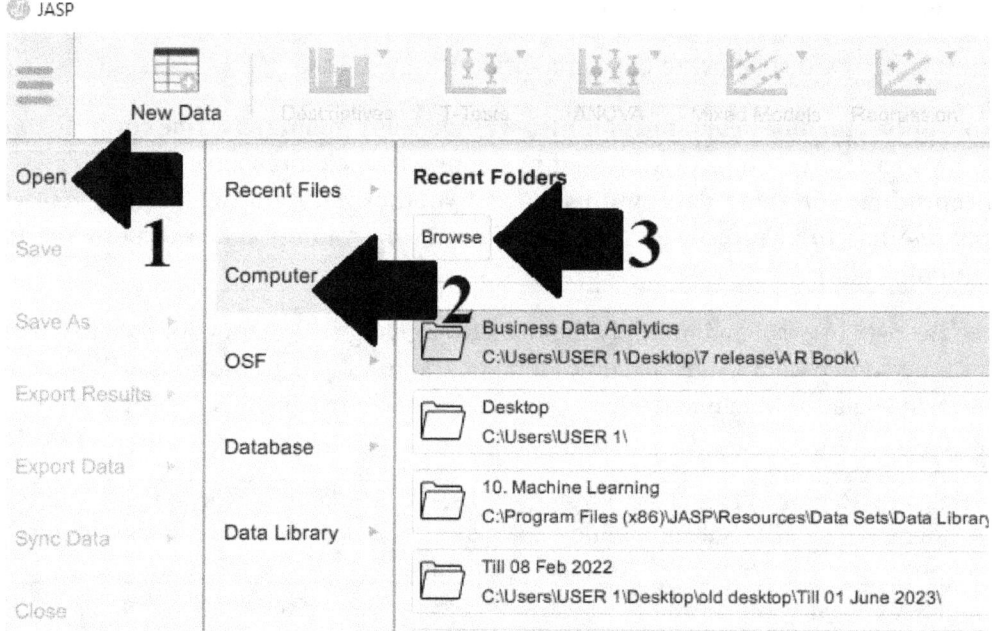

Now select the file

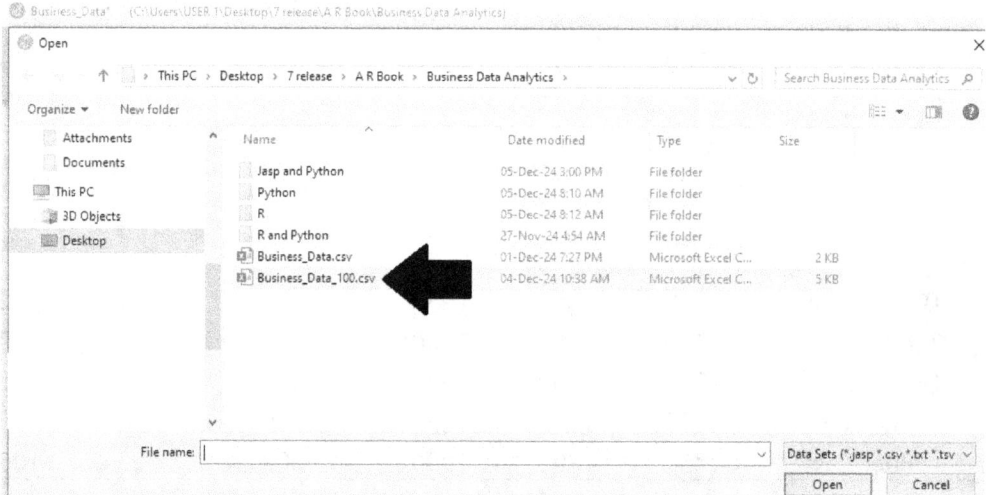

File will be loaded into JASP as shown below.

ID	Sales Amount	Region	Target Sales	Pre-Sales Amount	Post-Sales Amount	Marketing Spend	Customer Feedback Score	Sales Growth	Cust
1	1500	East	1600	1400	1550	500	4	50	Small
2	1800	West	1750	1700	1850	600	5	100	Medium
3	2200	East	2000	2100	2250	700	4	150	Large
4	2000	West	1900	1850	2050	550	3	100	Medium
5	1750	East	1700	1600	1800	450	4	50	Small
6	1900	West	1950	1900	2000	650	5	100	Medium
7	2100	East	2200	2050	2150	700	4	100	Large
8	2400	West	2300	2200	2400	600	5	200	Large
9	1600	East	1650	1500	1600	500	3	100	Small
10	2300	West	2400	2350	2500	750	4	150	Large
11	1950	East	2000	1900	1950	550	4	50	Medium
12	2050	West	2100	2000	2050	600	3	50	Medium
13	1750	East	1800	1700	1750	500	4	50	Small

3. **Activate the Machine Learning Module:**

Machine Learning Module is not a default module available in JASP. To activate Machine Learning Module, select the + symbol available on the right-hand side of the home screen.

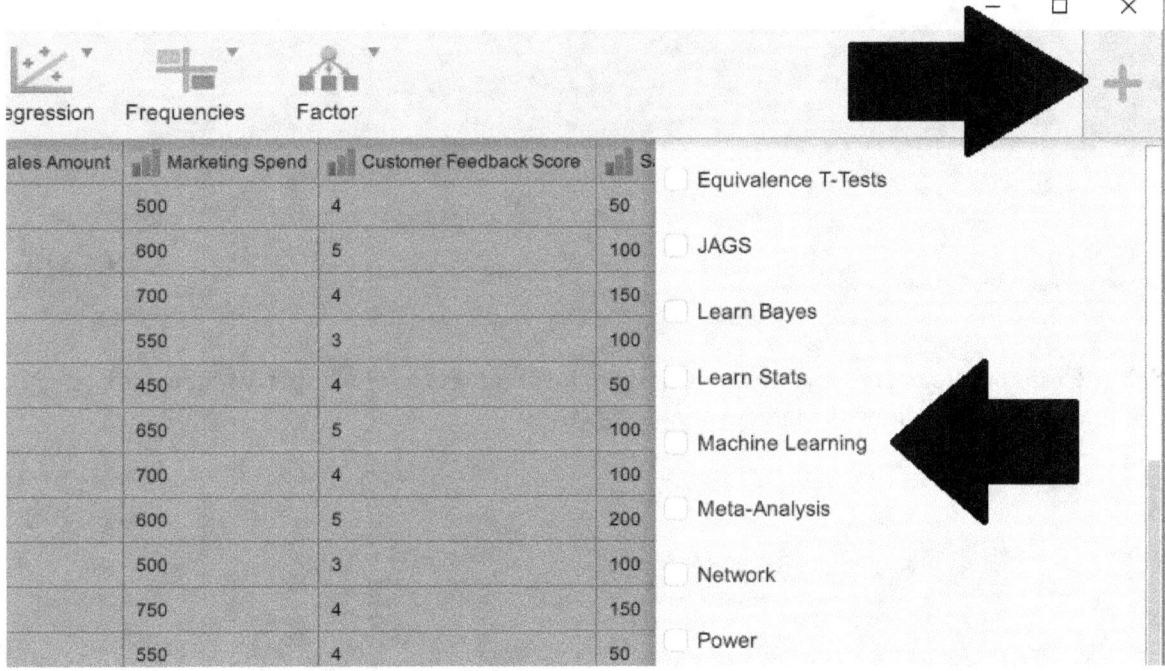

Now Machine Learning Tab will appear in the Tab as shown below.

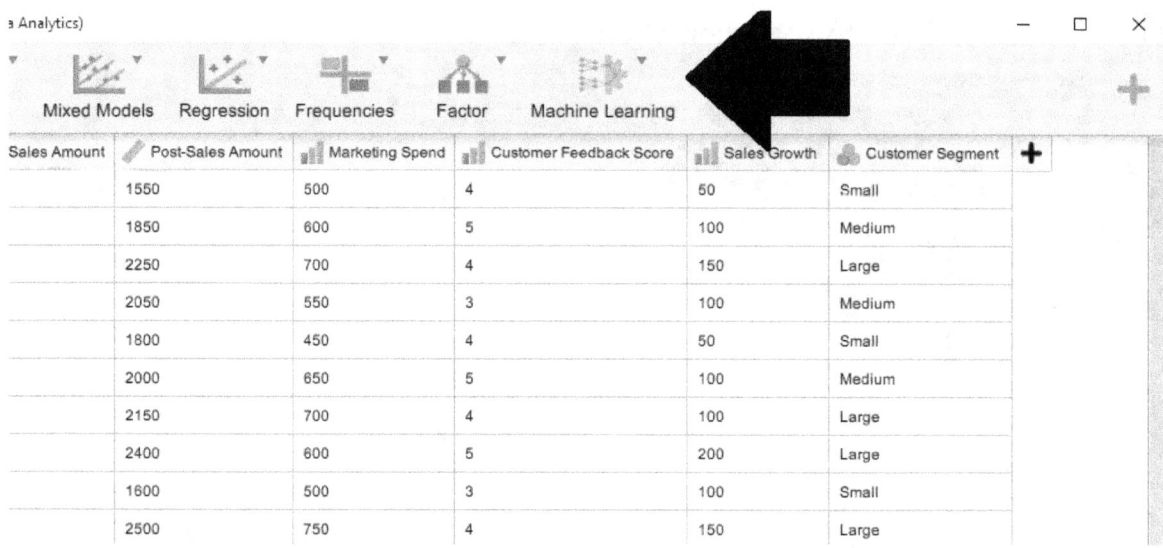

4. Select the **Decision Tree Classification** Menu

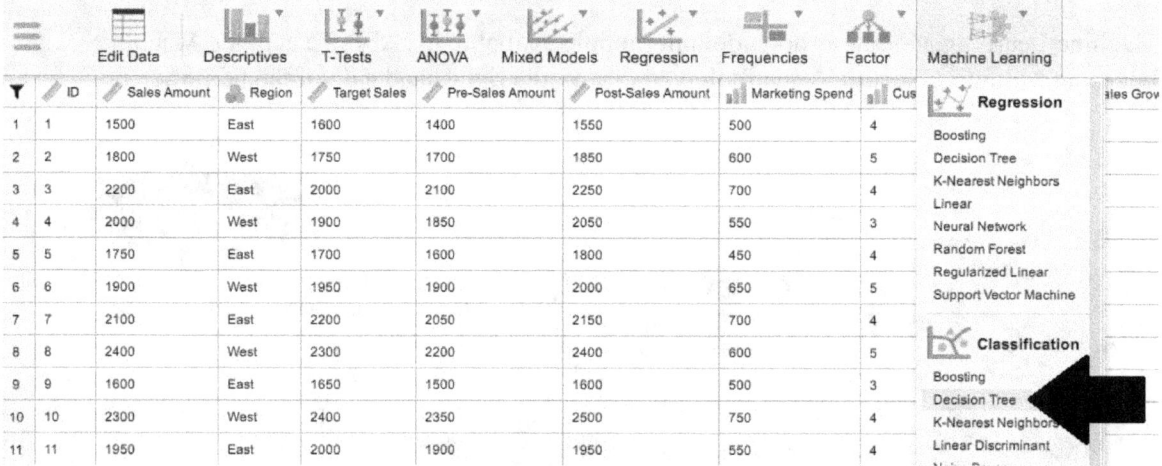

Select Customer Segment variable and Click the Play button near to Target Variable Box (or you can drag and position it on the target variable box)

With Press the Shift Key and Select All other variable Except ID. Click the Play button to move these variables to Features Block.

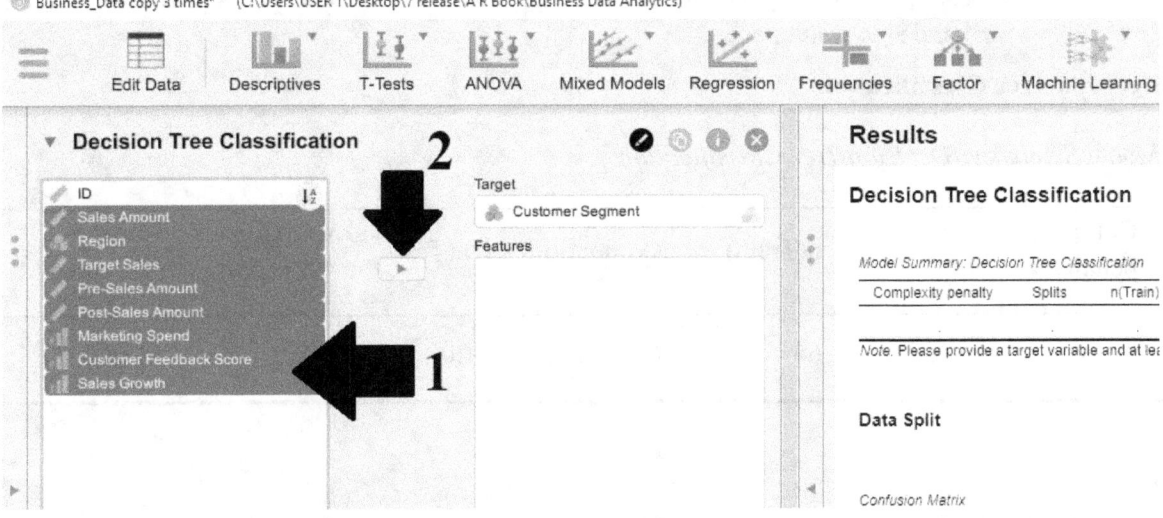

Scroll down and select Confusion Matrix under Tables, Data Split under Plots and decision Tree Under Plots. Result will be appeared in Result Pane on the Right- Hand side.

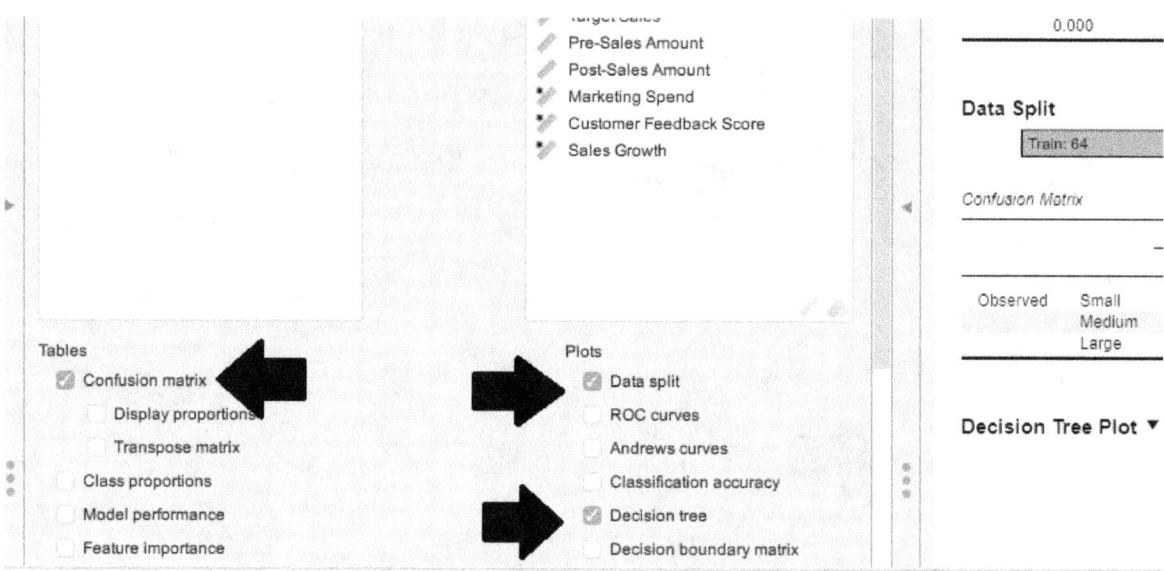

5. **View Results:**
   o JASP will display the plot and result in a table under the **Results** pane on the right-hand side result pane.

Decision Tree Classification

Model Summary: Decision Tree Classification

Complexity penalty	Splits	n(Train)	n(Validation)	n(Test)	Validation Accuracy	Test Accuracy
0.000	30	64	16	20	1.000	1.000

Data Split

| Train: 64 | Validation: 16 | Test: 20 | Total: 100 |

Confusion Matrix

		Predicted		
		Small	Medium	Large
Observed	Small	7	0	0
	Medium	0	9	0
	Large	0	0	4

Decision Tree Plot

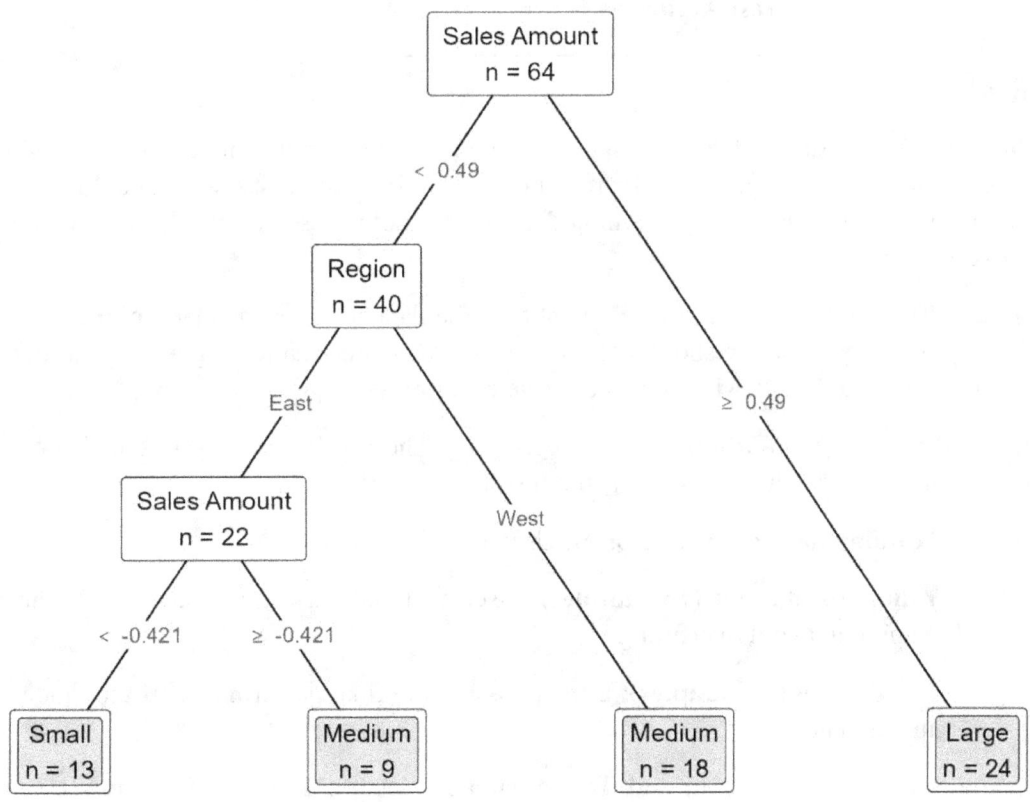

Let's break down and interpret the results of the Decision Tree Classification from the JASP output on the business dataset. The goal of the Decision Tree is to classify items into categories (Small, Medium, Large) based on certain features in the dataset.

1. Model Summary: Decision Tree Classification

Metric	Value
Complexity penalty	0.000
Splits	30
n(Train)	64
n(Validation)	16
n(Test)	20
Validation Accuracy	1.000
Test Accuracy	1.000

Explanation:

- **Complexity penalty (0.000)**: This penalty controls the depth and complexity of the decision tree. A value of 0 means there is no penalty for complexity, which could indicate that the tree is fully fitted to the training data. This is not necessarily ideal, as it could lead to overfitting.

- **Splits (30)**: The decision tree made 30 splits in the data. This means that the tree used 30 different decisions (or thresholds) to divide the data into smaller segments in order to classify them into Small, Medium, and Large categories.

- **n(Train) = 64, n(Validation) = 16, n(Test) = 20**: These values represent the size of the datasets used for training, validation, and testing, respectively:
  - **Training dataset (64 samples)**: Used to build the model.
  - **Validation dataset (16 samples)**: Used to tune and evaluate the model during training to avoid overfitting.
  - **Test dataset (20 samples)**: Used to assess the final performance of the model on unseen data.

- **Validation Accuracy (1.000)** and **Test Accuracy (1.000)**: These values show that the decision tree perfectly classified both the validation and test datasets. A perfect accuracy score of 1.000 suggests that the model is able to correctly classify all instances in both the validation and test datasets.

Interpretation:

The model appears to have performed perfectly on both the validation and test datasets, indicating high accuracy. However, the absence of a complexity penalty (0.000) and perfect accuracy could indicate overfitting, meaning the model might have learned the noise in the training data, which could affect its performance on new, unseen data.

2. Data Split

- **Train: 64, Validation: 16, Test: 20**.

Explanation:

These numbers show the distribution of the data into the three sets:

- The training set has 64 samples used to build the model.
- The validation set has 16 samples used to optimize the model during training.
- The test set has 20 samples used to assess the model's generalization capability.

This split seems appropriate for training, validating, and testing the model, though the size of the validation set (16 samples) is relatively small. Typically, a larger validation set might provide more robust evaluation during training.

3. Confusion Matrix

		Predicted	
	Small	Medium	Large
Small	7	0	0
Medium	0	9	0
Large	0	0	4

(Observed)

Explanation:

The confusion matrix provides a summary of the classification results:

- **Small**:
    - 7 samples were correctly predicted as Small.
    - 0 samples were incorrectly classified as Medium or Large.

- **Medium**:
    - 9 samples were correctly predicted as Medium.
    - 0 samples were misclassified as Small or Large.
- **Large**:
    - 4 samples were correctly predicted as Large.
    - 0 samples were misclassified as Small or Medium.

Interpretation:

- The confusion matrix shows that the decision tree perfectly predicted all the categories (Small, Medium, Large) with no misclassifications. The diagonal values (7, 9, and 4) represent the true positive classifications for each category.
- The absence of any off-diagonal values (misclassifications) further supports the perfect performance of the model.

4. Decision Tree Plot

The decision tree plot typically illustrates how the model splits the data based on different features and thresholds. Each node would represent a decision based on a feature, and each branch would represent a choice based on the feature's value.

Interpretation:

A well-constructed decision tree should visually reflect how different features contribute to predicting the categories (Small, Medium, Large). It might show which features are most important in classifying the categories. A fully grown tree without pruning could be complex and overly detailed, which might explain the perfect performance seen in this case.

Observations:

1. **Perfect Accuracy**: Both the validation and test accuracies are perfect (1.000), which suggests that the decision tree model fits the data very well. However, this could indicate overfitting, especially given the lack of a complexity penalty.
2. **Confusion Matrix**: No misclassifications occurred, which is a positive sign. This means the model was able to distinguish all categories without error.
3. **Data Split**: The data split is reasonable, though a larger validation set might give a better indication of how well the model generalizes to new data.

Business Implications:

1. **Overfitting Risk**: Although the model performs perfectly on the given datasets, overfitting is a concern. If the model was too complex, it could fail to generalize to new, unseen data. This is important for real-world applications where data may differ from the training set.

2. **Model Reliability**: If this perfect accuracy is consistent across other datasets or in cross-validation, the decision tree could be considered a reliable tool for classification. However, further validation using other techniques or larger datasets would be needed to confirm this.

3. **Feature Importance**: If we have access to the decision tree plot, we could analyze which features are most important in determining the categories (Small, Medium, Large). This could provide valuable business insights, helping prioritize certain business factors (e.g., price, location, or other metrics).

Business Decisions:

1. **Refinement of the Model**: Given the perfect accuracy but the risk of overfitting, businesses may want to tune the model further to avoid overly complex decision trees. Using a complexity penalty or pruning the tree could prevent the model from overfitting.

2. **Segmentation Strategy**: If the categories (Small, Medium, Large) represent different customer segments, the model's perfect classification could be used to tailor marketing strategies or product offerings for each segment.

3. **Data Collection**: If the model performs perfectly on this dataset, it suggests that the features used in the decision tree are highly predictive of the outcomes. This insight could help businesses focus on collecting more data on the important features identified by the tree, ensuring accurate classification in future scenarios.

In summary, while the decision tree shows excellent performance with perfect accuracy, it is crucial to assess the potential overfitting and generalization of the model, as it may not perform as well on new, unseen data. Additionally, businesses should consider using the insights gained from the decision tree to inform their strategies, while also refining the model to ensure its robustness.

10.3 Decision Tree Classification using Python

In this example, we'll apply a **classification model** (e.g., Decision Tree Classifier) to predict the **customer segment** based on the available features like sales, marketing spend, and customer feedback score.

We will also evaluate the model using:

- **Accuracy**: The proportion of correct predictions.
- **Confusion Matrix**: To understand the classification errors.
- **Classification Report**: To get more detailed metrics such as precision, recall, and F1-score.

Libraries to Install

You will need to install the relevant libraries. If you haven't already, you can do so via pip:

```
pip install numpy pandas matplotlib scikit-learn seaborn
```

Libraries Import

```python
# Import necessary libraries
import numpy as np
import pandas as pd
import matplotlib.pyplot as plt
from sklearn.tree import DecisionTreeClassifier, plot_tree
from sklearn.model_selection import train_test_split
from sklearn.metrics import accuracy_score, confusion_matrix, classification_report
from sklearn.preprocessing import StandardScaler
```

Explanation of Libraries:

- **NumPy**: For numerical operations (e.g., array handling).
- **Pandas**: For data manipulation and handling.
- **Matplotlib**: For visualizing the decision tree.
- **Scikit-learn**: Provides machine learning models and metrics:
    - **DecisionTreeClassifier**: A classification model that learns decision rules from the features.

- **train_test_split**: Used to split the dataset into training and testing subsets.
- **accuracy_score**, **confusion_matrix**, **classification_report**: Evaluation metrics for classification models.
- **StandardScaler**: To standardize the data (optional, but can help with models sensitive to feature scales).

Step-by-Step Code

1. Data Preparation

We'll start by preparing the data. Specifically, we'll define the features and target variable (i.e., **Customer Segment**).

```python
# Sample data (you can replace this with your own dataset)
data = {
    'Sales Amount': [1500, 1800, 2200, 2000, 1750, 1900, 2100, 2400, 1600, 2300, 1950, 2050, 1750, 2150, 1800, 2500, 1700, 1850, 2100, 2000, 1950, 2200, 1650, 1750, 1900],
    'Target Sales': [1600, 1750, 2000, 1900, 1700, 1950, 2200, 2300, 1650, 2400, 2000, 2100, 1800, 2200, 1850, 2450, 1750, 1900, 2150, 2050, 1900, 2250, 1700, 1800, 1850],
    'Pre-Sales Amount': [1400, 1700, 2100, 1850, 1600, 1900, 2050, 2200, 1500, 2350, 1900, 2000, 1700, 2100, 1750, 2400, 1650, 1800, 2050, 1950, 1850, 2150, 1600, 1700, 1800],
    'Post-Sales Amount': [1550, 1850, 2250, 2050, 1800, 2000, 2150, 2400, 1600, 2500, 1950, 2050, 1750, 2150, 1800, 2500, 1700, 1850, 2100, 2000, 1950, 2200, 1650, 1750, 1900],
    'Marketing Spend': [500, 600, 700, 550, 450, 650, 700, 600, 500, 750, 550, 600, 500, 650, 700, 800, 400, 500, 650, 600, 550, 700, 450, 500, 600],
    'Customer Feedback Score': [4, 5, 4, 3, 4, 5, 4, 5, 3, 4, 4, 3, 4, 5, 4, 5, 3, 4, 5, 4, 4, 5, 3, 4, 5],
    'Customer Segment': ['Small', 'Medium', 'Large', 'Medium', 'Small', 'Medium', 'Large', 'Large', 'Small', 'Large', 'Medium', 'Medium', 'Small', 'Large', 'Small', 'Large', 'Small', 'Medium', 'Large', 'Medium', 'Medium', 'Large', 'Small', 'Medium', 'Large']
}

# Create DataFrame
df = pd.DataFrame(data)
df.head()
```

Output

	Sales Amount	Target Sales	Pre-Sales Amount	Post-Sales Amount	Marketing Spend	Customer Feedback Score	Customer Segment
0	1500	1600	1400	1550	500	4	Small
1	1800	1750	1700	1850	600	5	Medium
2	2200	2000	2100	2250	700	4	Large
3	2000	1900	1850	2050	550	3	Medium
4	1750	1700	1600	1800	450	4	Small

```
# Map customer segments to numeric values for classification
df['Customer Segment'] = df['Customer Segment'].map({'Small': 0, 'Medium': 1, 'Large': 2})

# Define features (X) and target variable (y)
X = df[['Sales Amount', 'Target Sales', 'Pre-Sales Amount', 'Post-Sales Amount', 'Marketing Spend', 'Customer Feedback Score']]
y = df['Customer Segment']

# Standardize the data (important for many machine learning models)
scaler = StandardScaler()
X_scaled = scaler.fit_transform(X)
```

Explanation:

- We are using the **Customer Segment** as the target variable, which we map to numeric values (Small = 0, Medium = 1, Large = 2).
- The features are all the numerical columns except for the **Customer Segment**.
- **StandardScaler** is used to scale the feature data because certain models like Decision Trees may perform better with standardized data.

2. Train-Test Split

Next, we'll split the data into training and testing sets, where we train the model on the training data and test its performance on the testing data.

```
# Split the data into training and testing sets (80% training, 20% testing)
X_train, X_test, y_train, y_test = train_test_split(X_scaled, y, test_size=0.2, random_state=42)
```

```
# Check the dimensions of the split data
print(f"Training data shape: {X_train.shape}")
print(f"Testing data shape: {X_test.shape}")
```

Output

Training data shape: (20, 6)

Testing data shape: (5, 6)

Explanation:

- We use train_test_split to divide the data into a training set (80%) and a test set (20%) to evaluate the model's performance on unseen data.

3. Train a Decision Tree Classifier

Now, we will create and train a **Decision Tree Classifier**.

Create and train a Decision Tree Classifier

```
# Check unique classes in the target variable
print(f"Unique classes in y_test: {np.unique(y_test)}")


# Create and train a Decision Tree Classifier
clf = DecisionTreeClassifier(random_state=42)
clf.fit(X_train, y_train)


# Predict on the test set
y_pred = clf.predict(X_test)


# Evaluate the model
accuracy = accuracy_score(y_test, y_pred)
print(f"Accuracy: {accuracy:.4f}")
```

Output

Accuracy: 0.8000

Explanation:

- **Check for Unique Classes in y_test**: The line print(f"Unique classes in y_test: {np.unique(y_test)}") will show the unique classes in the test set. This allows you to verify if there are fewer than three classes (e.g., only Small and Medium).
- **Dynamic Target Names**: If the unique classes in y_test are fewer than three, the error should be resolved by adjusting the target_names list in the classification_report and decision tree visualization. However, if there are exactly three classes in the dataset, but only two in the test set, it could be because the split left out one of the segments. You may need to rebalance the dataset or collect more data
- We create a **DecisionTreeClassifier** and fit it to the training data.
- We then use predict to get the predicted labels for the test set.
- Finally, we compute the **accuracy** of the model by comparing the predicted labels (y_pred) with the true labels (y_test).

4. Evaluate the Model (Confusion Matrix, Classification Report)

Now, let's evaluate the model's performance by looking at the **Confusion Matrix** and the **Classification Report**.

```
# Confusion Matrix
conf_matrix = confusion_matrix(y_test, y_pred)
print("Confusion Matrix:")
print(conf_matrix)
```

Output

Confusion Matrix:

[[3 0]

 [1 1]]

Explanation:

- **Confusion Matrix**: Shows the number of correct and incorrect predictions for each class. It helps us understand how well the model is performing for each customer segment.

```
# Classification Report
# Ensure that target_names corresponds to the unique classes in y_test
```

```python
# If there are only 2 unique classes in y_test, adjust the target_names list to reflect that
unique_classes = np.unique(y_test)
print(f"Unique classes in y_test: {unique_classes}")
class_report = classification_report(y_test, y_pred, target_names=[str(i) for i in unique_classes])
print("Classification Report:")
print(class_report)
```

Output

```
Unique classes in y_test: [0 1]
Classification Report:
              precision    recall  f1-score   support

           0       0.75      1.00      0.86         3
           1       1.00      0.50      0.67         2

    accuracy                           0.80         5
   macro avg       0.88      0.75      0.76         5
weighted avg       0.85      0.80      0.78         5
```

Explanation:

- **Confusion Matrix**: Shows the number of correct and incorrect predictions for each class. It helps us understand how well the model is performing for each customer segment.
- **Classification Report**: Provides additional metrics such as:
    - **Precision**: The accuracy of positive predictions for each class.
    - **Recall**: The ability of the classifier to find all positive instances of each class.
    - **F1-score**: The harmonic mean of precision and recall, providing a balance between them.

5. Visualize the Decision Tree

Finally, let's visualize the trained decision tree.

```python
# Visualize the decision tree
plt.figure(figsize=(20, 10))
```

```
plot_tree(clf,
    filled=True,
    feature_names=list(X.columns),  # Convert Index to list
    class_names=['Small', 'Medium', 'Large'],
    rounded=True,
    proportion=True)
plt.show()
```

Output

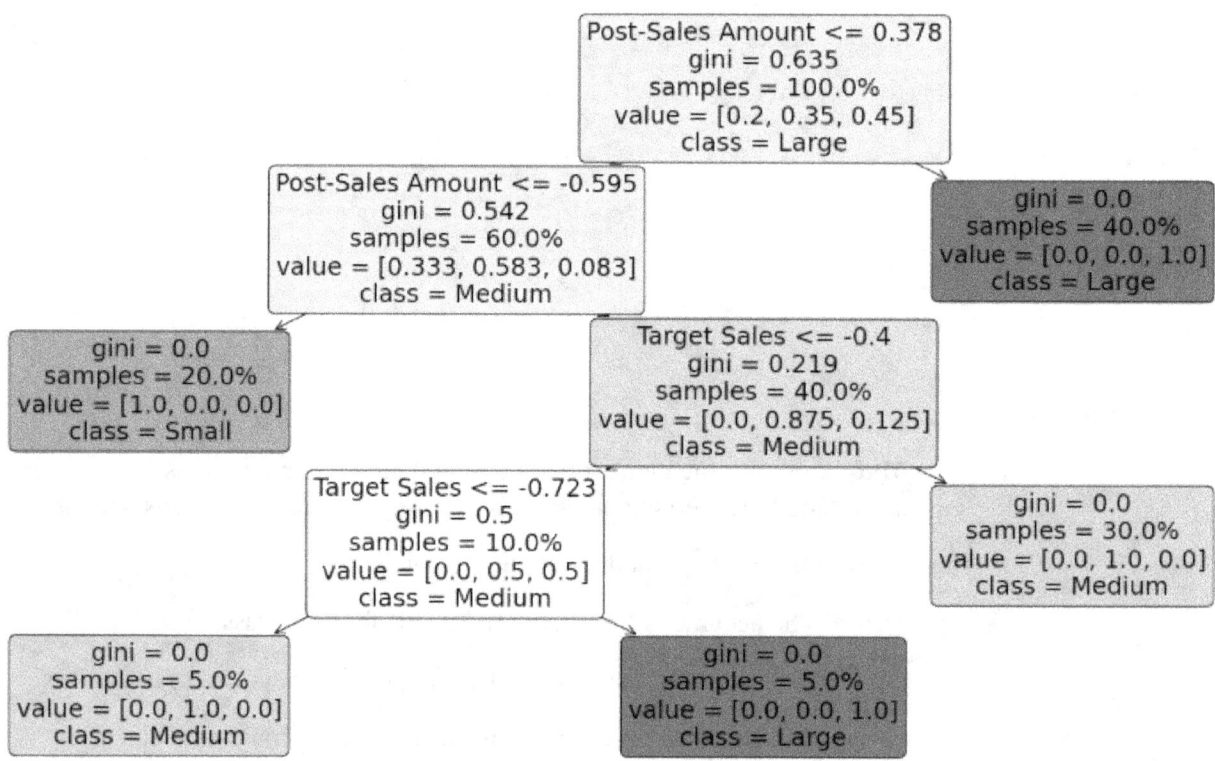

Explanation:

- **plot_tree**: Visualizes the decision tree model, showing how it splits the data based on different features. The nodes display the feature used for the split and the gini impurity of the node.

- **feature_names**: The feature names used to make splits at each node.

- **class_names**: The labels corresponding to the customer segments.

Full Code:

```
from sklearn.tree import DecisionTreeClassifier, plot_tree
from sklearn.model_selection import train_test_split
from sklearn.metrics import accuracy_score, confusion_matrix, classification_report
from sklearn.preprocessing import StandardScaler
import pandas as pd
import matplotlib.pyplot as plt


# Sample data
data = {
    'Sales Amount': [1500, 1800, 2200, 2000, 1750, 1900, 2100, 2400, 1600, 2300, 1950, 2050, 1750, 2150, 1800, 2500, 1700, 1850, 2100, 2000, 1950, 2200, 1650, 1750, 1900],

    'Target Sales': [1600, 1750, 2000, 1900, 1700, 1950, 2200, 2300, 1650, 2400, 2000, 2100, 1800, 2200, 1850, 2450, 1750, 1900, 2150, 2050, 1900, 2250, 1700, 1800, 1850],

    'Pre-Sales Amount': [1400, 1700, 2100, 1850, 1600, 1900, 2050, 2200, 1500, 2350, 1900, 2000, 1700, 2100, 1750, 2400, 1650, 1800, 2050, 1950, 1850, 2150, 1600, 1700, 1800],

    'Post-Sales Amount': [1550, 1850, 2250, 2050, 1800, 2000, 2150, 2400, 1600, 2500, 1950, 2050, 1750, 2150, 1800, 2500, 1700, 1850, 2100, 2000, 1950, 2200, 1650, 1750, 1900],

    'Marketing Spend': [500, 600, 700, 550, 450, 650, 700, 600, 500, 750, 550, 600, 500, 650, 700, 800, 400, 500, 650, 600, 550, 700, 450, 500, 600],

    'Customer Feedback Score': [4, 5, 4, 3, 4, 5, 4, 5, 3, 4, 4, 3, 4, 5, 4, 5, 3, 4, 5, 4, 4, 5, 3, 4, 5],

    'Customer Segment': ['Small', 'Medium', 'Large', 'Medium', 'Small', 'Medium', 'Large', 'Large', 'Small', 'Large', 'Medium', 'Medium', 'Small', 'Large', 'Small', 'Large', 'Small', 'Medium', 'Large', 'Medium', 'Medium', 'Large', 'Small', 'Medium', 'Large']
}


# Create DataFrame
df = pd.DataFrame(data)
```

```python
# Map customer segments to numeric values for classification
df['Customer Segment'] = df['Customer Segment'].map({'Small': 0, 'Medium': 1, 'Large': 2})

# Define features (X) and target variable (y)
X = df[['Sales Amount', 'Target Sales', 'Pre-Sales Amount', 'Post-Sales Amount', 'Marketing Spend', 'Customer Feedback Score']]
y = df['Customer Segment']

# Standardize the data
scaler = StandardScaler()
X_scaled = scaler.fit_transform(X)

# Split the data into training and testing sets
X_train, X_test, y_train, y_test = train_test_split(X_scaled, y, test_size=0.2, random_state=42)

# Create and train a Decision Tree Classifier
clf = DecisionTreeClassifier(random_state=42)
clf.fit(X_train, y_train)

# Predict on the test set
y_pred = clf.predict(X_test)

# Evaluate the model
accuracy = accuracy_score(y_test, y_pred)
print(f"Accuracy: {accuracy:.4f}")
```

```python
# Confusion Matrix
conf_matrix = confusion_matrix(y_test, y_pred)
print("Confusion Matrix:")
print(conf_matrix)


# Classification Report
# Ensure that target_names corresponds to the unique classes in y_test
# If there are only 2 unique classes in y_test, adjust the target_names list to reflect that
unique_classes = np.unique(y_test)
print(f"Unique classes in y_test: {unique_classes}")
class_report = classification_report(y_test, y_pred, target_names=[str(i) for i in unique_classes])
print("Classification Report:")
print(class_report)
# Visualize the decision tree
plt.figure(figsize=(20, 10))
plot_tree(clf,
    filled=True,
    feature_names=list(X.columns),  # Convert Index to list
    class_names=['Small', 'Medium', 'Large'],
    rounded=True,
    proportion=True)
plt.show()
```

Observations and Decisions in Business Analytics:

1. **Customer Segmentation**: The decision tree helps us identify key features (such as sales amount, marketing spend, and feedback score) that influence customer segmentation.

2. **Accuracy**: This score indicates the percentage of correct predictions. A high accuracy indicates that the model can reliably classify customer segments.

3. **Confusion Matrix**: Helps us understand where the model is making mistakes. If the model misclassifies a "Small" customer as "Large," it indicates a need for better features or model fine-tuning.

4. **Business Strategy**: Based on the classification model, the business can target specific customer segments with tailored marketing campaigns, improving resource allocation and ROI.

11. Introduction to Machine Learning Clustering in Business Analytics

Machine learning clustering is an unsupervised learning technique used to group similar data points into clusters. In business analytics, clustering can provide valuable insights into customer segmentation, product categorization, market trends, and operational efficiencies. Unlike supervised learning, where the model is trained on labeled data, clustering algorithms do not require predefined labels. Instead, they analyze the structure of the data itself to find natural groupings.

Applications of Clustering in Business Analytics:

1. **Customer Segmentation**: Businesses can use clustering to divide their customers into groups based on purchasing behavior, demographics, or other criteria. This enables targeted marketing, personalized offers, and better customer service.
2. **Market Research**: Clustering can help identify emerging market trends by grouping customers or products with similar attributes.
3. **Inventory Management**: By clustering products based on sales patterns, businesses can optimize inventory levels and distribution strategies.
4. **Fraud Detection**: In financial services, clustering can help detect anomalous behavior by grouping transactions and flagging outliers.

Types of Clustering Algorithms

1. **K-means Clustering**: This is one of the most commonly used algorithms, which partitions data into a predefined number of clusters based on similarity. It works by iteratively adjusting the cluster centroids to minimize the sum of squared differences between the data points and the centroids.
2. **Hierarchical Clustering**: This method builds a tree-like structure (dendrogram) that shows how data points can be grouped at different levels of similarity. It's useful when the number of clusters is not known in advance.
3. **DBSCAN (Density-Based Spatial Clustering of Applications with Noise)**: This algorithm groups together closely packed points, marking as outliers the points that are far away from others.
4. **Gaussian Mixture Model (GMM)**: A probabilistic model that assumes that the data is generated from a mixture of several Gaussian distributions. GMM is useful when the clusters are not spherical but may have different shapes.

Example with Sample Data

Let's consider an example where a retail company wants to segment its customers based on their spending behavior. The company has data on two attributes for each customer: **Annual Income** and **Spending Score** (a measure of how much they spend relative to their income).

Here's the sample data:

Customer ID	Annual Income (k)	Spending Score
1	60	40
2	80	50
3	120	90
4	200	40
5	220	80
6	180	60
7	150	70
8	300	50
9	500	90
10	450	60

Steps in Clustering

1. **Data Preparation**: Ensure the data is clean and normalized if necessary (e.g., scaling numerical values so that one feature doesn't dominate the clustering process).
2. **Choosing the Algorithm**: We will use **K-means clustering** in this case to segment the customers based on their **Annual Income** and **Spending Score**.
3. **Determining the Number of Clusters**: A common approach to determine the number of clusters (k) is the **Elbow Method**, which plots the sum of squared distances from each point to its assigned cluster center for different values of k. The point where the curve bends sharply (elbow) is the optimal number of clusters.

Running K-means Clustering

Let's assume we have already decided to use **k=3** clusters based on the Elbow Method. We apply K-means clustering to the dataset.

Clustered Data (Output):

Customer ID	Annual Income (k)	Spending Score	Cluster
1	60	40	1
2	80	50	1
3	120	90	2
4	200	40	1
5	220	80	3
6	180	60	2

7	150	70	2
8	300	50	3
9	500	90	3
10	450	60	3

Interpretation of the Results:

- **Cluster 1**: Customers with low annual income (60k - 200k) and low spending score. These customers might be more price-sensitive and could benefit from promotions and discounts to increase their spending.
- **Cluster 2**: Customers with mid-range income (120k - 180k) and moderate spending. This group may be targeted with loyalty programs, offering them value-added services or rewards for repeat purchases.
- **Cluster 3**: High-income customers (220k and above) with high spending scores. These customers are the most valuable and could be targeted with premium products, exclusive offers, or personalized experiences.

Business Implications and Decisions:

1. **Targeted Marketing**: Based on the clusters, marketing campaigns can be tailored. For example:
   - **Cluster 1** could receive more cost-effective promotions to increase their spending.
   - **Cluster 2** could receive rewards for loyalty, such as discounts on future purchases.
   - **Cluster 3** might be offered exclusive, high-end products or personalized services to retain their business.
2. **Product Offerings**: Different clusters may be interested in different types of products. **Cluster 1** may prefer budget-friendly items, while **Cluster 3** might lean towards luxury goods. By understanding these preferences, the company can improve its product offerings.
3. **Pricing Strategy**: Pricing models could be adjusted for different clusters. **Cluster 1** may be more responsive to price reductions, while **Cluster 3** may not be as sensitive to price and might appreciate more value-added services.
4. **Customer Retention**: The company can focus on retaining high-value customers from **Cluster 3** by offering personalized experiences or exclusive deals. They could also identify opportunities to move customers from **Cluster 1** to **Cluster 2** through targeted promotions and customer engagement.

Conclusion:

Clustering allows businesses to segment their customer base more effectively, enabling them to make data-driven decisions that improve marketing, sales, and customer retention. By leveraging machine learning clustering techniques, businesses can ensure that their strategies are more personalized, efficient, and impactful.

11.1 Understanding K-Means Clustering in Business Context

K-Means Clustering is an unsupervised machine learning algorithm used in business analytics to group a set of data points into a predefined number of clusters (denoted as K). The key idea behind K-Means is to partition data into distinct, non-overlapping groups based on the similarity of their features. Unlike classification, which is used for predicting categories, clustering is used to find natural groupings in data, making it a powerful tool for customer segmentation, market analysis, and other business insights.

Key Concepts in K-Means Clustering

1. **Unsupervised Learning**: Unlike supervised learning, where the output labels are known (e.g., predicting whether a customer will churn), clustering does not have predefined labels. It seeks to discover hidden patterns or groups in the data.

2. **Clusters**: These are groups of similar data points. Each data point belongs to one and only one cluster, and the points in the same cluster share similar characteristics.

3. **Centroids**: Each cluster is represented by a centroid, which is the average of all the data points in the cluster. The algorithm tries to minimize the distance between the data points and the centroid of their respective clusters.

4. **K**: The number of clusters, which is defined before the algorithm is run. A key challenge in K-Means clustering is determining the appropriate value of K.

5. **Iterative Process**: K-Means works by randomly assigning initial centroids and then iteratively refining them. During each iteration, it reassigns each data point to the nearest centroid and then recalculates the centroids based on the newly assigned points. This process continues until the centroids no longer change significantly.

6. **Distance Metric**: The most commonly used distance metric for K-Means is Euclidean distance, which measures how far apart two points are in the feature space.

Applications of K-Means Clustering in Business Analytics

K-Means clustering is widely used in business for various applications, including:

- **Customer Segmentation**: Businesses can segment customers based on purchasing behavior, demographics, or other attributes to target marketing campaigns effectively.

- **Market Basket Analysis**: Grouping items purchased together to understand product associations.

- **Sales and Revenue Prediction**: Identifying groups of stores or regions with similar sales trends for targeted strategies.

- **Risk Management**: Identifying groups of customers with similar credit behaviors for offering personalized services or managing risk.

Example of K-Means Clustering in Business Analytics

Let's consider a retail company that wants to segment its customers based on two features: **Annual Spending** and **Purchase Frequency**. The company believes that clustering customers into distinct groups will help create targeted marketing strategies and personalized offers.

Sample Data

Here's a small sample dataset of 10 customers:

Customer ID	Annual Spending ($)	Purchase Frequency (per year)
1	500	10
2	1500	5
3	2000	8
4	1200	6
5	800	12
6	2500	3
7	3000	2
8	600	15
9	1800	7
10	1000	9

Goal:

Segment customers into **K=3** clusters to understand different types of customers (e.g., high spenders, frequent buyers, etc.).

Steps in K-Means Clustering

1. **Choosing K**: The company decides to segment its customers into 3 groups (K=3) based on their spending and purchase frequency. The choice of K can be guided by domain knowledge, but it's often tested through methods like the Elbow Method.

2. **Initial Centroids**: The algorithm starts by selecting three random centroids from the data. These centroids represent the initial "center" of each cluster.

3. **Assigning Data Points to Clusters**: Each customer is assigned to the nearest centroid based on their annual spending and purchase frequency.

4. **Recalculating Centroids**: Once all customers are assigned to clusters, the centroid of each cluster is recalculated as the mean of all customers within the cluster.

5. **Repeat**: The algorithm repeats steps 3 and 4 iteratively until the centroids stabilize (i.e., no longer change significantly).

Output and Results

After running the K-Means clustering algorithm on the data with **K=3**, the resulting clusters may look like this:

Customer ID	Annual Spending ($)	Purchase Frequency (per year)	Cluster (Group)
1	500	10	1
2	1500	5	2
3	2000	8	2
4	1200	6	2
5	800	12	1
6	2500	3	3
7	3000	2	3
8	600	15	1
9	1800	7	2
10	1000	9	2

Centroids (final):

- **Cluster 1 (Low Spend, High Frequency)**: Customers who spend less annually but buy more frequently (e.g., Customer 1, 5, 8).
- **Cluster 2 (Moderate Spend, Moderate Frequency)**: Customers with moderate spending and moderate frequency (e.g., Customer 2, 3, 4, 9, 10).
- **Cluster 3 (High Spend, Low Frequency)**: Customers who spend more annually but purchase less frequently (e.g., Customer 6, 7).

Interpretation and Discussion

1. **Cluster 1 (Low Spend, High Frequency):**
    - These customers spend relatively less but buy often. They might be price-sensitive or frequent small-ticket item buyers.

- **Business Strategy**: Offering discounts or loyalty rewards could incentivize them to increase their overall spending. Promotions for frequent, smaller purchases might appeal to this group.

2. **Cluster 2 (Moderate Spend, Moderate Frequency)**:
   - These customers have a balanced pattern of spending and frequency. They are moderate in both aspects.
   - **Business Strategy**: Target these customers with regular offers to keep them engaged and increase either their frequency or spending. Special product bundles or personalized offers could work well.

3. **Cluster 3 (High Spend, Low Frequency)**:
   - These customers spend a lot but purchase less often. They may be occasional big spenders or luxury product buyers.
   - **Business Strategy**: Create personalized high-value offers or seasonal discounts to increase the frequency of their purchases. Exclusive VIP offers could encourage them to buy more frequently.

Business Decisions Based on K-Means Clustering Results

1. **Targeted Marketing Campaigns**: By understanding the different customer segments, the company can tailor its marketing efforts to each group. For example, offering loyalty programs to Cluster 1, personalized high-value promotions to Cluster 3, and general product bundles to Cluster 2.

2. **Customer Retention**: Identifying low-frequency, high-spend customers (Cluster 3) provides an opportunity to increase retention by encouraging more frequent purchases through exclusive offers.

3. **Resource Allocation**: The company can allocate marketing resources efficiently by focusing on high-potential groups (like Cluster 3), who may have higher profitability if their purchase frequency is increased.

4. **Product Customization**: Understanding customer clusters allows businesses to customize product offerings to suit the needs of different segments, improving customer satisfaction and increasing sales.

Conclusion

K-Means clustering is a powerful tool for identifying natural groupings in data, particularly useful for customer segmentation in business analytics. By segmenting customers into distinct groups based on common features, businesses can develop targeted strategies that improve customer engagement, retention, and overall profitability. While the process requires careful selection of K and thoughtful interpretation of clusters, the insights gained from clustering can significantly enhance business decision-making.

11.2 K-Means Clustering in JASP

In this example, we will apply **K-Means Clustering in JASP**, a common unsupervised learning algorithm used to group data points into clusters based on their features. We'll also compute the **Silhouette Score**, which is a metric used to evaluate the quality of the clusters.

Follow the steps provided below to create modified Business Data.

> **Note:** To apply machine learning module, we need approximately 100 rows of data. The business dataset (Refer Chapter 1.2) used in the previous chapter have only 25 rows. Hence, we will reproduce the same data and use it as hypothesized data for learning. However, in real time, one has to ensure large number of data for training and testing of the machine learning model

Now open the data in excel and multiply the rows by copying the first 25 rows of data and pasting in the end. Now, 3-time copy and paste (25 x 3) becomes a total of 100 rows of data. Next, we will use this data as a hypothesized data for Machine learning purposes. We will rename this dataset as **Business_data_100.CSV**

ID	Sales Amount	Region	Target Sales	Pre-Sales Amount	Post-Sales Amount	Marketing Spend	Customer Feedback Score	Sales Growth	Customer Segment
1	1500	East	1600	1400	1550	500	4	50	Small
2	1800	West	1750	1700	1850	600	5	100	Medium
3	2200	East	2000	2100	2250	700	4	150	Large
4	2000	West	1900	1850	2050	550	3	100	Medium
5	1750	East	1700	1600	1800	450	4	50	Small
95	1950	East	1900	1850	1950	550	4	50	Medium
96	2200	West	2250	2150	2200	700	5	100	Large
97	1650	East	1700	1600	1650	450	3	50	Small
98	1750	West	1800	1700	1750	500	4	50	Medium
100	1900	East	1850	1800	1900	600	5	100	Large

Steps to use Machine Learning Decision Tree Classification in JASP

1. **Open JASP:**

- If you haven't already, open JASP and load your dataset (e.g., a CSV, Excel, or SPSS file).

2. **Load the Data**:
   - Click **"File" > "Open"** to load your dataset into JASP.

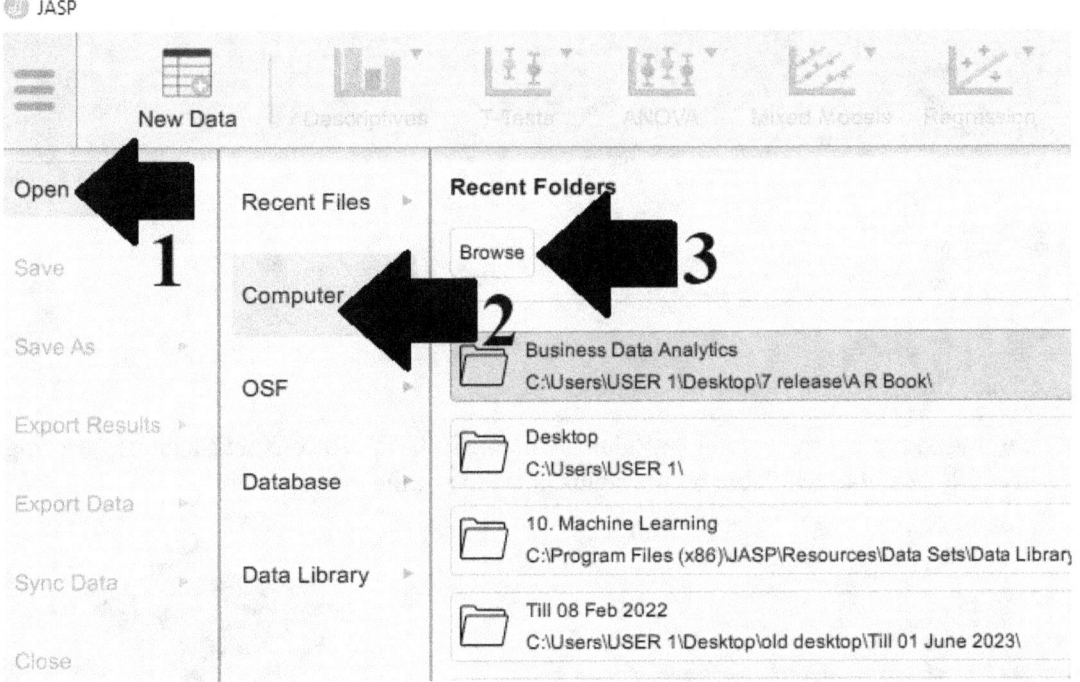

Now select the file

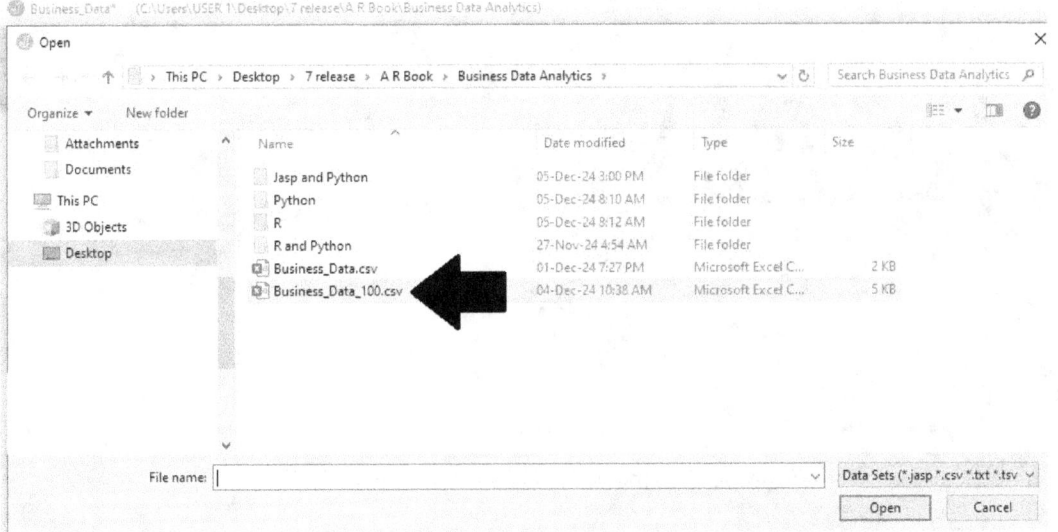

File will be loaded into JASP as shown below.

ID	Sales Amount	Region	Target Sales	Pre-Sales Amount	Post-Sales Amount	Marketing Spend	Customer Feedback Score	Sales Growth	Cust...
1	1500	East	1600	1400	1550	500	4	50	Small
2	1800	West	1750	1700	1850	600	5	100	Medium
3	2200	East	2000	2100	2250	700	4	150	Large
4	2000	West	1900	1850	2050	550	3	100	Medium
5	1750	East	1700	1600	1800	450	4	50	Small
6	1900	West	1950	1900	2000	650	5	100	Medium
7	2100	East	2200	2050	2150	700	4	100	Large
8	2400	West	2300	2200	2400	600	5	200	Large
9	1600	East	1650	1500	1600	500	3	100	Small
10	2300	West	2400	2350	2500	750	4	150	Large
11	1950	East	2000	1900	1950	550	4	50	Medium
12	2050	West	2100	2000	2050	600	3	50	Medium
13	1750	East	1800	1700	1750	500	4	50	Small

3. **Activate the Machine Learning Module:**

Machine Learning Module is not a default module available in JASP. To activate Machine Learning Module, select the + symbol available on the right-hand side of the home screen.

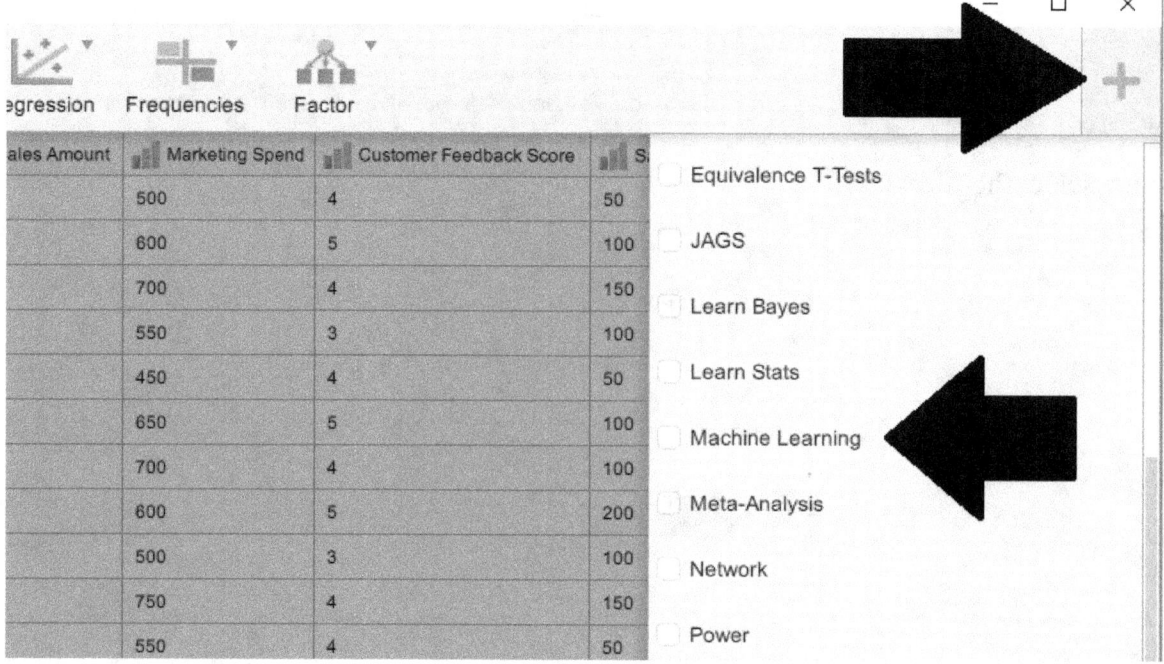

Now Machine Learning Tab will appear in the Tab as shown below.

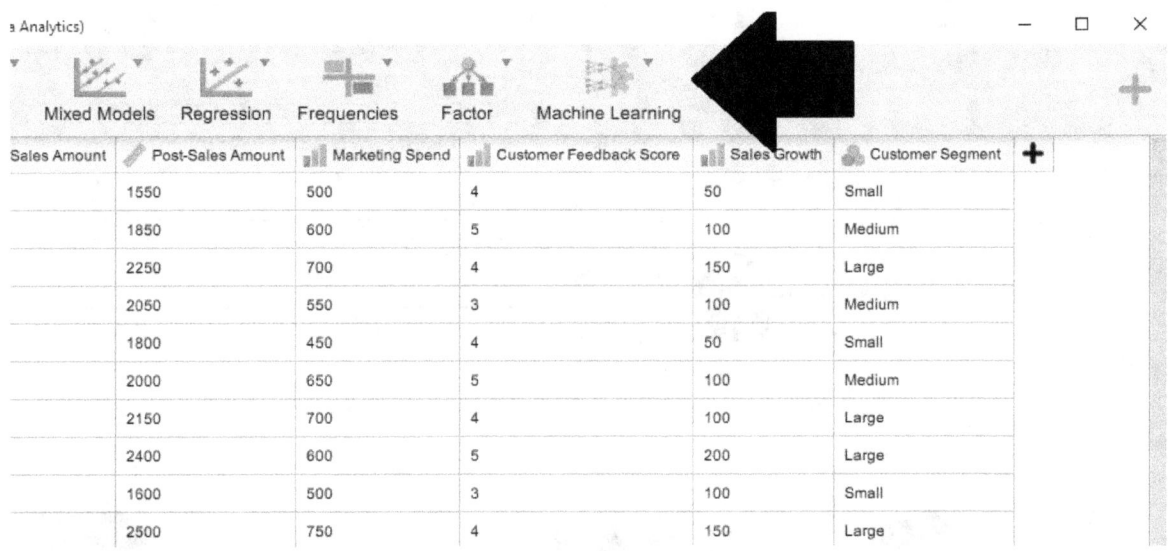

4. Select the **Neighborhood-Based Clustering** Menu

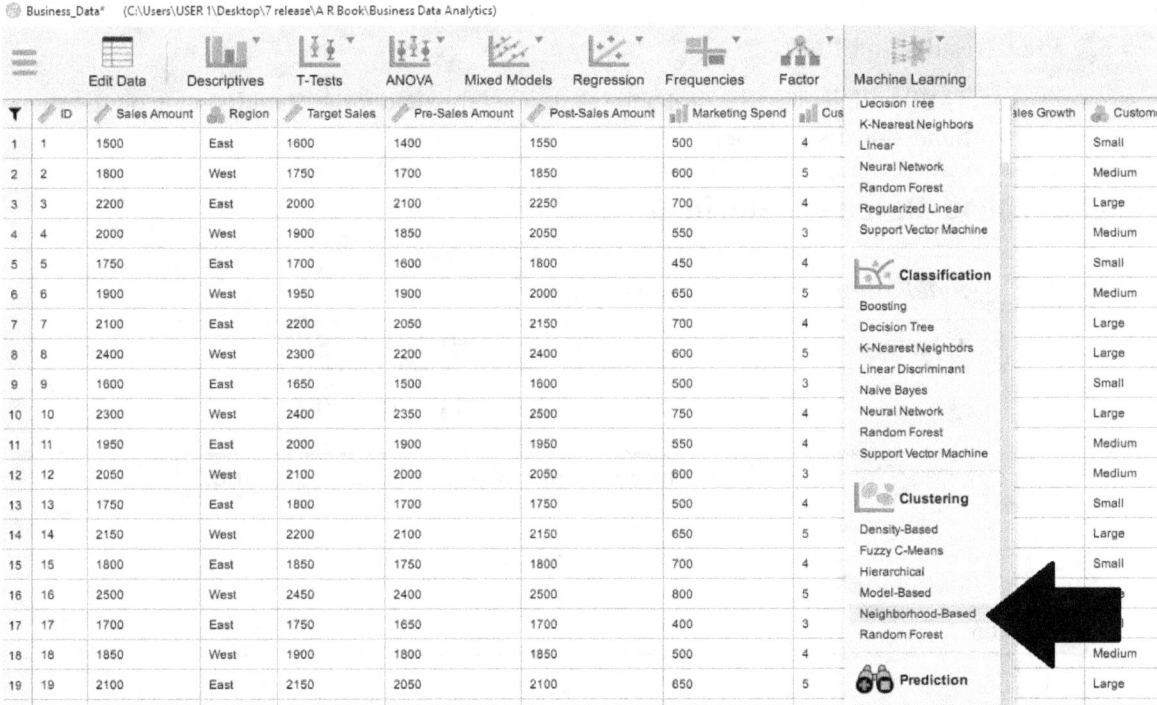

Select and transfer the numerical variables to Features block. Select the required tables and plots from the options.

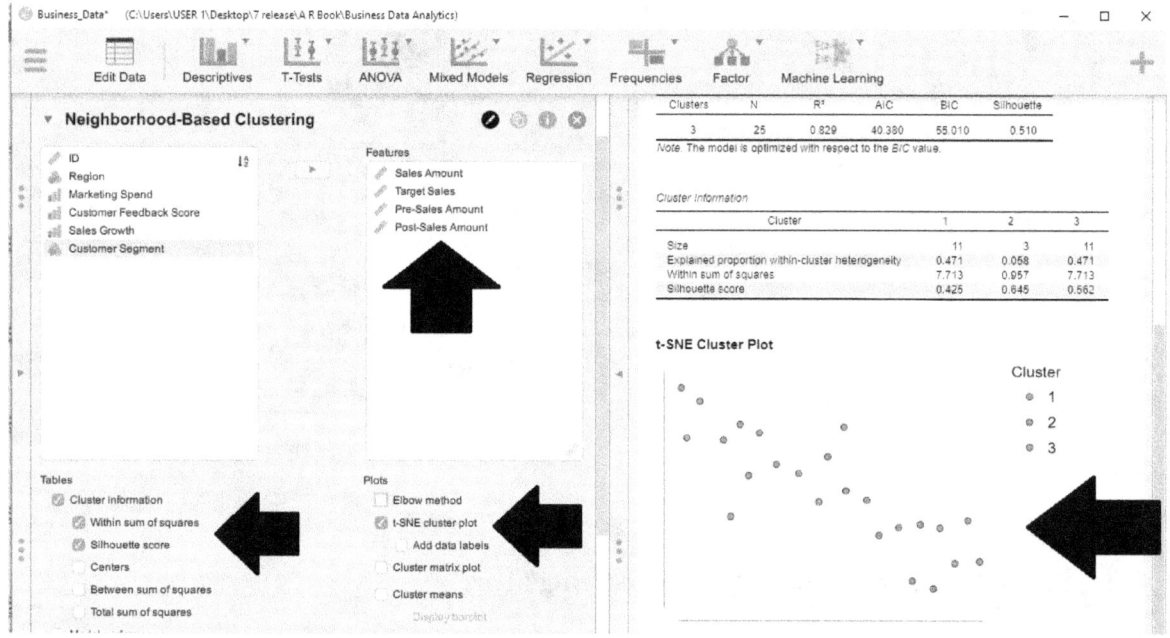

5. **View Results and Plot:**
    o JASP will display the plot and result in a table under the **Results** pane on the right-hand side result pane.

Neighborhood-Based Clustering

Model Summary: K-Means Clustering					
Clusters	N	R^2	AIC	BIC	Silhouette
3	25	0.829	40.380	55.010	0.510
Note. The model is optimized with respect to the *BIC* value.					

Cluster Information

Cluster	1	2	3
Size	11	3	11
Explained proportion within-cluster heterogeneity	0.471	0.058	0.471
Within sum of squares	7.713	0.957	7.713
Silhouette score	0.425	0.645	0.562

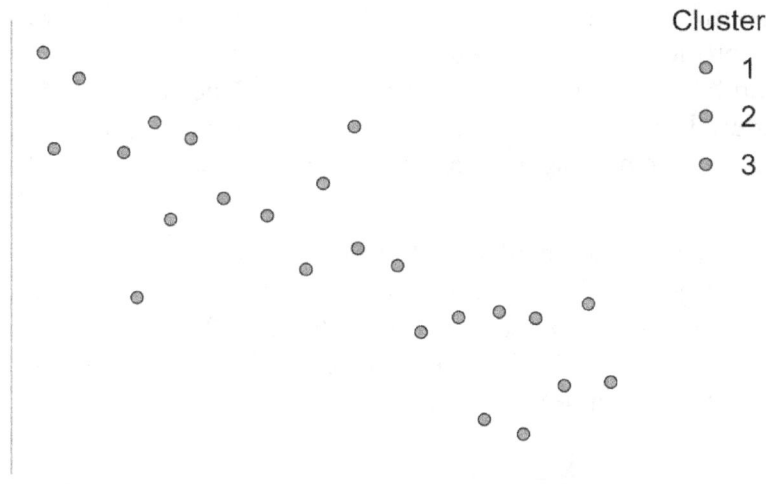

Explanation and Interpretation of the Results in K-Means Clustering

The results of the K-Means clustering model applied to the business dataset provide key insights into how well the data has been divided into clusters, and how the clusters perform in terms of homogeneity, separability, and the effectiveness of the model. Let's go through each table and explain the results step by step.

Model Summary: K-Means Clustering

Clusters	N	R^2	AIC	BIC	Silhouette
3	25	0.829	40.380	55.010	0.510

Explanation of each metric:

1. **Clusters**: This indicates that the dataset has been divided into 3 distinct clusters. K-Means clustering was applied with **K = 3**.

2. **N**: The total number of data points in the dataset is 25.

3. **R^2 (Coefficient of Determination)**: The R^2 value of 0.829 suggests that 82.9% of the variance in the data is explained by the model. A higher R^2 value indicates that the clustering algorithm has done a good job in grouping similar data points together, meaning the clusters are well-defined and distinct.

4. **AIC (Akaike Information Criterion)**: The AIC value is 40.380. The AIC is a measure of the relative quality of the model for a given set of data. Lower AIC values indicate a better model fit. In clustering, the AIC can be used to compare models with different numbers of clusters; here, the AIC suggests that the chosen model (K=3) is optimal.

5. **BIC (Bayesian Information Criterion)**: The BIC value is 55.010. Similar to AIC, BIC is a criterion for model selection, but it includes a penalty for model complexity (i.e., the number of parameters). The model with the lowest BIC value is typically considered the best. In this case, the model is optimized with respect to the BIC, meaning it has been selected because it balances fit and complexity well.

6. **Silhouette Score**: The silhouette score of 0.510 indicates that the clustering solution has moderate quality. A silhouette score ranges from -1 to +1, where higher values indicate better-defined clusters. A score closer to 0 suggests that some data points may be on the border between clusters. While 0.510 is not perfect, it shows a reasonable separation of clusters.

Cluster Information Table

Cluster	1	2	3
Size	3	11	11
Explained Proportion of Within-Cluster Heterogeneity	0.058	0.471	0.471
Within Sum of Squares	0.957	7.713	7.713
Silhouette Score	0.645	0.562	0.425

Explanation of each metric:

1. **Size**:
    - Cluster 1 has 3 data points, Cluster 2 has 11 data points, and Cluster 3 also has 11 data points.
    - The clusters have relatively small and balanced sizes, though Cluster 1 is much smaller compared to Clusters 2 and 3.

2. **Explained Proportion of Within-Cluster Heterogeneity**:
    - This shows how much of the variability (heterogeneity) within each cluster is explained by the model.
    - Cluster 1 explains only 5.8% of its internal variability, indicating that Cluster 1 may be less homogeneous compared to the other two clusters.
    - Clusters 2 and 3 explain 47.1% of their internal variability, suggesting that these clusters are more homogeneous and that the data within these clusters are more similar.

3. **Within Sum of Squares**:
    - The sum of squares represents the variance within each cluster. A higher value of sum of squares indicates more spread or greater variability within the cluster.
    - Cluster 1 has the lowest value (0.957), indicating it is the least spread-out cluster, possibly because of the smaller number of data points.
    - Clusters 2 and 3 have much higher values (7.713), suggesting that they are more spread out or have higher variability in the data.
4. **Silhouette Score for Each Cluster**:
    - **Cluster 1** has a silhouette score of 0.645, which is relatively high, indicating that the points in Cluster 1 are well-separated from other clusters and are relatively cohesive within the cluster.
    - **Cluster 2** has a score of 0.562, which is also reasonable, suggesting good cohesion and separation but less so than Cluster 1.
    - **Cluster 3** has a lower silhouette score of 0.425, which indicates that this cluster is less cohesive, with some data points possibly being near the boundary with other clusters.

t-SNE Cluster Plot

The **t-SNE** (t-Distributed Stochastic Neighbor Embedding) plot is a dimensionality reduction technique used to visualize high-dimensional data in a 2D space. In the context of clustering, it helps to visualize how well-separated the clusters are.

Interpretation:

- The t-SNE plot shows the spatial separation of the 3 clusters in a 2D space, with each point representing a data point and different clusters shown in distinct colors.
- If the clusters are well-separated in the t-SNE plot, it visually confirms that the clustering algorithm did a good job in finding meaningful groupings in the data. If the clusters overlap significantly, it would indicate poor clustering.

Observations:

- **Cluster Distribution**: Clusters 2 and 3 are much larger in size compared to Cluster 1, with 11 members each compared to just 3 in Cluster 1. This suggests that the data is not evenly distributed across clusters.

- **Cluster Homogeneity**: Clusters 2 and 3 are more homogeneous, as reflected in the higher explained proportion of within-cluster heterogeneity and higher silhouette scores compared to Cluster 1.
- **Cluster Separation**: Although the silhouette scores suggest moderate cluster separation, Cluster 3's lower silhouette score indicates that some points may not fit as well in this cluster. The overall silhouette score of 0.510 suggests that there is room for improvement in terms of clustering cohesion and separation.

Business Implications:
- **Targeting Different Customer Segments**: The clustering model can be used for segmenting customers or users in the business dataset. With three distinct clusters, businesses can tailor their marketing, product offerings, or customer service to better suit each group.
- **Optimizing Product Development**: Cluster 1, with only 3 members, may represent a niche or specialized customer segment. The business may want to investigate this segment further to understand its needs better.
- **Resource Allocation**: Clusters 2 and 3, being larger, could represent the majority of the customer base. The business may want to focus more resources on understanding and targeting these clusters effectively.

Business Decisions:
- **Customer Profiling**: The business should profile the customers in each cluster to determine key characteristics and develop targeted strategies. For example, Cluster 1 may require specialized products or services, while Clusters 2 and 3 might need more standardized offerings.
- **Optimizing Marketing Efforts**: With clear segmentation, marketing campaigns can be customized to suit each cluster's needs, increasing conversion rates and customer satisfaction.
- **Refinement of Clusters**: The moderate silhouette score indicates potential overlap or poor fit in some clusters, particularly Cluster 3. The business may consider experimenting with other clustering algorithms (like hierarchical clustering or DBSCAN) or adjusting the number of clusters to improve the model's fit.

In conclusion, while the K-Means clustering model provides valuable insights into customer segments, the results suggest areas for further refinement, and the business can use these insights to make targeted and informed decisions.

11.3 K-Means Clustering in Python

In this example, we will apply **K-Means Clustering**, a common unsupervised learning algorithm used to group data points into clusters based on their features. We'll also compute the **Silhouette Score**, which is a metric used to evaluate the quality of the clusters.

Libraries to Install and Load

First, you'll need to install the necessary libraries. For clustering and silhouette scores, we need **Scikit-learn** and **Matplotlib** (for visualizations).

If you haven't installed these libraries yet, you can do so using pip:

```
pip install numpy pandas matplotlib scikit-learn seaborn
```

Libraries Import

```python
# Import necessary libraries
import numpy as np
import pandas as pd
import matplotlib.pyplot as plt
from sklearn.cluster import KMeans
from sklearn.metrics import silhouette_score
from sklearn.preprocessing import StandardScaler
from sklearn.decomposition import PCA
import seaborn as sns
```

Explanation of Libraries:

1. **NumPy**: Used for numerical operations, especially for working with arrays.
2. **Pandas**: Provides powerful data structures like DataFrames for data manipulation.
3. **Matplotlib/Seaborn**: Used for data visualization.
4. **Scikit-learn**: A machine learning library that provides tools for data preprocessing, clustering (like KMeans), and evaluating clustering (e.g., Silhouette Score).
    - **KMeans**: Implements the K-Means algorithm to perform clustering.

- **Silhouette Score**: Measures the quality of the clusters by comparing the cohesion (how close the points in a cluster are) and separation (how distinct the clusters are).
- **StandardScaler**: Standardizes features to have zero mean and unit variance, improving the performance of K-Means.
- **PCA**: Reduces the dimensionality of data, helping with visualization of high-dimensional clustering results.

Step-by-Step Code

Here's how you would implement clustering using **K-Means** and evaluate it using the **Silhouette Score**.

1. Data Preparation

Assuming we are working with your dataset (or a similar one) for clustering, we'll first preprocess the data by selecting relevant features and scaling them.

```
# Sample data (substitute with your DataFrame)
data = {
    'Sales Amount': [1500, 1800, 2200, 2000, 1750, 1900, 2100, 2400, 1600, 2300, 1950, 2050, 1750, 2150, 1800, 2500, 1700, 1850, 2100, 2000, 1950, 2200, 1650, 1750, 1900],
    'Target Sales': [1600, 1750, 2000, 1900, 1700, 1950, 2200, 2300, 1650, 2400, 2000, 2100, 1800, 2200, 1850, 2450, 1750, 1900, 2150, 2050, 1900, 2250, 1700, 1800, 1850],
    'Pre-Sales Amount': [1400, 1700, 2100, 1850, 1600, 1900, 2050, 2200, 1500, 2350, 1900, 2000, 1700, 2100, 1750, 2400, 1650, 1800, 2050, 1950, 1850, 2150, 1600, 1700, 1800],
    'Post-Sales Amount': [1550, 1850, 2250, 2050, 1800, 2000, 2150, 2400, 1600, 2500, 1950, 2050, 1750, 2150, 1800, 2500, 1700, 1850, 2100, 2000, 1950, 2200, 1650, 1750, 1900],
    'Marketing Spend': [500, 600, 700, 550, 450, 650, 700, 600, 500, 750, 550, 600, 500, 650, 700, 800, 400, 500, 650, 600, 550, 700, 450, 500, 600],
    'Customer Feedback Score': [4, 5, 4, 3, 4, 5, 4, 5, 3, 4, 4, 3, 4, 5, 4, 5, 3, 4, 5, 4, 4, 5, 3, 4, 5],
}


df = pd.DataFrame(data)
df.head()
```

Output

	Sales Amount	Target Sales	Pre-Sales Amount	Post-Sales Amount	Marketing Spend	Customer Feedback Score
0	1500	1600	1400	1550	500	4
1	1800	1750	1700	1850	600	5
2	2200	2000	2100	2250	700	4
3	2000	1900	1850	2050	550	3
4	1750	1700	1600	1800	450	4

```
# Select features for clustering
X = df[['Sales Amount', 'Target Sales', 'Pre-Sales Amount', 'Post-Sales Amount', 'Marketing Spend', 'Customer Feedback Score']]


# Standardize the data (important for K-Means)
scaler = StandardScaler()
X_scaled = scaler.fit_transform(X)


# Check the scaled data
print("Scaled data:")
print(X_scaled[:5])  # Display first 5 rows
```

Output

```
Scaled data:
[[-1.84754453 -1.58397189 -1.93301689 -1.66578584 -0.9         -0.16876319]
 [-0.62670013 -0.93833117 -0.72989434 -0.49817894  0.1          1.23759669]
 [ 1.00109241  0.13773669  0.87426905  1.05863025  1.1         -0.16876319]
 [ 0.18719614 -0.29269046 -0.12833307  0.28022566 -0.4         -1.57512306]
 [-0.83017419 -1.15354475 -1.13093519 -0.69278009 -1.4         -0.16876319]]
```

Explanation:

- **Data Selection**: We are selecting columns related to sales, marketing, and customer feedback as features for clustering.

- **Scaling**: K-Means clustering is sensitive to the scale of data, so we use StandardScaler to standardize the features (mean=0, standard deviation=1). This ensures that each feature contributes equally to the clustering process.

2. Apply K-Means Clustering

Next, we apply **K-Means** with a specified number of clusters (let's choose k=3 for simplicity).

```
# Apply K-Means clustering
kmeans = KMeans(n_clusters=3, random_state=42)
kmeans.fit(X_scaled)

# Add the cluster labels to the original data
df['Cluster'] = kmeans.labels_

# Display the first few rows of the data with the cluster labels
print(df.head())
```

Output

```
   Sales Amount  Target Sales  Pre-Sales Amount  Post-Sales Amount
0          1500          1600              1400               1550
1          1800          1750              1700               1850
2          2200          2000              2100               2250
3          2000          1900              1850               2050
4          1750          1700              1600               1800

   Marketing Spend  Customer Feedback Score  Cluster
0              500                        4        1
1              600                        5        2
2              700                        4        0
3              550                        3        2
4              450                        4        1
```

Explanation:

- **KMeans(n_clusters=3)**: We specify that we want to create 3 clusters. This is a common choice, but you can experiment with different values of k based on your data.
- **kmeans.labels_**: These are the cluster labels assigned to each data point.
- We then add the cluster labels to the original DataFrame for easy inspection.

3. Silhouette Score

Now, let's compute the **Silhouette Score**, which measures the quality of the clustering.

```
# Compute the Silhouette Score
sil_score = silhouette_score(X_scaled, kmeans.labels_)
print(f"Silhouette Score: {sil_score}")
```

Output

Silhouette Score: 0.36047728216019875

Explanation of Silhouette Score:

- The **Silhouette Score** is a metric that quantifies how well each data point has been clustered. It combines two factors:
    - **Cohesion**: How close the data points within the same cluster are to each other.
    - **Separation**: How far the data points in one cluster are from those in other clusters.

The score ranges from -1 to +1:

- A **high score** indicates that the clusters are well separated and cohesive.
- A **low or negative score** suggests that the clustering may be poor (e.g., clusters overlap).
- Here, Silhouette Score is 0.36047728216019875 indicate near to average cluster separations can be achieved. One of the reasons is that we used very less data(only 24 rows) for applying clustering techniques. Minimum suggested number must be 120 rows of data, to get better results.

4. Visualizing the Clusters (Optional)

To visualize the clustering, we can reduce the dimensionality of the data using **PCA (Principal Component Analysis)** and then plot the clusters.

```
# Reduce dimensionality for visualization
pca = PCA(n_components=2)
X_pca = pca.fit_transform(X_scaled)


# Plot the clusters
```

```
plt.figure(figsize=(8, 6))

sns.scatterplot(x=X_pca[:, 0], y=X_pca[:, 1], hue=df['Cluster'], palette='viridis', s=100, alpha=0.7)

plt.title('K-Means Clusters (PCA-reduced)')

plt.xlabel('Principal Component 1')

plt.ylabel('Principal Component 2')

plt.show()
```

Output

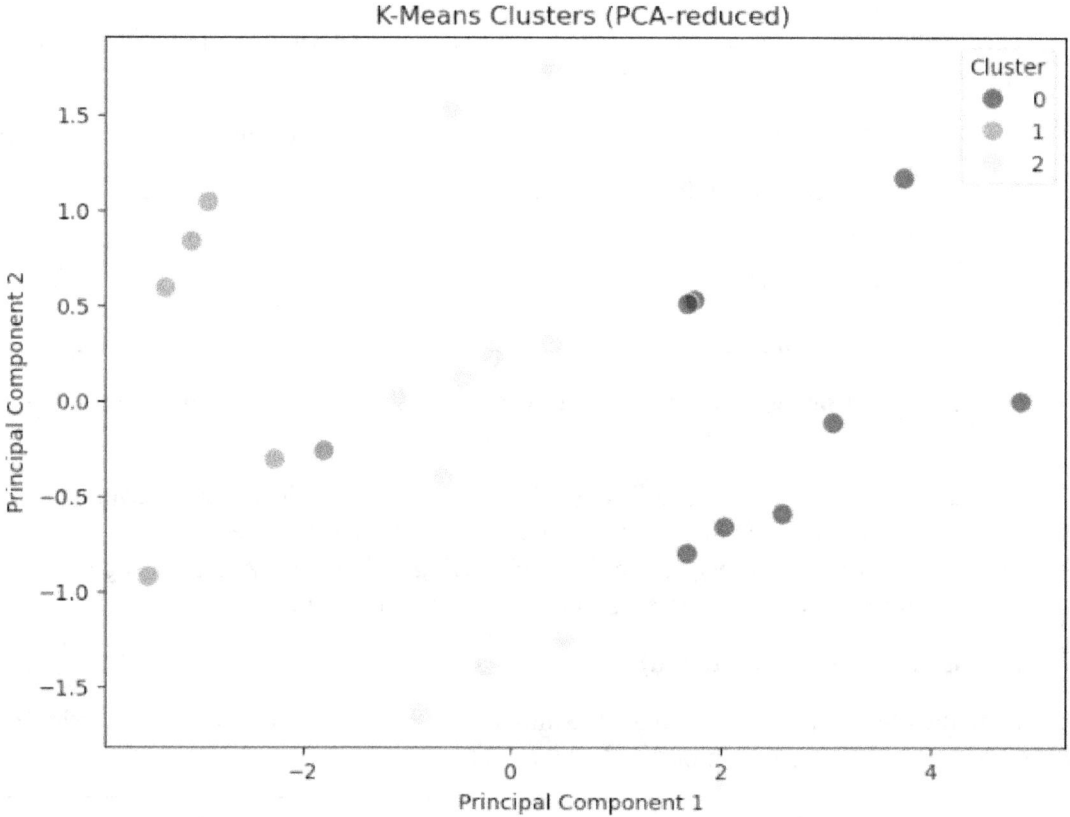

Explanation:

- **PCA**: We reduce the features to 2 components to make the clustering results visualizable in a 2D scatter plot.
- **Scatterplot**: We use seaborn to plot the clusters, with different colors representing different clusters.

Full Code:

```python
from sklearn.cluster import KMeans

from sklearn.metrics import silhouette_score

from sklearn.preprocessing import StandardScaler

from sklearn.decomposition import PCA

import pandas as pd

import seaborn as sns

import matplotlib.pyplot as plt


# Data (same as defined earlier)

data = {
    'Sales Amount': [1500, 1800, 2200, 2000, 1750, 1900, 2100, 2400, 1600, 2300, 1950, 2050, 1750, 2150, 1800, 2500, 1700, 1850, 2100, 2000, 1950, 2200, 1650, 1750, 1900],

    'Target Sales': [1600, 1750, 2000, 1900, 1700, 1950, 2200, 2300, 1650, 2400, 2000, 2100, 1800, 2200, 1850, 2450, 1750, 1900, 2150, 2050, 1900, 2250, 1700, 1800, 1850],

    'Pre-Sales Amount': [1400, 1700, 2100, 1850, 1600, 1900, 2050, 2200, 1500, 2350, 1900, 2000, 1700, 2100, 1750, 2400, 1650, 1800, 2050, 1950, 1850, 2150, 1600, 1700, 1800],

    'Post-Sales Amount': [1550, 1850, 2250, 2050, 1800, 2000, 2150, 2400, 1600, 2500, 1950, 2050, 1750, 2150, 1800, 2500, 1700, 1850, 2100, 2000, 1950, 2200, 1650, 1750, 1900],

    'Marketing Spend': [500, 600, 700, 550, 450, 650, 700, 600, 500, 750, 550, 600, 500, 650, 700, 800, 400, 500, 650, 600, 550, 700, 450, 500, 600],

    'Customer Feedback Score': [4, 5, 4, 3, 4, 5, 4, 5, 3, 4, 4, 3, 4, 5, 4, 5, 3, 4, 5, 4, 4, 5, 3, 4, 5],
}


df = pd.DataFrame(data)


# Standardize the data

X = df[['Sales Amount', 'Target Sales', 'Pre-Sales Amount', 'Post-Sales Amount', 'Marketing Spend', 'Customer Feedback Score']]
```

```python
scaler = StandardScaler()
X_scaled = scaler.fit_transform(X)

# Apply K-Means clustering
kmeans = KMeans(n_clusters=3, random_state=42)
kmeans.fit(X_scaled)

# Add cluster labels
df['Cluster'] = kmeans.labels_

# Compute Silhouette Score
sil_score = silhouette_score(X_scaled, kmeans.labels_)
print(f"Silhouette Score: {sil_score}")

# Visualizing clusters (PCA-reduced)
pca = PCA(n_components=2)
X_pca = pca.fit_transform(X_scaled)

plt.figure(figsize=(8, 6))
sns.scatterplot(x=X_pca[:, 0], y=X_pca[:, 1], hue=df['Cluster'], palette='viridis', s=100, alpha=0.7)
plt.title('K-Means Clusters (PCA-reduced)')
plt.xlabel('Principal Component 1')
plt.ylabel('Principal Component 2')
plt.show()
```

Explanation of Outputs and Results:

1. **Silhouette Score**: A **higher score** (close to 1) indicates well-separated clusters, while a **score closer to 0** suggests overlapping clusters. Negative scores indicate poor clustering (overlap with other clusters).
2. **Cluster Visualization**: Using PCA, the clusters are visualized in 2D space, showing how the samples are grouped based on the features. The different colors represent different clusters.

Business Analytics Insight:

- **Cluster Identification**: After performing clustering, each cluster represents a distinct group of customers based on sales, feedback, and other factors.
- **Targeting Strategies**: By analyzing the clusters, businesses can tailor marketing efforts to each cluster based on shared characteristics (e.g., high-spending customers vs. low-spending ones).
- **Improved Decision Making**: Understanding customer segmentation helps in making data-driven decisions for product offerings, customer service, and promotional activities.

12. Final Project: Business Analytics Strategy for a Real-World Business Problem

The **Final Project** serves as the culmination of the knowledge and skills you've acquired throughout this book. In this project, you will apply business analytics techniques using Python to solve a real-world business problem. This project will encourage you to use the full range of tools available in Python —ranging from data wrangling and visualization to building predictive models and deriving actionable business insights.

Project Overview:

You will choose a real or hypothetical business problem, gather and prepare the data, apply business analytics techniques, and then use R to analyze and model the data. The end goal of the project is to deliver actionable insights that the business can use to improve its operations, optimize strategies, or solve a particular challenge.

Key Steps in the Final Project:

1. **Define the Business Problem:**
    - Choose a specific business problem or question. Examples could include:
        - Forecasting sales for a product line.
        - Optimizing inventory management.
        - Understanding customer churn and creating a retention strategy.
        - Analyzing customer behavior to improve marketing strategies.

2. **Data Collection and Preparation:**
    - Collect relevant data for the chosen problem (e.g., sales data, customer data, operational data).
    - Clean and preprocess the data (handle missing values, outliers, and data transformation).

3. **Exploratory Data Analysis (EDA):**
    - Use Python's powerful data visualization tools to explore and summarize the data.
    - Identify key trends, correlations, and patterns that might inform your business solution.

4. **Modeling and Analytics:**
    - Depending on the problem, you may apply:
        - **Descriptive Analytics**: Summarizing past performance.

- **Predictive Analytics**: Using models like ARIMA for time series forecasting, linear regression for trend analysis, or classification models to predict customer churn.
- **Prescriptive Analytics**: Using optimization techniques to recommend business actions.

5. **Model Evaluation:**
   - Evaluate your model using key metrics (e.g., RMSE, MAPE, AUC) to assess its predictive accuracy and business relevance.
   - If necessary, iterate on the model to improve its performance.

6. **Business Insights and Recommendations:**
   - Derive actionable insights from your analysis.
   - Present recommendations that the business can use to address the problem or capitalize on the opportunities identified.

7. **Final Report and Presentation:**
   - Prepare a comprehensive report that includes your methodology, analysis, results, and business recommendations.
   - Prepare a presentation to communicate your findings and recommendations to stakeholders.

Case Studies in Business Analytics

To help you understand the application of business analytics in a variety of industries, the following **case studies** will provide real-world examples of how companies have used data analytics to solve business problems, improve efficiency, and drive success. Each case study highlights the different phases of the analytics lifecycle, from data collection to decision-making.

Case Study 1: Sales Forecasting for a Retail Chain

Business Problem: A retail chain wants to forecast future sales across its stores to optimize inventory, plan marketing campaigns, and manage staffing levels during peak seasons.

Analytics Approach:

1. **Data Collection**: The company collects historical sales data for each store, including factors such as store size, geographic location, and seasonal promotions.
2. **Data Preparation**: The data is cleaned and prepared by addressing missing values, removing duplicates, and transforming sales figures into monthly aggregates.
3. **Exploratory Data Analysis (EDA):**
   - Visualizations of sales trends over time are created using ggplot2.

- Seasonal patterns and trends are identified in the data.

4. **Time Series Forecasting**:
   - The ARIMA model is applied to the sales data to predict future sales trends for each store.
   - Seasonal adjustments are made using SARIMA (Seasonal ARIMA) models to account for yearly fluctuations.

5. **Model Evaluation**:
   - The performance of the ARIMA model is evaluated using **RMSE** and **MAPE**.
   - The model is refined by adjusting the parameters to minimize forecasting error.

6. **Business Insights**:
   - The model identifies key periods of high sales demand, such as holidays and promotional events.
   - Based on the forecast, the company can adjust inventory, staffing, and marketing efforts to maximize profitability.

Key Business Outcome:

The retail chain successfully forecasts future sales with an average MAPE of 5%, allowing it to improve inventory management, reduce stockouts, and increase overall efficiency.

Case Study 2: Customer Segmentation for Marketing Campaigns

Business Problem: A marketing team wants to improve the targeting of its promotional campaigns by segmenting its customer base according to purchasing behavior.

Analytics Approach:

1. **Data Collection**: The company collects customer data from its loyalty program, including purchase frequency, total spending, and product preferences.

2. **Data Preparation**:
   - Missing values are handled, and the data is scaled for clustering analysis (e.g., normalization of purchase amounts).

3. **Exploratory Data Analysis (EDA)**:
   - A segmentation of customers based on spending behavior is visualized using histograms and box plots.

4. **Clustering Analysis**:
   - K-means clustering is applied to the data, with the number of clusters determined using the Elbow method.

- Customers are grouped into segments such as "high-value frequent shoppers," "occasional buyers," and "price-sensitive shoppers."

5. **Model Evaluation**:
   - The clustering performance is evaluated using **Silhouette Scores** to ensure that customers within each group are similar, and groups are distinct.

6. **Business Insights**:
   - Marketing strategies are tailored for each customer segment. For example, high-value customers are targeted with exclusive offers, while price-sensitive customers are given discounts to increase loyalty.

Key Business Outcome:

Customer segmentation helps the company improve the conversion rate of its marketing campaigns by 20%, leading to more effective targeting and better ROI on marketing spend.

Case Study 3: Predicting Customer Churn in a Telecom Company

Business Problem: A telecom company wants to predict which customers are likely to churn (cancel their subscriptions) so that retention efforts can be focused on high-risk customers.

Analytics Approach:

1. **Data Collection**: The company gathers customer data, including subscription details, service usage patterns, and customer service interactions.

2. **Data Preparation**:
   - Data is cleaned and preprocessed, with categorical variables encoded and features engineered (e.g., churn history, customer tenure).

3. **Exploratory Data Analysis (EDA)**:
   - EDA is performed to identify relationships between churn and factors like contract length, service type, and number of complaints.

4. **Predictive Modeling**:
   - A **logistic regression** model is used to predict the likelihood of churn, based on customer attributes.
   - The model is tuned using cross-validation to improve accuracy.

5. **Model Evaluation**:
   - The model's performance is assessed using **AUC-ROC** and **Confusion Matrix**, showing the model's ability to predict churn correctly.

6. **Business Insights**:

- The model identifies key predictors of churn, such as poor customer service interactions and contract expiry.
- The company implements targeted retention strategies, such as offering loyalty rewards to at-risk customers and improving service quality in high-churn segments.

Key Business Outcome:

The predictive churn model enables the telecom company to reduce churn by 15% within the first quarter of implementation, by proactively addressing issues with high-risk customers.

Conclusion

The final project and case studies illustrate the wide range of applications for business analytics in real-world scenarios. From forecasting and segmentation to churn prediction, data-driven insights play a crucial role in guiding business strategies and decisions. By applying the tools and techniques you have learned in this book—using Python for data analysis, modeling, and visualization—you are now equipped to tackle complex business problems and deliver solutions that drive business success.

Whether you are working on your final project or analyzing a business case, always remember that the value of analytics lies in its ability to uncover insights that lead to informed, impactful decisions. By continuing to refine your analytical skills and approach, you can make a significant contribution to any organization, turning data into a strategic asset.

12.1 Building a Business Analytics Project: Planning and Executing a Comprehensive Business Analytics Project

When undertaking a Business Analytics project using Python, the key is to follow a structured approach to ensure comprehensive and actionable insights. Below is a step-by-step breakdown of how to plan and execute a Business Analytics project in Python, using an example dataset.

Steps in Business Analytics Project:

1. Define the Business Problem

Before diving into data, it's essential to clearly define the business problem you're trying to solve. This allows you to align your analytics with the overall business strategy and goals.

Example Problem:
A car manufacturing company wants to predict car fuel efficiency (mpg) based on car attributes (e.g., horsepower, weight, number of cylinders).

Business Objective:

- Predict mpg (miles per gallon) to help the company optimize car designs for fuel efficiency.

2. Data Collection

The next step is to gather all the relevant data for analysis. This data can come from various sources such as internal databases, external public datasets, or libraries.

For this example, we'll use the **mtcars** dataset, which is available in Python as part of several libraries or can be directly loaded from seaborn.

3. Data Cleaning and Preprocessing

Before jumping into the analysis, we need to clean and preprocess the data to ensure its quality. This involves:

- Handling missing values
- Removing duplicates
- Encoding categorical variables
- Scaling numerical data (if necessary)

4. Exploratory Data Analysis (EDA)

EDA involves understanding the dataset by calculating descriptive statistics, visualizing the data, and identifying any patterns or relationships. The key goal is to understand the structure of the data before building a model.

Tasks:

- Visualize data using plots like histograms, boxplots, and scatter plots.
- Calculate descriptive statistics (mean, median, mode).
- Check for correlations between numerical variables.

5. Modeling and Analytics

Choose an appropriate model based on the business problem. For a regression problem like predicting mpg, we will use a **linear regression** model.

Tasks:

- Split the dataset into training and testing subsets.
- Train a machine learning model.
- Validate the model on the test data.

6. Model Evaluation

After building the model, we need to evaluate its performance using appropriate metrics like:

- **RMSE (Root Mean Squared Error)** for regression tasks.
- **R²** (R-squared) for how well the model explains the variance in the target variable.

7. Business Insights and Recommendations

Once the model is evaluated, you can extract actionable business insights from the results. These insights are crucial for decision-making.

Example Insights:

- How the features (e.g., weight, horsepower) influence fuel efficiency.
- Recommendations for improving vehicle design to optimize fuel consumption.

8. Final Report and Presentation

Document your findings, conclusions, and recommendations in a final report. Prepare a

12.2 Showcasing Your Findings in Business Analytics: Best Practices for Presenting Analytical Results and Insights

Presenting your **analytical findings** effectively is one of the most crucial aspects of Business Analytics. The ultimate goal of any analytics project is to provide clear, actionable insights that can guide business decisions. How you present your findings can significantly impact how your audience understands, engages with, and acts upon your recommendations.

The presentation of business analytics should be structured, compelling, and tailored to the audience. Whether you're presenting to **executives**, **managers**, or **data scientists**, the communication approach should vary based on their familiarity with the subject and their decision-making needs.

Below, we will outline the **best practices** for showcasing your findings, along with strategies to make your presentation more effective.

1. Understand Your Audience

The first step in any presentation is to understand your **audience**:

- **Executives/Stakeholders**: These are often non-technical individuals interested in strategic insights and actionable recommendations.
- **Managers**: Managers may want more granular details that tie to operational decisions and team-level outcomes.
- **Technical Teams/Analysts**: Technical audiences may require deeper insights into the model-building process, methodology, and data.

Key considerations:

- **Executive Presentations**: Focus on the **big picture**, the **business impact**, and actionable recommendations.
- **Managerial Presentations**: Provide more detailed insights that help in decision-making and operational improvements.
- **Technical Presentations**: Dive into the methodology, metrics, and statistical significance of your analysis.

2. Start with the Business Problem

Before diving into numbers and models, **frame the problem** from a business perspective. This helps set the context and gives your audience a clear understanding of the **purpose** of the analysis.

- **Problem Definition**: Clearly state the business question you're answering. For example:
    - "How can we reduce customer churn in the next quarter?"
    - "What are the key drivers of sales growth in Region X?"

Example: If you're analyzing customer churn, begin by highlighting the impact of churn on revenue and the need for better retention strategies.

3. Visual Storytelling with Data

Visualization is one of the most powerful tools for presenting analytical results. Well-designed charts and graphs can help simplify complex information and make it more digestible for your audience. Use visualizations to tell a **story**, not just to display data.

Best Practices in Visualization:

- **Keep it Simple**: Use clear, intuitive charts. Avoid cluttered or overly complex visualizations.
- **Choose the Right Chart Type**: Different charts serve different purposes.
  - **Bar/Column charts**: Great for comparing categories (e.g., sales by region).
  - **Line charts**: Best for trends over time (e.g., sales performance month-over-month).
  - **Pie charts**: Useful for showing proportions but should be used sparingly.
  - **Heatmaps**: Excellent for correlation analysis or performance indicators.
  - **Scatter plots**: Ideal for showing relationships between two variables.

Example:

- A **bar chart** showing the percentage of churned vs. retained customers in different segments.
- A **line graph** showing sales growth trends across regions over several months.

Tools for Visualization:

- **R** has powerful visualization libraries such as **ggplot2** and **plotly**, which can be used to create interactive and informative charts.
- **Power BI** or **Tableau** are business intelligence tools that are widely used for creating impactful dashboards and visualizations.

4. Focus on Key Insights and Actionable Recommendations

The goal of the analysis is not just to present numbers but to **translate** those numbers into actionable **insights**. Focus on what the data **reveals** and what it **means** for the business.

Key Insights:

- **Summary of findings**: Highlight the main takeaways from the analysis. For example:
  - "We found that customer churn increases significantly when service response time exceeds 48 hours."

- "Marketing spend has a high positive correlation with sales growth in Region X."

Actionable Recommendations:

- Provide **concrete recommendations** based on the insights.
    - "To reduce churn, we should implement a 24-hour response time SLA."
    - "Increase marketing spend by 10% in Region X to further drive sales growth."

Recommendations should be **clear**, **specific**, and **feasible** based on the data.

5. Communicate Uncertainty and Limitations

Be transparent about the **uncertainties** in your analysis and the **limitations** of your models. This adds credibility to your work and sets realistic expectations.

- **Model limitations**: "The random forest model we used predicts churn with 85% accuracy, but there is still room for improvement."
- **Data limitations**: "Some data from our CRM system was missing, which could slightly impact the results."

6. Provide Context with Benchmarks or Historical Data

Providing **benchmarks** or **historical data** helps contextualize your findings and allows stakeholders to compare current performance against past trends or industry standards.

- **Example**: "Our sales growth of 5% this quarter is in line with the industry average of 4%, but slightly below our target of 7%."

7. Use Clear and Concise Language

Avoid jargon and overly technical terms, especially if your audience is not familiar with advanced analytics or statistics. Focus on **clarity** and **simplicity**.

- Instead of: "The p-value for the hypothesis test was 0.03, suggesting a statistically significant result."
- Say: "We found that the difference in sales between the two regions is statistically significant, with a 97% confidence level."

8. Tailor the Presentation to the Audience

Different stakeholders have different needs:

- **Executives**: Focus on high-level insights and business impact.
- **Managers**: Provide more detailed operational recommendations.
- **Technical Teams**: Dive into methodology, model performance, and data sources.

Example: If you're presenting to a marketing team, you might want to focus on insights around customer segments, marketing ROI, and engagement strategies. For a sales team, focus on lead generation, sales trends, and sales cycle insights.

9. Tell a Story with Your Data

Effective analytics presentations are not just about numbers—they're about telling a **story**. Use a narrative arc to guide the audience through your analysis:

1. **Set the Scene**: Start with the business problem or challenge.
2. **Present the Journey**: Walk through the data exploration, methodology, and analysis.
3. **Present the Conclusion**: Provide the key insights and actionable recommendations.
4. **Provide Next Steps**: What actions should the business take based on your analysis?

10. Practice and Refine Your Presentation

- **Rehearse** your presentation to ensure it flows smoothly and that you're able to answer questions confidently.
- **Seek Feedback**: Before presenting to stakeholders, practice with colleagues or mentors and get feedback.
- **Use Visual Aids**: Use slides or dashboards as a **visual aid**, but don't rely solely on them. You should be able to explain your insights without reading directly from your slides.

Example of a Structured Analytics Presentation

Slide 1: Title

- Title: "Customer Churn Prediction: Key Drivers and Actionable Insights"
- Your name, date, and company logo

Slide 2: Problem Statement

- **Business Problem**: "The company has seen an increase in churn, leading to a decline in revenue. We need to identify the key drivers of churn to take proactive measures."

Slide 3: Data Overview

- Briefly describe the dataset used (e.g., customer demographics, usage data, support interactions).
- "We analyzed data from 10,000 customers over the last 12 months."

Slide 4: Key Findings

- "Churn rates are highest among customers with low engagement and those who contacted customer support more than 3 times."
- "Price sensitivity is a major factor in churn for customers in the 25-35 age group."

Slide 5: Insights and Visuals

- Show charts of churn by customer segment (age, engagement, support calls).
- "Customers who have contacted support more than 3 times are 40% more likely to churn."

Slide 6: Recommendations

- "Introduce a loyalty program for high-engagement customers."
- "Provide additional support and personalized offers to customers with more than 3 support tickets."

Slide 7: Next Steps

- "Implement the loyalty program in the next quarter and track its impact on churn."
- "Investigate further into the reasons behind high support calls and implement a customer satisfaction survey."

Slide 8: Q&A

- Open the floor for questions and discussion.

Conclusion

The ability to present your analytical findings in a compelling way is as important as the analysis itself. By following these best practices, you can ensure that your insights resonate with your audience and lead to informed business decisions. Keep your presentations **clear**, **concise**, and **actionable**, and always tailor your message to the audience's level of expertise and business needs.

12.3 Future Directions in Business Analytics: Emerging Trends and Technologies

The field of **Business Analytics (BA)** is evolving rapidly, with new **technologies**, **techniques**, and **approaches** transforming how businesses leverage data for decision-making. In this section, we'll discuss the key **emerging trends** and **technologies** shaping the future of business analytics.

1. Artificial Intelligence (AI) and Machine Learning (ML) Integration

AI and **ML** are set to revolutionize business analytics by enhancing predictive capabilities, automating decision-making, and uncovering insights from complex datasets. While AI and ML have been part of the analytics landscape for years, their integration into everyday business processes is rapidly accelerating.

Key Developments:

- **Predictive Analytics**: Machine learning models can predict future trends with greater accuracy. For instance, **customer churn prediction**, **sales forecasting**, and **inventory optimization** are all applications powered by ML algorithms.

- **Natural Language Processing (NLP)**: NLP is enabling more intuitive interactions with data. Businesses can use conversational AI to analyze data, generate reports, and answer business questions directly from unstructured data sources like emails, chat logs, and social media.

- **Automated Decision Making**: AI-powered systems can make autonomous decisions based on data analysis, streamlining processes and improving efficiency in areas like marketing optimization and fraud detection.

Example:

- In retail, AI can be used to **forecast demand** based on historical trends, seasonality, and market conditions, which helps businesses optimize their supply chain and reduce excess inventory.

2. Augmented Analytics

Augmented Analytics refers to the use of AI, ML, and NLP to automate data preparation, data discovery, and insight generation. The goal is to make data analysis more accessible to non-technical users while improving the productivity of data scientists.

Key Developments:

- **Automated Data Preparation**: Augmented analytics tools help automate data cleaning, transformation, and integration tasks, which are typically time-consuming and require technical expertise.

- **Self-Service BI**: With augmented analytics, business users can generate reports, dashboards, and insights without needing advanced technical skills. AI-driven insights can also help uncover hidden patterns in the data.
- **Advanced Insights Discovery**: Tools now enable automatic identification of trends, anomalies, and patterns, reducing the need for manual hypothesis testing and exploratory analysis.

Example:

- A marketing team could use an augmented analytics platform to automatically generate customer segmentation reports, uncovering insights like high-value customers who may require a loyalty program without needing to rely on IT or data scientists for analysis.

3. Cloud Analytics

Cloud computing has already reshaped how businesses store and process data, but the future of cloud-based analytics is even more promising. Cloud analytics platforms are becoming more powerful, scalable, and cost-effective, enabling businesses to store vast amounts of data and run complex analyses without significant investment in on-premise infrastructure.

Key Developments:

- **Scalable Data Processing**: Cloud platforms like **AWS**, **Azure**, and **Google Cloud** offer on-demand compute resources, making it easier for businesses to scale their analytics as data volumes grow.
- **Cloud Data Lakes**: Instead of storing data in siloed databases, organizations are moving towards cloud-based **data lakes** to consolidate all types of structured and unstructured data. This enables easier access and analysis of large, diverse datasets.
- **Integration with Other Cloud Services**: Cloud analytics tools now integrate seamlessly with other cloud services, such as machine learning tools, CRM platforms, and business intelligence applications.

Example:

- A large e-commerce company may use cloud analytics to collect and process real-time transaction data, customer browsing behavior, and inventory levels across various platforms, using that data for real-time decision-making.

4. Edge Analytics and IoT

With the explosion of Internet of Things (**IoT**) devices and the increase in real-time data generation, **edge analytics** has emerged as a key trend. Instead of sending all raw data to the cloud for processing, edge analytics involves processing data at or near the source (on the device or local server), enabling faster insights and more efficient decision-making.

Key Developments:

- **Real-Time Data Processing**: For industries such as manufacturing, transportation, and healthcare, edge analytics enables the real-time monitoring of equipment, machinery, and patient health. This reduces latency and allows businesses to act on insights quickly.
- **Autonomous Systems**: In IoT-driven environments, edge analytics can be used to optimize processes without human intervention, such as monitoring factory machines and automatically adjusting operations based on real-time performance data.

Example:

- In **smart cities**, IoT sensors and edge computing can collect data on traffic, air quality, and energy consumption. This data is processed locally to optimize traffic flow or detect potential hazards before sending summaries to the central system for further analysis.

5. Data Privacy and Governance

As data privacy concerns grow, **data governance** and **privacy protection** will continue to be a major focus for businesses. The rise of **GDPR (General Data Protection Regulation)** and similar regulations worldwide will drive the need for businesses to implement stronger data governance frameworks.

Key Developments:

- **Data Sovereignty**: The demand for local data storage and processing is increasing to comply with regional data protection regulations.
- **Data Anonymization**: Businesses are focusing on developing techniques for **anonymizing** or **pseudonymizing** sensitive customer data to ensure compliance with privacy laws.
- **Governance Automation**: Automation tools will be used to enforce policies and monitor data usage across the organization, ensuring that data is used ethically and in compliance with regulations.

Example:

- A healthcare provider that uses patient data for analysis would need to ensure that all data is anonymized or securely encrypted to comply with **HIPAA** (Health Insurance Portability and Accountability Act) regulations in the U.S.

6. Explainable AI (XAI)

As businesses increasingly rely on **AI** and **ML** models for decision-making, **explainability** of these models is becoming more critical. **Explainable AI (XAI)** focuses on creating machine learning models that can provide **clear and understandable explanations** for their predictions, making them more transparent and trustworthy.

Key Developments:

- **Model Interpretability**: Tools are being developed to allow users to interpret the outcomes of black-box models (like deep learning and random forests) by identifying which features contributed to predictions.
- **Regulatory Compliance**: Many sectors, such as finance and healthcare, require transparency and accountability in AI-driven decision-making, making **XAI** an essential development.

Example:

- A **loan approval** system powered by AI could use explainable AI to show why an application was approved or denied, such as "The applicant's credit score was a major factor, and the employment history was a key consideration."

7. Automated Machine Learning (AutoML)

AutoML is making machine learning more accessible to non-technical users by automating the process of model selection, training, and evaluation. Rather than requiring extensive knowledge of algorithms and hyperparameters, **AutoML platforms** allow business users and analysts to apply machine learning models to their data with minimal effort.

Key Developments:

- **End-to-End Automation**: AutoML tools can handle the entire machine learning pipeline—from data preprocessing to model deployment—without requiring human intervention.
- **Lowering Barriers**: By automating much of the machine learning workflow, AutoML makes it easier for businesses of all sizes to apply machine learning without needing specialized expertise.

Example:

- A retail business could use **AutoML** tools to predict customer purchase behavior by uploading historical sales data, and the system would automatically select and tune the best machine learning model for prediction.

8. Blockchain in Data Analytics

Blockchain technology, best known for its role in cryptocurrency, is emerging as a tool for enhancing **data security** and **transparency** in analytics. Blockchain's decentralized nature ensures that data is immutable and verifiable, making it particularly useful in industries that rely heavily on data integrity.

Key Developments:

- **Data Provenance**: Blockchain can be used to track the origin of data and ensure its integrity, which is crucial in industries like finance, healthcare, and supply chain.

- **Smart Contracts**: In data analytics, blockchain-based smart contracts could automate data sharing between organizations and ensure that data is used in accordance with agreed-upon rules.

Example:

- A **supply chain** company could use blockchain to track the provenance of raw materials from farm to factory, ensuring the data's accuracy and transparency while protecting the privacy of suppliers.

9. Real-Time Analytics

Real-time or **streaming analytics** allows businesses to analyze and act on data as it is generated. This is critical in industries where time-sensitive decisions are crucial, such as in **financial trading**, **online advertising**, and **IoT applications**.

Key Developments:

- **Real-Time Decision Making**: Businesses can instantly detect trends, anomalies, or opportunities and take immediate action. For example, fraud detection systems in banking can flag suspicious transactions in real-time.
- **Integration with IoT**: Real-time analytics allows businesses to monitor IoT devices and sensors continuously, making it possible to optimize operations instantly.

Example:

- An **e-commerce platform** could use real-time analytics to recommend products to users as they browse, adjusting in real-time based on user behavior and preferences.

Conclusion

The future of **Business Analytics** is marked by an increasing integration of **advanced technologies** such as AI, machine learning, cloud computing, and edge analytics. As businesses continue to adopt and harness these technologies, they will gain deeper, more actionable insights that can drive **operational efficiency, enhanced customer experiences**, and **innovative business strategies**.

Key trends to watch out for in the future of business analytics include **augmented analytics**, **automated machine learning**, **real-time analytics**, and **blockchain**, all of which will shape the ways companies make data-driven decisions. Staying ahead of these trends and embracing emerging technologies will be critical for businesses aiming to stay competitive in the data-driven world of tomorrow.

www.ingramcontent.com/pod-product-compliance
Lightning Source LLC
Chambersburg PA
CBHW082243220526
45469CB00009B/2859